THE PHILIPPINES

D0870588

The Philippines

The Political Economy of Growth and Impoverishment in the Marcos Era

James K. Boyce
Associate Professor of Economics
University of Massachusetts, Amherst

University of Hawaii Press
Honolulu

in association with the
OECD Development Centre

Published in North America by
UNIVERSITY OF HAWAII PRESS
2840 Kolowalu Street
Honolulu, Hawaii 96822

First published 1993 by
THE MACMILLAN PRESS LTD
Houndmills, Basingstoke, Hampshire RG21 2XS
and London

and

Organization for Economic Cooperation and Development
94, rue Chardon-Lagache
75016 Paris
France

Library of Congress Cataloging-in-Publication Data
Boyce, James K.
The Philippines: the political economy of growth and
impoverishment in the Marcos era / James K. Boyce in association
with the OECD Development Centre.
p.   cm.
Includes bibliographical references and index.
ISBN 0–8248–1521–1. — ISBN 0–8248–1522–X (pbk.)
1. Philippines—Economic conditions—1946–1986.   2. Economic
assistance, American—Philippines.   3. Poor—Philippines.
4. Marcos, Ferdinand E. (Ferdinand Edralin), 1917–1989.
I. Organization for Economic Co-operation and Development.
Development Centre.   II. Title.
HC455.B69   1993
338.9599'009'045—dc20   92–26934
                                                                          CIP

Printed in Hong Kong

Contents

List of Tables

List of Figures

Foreword

This volume forms part of a series on economic choices before the developing countries. The experience of economic development over more than four decades is varied and rich, and it is possible to learn much from it, both analytically and in terms of economic policy. It is clear that there are many paths to development, although some, no doubt, are more circuitous than others. Enough time has elapsed and enough data are available to make it possible to test the strengths and limitations of the most widely advocated policy approaches or development strategies against actual practice.

This was done within a comparative framework in my own contribution to the series entitled *Alternative Strategies for Economic Development*. That volume, as well as this one on *The Philippines: The Political Economy of Growth and Impoverishment in the Marcos Era*, are a part of a much larger research programme on the economic choices or alternatives facing the Third World in the closing years of this century. The research programme and this series, which reports results, were sponsored by the OECD Development Centre in Paris and received the personal and unstinting support of the Centre's President, Louis Emmerij.

The study of the Philippines by James Boyce is of more than usual interest, for the Philippines is the home of the green revolution in rice and, in addition, the country has an important agricultural export sector. The development strategy in the Philippines is distinctive in that it has concentrated much attention on agriculture, as many developing countries have been advised to. The high-yielding varieties of rice were developed at the International Rice Research Institute in Los Banos and three-quarters of the rice acreage is sown to the improved varieties. Indeed, new technology was seen as the spearhead of an agricultural transformation and as an alternative to redistributive land reforms and other policies intended to benefit the poor directly.

The agricultural export sector consists of the traditional plantation crops of coconuts and sugar, plus the more recent banana and pineapple crops developed by transnational corporations and, finally, forestry products, notably tropical hardwoods. Between them, agricultural exports account for about 30 per cent of the country's export earnings. The expansion of plantation crops often has occurred in sparsely settled regions by displacing peasant farmers and tribal people from their land. The export of forest products has been based on an unregulated extraction of timber: neither

the need to replace the felled trees nor the environmental effects, such
as flooding, nor the consequences for those who previously depended on
the forests for a living have been taken into account. Beyond this, James
Boyce shows in great detail that the interests of those who work in export
agriculture and depend upon it for a livelihood have been neglected both
by the large landowners and by the government. Going further, the author
argues persuasively that in general social costs and benefits have not been
taken into account by policy makers in the Philippines and are unlikely to
be in the future until the country becomes genuinely more democratic and
responsive to the needs of the poor.

An attempt was made by policy makers in the Philippines to marry a
green revolution strategy of development to a strategy of open economy
industrialisation. The latter, however, was poorly implemented and hence
was not given a chance to succeed. Indeed, the author shows that the
Philippines achieved nether a non-interventionist, free-market policy nor
a policy of rational interventions designed to serve a wide public interest.
Growth, however, was achieved and average incomes rose, but in the period
1962 to 1986, on which the author focuses, the rise in per capita income
was accompanied by 'declining incomes for a substantial segment of the
poor and middle classes'. Inequality in the distribution of income increased;
the increase in inequality was so great that many people experienced an
absolute decline in their standard of living.

Although the economy was not really 'open' as far as international trade
is concerned, it certainly was open to foreign capital. Overseas borrowing
rose rapidly, debt servicing problems soon followed and shortly after the
assassination of Benigno Aquino in 1983, the net transfer of resources
to the Philippines became negative. James Boyce shows that for the
period 1971 to 1983, the heyday of foreign borrowing, there was a strong
negative relationship between foreign capital inflows and the growth of
output, largely because of the adverse effect of foreign capital on the
efficiency of investment. The author also shows that capital flight from
the Philippines was equivalent to four-fifths of the country's external debt
and, furthermore, that capital flight rose and fell directly with foreign
borrowing. More than three-quarters of the foreign debt by the end of the
Marcos era was public debt and much had been used to fuel an enormous
expansion of state activities.

The development policies pursued in the Philippines resulted in the
impoverishment of the already poor, the plunder of the economy's natural
resources, massive foreign indebtedness by the state to finance private
capital flight and an enormous enrichment of a tiny minority. The advanced
technology of a green revolution and, more generally, economic policy-

making by technocrats within an authoritarian system, were supported abroad and proclaimed at home as the solution to underdevelopment. In the event, underdevelopment was accentuated, the country was led to financial ruin and the political regime collapsed. The search for a viable development strategy in the Philippines continues.

This volume will naturally be of interest to those concerned with economic policy and prospects in the Philippines. It will be of equal interest, however, to three other groups of people – namely, those who advocate a technology-led agricultural development stategy; those trying to understand how foreign capital and borrowing can aggravate the problems they are thought to solve; and those struggling with other cases of pathological development in which growth is accompanied by immiseration. There is much that can be learned from a careful study of the Philippines.

KEITH GRIFFIN
Series Editor
Paris

Acknowledgements

This study was commissioned by the Development Centre of the Organization for Economic Co-operation and Development as a component of its Research Program on Economic Choices before the Developing Countries. I am grateful to the Development Centre for its support and to Dr. Keith Griffin for his encouragement.

I am also grateful to the Philippine Institute for Development Studies for the research facilities generously extended to me, and to the University of Massachusetts at Amherst and the Joint Committee on Southeast Asia of the Social Science Research Council and American Council of Learned Societies for grants to finance research assistance.

I have benefitted from the advice and efforts of many people in the course of my research, and it is a pleasure to acknowledge them. Keith Griffin and José E. R. Ledesma read the entire manuscript and provided many helpful criticisms. Howarth Bouis, Gary Hawes, Benedict Kerkvliet, David Kummer, Benito Legarda, Jr., Manuel Montes, James Putzel, Agnes Quisumbing and J. Mohan Rao read various draft chapters and offered valuable comments. Walden Bello, John Cavanagh, and Robin Broad provided access to a number of crucial documents. Craig Nelson of the National Security Archive in Washington, D.C., supplied several important documents obtained from the United States government under the Freedom of Information Act, and assisted me in submitting my own requests under that Act. Annette Balaoing, Linda Balaoing, Stephen Beam, Lynn Duggan, Lester Henry, Thomas Hutcheson, José E. R. Ledesma, Tania Meisner, Beng Tan of IBON Databank, Throadia Santos and Lyuba Zarsky provided valuable research assistance. In addition, I wish to record my thanks to the many individuals who agreed to be interviewed for this research.

Responsibility for the views expressed in this book is, of course, mine alone.

J. K. BOYCE
Amherst, Massachusetts

1 The Setting

INTRODUCTION

The Philippines is rich country, yet the majority of its people are poor. Their poverty is not a result of neglect by the country's wealthy minority, the outside world, or would-be developers. On the contrary, it is in no small measure the result of their unwanted attentions.

When President Ferdinand Marcos was airlifted from the Philippines on a United States Air Force jet in February 1986, he left behind an economy in shambles. The average yearly income was US $540 per person, and like many averages, this concealed vast disparities. While the rich lived in an ostentatious splendor symbolized by the legendary extravagance of the Marcoses, the majority of Filipinos could not afford to consume the minimum daily calorie requirement.

In the two decades of Marcos's rule, Philippine economic development strategy had three central pillars. The first was a 'green revolution' in rice agriculture, which successfully doubled production of the country's basic food staple. The second was a continued reliance on export agriculture as a major source of income and foreign exchange earnings. The third was large-scale borrowing from foreign banks and official lenders.

This strategy was enthusiastically backed by the Marcos regime's international allies, who not only tolerated the President's authoritarian rule, but welcomed it. The World Bank (1973, Vol. 1, p. 1) greeted Marcos's 1972 declaration of Martial Law with the statement that 'recent developments offer an opportunity for a more serious attack on the very difficult social and economic problems presently confronting the Philippines'. In 1981, after Marcos's re-election with an ostensible 86 per cent of the vote, United States Vice-President George Bush offered his famous inaugural toast: 'We stand with you sir . . . We love your adherence to democratic principles and to democratic processes.'[1]

Diplomatic talk can be cheap, but these were not hollow expressions of support. Between 1962 and 1983, the United States government provided $3 billion in economic and military assistance to the Philippines.[2] In the same period, the World Bank lent $4 billion to the Philippine government.[3]

The magnitude of the Philippine development strategy's failure can be appreciated by comparisons with neighboring countries. In 1962, per capita

TABLE 1.1 *Development Indicators for Selected Southeast and East Asian Countries, 1962 and 1986*

Country	Gross national product per capita (1986 U.S. $)[1]		Growth rate, 1962–86 (per cent per year)			Infant mortality rate (per thousand live births)	
	1962	*1986*	*GNP*	*Population*	*GNP per capita*	*1965*	*1988*
Philippines	495	540	3.1	2.7	0.4	72	44
China	105	300	6.8	1.7	5.1	90	31
Indonesia	190	490	6.9	2.3	4.6	128	68
Japan	2,005	16,200	9.7	1.0	8.7	18	5
Korea (S.)	330	2,345	10.1	1.9	8.2	62	24
Malaysia	820	1,730	5.7	2.6	3.1	55	23
Singapore	1,500	6,765	8.0	1.7	6.3	26	7
Taiwan	505	3,790	10.6	2.2	8.4	NA	NA
Thailand	345	760	5.9	2.6	3.3	88	30
Vietnam	NA	300	NA	2.8	NA	NA	44

NA = not available

NOTE

1. Data for China and Indonesia refer to the years 1965–86. Data for Singapore refer to gross domestic product. Data for Vietnam refer to the year 1984.

SOURCES

Gross national product: GNP at current prices converted to US dollars using period-average exchange rates and to 1986 dollars using US wholesale price index, all as reported in International Monetary Fund (1989). China's and Indonesia's GNP from World Bank (1988b, p. 222). Taiwan's GNP from United Nations Economic Commission on Asia and the Far East (1965, p. 231) and Asian Development Bank (1988, p. 305). Vietnam's GNP from US Central Intelligence Agency (1987, p. 263).

Population: China's 1965 population and Japan's 1986 population interpolated from data in United Nations (1988, pp. 252, 274); Vietnam's 1986 population from World Bank (1988b, p. 222). All other 1962 populations from United Nations Economic Commission on Asia and the Far East (1965, p. 228); all other 1986 populations from Asian Development Bank (1988).

Infant mortality rate: World Bank (1990b, pp. 232–3).

TABLE 1.2 *Debt Indicators for Selected Southeast and East Asian Countries, 1986*

Country	External debt outstanding at end of 1986 (US$ billion)	Debt-to-GNP ratio	Debt per capita (US$)
Philippines	27.2	0.90	485
China	26.6	0.08	25
Indonesia	42.2	0.51	250
Korea (S.)	54.4	0.56	1,310
Malaysia	22.9	0.82	1,420
Singapore	4.4	0.25	1,710
Taiwan	12.7	0.17	655
Thailand	18.7	0.47	355
Vietnam	7.9	0.44	125

SOURCES Debt from OECD (1987, pp. 12–17); GNP and population as in Table 1.1.

income in the Philippines was comparable to that in Taiwan, and one-quarter of that in Japan (see Table 1.1). In 1986, it was one-seventh of Taiwan's and three per cent of Japan's. Infant mortality in the Philippines in 1986 was equal to that in Vietnam, a country on which the US had rained bombs rather than banknotes.[4] The Philippine external debt burden, measured by its ratio to national income, was the heaviest in East and Southeast Asia (see Table 1.2).

Although per capita income in the Philippines rose between the early 1960s and the mid-1980s, the incomes of the country's poor majority declined. Real wages fell sharply in both rural and urban areas, even in periods when the country was experiencing relatively rapid growth in national income.[5] This phenomenon is sometimes called 'immiserizing growth'.[6] The term can be used not only to describe a situation in which the poor become poorer even as income per person grows, but also in a stronger, causal sense to mean that growth itself is a cause of impoverishment. The latter is what economist Ian Little (1976, p. 101) derides as the 'fashionable neo-populist doctrine of immiserizing growth'.

At the risk of annoying those who axiomatically reject any connection between growth and impoverishment, I argue in this book that in the Philippines the two went hand-in-hand. Both growth and impoverishment resulted from the policies pursued by the Philippine government and its international backers. This is not to say that growth *in general* is undesirable. On the contrary, a further criticism of the Philippine development strategy is that the country could have achieved more rapid growth under alternative policies. Equity was not 'traded off' for growth in the Philippines. Rather, both were sacrificed to a technocratic development strategy wedded to an unjust political and economic order.

HISTORICAL BACKGROUND

It is more than four centuries since the Portuguese explorer Ferdinand Magellan discovered the Philippine archipelago for the European world. The islanders killed him, inspired perhaps by some preternatural inkling of what this discovery would augur for future generations of Filipinos. Four decades after Magellan's death, the Spanish returned and conquered the Philippines by force of arms.

Colonial rule died slowly in the Philippines, and some of its vestiges survive to the present day. At the end of the nineteenth century, Filipino revolutionaries finally defeated the Spanish rulers who left behind their surnames, their religion, and a rigid class structure based on control of agricultural land. Spain was immediately supplanted, however, by a new colonial power: the United States.

In January 1900, US Senator Alfred Beveridge elaborated the vital US interests in the Philippines. 'I have ridden hundreds of miles on the islands', he declared, 'every foot of the way a revelation of vegetable and mineral riches'. He waxed eloquent about the fertility of the land, its lush crops of rice, coffee, sugarcane, and coconuts, and its verdant forests with enough wood to 'supply the furniture of the world for a century to come'. But the greatest lure of the Philippines was strategic:

> [T]he Pacific is the ocean of commerce of the future. Most future wars will be conflicts for commerce. The power that rules the Pacific, therefore, is the power that rules the world.

'With the Philippines', Beveridge concluded, 'that power is and will forever be the American Republic'.[7]

The Americans, like the Spanish, took the Philippines by force of arms. No one knows how many Filipinos died during the US conquest, but a US general estimated in 1901 that 'one-sixth of the natives of Luzon have either been killed or have died of the dengue fever in the last two years'[8] (see map, Figure 1.1). Francisco (1987, p. 19) concludes that a total estimate of

Figure 1.1: Map of the Philippines

a million dead – more than one-tenth of the country's population – 'might conceivably err on the side of understatement'.[9]

US rule proved a boon to the *hacenderos*, the Philippines' landowning elite. Agricultural exports thrived as the country was brought inside US tariff barriers.[10] At the same time, US manufactures enjoyed free access to the Philippine market, limiting prospects for domestic industrialization. The *hacendero*-dominated colonial legislature, established by the US, brought leading members of the elite together in the capital, diluting their provincialism and forging them into 'a self-conscious *ruling* class' (Anderson, 1988, p. 11; emphasis in original).

In 1946, following three years of Japanese occupation during World War Two, the US granted independence to the Philippines. Close economic ties between the Philippines and the US persisted under agreements providing for preferential tariffs, special treatment for US investors in the Philippines, and a fixed peso/dollar exchange rate.[11] Military ties also persisted: the US retained Clark Air Base, Subic Bay Naval Base, and a number of smaller bases in the Philippines, and established a permanent Military Advisory Group for the Philippine armed forces.[12]

In the 1950s the country experienced a burst of industrialization, sparked by government import controls. Initially imposed in response to a balance-of-payments crisis in 1949, the controls quickly became an instrument to protect domestic manufacturers of consumer goods from foreign competition.[13] Between 1949 and 1958, manufacturing output grew at an average annual rate of 12 per cent.[14] This growth brought the emergence a 'new industrial class', drawn from 'the more enterprising members of the moneyed class, including sugar-associated interests' (Power and Sicat, 1971, p. 61). On certain issues, the interests of the industrialists clashed with those of the agricultural exporters. In particular, the two groups had opposing interests on exchange rate policy. The industrialists favored a strong peso (that is, a low peso/dollar rate), which allowed them to import capital goods cheaply while keeping out imported consumer goods with the controls. The agro-exporters favored a weak peso (a high peso/dollar rate), which would increase the peso earnings from their exports.

In 1961, with support from discontented industrialists whose access to import licenses was blocked by political favoritism, the agro-exporters elected a president, Diosdado Macapagal, committed to the immediate abolition of exchange controls.[15] The decontrol of imports and foreign exchange in 1962, and the ensuing devaluation of the peso by almost 100 per cent, brought windfall profits to agro-exporters. In following years, acreage under export crops rose sharply, while that under domestic food crops stagnated (Treadgold and Hooley, 1967). Food price increases lowered the real incomes of consumers in general, and of industrial wage-earners in particular.[16] The redistribution of national income towards agricultural exporters marked a reassertion of power by the traditional oligarchy. For this reason, the year 1962 is often taken as a starting point in the analysis which follows.

The election of Ferdinand Marcos as President of the Philippines in 1965 continued the traditional rotation of national office among regional power brokers. Marcos, however, would soon defy the rules of the political game. He built a domestic power base among military officers, civilian technocrats, and a fraction of the elite who became known as the President's 'cronies'. At the same time, he secured crucial external backing from the US government, skillfully manipulating its preoccupation with the military bases, and personally investing in the electoral campaigns of key US politicians.[17] In 1969 Marcos was re-elected. His opponent complained that he was 'outgunned, outgooned, and outgold'.[18] In 1972 Marcos consolidated his grip on power by declaring Martial Law. In the end, he ruled the Philippines for twenty years, until at last he was driven into exile by the 'people's power' revolution of February 1986.

In one important respect, however, the Marcos regime maintained continuity with established political tradition. At the turn of the century, George Washington Plunkitt, the political boss of New York City, had coined the term 'honest graft' to describe his philosophy of the use of state power as vehicle for personal enrichment. Plunkitt's motto was: 'I seen my opportunities and I took 'em'.[19] This feature of US politics flourished in the Philippines. In another declaration memorable for its indelicacy, a member of the Philippine Senate exclaimed in the 1950s: 'What are we in power for? We are not hypocrites. Why should we pretend to be saints when in reality we are not?'[20]

Ferdinand Marcos certainly did not invent the exploitation of public office for private ends. But many Filipinos shared the opinion of a 1985 US Senate staff report that 'the extent of the President's intervention on behalf of family and friends has well exceeded social norms'.[21] In particular, Marcos taught his rivals in the oligarchy that 'property was not power, since at the stroke of the martial pen it ceased to be property' (Anderson, 1988, p. 22). In so doing, he pursued the logic of individual self-interest to its ultimate conclusion.

THE DEVELOPMENT STRATEGY

The technocrats who formulated Philippine development strategy under President Marcos did not challenge the country's inegalitarian economic and political order. On the contrary, that order provided the fulcrum for their pursuit of development 'from above'. Development, in a technocratic strategy, is something done *to* or *for* its putative beneficiaries, but not *by* them, unless in response to commands or incentives issued by the technocrats. The poor are the objects of the development process, not its subjects.

Although powerful, technocrats are not omnipotent. A democratic movement can challenge the basic structure of wealth and power in a society. Technocrats cannot. Redistribution, insofar as it figures at all among their strategic objectives, is confined to the expanding margin of the economy: new income streams can be channeled to specific target groups, but existing income streams cannot be redirected to the poor.[22]

The three pillars of Philippine development strategy epitomized the technocratic approach.

The Green Revolution
The 'green revolution' is the popular term for the agricultural development strategy promoted by international agencies in Asia, Latin America, and Africa since the mid-1960s, the central objective of which is increased food production per unit land area.[23] Its key instrument is a technological package comprised of highly fertilizer-responsive crop varieties, fertilizers, pesticides, and water control. Notably absent from the green revolution strategy are changes in the institutions which govern the production of food and its distribution. Institutional changes, such as land reform, are not viewed as necessary for increased production.

Indeed, some proponents of the strategy claim that institutional changes are not necessary to reduce poverty either. For example, S. Shahid Husain, the chairman of the Consultative Group for International Agricultural Research, stated in 1985 that 'added emphasis on poverty alleviation is not necessary', because increasing food production automatically has 'a major impact' on the poor.[24]

The Philippines was the birthplace of the green revolution in rice agriculture. The new 'high-yielding' varieties were bred at the International Rice Research Institute in Los Baños, and the country's rice farmers have led the world in the adoption of the new rice technology. Although limited institutional changes were instituted under the banner of land reform, the basic dichotomy between ownership of land and labor on it has survived. The outcome of the green revolution in the Philippines reveals much about the efficacy of the technocratic food strategy within the context of an inegalitarian agrarian structure.

Export Agriculture and Forestry
The traditional economic mainstay of the Philippine ruling elite has been export agriculture. Development strategy in the Marcos era continued to rely

on this sector as a major source of income and foreign exchange. Between 1962 and 1985, export crop acreage more than doubled. Earnings did not rise commensurately, however, owing to worsening terms of trade.

The Marcos regime cornered an increasing share of the profits from the traditional export crops, sugarcane and coconut. The result was a redistribution of income from the agro-export elite as a whole to a politically well-connected subset of that elite. At the same time, two non-traditional export crops, bananas and pineapples, became increasingly important under the aegis of transnational firms. Forestry exports also brought in substantial foreign exchange earnings. Here, too, the benefits were highly concentrated, while the 'external costs' of deforestation were imposed on the Filipino people as a whole.

Foreign Borrowing

To finance both agricultural and industrial growth, the Philippine development strategy relied heavily on foreign borrowing from official and private lenders. The country's external debt rose from US $360 million in 1962 (equivalent to $1.1 billion in 1986 dollars) to $28.3 billion in 1986, making the Philippines one of the most heavily indebted countries in Asia, Africa, and Latin America.

When a government borrows money from abroad, it knows that one day it will have to repay the loans with interest. The rationale for foreign borrowing must be either that the funds will be invested to generate a rate of return at least equal to the rate of interest on the loan, or that the short-term benefits justify the eventual longer-term costs. Although official rhetoric stressed the first, in practice the second rationale predominated in Philippine debt policy. The long-term costs began to arrive in the final years of the Marcos regime, when the net transfer – new money minus debt service on previous loans – turned negative. Those who reaped the short-term benefits are not those who now bear the long-term costs.

The literature on Philippine industrialization has focused mainly on trade policy.[25] International agencies, notably the World Bank and the International Monetary Fund, have long pressed for trade liberalization in the Philippines (see Broad, 1988), arguing that protection reduces export competitiveness, depresses labor absorption, and fosters unproductive 'rent-seeking' activity. Relatively little attention has been paid to the impact of external borrowing, despite the fact that it can breed many of the same maladies ascribed to protection. By increasing the supply of foreign exchange, foreign loans strengthen the currency of the borrowing country, making its exports less competitive on the world market. By cheapening capital, foreign loans bias the direction of technological change against labor absorption.

And insofar as public debts finance the acquisition of private assets, foreign loans divert entrepreneurial energies into rent seeking.

Grafted to the rootstock of an unjust social order, the technocratic development strategy in the Philippines bore the bitter fruit of impoverishment. Chapter 2 summarizes the results: modest growth in per capita income coupled with declining incomes for the poor. Subsequent chapters analyze the elements of the development strategy sketched above. Chapters 3 to 5 examine the green revolution in Philippine rice agriculture. Chapters 6 to 8 examine export agriculture and the forestry sector. Chapters 9 to 11 examine foreign borrowing. In conclusion, Chapter 12 suggests some implications of this study for the future of the Philippines and, more generally, for the political economy of development.

NOTES

1. Quoted in Kessler (1986, p. 57).
2. This included $1,366 million in economic assistance, $777 million in military assistance, and $860 million in other loans (United States Agency for International Development, 1983, p. 77).
3. The Asian Development Bank provided a further $1.6 billion. These multilateral loans are summarized by the United States Agency for International Development (1983, p. 212).
4. The infant mortality data in Table 1.1 should be treated with some caution. For example, two recent editions of the World Bank's *World Development Report* present conflicting figures for Philippine infant mortality in 1965: 90 versus 72 per 1,000 live births (World Bank, 1985c, p. 218; 1990b, p. 232).
5. For details, see Chapter 2. Similar conclusions are reached by Fields (1980, Tables 7.1 and 7.2) and Oshima, de Borja and Paz (1986).
6. Bhagwati (1958) coined the term in a different context, to describe a theoretical case in which output growth leads to lower real income via deterioration in the terms of trade.
7. 'Our Philippine Policy', *Congressional Record*, 9 January 1900, reprinted in Schirmer and Shalom, eds (1987, pp. 24–5).
8. The statement is usually attributed to General J. Franklin Bell, who as commander of US troops in southern Luzon ordered the confinement of the population in detention camps and declared what would be termed, in modern military parlance, a free-fire zone outside the camps. Gates (1983, p. 368) attributes the statement to a different General Bell.
9. The 1903 census reported a surviving population of 7.6 million (NEDA, 1976, p. 37). Gates (1983, pp. 373–4) advances a more conservative, 'highly tentative' estimate of war-related deaths, as of 1903, at between 128,000 and 363,000.

10. Under the Payne-Aldrich Act of 1909, quotas were initially imposed on the entry of Philippine sugar and tobacco in response to US producer interests. These were lifted under the Underwood-Simmons Act of 1913. For discussion, see Constantino (1975, pp. 296–7), Hawes (1987, pp. 86–7), and Pomeroy (1970, pp. 177–9).

11. The Bell Trade Act of 1946 required the Philippines to amend its Constitution to give US citizens 'parity' with Filipinos in the right to own public utilities and corporations engaged in natural resource exploitation. The Laurel-Langley Agreement of 1955 extended these preferential arrangements. Relevant provisions are reprinted in Schirmer and Shalom, eds (1987, pp. 88–90, 95–6).

12. The relevant agreements are reprinted in Schirmer and Shalom, eds (1987, pp. 97–103).

13. See Power and Sicat (1971, pp. 33–38), Baldwin (1975, pp. 22–45), and Bello *et al.* (1982, pp. 128–31).

14. Calculated from index of physical production reported by Golay (1961, p. 103.)

15. See Grossholtz (1964, p. 268), Payer (1974, pp. 62–6), and Baldwin (1975, p. 62).

16. See Treadgold and Hooley (1967), Power and Sicat (1971, pp. 46–7), Payer (1974, p. 67), and Baldwin (1975, pp. 60–1).

17. Bonner (1987, p. 141) reports, for example, that Marcos contributed US $1 million to Richard Nixon's 1968 and 1972 presidential campaigns.

18. Senator Sergio Osmena, Jr., in *The New York Times*, 16 November 1969, quoted by Anderson (1988, p. 18).

19. Turn-of-the-century Tammany Hall boss George Washington Plunkett, quoted by Tolchin (1990).

20. Attributed by President Quirino to Senator Avelino in 1957; quoted in Grossholtz (1964, p. 167, n. 12). 'The question "What are we in power for?" is heard all over the islands now', Grossholtz reported, 'usually in a humorous context but with a measure of acceptance of the idea it contains'.

21. *The Philippines: A Situation Report*, Staff Report to the Senate Select Committee on Intelligence, United States Senate, 1 November 1985, p. 6.

22. This is the strategy advanced in the reformist World Bank manifesto, *Redistribution with Growth* (Chenery *et al.*, 1974; see especially pp. 47–9).

23. Africa has lagged behind Asia and Latin America, but is now squarely on the green revolutionaries' agenda; see, for example, Borlaug (1990).

24. Husain (1985, p. 2). From its headquarters at the World Bank, the Consultative Group coordinates finance for the international agricultural research centers, including the International Rice Research Institute in the Philippines.

25. See, for example, Power and Sicat (1971), International Labor Organization (1974), Baldwin (1975), and Bautista, Power, *et al.* (1979).

2 Growth and Distribution: An Overview

INTRODUCTION

Income per person in the Philippines rose between 1962 and 1986. Such averages can be deceptive, however. For the country's poor majority, this was not an era of rising income, but of deepening impoverishment.

Five possible ways of dividing a larger income pie can be distinguished:

1. *unchanged distribution*, in which all slices grow at the same rate;
2. *mild equalization*, in which all slices grow, but those of the poor increase more rapidly than those of the rich;
3. *strong equalization*, in which the slices of the poor grow, while those of the rich shrink;
4. *mild polarization*, in which all slices grow, but those of the rich increase more rapidly than those of the poor; and
5. *strong polarization*, in which the slices of the rich grow, while those of the poor shrink.

In the first four cases, the absolute incomes of the poor rise. In the last case, their absolute incomes decline.

Many economists do not find mild polarization terribly disturbing. Indeed, some contend that it is a natural, if not inevitable, corollary of rising per capita incomes at early stages of development.[1] As long as some absolute income increments 'trickle down' to the poor, they are arguably better off than they were before. Strong polarization is much more controversial. If the poor get poorer while the rich get richer, then it can be argued that social welfare has declined despite growth in average income.[2]

The evidence reviewed in this chapter indicates that the distribution of income in the Philippines underwent strong polarization between 1962 and 1986. In other words, the country experienced immiserizing growth, at least in the descriptive sense. Successive sections examine trends in growth and productivity, wages and employment, and income distribution and poverty. Subsequent chapters will explore whether economic growth in the Philippines was immiserizing in the causal sense, too.

GROWTH AND PRODUCTIVITY

The conventional measure of a country's overall economic performance is the rate of growth of its gross national product (GNP) or national income. The deficiencies of this measure are well known. Not only does it omit other information about economic well-being – notably, how the income is distributed among individuals – but also it fails for numerous reasons to provide an accurate measure of aggregate income itself. For example, national income accounts often exclude non-market activities, such as food production by a household for its own consumption. If the land changes hands, and the new owners sell the same produce on the market while the old owners now buy their food, GNP registers an increase. More generally, in periods of commercialization, recorded GNP growth may overstate actual growth in income.

The treatment, or non-treatment, of natural resource depletion is a further defect in the national income accounts. When a forest is cut and the soil on which it grew washes away, GNP records only the income gained in selling the trees. Depreciation of chain saws and logging trucks is counted as a cost in the calculation of net national product, but depreciation of 'nature's capital' is not. The resulting discrepancies can be large. In the case of Indonesia, for example, Repetto (1989) reports that correction for depletion of forests and petroleum reserves lowers that country's rate of income growth in 1971–84 by three per cent per year.[3]

Comparisons of national income over time and across countries pose additional problems in the choice of price indexes and exchange rates. For example, official statistics in the Philippines show per capita GNP in 1986 to be 36 per cent higher than in 1962, when converted into constant pesos using the GNP deflator (see Table 2.1). However, estimates for the same years in US dollars, reported by the World Bank, indicate that real per capita income was only 9 per cent higher (see Table 1.1).[4]

Bearing these limitations in mind, let us examine the growth record of the Philippine economy in 1962–86 as reported in the national income accounts. Table 2.1 presents annual estimates of GNP (in constant pesos), population, and GNP per capita. Recorded per capita income rose steadily until 1981, when it was 65 per cent higher than its 1962 level. Thereafter per capita income contracted sharply, however, so that in 1986 it was only 36 per cent above its 1962 level. The sharpest drop came after 1983, when the most severe economic crisis in post-war Philippine history began.

Fitting an exponential trend line to the 25-year period as a whole, we find that GNP grew at an annual rate of 4.8 per cent, population at 2.7 per cent, and GNP per capita at 2.0 per cent.[5] Partitioning this 25-year period into two

TABLE 2.1　*GNP and Population, 1962–1986 (constant 1985 pesos)*

Year	GNP (billion pesos)	Population (millions)	GNP Per Capita (pesos)
1962	231.4	29.0	7,979
1963	247.5	30.0	8,260
1964	256.0	30.9	8,278
1965	268.9	31.9	8,433
1966	280.6	32.8	8,543
1967	294.0	33.8	8,699
1968	309.8	34.8	8,912
1969	326.3	35.7	9,134
1970	340.4	36.7	9,279
1971	360.0	37.9	9,508
1972	377.7	39.5	9,558
1973	415.8	39.4	10,555
1974	439.1	40.7	10,799
1975	464.5	42.1	11,041
1976	498.9	43.4	11,493
1977	530.5	44.6	11,899
1978	561.1	45.8	12,252
1979	599.7	47.0	12,750
1980	629.5	48.1	13,087
1981	651.2	49.5	13,146
1982	663.5	51.3	12,939
1983	670.9	52.1	12,888
1984	623.4	53.4	11,686
1985	597.7	54.7	10,934
1986	608.9	56.0	10,872
Growth Rates (per cent per annum)			
1962–1986	4.8	2.7	2.0
1962–1974	6.0	2.9	3.1
1974–1986	3.6	2.6	1.0

SOURCES　GNP from IMF (1989, pp. 586–7). Population from NSCB (1989, p. 1/14); population interpolated in missing years.

Growth rates in this and following tables are estimated from exponential and kinked exponential models by ordinary least squares (see Boyce, 1986, for methodology).

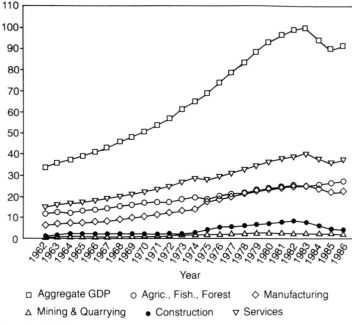

□ Aggregate GDP   o Agric., Fish., Forest   ◇ Manufacturing

△ Mining & Quarrying   ● Construction   ▽ Services

Sources: See Table 2.2.

Figure 2.1:   Aggregate and Sectoral GDP, 1962 – 1986
(billions of constant 1972 pesos)

subperiods of equal length, we find that per capita GNP grew at 3.1 per cent per year in 1962–74, and at 1.0 per cent in 1974–86.[6]

Table 2.2 and Figure 2.1 report the composition of gross domestic product (GDP) by major economic sectors. The two largest sectors – services and agriculture – grew more slowly than total GDP, while manufacturing and construction grew more rapidly. The most notable feature of the sectoral composition of output, however, is its stability. Services and agriculture remained dominant throughout the period, their combined share in total GDP slipping from 78 per cent in 1962 to 71 per cent in 1986. The share of manufacturing rose only modestly from 18 to 24 per cent. Thus the Philippine economy did not experience rapid structural change.

The available data do not permit calculation of output growth rates at the regional level, owing to boundary changes during the period.[7] Large disparities among regions in the level of per capita income are apparent, however, in the data for 1980 reported in Table 2.3. Average income in the National Capital Region was more than double that in the next highest

TABLE 2.2 GDP by Sector, 1962–1986 (constant 1972 prices in billions of pesos)[1]

Year	Agriculture Fishery & Forestry	Manufacturing	Mining & Quarrying	Construction	Services[3]	GDP
		Sector[2]				
1962	11.4	5.9	0.5	1.0	14.7	33.5
1963	12.1	6.3	0.5	1.3	15.5	35.7
1964	12.0	6.5	0.5	1.5	16.4	36.8
1965	12.9	6.8	0.5	1.6	17.0	38.8
1966	13.4	7.3	0.6	1.5	17.9	40.7
1967	13.9	8.0	0.7	1.6	19.0	43.2
1968	14.9	8.6	0.8	1.4	19.9	45.6
1969	15.8	9.1	0.9	1.6	20.6	48.0
1970	16.6	9.9	1.1	1.3	22.1	50.9
1971	16.9	10.9	1.3	1.3	23.6	53.9
1972	17.0	11.5	1.4	1.8	24.8	56.5
1973	18.6	13.0	1.5	1.9	26.7	61.7
1974	19.3	13.5	1.5	2.2	28.3	64.8
1975	18.3	17.3	1.4	4.0	27.4	68.4
1976	19.8	18.3	1.5	5.3	29.1	73.9
1977	20.8	19.7	1.7	5.8	30.5	78.5
1978	21.6	21.1	1.8	5.9	32.3	82.8
1979	22.6	22.2	2.1	6.8	34.2	88.0
1980	23.7	23.2	2.2	7.1	36.4	92.6

| Year | Sector[2] | | | | | |
	Agriculture Fishery & Forestry	Manufacturing	Mining & Quarrying	Construction	Services[3]	GDP
1981	24.6	24.0	2.2	7.8	37.6	96.2
1982	25.4	24.5	2.0	8.1	39.0	99.0
1983	24.8	25.1	2.0	7.7	40.3	99.9
1984	25.4	23.3	1.8	5.9	37.6	93.9
1985	26.3	21.5	1.8	4.3	36.1	89.9
1986	27.1	21.7	1.6	3.4	37.4	91.2
Growth Rates (per cent per annum)						
1962–1986	3.7	6.7	6.5	8.5	4.3	4.9
1962–1974	4.3	8.9	11.4	9.5	5.5	6.2
1974–1986	3.1	4.6	1.5	7.6	3.1	3.6

NOTES

1. Data for the years 1962–1974 converted from 1967 pesos to 1972 pesos using the ratio of 1972 GDP reported according to the two base years in NEDA (1976, p. 119) and NSCB (1989, p. 3/26), respectively.

2. For the years 1962–1974, gross sector output is calculated from net output data by pro-rating capital consumption allowance and indirect taxes across sectors according to their shares in net domestic product.

3. Service sector includes transportation, communication, storage, utilities, commerce, and other services.

SOURCES   NEDA (1976, pp. 118–19); NSCB (1989, pp. 3/26 to 3/27).

TABLE 2.3 *GDP and Population by Region, 1980*

Region		GDP (billions of pesos)	Population (millions)	GDP Per Capita (pesos)
	Philippines	264.7	48.1	5502
NCR.	Metro Manila	79.7	5.9	13449
I.	Ilocos	10.7	3.5	3025
II.	Cagayan Valley	7.7	2.2	3460
III.	Central Luzon	24.6	4.8	5115
IV.	Southern Tagalog	39.7	6.1	6480
V.	Bicol	9.1	3.5	2606
VI.	Western Visayas	20.3	4.5	4478
VII.	Central Visayas	18.5	3.8	4877
VIII.	Eastern Visayas	6.2	2.8	2225
IX.	Western Mindanao	9.1	2.5	3599
X.	Northern Mindanao	12.8	2.8	4628
XI.	Southern Mindanao	18.4	3.3	5509
XII.	Central Mindanao	8.0	2.3	3537

SOURCES GDP from NEDA (1986, p. 206); population from NEDA (1986, pp. 20–7).

income region, Southern Tagalog (which adjoins metropolitan Manila). In the two poorest regions, Bicol and Eastern Visayas, per capita income was less than half the national average, and less than one-fifth that of the National Capital Region.

Combining output and employment data, we can examine trends in labor productivity. Table 2.4 presents official data on total and sectoral employment. Although their reliability is open to question, as discussed below, these data provide a useful first approximation of overall trends. Total employment grew at 3.3 per cent per year in 1962–86. Employment in agriculture and manufacturing grew more slowly, at only 2.6 per cent. Employment in the services sector, by contrast, grew at 4.7 per cent, lifting that sector's share in total employment from 25 per cent in 1962 to 37 per cent in 1986.

Relatively rapid employment growth in services can occur under three different scenarios. In the first, the service sector plays a leading role in the growth process, pulling labor from other sectors and generating rising per capita output. In the second, the service sector provides highly elastic accommodation for a growing labor force, so that per capita output in the

TABLE 2.4 *Employment by Sector, 1962–1986.*
(thousands of employed persons)

| Year | Sector | | | | | Rural | Urban | Total Employed Labor Force |
	Agriculture Fishery & Forestry	Manu-facturing	Mining & Quarrying	Con-struction	Services			
1962	5898	1052	40	236	2378	NA	NA	9603
1963	5779	1139	29	271	2547	NA	NA	9764
1965	5725	1101	24	295	2957	7143	2958	10101
1966	6290	1229	26	283	3109	7714	3223	10937
1967	6330	1223	45	276	2993	7742	3124	10866
1968	5631	1234	43	342	3220	7124	3347	10471
1970	6100	1354	51	438	3415	NA	NA	11358
1971	6321	1439	59	420	4304	8745	3797	12542
1972	6863	1323	36	432	3927	8823	3759	12582
1973	7766	1396	51	350	4302	9600	4265	13865
1974	7684	1423	47	403	4269	9583	4242	13825
1975	7768	1651	54	456	4589	10073	4444	14517
1976	7659	1598	81	428	4471	9690	4548	14238
1977	7474	1515	52	484	4810	9739	4595	14334
1978	8422	1742	61	519	5375	11020	5081	16101
1980	8453	1814	94	588	5485	11614	4820	16434

Year	Sector					Rural	Urban	Total Employed Labor Force
	Agriculture Fishery & Forestry	*Manu-facturing*	*Mining & Quarrying*	*Con-struction*	*Services*			
1981	8928	1807	80	592	6044	12339	5112	17451
1982	8920	1741	74	604	6031	12211	5160	17371
1983	9880	1887	102	697	6646	13709	5502	19211
1984	9740	1931	138	759	7065	12738	6935	19673
1985	9698	1922	128	684	7365	12841	6960	19801
1986	10289	1905	150	629	7623	13480	7115	20595
Growth Rates (per cent per annum)								
1962–1986	2.6	2.6	6.4	4.5	4.7	3.2	3.9	3.3
1962–1974	2.2	2.8	4.3	4.6	4.7	3.2	3.6	3.1
1974–1986	2.9	2.4	8.3	4.4	4.6	3.1	4.0	3.5

NA = not available

NOTE   Sectoral data by industry for 1964, 1969 and 1979 not available.

SOURCES   NEDA (1976, pp. 54–5, 58) and NSCB (1989, pp. 11/8–9, 11/12–15).

sector remains constant, a phenomenon sometimes termed 'involution'.[8] In the third, the service sector serves as a 'parking lot for the poor', in which per capita output declines as more and more labor is pushed into it.

In the Philippine economy as a whole, labor productivity registered modest growth until 1983, whereupon it fell sharply (see Table 2.5). Labor productivity in the services sector held fairly constant from the early 1960s to the early 1980s. On the whole, then, the sector could be characterized as involutionary in this period. The services sector in the Philippines is quite heterogeneous, however, and this could reflect offsetting productivity increases and declines in different subsectors.[9] Following the onset of the economic crisis in 1983, employment in services grew substantially, and labor productivity dropped so sharply that by 1986 it was 20 per cent lower than it had been in 1963. During the crisis, the 'parking lot' scenario apparently predominated.

Table 2.6 reports trends in capital formation and the incremental output-capital ratio. Real net fixed capital formation rose in the 1960s, contracted in the wake of the 1970 balance-of-payments crisis, then rose sharply in the era of 'debt-led growth', and finally collapsed when the debt crisis struck in 1983, a course of events described more fully in Chapter 9.

The incremental output-capital ratio (IOCR), here calculated as the ratio of increase in GDP to net fixed capital formation in the current year, provides a measure of the marginal efficiency of capital. This is a rather crude measure, since investment may also contribute to output growth in later years, and variations in capacity utilization can lead to curious results as in the years 1984–86. Nevertheless, it provides a reasonable notion of the general trend in capital productivity. The IOCR ranges between 0.4 and 0.5 in much of the period, rising briefly in the early 1970s when new investment declined while output growth continued under the impact of prior investment. In the late 1970s, however, the IOCR began to decline. In 1984 and 1985 we find negative IOCRs, owing to the contraction of GDP, while in 1986 we find an anomalously high figure, as GDP recovers slightly with virtually zero net capital formation in that year. A noteworthy feature of these data is that the IOCR decline began several years *before* the onset of the debt crisis in 1983.

WAGES AND UNEMPLOYMENT

The failure of rising GNP per capita to 'trickle down' to the poor in the Philippines in 1962–86 emerges most clearly from an examination of trends in real wages and unemployment. In both rural and urban areas, the incomes of Filipino wage laborers declined substantially.

TABLE 2.5 *Labor Productivity by Sector,*
1962–1986 (constant 1972 pesos per worker)

Year	Sector					Total Employed Labor Force
	Agri-culture Fishery & Forestry	Manu-facturing	Mining & Quarrying	Con-struction	Services	
1962	1,928	5,572	11,632	4,323	6,191	3,485
1963	2,092	5,537	16,855	4,812	6,101	3,659
1965	2,246	6,116	21,647	5,421	5,751	3,838
1966	2,128	5,933	22,443	5,389	5,757	3,720
1967	2,194	6,563	14,523	5,940	6,336	3,973
1968	2,647	6,993	17,871	4,179	6,170	4,355
1970	2,713	7,304	21,182	2,904	6,478	4,483
1971	2,672	7,541	21,750	3,187	5,472	4,298
1972	2,480	8,674	37,524	4,253	6,311	4,488
1973	2,395	9,290	28,612	5,477	6,210	4,447
1974	2,510	9,512	30,909	5,454	6,627	4,684
1975	2,359	10,486	26,759	8,680	5,969	4,714
1976	2,584	11,451	18,407	12,325	6,501	5,192
1977	2,779	12,985	33,500	11,946	6,341	5,474
1978	2,568	12,117	29,656	11,453	6,008	5,136
1980	2,799	12,776	23,787	12,141	6,628	5,633
1981	2,756	13,259	27,187	13,226	6,227	5,513
1982	2,845	14,092	27,243	13,376	6,465	5,699
1983	2,515	13,306	19,275	11,032	6,066	5,201
1984	2,609	12,076	12,717	7,729	5,319	4,784
1985	2,707	11,208	13,813	6,225	4,900	4,540
1986	2,653	11,400	10,493	5,377	4,906	4,427
Growth Rates (per cent per annum)						
1962–86	1.1	4.0	−0.1	3.9	−0.4	1.5
1962–74	2.0	6.0	7.2	4.9	0.8	3.0
1974–86	0.2	2.1	−6.8	2.9	−1.5	0.1

NOTE
Productivity calculated from the ratio of GDP to employed labor force given in
Tables 2.2 and 2.4.

TABLE 2.6 *Capital Formation and Incremental Output-Capital Ratios,
1962–1986 (constant 1972 prices in millions of pesos)*

Year	Gross Fixed Capital Formation	Depreciation	Net Fixed Capital Formation	Incremental Output-Capital Ratio
1962	4,883	1,628	3,255	0.49
1963	5,801	1,874	3,927	0.58
1964	6,815	2,142	4,673	0.24
1965	7,129	2,444	4,685	0.41
1966	7,206	2,722	4,483	0.43
1967	8,811	3,019	5,791	0.43
1968	9,102	3,396	5,706	0.43
1969	9,116	3,839	5,277	0.46
1970	8,625	4,308	4,317	0.67
1971	9,084	4,848	4,236	0.71
1972	9,231	5,303	3,928	0.65
1973	10,070	5,762	4,308	1.21
1974	11,966	6,019	5,947	0.52
1975	14,974	6,324	8,650	0.42
1976	17,224	6,910	10,314	0.53
1977	17,553	7,480	10,073	0.45
1978	19,035	7,981	11,054	0.39
1979	21,270	8,757	12,513	0.41
1980	22,737	9,440	13,297	0.35
1981	23,542	10,544	12,998	0.28
1982	23,687	11,149	12,538	0.22
1983	23,102	11,394	11,708	0.08
1984	15,594	10,936	4,658	−1.29
1985	11,826	10,726	1,100	−3.66
1986	10,057	9,966	91	14.02

NOTE

For the years 1962–74, gross fixed capital formation and depreciation were converted
from 1965 pesos to 1972 pesos using the ratio of 1972 gross fixed capital formation
and 1972 depreciation reported according to the two base years in NEDA (1976,
pp. 119, 123) and NSCB (1989, pp. 3/20, 3/26, respectively).

SOURCES   NEDA (1976, pp. 118–19, 122–3) and NSCB (1989, pp. 3/20–21,
3/26–27).

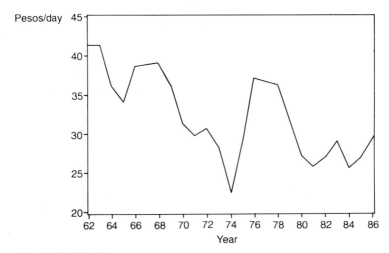

Sources: See Table 2.7.

Figure 2.2: **Real Agricultural Wage, 1962 – 1986**
(daily wage, without meals, constant 1986 pesos)

Agricultural wages fell by roughly one third in the 25-year period. Table 2.7 reports real daily wages for agricultural laborers in the country's four main crops – rice, corn, sugarcane, and coconut – based on data collected by the Bureau of Agricultural Economics (BAEcon) of the Ministry of Agriculture and Food.[10] To adjust for inflation, nominal wages are converted into constant 1986 pesos using the consumer price index for the country as a whole.[11] An overall agricultural wage index is constructed by averaging the rice and corn wages, which BAEcon officials consider the most reliable.[12]

Figure 2.2 depicts the trend in the real agricultural wage. It dropped sharply from 1962 to 1974, recovered partially in 1975 and 1976, and then slid again in the late 1970s and early 1980s. Lags in adjustment to price inflation explain some of the year-to-year variation; the 1974 trough, for example, coincided with exceptionally rapid inflation.[13] The overall trend is clearly downward. In the period as a whole, the real agricultural wage declined at 1.6 per cent per year.[14] In real (1986) US dollars, it fell from roughly $2.00/day in 1962 to $1.40/day in 1986.[15]

This conclusion is consistent with the findings of previous studies. Precise estimates of the extent of the wage decline vary, depending on the time period, the crops included, and the price index used. Of nine time series on real agricultural wages culled from various sources by the World Bank (1979c), pertaining to various periods from 1950 through 1977,

TABLE 2.7 *Agricultural Wage Rates, 1962–1986*
(daily wage, without meals, constant 1986 pesos)[1]

Year	Crop				Agriculture[2]	
	Rice	Corn	Sugar-cane	Coconut	1986 pesos	Index (1962=100)
1962					41.31	100.0
1963					41.37	100.1
1964					36.16	87.5
1965					34.07	82.5
1966	40.07	37.29			38.68	93.6
1967	40.19	37.80			38.99	94.4
1968	39.28	38.81			39.04	94.5
1969	37.37	35.41			36.39	88.1
1970	34.02	28.70	31.91	33.92	31.36	75.9
1971	31.17	28.36	27.45	34.81	29.76	72.0
1972	32.39	28.96	28.04	33.69	30.68	74.3
1973	29.04	27.34	33.56	31.01	28.19	68.2
1974	22.57	22.23	28.73	31.07	22.40	54.2
1975	28.92	29.33	35.60	33.54	29.13	70.5
1976	37.59	36.75	30.51	36.59	37.17	90.0
1977	37.59	35.64	41.78	35.15	36.62	88.6
1978	37.02	35.38	35.49	36.17	36.20	87.6
1979	32.37	31.38	33.25	32.10	31.87	77.2
1980	27.11	27.26	28.05	27.39	27.18	65.8
1981	26.93	24.42	26.87	30.42	25.68	62.2
1982	27.53	26.14	26.18	31.43	26.84	65.0
1983	29.57	28.34			28.96	70.1
1984	28.08	22.95			25.51	61.8
1985	30.43	23.20			26.82	64.9
1986	32.72	25.69			29.20	70.7

NOTES
1. Converted to 1986 pesos using consumer price index as reported in IMF (1987, pp. 560–1).
2. Simple average of rice and corn wages; estimates for the years 1962–1965 derived by splicing with 7-crop averages reported by Balagot and Librero (1975, Table 18). See text.

SOURCES   Rice and corn wages from unpublished data provided by the Bureau of Agricultural Economics. Sugarcane and coconut wages from World Bank (1985a, p. 29).

all but the earliest one, for the years 1950–63, display clear downward trends.[16]

Urban wages declined even more dramatically. From 1949 to 1980, the Central Bank of the Philippines collected and published data on wages for skilled and unskilled workers in industrial establishments in Manila and its suburbs.[17] Table 2.8 presents these data, converted into 1986 pesos by the consumer price index, for the years from 1962 onwards.[18] The Central Bank data reveal that skilled and unskilled urban workers experienced a remarkable decline in real wages during the 1970s. In 1980, their real wages were less than half the 1962 level.

The Central Bank series was discontinued by order of President Marcos in 1980 (World Bank, 1985a, p. 64), a step Lande and Hooley (1986, p. 1089) attribute to the embarrassment the data caused the government. Fragmentary data for subsequent years suggest that real wages of urban workers continued to deteriorate in the early 1980s. The World Bank (1985a, p. 103) reports nominal wages as of March 1983 for unskilled workers and for nine of the fifteen occupational groups included in the erstwhile Central Bank skilled-labor index. Montes (1987, p. 30b) reports quarterly data on wage movements from 1983 to 1986, based on unpublished small-scale 'skim' surveys undertaken by the government's National Census and Statistics Office (NCSO) to monitor the 'adjustment' process. Both sources indicate sharp real wage declines, as one might expect in a time of currency devaluation and severe contraction of economic activity.[19] The urban wage series in Table 2.8 is extended to 1986 using the World Bank and NCSO data.[20] The trends, depicted graphically in Figure 2.3, indicate a truly staggering decline in the purchasing power of urban wages, one which began well before the economic collapse of the mid-1980s.

Between 1962 and 1986, real wages of unskilled laborers in metropolitan Manila declined at an annual rate of 5.8 per cent, and real wages of skilled laborers declined almost as rapidly, at 5.2 per cent.[21] In real (1986) US dollars the daily wage of an unskilled worker fell from $4.37 in 1962 to $1.12 in 1986, while that of a skilled worker fell from $6.18 to $1.72. Comparing these trends to those for agricultural wages, we find a convergence. Both agricultural and urban real wages fell, but the latter fell more sharply, narrowing the initial gap between the two. Indeed, the wage for unskilled urban workers appears to have fallen below the agricultural wage in 1985 and 1986.

The precision of these data is open to challenge. A defect of the Central Bank's wage series, for example, is that it was based on an unchanging sample of firms, rather than on a representative sample selected anew in successive years. If real wages fell more rapidly in older firms than in newer ones, this could impart a downward bias to the data. It strains belief,

TABLE 2.8 *Urban Wage Rates, 1962–1986 (daily wage, constant 1986 pesos)*[1]

Year	Unskilled workers		Skilled workers[2]	
	1986 pesos	*Index (1962=100)*	*1986 pesos*	*Index (1962=100)*
1962	89.50	100.0	126.74	100.0
1963	87.31	97.6	120.77	95.3
1964	80.92	90.4	112.94	89.1
1965	84.07	93.9	112.76	89.0
1966	86.02	96.1	112.90	89.1
1967	85.19	95.2	111.81	88.2
1968	92.95	103.9	118.38	93.4
1969	96.06	107.3	123.03	97.1
1970	92.42	103.3	113.37	89.5
1971	81.27	90.8	98.25	77.5
1972	79.61	89.0	95.27	75.2
1973	70.08	78.3	86.08	67.9
1974	56.41	63.0	70.12	55.3
1975	57.27	64.0	68.31	53.9
1976	55.11	61.6	65.01	51.3
1977	52.79	59.0	65.36	51.6
1978	51.23	57.2	68.40	54.0
1979	45.92	51.3	64.12	50.6
1980	40.37	45.1	57.69	45.5
1981	NA	NA	NA	NA
1982	NA	NA	NA	NA
1983	36.83	41.1	61.81	48.8
1984	27.29	30.5	43.42	34.3
1985	23.21	25.9	35.55	28.0
1986	23.04	25.7	35.28	27.8

NA = not available

NOTES

1. Converted to 1986 pesos using consumer price index as reported in IMF (1987, pp. 560–1).
2. Skilled wage = simple average of fifteen occupations, as reported in Central Bank statistics.

SOURCES   Wage data for 1962–80 from Central Bank (1973, pp. 384–8; 1980, pp. 268–70). Wage estimates for 1983–86 calculated from March 1983 data in World Bank (1985a, p. 103) and quarterly nominal wage growth rates for 1983–86 reported in Montes (1987, p. 30b).

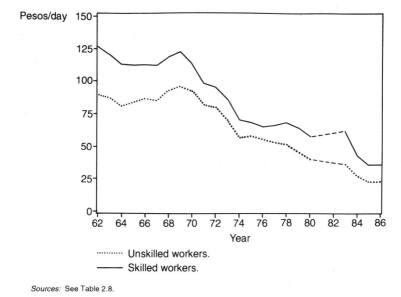

Sources: See Table 2.8.

Figure 2.3: **Real Wage of Urban Unskilled and Skilled Workers, 1962 – 1986 (daily wage, constant 1986 pesos)**

however, to imagine that such biases could explain away the negative trend. The conclusion seems inescapable: wage laborers in metropolitan Manila experienced a collapse in real wages in the 1970s and 1980s, on a magnitude with few precedents in modern economic history.

Employment data show substantial unemployment throughout the period. There is no evidence that the impact of real wage declines on worker incomes was mitigated significantly by increased employment per worker. Labor force participation rates increased, particularly among women. This helped to cushion the decline in real income per household, but did not reverse it.

In the Philippines, open unemployment is a somewhat misleading indicator of economic well-being, for the simple reason that the poor cannot afford it.[22] The poorest Filipinos cannot claim unemployment benefits from the government, nor can their families easily support them while they search for work. Instead they try to bring in some income, one way or another. The cigarette and candy vendors who ply their wares among the automobiles stuck in Manila's traffic jams are working, but they are not fully employed.

Such 'disguised unemployment', or underemployment, is difficult to measure. Household surveys conducted by the Philippine government's

National Census and Statistics Office (NCSO) distinguish two types of underemployment: the 'visibly underemployed', who work less than the full-time norm (40 hours per week prior to 1976; 64 days per quarter thereafter) and wanted additional work; and the 'invisibly underemployed', who work the full-time norm or more, but still wanted additional work.[23] Although these data provide some indication of the extent of underemployment, they are not ideal for assessing the extent to which lower wages were offset by longer hours, since a persons's desire for additional work might vary with the wage.

The official data on open unemployment and underemployment are reported in Table 2.9. To estimate total unemployment, the head-count measure of underemployment must be converted to a full-time equivalent. Here, following Tidalgo and Esguerra (1984, p. 91), this is done on the assumption that the average underemployed person was 67.5 per cent unemployed throughout the period.[24] In reality, the average degree of under-employment may have varied over time. For these reasons, the estimates of total unemployment reported in the table should be regarded as only rough approximations.

A further complication arises from changes in the official definition of employment over the years. In 1976, the survey reference period was changed from the past week to the past quarter, and the age cut-off for the working-age population was changed from 10 years and older to 15 years and older (World Bank, 1985a, pp. 62–3). Critics claimed that the Marcos government instituted these changes 'to conceal the rising number of unem-ployed'.[25] The former change could be expected to reduce the estimate of open unemployment, since a person is more likely to have been employed at some time in the past three months than in the past week. Both changes could be expected to increase the measured labor force participation rate (LFPR).[26]

The two series overlapped in 1976, as reported in Table 2.9, but they cannot be accurately spliced, among other reasons, because the new data pertain only to the third quarter. The new methodology may have increased the estimates of underemployment, but the extent to which this explains the higher reported underemployment rates in the late 1970s and 1980s cannot be readily ascertained. The World Bank (1988a, p. 41) states that 'if one defines underemployment as those working less than 65 days in a quarter and reporting their willingness to work additional time, underemployment in the 1980s more than doubled compared to its 1970 levels', implying that the methodological changes did not greatly affect the comparability of the pre- and post-1976 estimates.

More cautiously, we can conclude that total unemployment declined in the 1960s and early 1970s, and that it rose in the late 1970s and early

TABLE 2.9 *Labor Force Participation, Unemployment, and Underemployment,*
1961–1986

Year	Labor force participation rate	Open unem- ployment	Underemployment		Total unem- ployment[2]
			Head- count	Full- time equivalent[1]	
	(% of working- age population)		(% of labor force)		
1961	57.6	7.5	21.2	14.3	21.8
1966	55.9	7.1	22.1	14.9	22.0
1971	50.0	5.2	14.4	9.7	14.9
1972	50.8	6.3	11.9	8.0	14.3
1973	49.9	4.9	11.8	8.0	12.9
1974	50.2	4.0	9.8	6.6	10.6
1975	50.2	3.9	11.2	7.6	11.5
1976a	51.8	5.0	10.1	6.8	11.8
1976b[3]	60.5	5.2	24.2	16.3	21.5
1977	59.7	5.1	18.9	12.8	17.9
1978	61.8	5.2	14.1	9.5	14.7
1979	62.8	4.2	NA	NA	NA
1980	61.8	4.7	21.4	14.4	19.1
1981	62.6	5.4	22.8	15.4	20.8
1982	63.6	5.5	27.6	18.6	24.1
1983	63.8	4.9	30.3	20.5	25.4
1984	63.3	7.0	24.3	16.4	23.4
1985	63.9	6.1	17.5	11.8	17.9
1986	64.2	6.4	16.5	16.5	22.9

NA = not available

NOTES

1. Full-time equivalent calculated as 67.5 per cent of head-count.
2. Total unemployment = open unemployment plus full-time equivalent underemployment.
3. 1976a = old basis; 1976b = new basis, third quarter only (see text).

SOURCES Tidalgo and Esguerra (1984, pp. 84–5); World Bank (1985a, p. 22);
World Bank (1988a, pp. 127–8).

1980s. What happened between the early 1970s and the late 1970s is not entirely clear, owing to the changes in methodology in 1976, but on the face of it the numbers indicate a rise in total unemployment. It seems safe to conclude that if employment per member of the labor force grew at all between 1962 and 1986, it did not grow much. The impact of real wage declines on income per worker was not offset by dramatic reductions in unemployment.

Whatever the precise trend, the unemployment data reveal large-scale underutilization of the country's labor resources. The data indicate that in the 1980s one-fifth to one-fourth of the labor force was idle. Similarly, the International Labour Office (1974, p. 7) 'guesstimated' total unemployment at 25 per cent of the Philippine labor force in the early 1970s. Tidalgo and Esguerra (1984, pp. 91–3) report 18 per cent unemployment in the late 1970s. They also calculate a broader measure of labor underutilization, which includes reserves outside the officially counted labor force (primarily housekeepers and students); by this measure, 31 per cent of the potential labor force was unemployed in the late 1970s.

Labor force participation rates (LFPRs) declined from the early 1960s to the early 1970s, and then rose from the mid-1970s onwards, as reported in Table 2.9. The main source of LFPR growth in the latter period was the entry of more women into the labor force. Data presented by Reyes, Milan and Sanchez (1988, Table 5) indicate that between 1976 and 1986 the male LFPR remained fairly constant at about 80 per cent, while the female LFPR rose from 40 per cent to 48 per cent.

In theory, the increase in female labor force participation could be attributable to one or more of three factors: (1) the increasing emancipation of women from gender-related employment constraints; (2) the erosion of non-market economic activities which to some extent are omitted from labor-force measures; and (3) a survival strategy adopted in response to decreasing household incomes. The fact that female LFPR rose at a time of declining real wages and rising underemployment suggests that the third factor played an important role in the Philippines.

This inference is supported by the testimony of women workers. Women on a Negros sugarcane plantation, for example, explained to Rutten (1982, p. 54) that they worked on the hacienda 'only because their husband's wage is not sufficient to support their household, and that they would gladly stop doing this ill-paid tiresome work if his wages were much higher'.[27] A study of women's labor force participation in two rice-growing villages in Bicol similarly found that 'the concern to prevent a further deterioration in their family's standard of living when returns to labor are falling pervades among the village women' (Illo, 1985, p. 88).

Asian Development Bank economist J. M. Dowling (1984, p. 62) concludes: 'It is doubtful whether increased labor force participation could have offset the decline in real wages per worker'. A comparison of the magnitudes involved reinforces this conclusion. While real wages declined in 1962–86 at an annual rate of 1.6 per cent in agriculture, and at more than 5 per cent in metropolitan Manila, employment per capita grew at 0.6 per cent per year.[28] It seems unlikely, therefore, that increased female labor force participation could have prevented an increase in poverty among wage-earning families.

INCOME DISTRIBUTION AND POVERTY

The Philippine government periodically conducts family income and expenditure surveys which have been used by the World Bank, among others, to analyze changes over time in income distribution and poverty. The reliability of these data is quite low. In the view of a leading analyst of Philippine income distribution, this reflects the 'relative lack of serious attention in Philippine development planning and economic policy-making to the poverty problem' (Mangahas, 1982, p. 126). A review of the survey data is useful, however, if only to warn against the spurious conclusions to which their incautious use can lead.

Data Problems

The main source of income distribution data in the Philippines is the Family Income and Expenditures Survey (FIES) conducted approximately every five years since 1956 by the NCSO. In addition, in 1979 the NCSO began a quarterly Integrated Survey of Households (ISH) based on a smaller sample.[29]

The accuracy of these data at any point in time is quite doubtful, as is their comparability over time. Income and expenditure appear to be seriously underestimated in the surveys. Total personal income estimated by the FIES and ISH has ranged from 42 to 71 per cent of the total reported in the National Accounts (see Table 2.10).[30] There is no reason to suppose that the degree of underestimation has been uniform across income classes, nor that the pattern of underestimation across classes remained constant through time.

Inferences from the survey data are highly sensitive to assumptions regarding the pattern of underestimation and its variation over time. 'The problem of gross undercoverage makes it highly inadvisable to use this

TABLE 2.10 *Survey Estimates of Income Shares of Upper and Lower Quintiles,*
1956–1985

Year	Share of bottom 20% of families	Share of top 20% of families	Ratio of survey to national accounts income
1956	4.9	54.8	0.71
1961	4.7	56.5	0.65
1965	3.6	55.4	0.67
1971	4.0	54.5	0.62
1978–79	3.3	57.6	0.42–0.54
1980–83	3.0	58.8	0.54–0.66
1985	5.7	50.3	0.65

SOURCES
Income shares based on Family Income and Expenditure Surveys and Integrated
Surveys of Households (for 1978–9 and 1980–3), as reported by Dowling (1984,
p. 54) for 1956, 1965 and 1978–9; World Bank (1985a, p. 16) for 1980–3; and World
Bank (1988a, p. 123) for 1961, 1971 & 1985.

Ratios of survey estimates of total personal income to National Accounts estimates
are from Berry (1978, p. 315) for 1956; Mangahas (1981, p. 60) for 1978–9;
World Bank (1985a, p. 16) for 1980–3; and World Bank (1988a, p. 159) for
remaining years.

series of surveys for establishing the trend in income distribution', Mangahas
(1982, pp. 134, 138) remarks. 'If the sample mean income is grossly out
of reality, I would not regard the sample variance, the decile shares, the
Gini ratio, or any other distributive parameters as of any *substantive* value'.
Mangahas concludes that all that can be ascertained from the data is that 'the
degree of inequality has been high for some time, and that there is as yet no
indication of any tendency for it to decline'.

Others have been less cautious. The World Bank (1980b, 1985a, 1988a),
has reported distributional trends based on the survey data in three successive
'Philippine poverty reports'. These reports have been widely disseminated
among officials, and summaries of the Bank's findings have appeared in
the press.[31] However doubtful their substantive value, the survey data have
helped to shape official and public perceptions of distributional trends in the
Philippines.

Several methodological issues are inescapable in any attempt to infer
distributional trends from the survey data:

(i) *Income v. expenditure data*
The first issue is whether to use data on family income or family expenditure. An argument in favor of expenditure-based measures of distribution is that deliberate under-reporting (owing, for example, to tax avoidance) tends to be more serious in the income data. On the other hand, income data clearly are preferable on theoretical grounds. Expenditure data tend to understate the incomes of the rich, since savings rates tend to rise with income. At the same time, among the poor we tend to find an excess of expenditure over income, financed by dissaving (or borrowing). Moreover, Khan (1977, pp. 240–1) reports that the NCSO's method of valuation of food tends to overstate the expenditure of the poor, while its method of valuation of durable goods understates the expenditure of the rich.[32]

Comparisons with National Accounts data reveal that in the 1985 FIES, total expenditure was *more* seriously underestimated than income.[33] The ISH surveys report only income data. Hence analyses of distributional trends extending to the 1980s, such as those of the World Bank (1985a, 1988a), have used the income data rather than the expenditure data. The analysis below does the same.

(ii) *Variations in aggregate understatement of income*
The reliability of the survey data on family income, never high, has varied through time. The ratio of total personal income as estimated by the surveys to that in the National Accounts, reported in Table 2.10, provides an indicator of the extent of understatement, albeit an imperfect one since the National Accounts are themselves subject to measurement errors.[34] The 1975 and 1979 FIES 'encountered difficulties such that the resulting data have not been published' (NCSO, 1986, p. iii), and hence are not included in the discussion below.[35] The ISH data are considered to be less reliable than the FIES data due to the smaller sample size, and are less consistent with the National Accounts estimates of total personal income.

(iii) *The pattern of understatement across income classes*
While the National Accounts provide some indication of the extent of aggregate income understatement in the surveys, we have no comparable information about the pattern of understatement across income classes, nor about changes in this pattern over time. If income understatement were uniform among all classes – that is, if the income of the poor were underestimated by the same percentage as that of the rich – then the survey data would accurately reflect the true level of inequality. If the degree of understatement varied across classes, but this pattern remained constant over time, then the survey data at least would reveal the trend in inequality, if not

its true level. Unfortunately, there is no empirical basis whatsoever for either assumption.

Differences in the degree of understatement across income classes can arise from three sources. The first is variation in the extent of under-reporting by survey respondents. Rich people typically have a higher propensity to understate their incomes than poor people, for the simple reason that they have more to hide.[36] The second is differences in the relative importance of non-cash income sources, and in the extent to which these are captured in the survey. The third is sampling error, that is, a non-proportional coverage of different income classes uncorrected by the use of different 'blowing-up' factors.[37]

There are grounds to suspect that income understatement for the rich increased over time, while income understatement for the poor decreased. Khan (1977, p. 240) reports that FIES coverage of non-cash incomes, which are relatively more important for poorer families, improved between 1961 and 1971. Yet the ratio of FIES to National Account income declined, implying greater understatement in the upper-income brackets.[38]

There are good *a priori* reasons to suspect that this shift in the pattern of understatement continued in subsequent years. Increasing commercialization would increase the cash component of incomes, which is more likely to be recorded than the non-cash component; hence understatement of the incomes of the poor would tend to decrease. At the same time, if intentional under-reporting is positively correlated with income, its extent among the rich could be expected to worsen as the their incomes rise. Furthermore, the predations of the martial law regime in the 1970s, and the economic and political crises of the 1980s, may have heightened the incentives for income concealment on the part of the rich. As documented in Chapter 10 of this book, the Philippines experienced large-scale illicit capital flight during this period. The relatively wealthy individuals spiriting their money out of the country had an extra motive for understating their true incomes.

The World Bank's third Philippine poverty report (1988a, pp. 5, 123) presents estimates of trends in real incomes by decile for the years 1961, 1971, and 1985. In so doing, it simply ignores this issue, assuming, in effect, that the pattern of income understatement remained constant over time. The sensitivity of the World Bank's results to alternative assumptions is demonstrated below.

(iv) *Price indexes*
The choice of price indexes for the conversion of nominal to real income affects trend estimates of income, poverty, and inequality. The use of a single consumer price index (CPI) for all income classes – as, for example, in the

World Bank's (1988a, pp. 5, 123) calculation of average real income by decile – masks the distributional effects of changes in relative prices.

Table 2.11 reports the overall Philippine CPI and its food and non-food price components. Two CPI series are reported: one published by the International Monetary Fund (IMF) with 1980 as the base year, and the other from the government's National Economic and Development Authority (NEDA) with 1978 as the base year.[39] The food price index (more precisely, the index for food, beverage, and tobacco prices) appears along with NEDA's CPI. The non-food price index is here derived on the assumption that the food items receive a weight of 55 per cent in the CPI. [40]

Food prices rose more rapidly than non-food prices between 1962 and 1974, and thereafter more slowly. Since the poor devote a larger fraction of their income to food than do the rich, the use of the overall CPI tends to understate the degree to which real income distribution became more unequal in the years prior to 1974, and to overstate the growth in inequality thereafter.[41] The data in Table 2.11 permit rough adjustments for this relative price effect, and these are carried out below.

(v) *Family v. per capita income*
A final issue is the difference between family income and per capita income. In theory, per capita income is preferable for distributional measures, since family size may vary systematically across family income classes. If household size is positively related to income, as is often assumed to be the case, then per capita income measures will show less inequality than family income measures. In the Philippines, however, there is some evidence that the reverse is true: poor households tend to be larger than rich ones.[42]

In practice, Philippine government publications report only family income data. If this is inversely related to family size, the official data understate the degree of inequality at any given time.[43] Changes over time in the family size-income relationship would bias trend estimates based on family income, but little evidence is available on this point. The World Bank (1988a), however, presents revised distributional profiles based on per capita income, specially tabulated for the Bank from the raw survey data. These data are examined below.

Income Distribution

We now turn to the evidence. Table 2.10 reports the share in total income of the top and bottom quintiles – that is, the richest 20 per cent and poorest

The Philippines

TABLE 2.11 *Consumer, Food, and Non-food Price Indexes, 1962–1986*

Year	CPI		Food prices	Non-food prices
	IMF	*NEDA*		
	(1980=100)	*(1978=100)*	*(1978=100)*	*(1978=100)*
1962	15.9	23.7	20.4	27.8
1963	17.2	25.0	22.4	28.2
1964	18.7	27.0	25.4	28.9
1965	19.3	27.7	25.8	29.9
1966	20.2	28.5	27.6	29.6
1967	21.4	30.3	29.8	30.9
1968	21.8	31.1	29.7	32.8
1969	22.1	31.6	30.2	33.3
1970	25.5	34.6	33.4	36.1
1971	30.9	39.8	40.1	39.4
1972	33.5	46.4	48.1	44.3
1973	39.0	53.9	55.4	52.1
1974	52.3	72.5	74.5	70.1
1975	55.9	77.5	78.5	76.3
1976	61.0	85.0	86.0	83.8
1977	67.1	93.4	94.4	92.2
1978	72.0	100.0	100.0	100.0
1979	84.6	117.5	115.6	119.8
1980	100.0	138.9	132.9	146.2
1981	113.1	157.1	149.8	166.0
1982	124.6	173.2	162.5	186.3
1983	137.1	190.5	176.5	207.6
1984	206.2	286.4	271.4	304.7
1985	253.8	352.6	332.0	377.8
1986	255.7	355.3	329.1	387.3

SOURCES Column 1: IMF (1987, pp. 560–1). Columns 2–4: NEDA (1986, pp. 116–17) and NSCB (1989, p. 2, 25), with 1962–9 figures for Metropolitan Manila area scaled to all-Philippines basis using their average ratio in 1970–2.

20 per cent of Philippine families – as estimated by successive FIES and ISH surveys. These estimates are not corrected for income understatement, relative price changes, or differences in family size. They indicate that the richest fifth of Philippine families consistently received more than half of total income, while the poorest fifth received as little as three per cent.

This income distribution ranks among the most inequitable in the world. The World Bank (1988a, p. iii) notes that the country 'has one of the most unequal income distributions among middle-income countries', and that it is 'particularly unequal when compared with some other developing countries in the region'. In its previous poverty report, the World Bank (1985a, p. 18) similarly observed that the Philippine income distribution is 'closer to those of the Latin American countries than [to those of the] East Asian countries'.

Income inequality in the Philippines is exacerbated by regressive government tax policy. According to the World Bank (1988a, p. iii), revenue collections fall more heavily on the poor than the rich, and hence, 'inequality of income after taxes is also much worse when compared with similar indicators in other countries'. The regressive impact of Philippine government policy has extended far beyond the tax structure, as documented elsewhere in this book, but it is noteworthy that this impact was sharpened rather than moderated by taxation.

Regarding the trend in inequality, as opposed to its level, the survey evidence is highly suspect for the reasons noted above. Taking the data in Table 2.10 at face value, they indicate that inequality widened until the early 1980s, at which time the richest quintile received nearly 59 per cent of total income, while the poorest quintile received only 3 per cent. The trend towards greater inequality appears to have been reversed in 1985, when the estimated income share of the poorest quintile rose to an all-time high of 5.7 per cent, while that of the top quintile dropped to an all-time low of 50.3 per cent. Whereas the ISH surveys of 1980–83 found that the family incomes of the richest quintile were twenty times as high as those of the poorest quintile, the 1985 FIES found they were only nine times as high.

Indeed, the 1985 estimates show not only an increase in equality, but a rise in the real incomes of the poor since 1971, coupled with a decline in the real incomes of the rich (see Table 2.12, series A). The ostensible gain for the poor is rather extraordinary, since in 1985 the Philippines was mired in the worst economic crisis in its postwar history. Between 1982 and 1985, the country's GNP plunged by 10 per cent, and GNP per capita by 15 per cent. Following the devaluation of the peso, inflation ran at 50 per cent in 1984 and 23 per cent in 1985. According to the World Bank (1988a, p. 21), this inflation was 'a regressive tax since it lowered the incomes of the lower six deciles while increasing incomes of the highest two deciles'. As documented in the previous section, real wages had declined even during the 1970s, and continued to do so in the 1980s.

The World Bank (1988a, pp. 4–5) nevertheless chooses not to challenge the accuracy of the 1985 FIES figures in its third poverty report, and draws the remarkable conclusion that 'although average family income fell in real

TABLE 2.12 *Trends in Real Income Distribution, 1961–1985: Three Alternative Estimates (average annual family income; thousands of 1978 pesos)*

	A			B			C		
	1961	1971	1985	1961	1971	1985	1961	1971	1985
(a) Total									
Richest 10%	46.4	56.5	47.4	42.9	56.7	46.1	39.9	55.9	49.9
Poorest 30%	3.1	3.7	4.5	3.3	3.7	4.6	4.3	4.0	3.3
Rich/poor ratio	15.2	15.1	10.6	13.1	15.2	10.1	9.3	13.9	15.2
(b) Rural									
Richest 10%	24.1	39.4	29.0	22.3	39.6	28.2	20.7	39.0	30.5
Poorest 30%	2.6	3.1	3.7	2.8	3.1	3.8	3.4	3.3	3.0
Rich/poor ratio	9.2	12.6	7.8	7.9	12.7	7.5	6.2	11.7	10.2
(c) Urban									
Richest 10%	77.0	82.2	69.7	71.2	82.7	67.9	66.1	81.3	73.5
Poorest 30%	4.2	6.4	6.5	4.5	6.4	6.6	6.2	6.8	4.7
Rich/poor ratio	18.5	12.8	10.8	16.0	12.9	10.3	10.7	11.9	15.6

Series A = World Bank data scaled up assuming uniform income understatement across deciles (given by FIES/National Accounts family income ratios of 0.65 in 1961, 0.62 in 1971, and 0.65 in 1985).

Series B = Series A adjusted for effects of changes in relative price of food [see text for details].

Series C = Series B recalculated assuming that understatement of the incomes of the richest 10% rose over time (reported/actual income ratio declining from 0.70 in 1961 to 0.63 in 1971 and to 0.60 in 1985), with a compensating decrease in understatement of the incomes of the poorest 30% [see text for details].

SOURCES   FIES income distribution data from World Bank (1988a, p. 123); price index data from NEDA (1986, pp. 116–17); food weights for relative price adjustment from NCSO (1986b, p. 99).

terms from 1971 to 1985, it increased for the lowest five deciles, and declined for the top five deciles'. In other words, the country purportedly experienced strong equalization in the distribution of income.

Before we celebrate this achievement, let us consider other plausible explanations for the 1985 family income estimates. In particular, it would seem prudent to consider the possible impact of changes in the relative prices of food and non-food items, and of changes in the pattern of income understatement across income classes. As noted above, there are reasonable grounds to suspect biases on both counts.

Table 2.12 presents estimates of the trend in real incomes for the richest 10 per cent of Philippine families and for the poorest 30 per cent, who are termed the 'core poor' by the World Bank (1988a, p. 8). The estimates are based on FIES data for 1961, 1971 and 1985, with families grouped into deciles based on their per capita incomes (World Bank, 1988a, pp. 5, 123).[44] As a summary measure of relative inequality, the table also reports the ratio of the average income of the richest 10 per cent to that of the poorest 30 per cent.

Three alternative sets of estimates are presented in Table 2.12:

Series A
These are the estimates reported by the World Bank, with the sole difference that they are scaled up by the survey/national-account income ratio by assuming *uniform* income understatement across classes. Since this ratio changed little in the years in question (it was 0.65 in 1961 and 1985, and 0.62 in 1971), the trends depicted in Series A correspond closely to those reported by the World Bank (1988a, pp. 5, 123).[45] Since the same scalar adjustments are applied to rich and poor alike, relative inequality is identical to that reported by the World Bank. Real income is here derived from the nominal data by applying the overall consumer price index to all income classes.[46]

Series B
Real income as reported in Series A is here recalculated to capture the effects of changes over time in the relative price of food. Separate price indexes were computed for the richest 10 per cent and for the poorest 30 per cent, incorporating different weights on food and non-food items derived from the 1985 FIES expenditure data.[47] The most striking impact of this adjustment is on the trend between 1961 and 1971, when food prices rose considerably faster than non-food prices (see Table 2.11). Whereas Series A shows a slight *decrease* in relative inequality in the country as a whole between 1961 and 1971, Series B shows an noticeable *increase*.

Series C

Real income as reported in Series B is here recalculated on the assumptions that income understatement was *not* uniform across classes and that the pattern of understatement *shifted* over time. Specifically, it is assumed that income understatement for the richest decile increased, such that the ratio of their survey to actual income declined from 0.70 in 1961 to 0.63 in 1971 and to 0.60 in 1985. The National Accounts income data indicate aggregate ratios in these years of 0.65, 0.62, and 0.65, respectively (see Table 2.10). The assumed extent of understatement by the rich thus does not diverge all that greatly from the average figures. A compensating shift towards less income understatement for the poorest 30 per cent is assumed, such that the ratio of their survey-to-actual income rose from 0.50 in 1961 to 0.57 in 1971 and to 0.90 in 1985.[48]

The impact of these alternative assumptions on the trends in income distribution is quite striking. Rather than the reduction in inequality reported by the World Bank, Series C shows a substantial increase in inequality. Rather than a 45 per cent rise in the real incomes of the poorest 30 per cent between 1961 and 1985, Series C shows a 23 per cent decline. One could, of course, assume a wide variety of patterns of income understatement and shifts in them through time. Series C merely illustrates the implications of one such assumption. The precise ratios chosen are quite arbitrary. However, the World Bank's implicit assumptions that the degree of understatement was identical for each income class, and that this pattern remained unchanged over time, are no less arbitrary. The sensitivity of the findings to these assumptions underscores the extremely tenuous nature of *any* conclusions about distributional trends based on the survey data.

As discussed above, it seems likely that the pattern of income under-statement did shift over time, as increasing commercialization and better coverage of non-cash incomes reduced understatement for the poor, while rising incomes, political and economic risks, and massive capital flight led to increased understatement for the rich. If so, Series C may provide a better approximation of reality than series A. Series C is also far more consistent with the real wage evidence examined in the previous section.

The overall picture in Series C is one of immiserizing growth. Between 1961 and 1971, the rich became much richer, while the poor became a bit poorer.[49] Between 1971 and 1985, both rich and poor experienced real income declines, but in percentage terms the incomes of the poor fell more than the incomes of the rich. Hence inequality continued to widen.

The sole exception to the general widening of inequalities in Series C is an apparent narrowing of inequality in rural areas between 1971 and 1985.

Remarking on this finding in its own series (which, in terms of relative distribution, is identical to Series A), the World Bank (1988a, p. 6) states that this improvement 'may be due to the fact that large landlords, who were previously surveyed in the rural areas, have now moved into the cities because of the insurgency situation'.

The urban income estimates in Series C illustrate the possibility that two successive periods of weak polarization – one in which the incomes of the rich rise faster than those of the poor, and the other in which the incomes of the poor fall faster than those of the rich – can produce an overall result of strong polarization, in which the rich become absolutely richer, and the poor absolutely poorer.

All three sets of estimates in Table 2.12 show that rural–urban income differentials narrowed over time.[50] No great confidence can be placed in this finding. Just as the pattern of understatement across income classes is likely to have varied over time, so too the pattern may have varied between rural and urban areas. Comparing 1975 FIES and early 1980s ISH data, the World Bank (1985a, p. 18) concluded that the rural-urban income gap was in fact widening. On the other hand, the sharper wage decline in metropolitan Manila than in agriculture, discussed above, is consistent with a narrowing of the income gap. Since evidence on this point is sparse and inconclusive, no revision of the survey estimates of rural-urban income differentials is attempted here.[51]

In sum, survey data on family income in the Philippines provide a slender basis on which to assess distributional trends. Any conclusions drawn from the available data are necessarily conjectural, resting in particular on assumptions as to the pattern of income understatement. The estimates presented in Table 2.12 are consistent with the level of national income as reported in the National Accounts. Series B and C incorporate an adjustment for relative price effects. Series C also incorporates an adjustment for shifts over time in the pattern of understatement, and may be the more plausible depiction of actual trends.

Poverty

Most estimates of the extent of poverty in the Philippines have been based on the official family income surveys, and hence are subject to the data deficiencies reviewed above. Changes over time in the extent of income understatement for low-income families, for example, could dramatically affect estimates of poverty trends.

In addition, poverty measurement poses two distinct methodological problems: how to draw the 'poverty line' to define who is poor, and how to add up the individuals or households below it to get a measure of the overall magnitude of poverty. In the Philippines, poverty lines typically have been based on estimates of the income needed to meet nutritional requirements.[52] Most studies have used the simple headcount measure – the percentage of individuals or households who live below the line – to solve the aggregation problem. Although this measure has the virtue of simplicity, it has the obvious defect that it says nothing about *how far* below the line people are living.[53]

Table 2.13 presents nationwide and regional poverty estimates for the Philippines, compiled from several sources. The estimates for 1965, 1971 and 1975 are based on FIES data analyzed by Tan and Holazo (1979). The authors used regional price data to construct two poverty lines for each region, one based on a least-cost food budget and the other on a food budget constrained by variety considerations. The latter (their 'Series B') is reported here.[54]

Two sets of estimates are reported for the year 1983. The first, from the World Bank (1985a), is based on ISH data, using region-specific price indexes.[55] The World Bank's estimates show lower poverty incidence in 1983 as compared to earlier years. The second set of estimates for 1983 is based on 'self-rating' surveys reported by Mangahas (1985a). This approach departs quite radically from traditional income surveys, for it assesses the extent of poverty simply by asking people whether they consider themselves to be poor.[56] Self-rating data for the Philippines are not available prior to the 1980s, however, and hence do not provide an alternative basis for the assessment of earlier time trends. Finally, the poverty estimates for 1985 are based on FIES data analyzed by NEDA's Technical Working Group on Poverty (1988). These too were derived using region-specific price indexes.

The estimates consistently indicate less poverty in metropolitan Manila than elsewhere. The differential diminished over time, however, a finding consistent with the evidence on urban and rural wages. Among the other regions, Southern Tagalog and Central Luzon, the two nearest to Manila, also recorded below-average poverty incidence in all years. The regions with the most poverty varied over time. The earlier data show relatively high poverty incidence in northern Luzon (Cagayan Valley and Ilocos), Eastern and Western Visayas, and Mindanao. The 1985 data show the highest poverty incidence in Bicol and Western Visayas. The self-rating approach, which Mangahas (1985a, p. 112; 1987, p. 11) contends yields the most plausible regional comparisons, shows the highest poverty levels in Northern and Western Mindanao, followed by the Visayas and Cagayan Valley.

TABLE 2.13 Estimates of Poverty Incidence by Region, 1965–1985
(per cent of families living below poverty line)

Region	1965	1971	1975	1983 World Bank	1983 Mangahas	1985 Total	1985 Urban	1985 Rural
Manila & suburbs	10.6	16.0	40.6	11.2	31	43.9	43.9	–
Ilocos	57.3	56.3	51.7	40.3	53	51.6	55.4	50.6
Cagayan Valley	67.6	65.5	56.5	43.1	67	55.7	49.7	56.7
Central Luzon	32.3	30.7	37.8	27.4	46	43.5	44.5	42.8
Southern Tagalog	34.0	39.8	50.9	31.3	43	55.2	50.0	58.4
Bicol	38.5	49.8	55.9	42.7	58	73.5	62.6	76.3
Western Visayas	37.7	36.9	53.5	50.0	66	73.4	66.0	76.3
Eastern Visayas	{ 52.3	{ 61.5	{ 54.9	33.0	66	70.2	69.6	70.4
Central Visayas				48.1	69	69.9	60.9	74.1
Northern Mindanao	{ 47.8	{ 51.5	{ 65.6	38.6	75	63.0	60.1	63.6
Central Mindanao				28.4	52	60.2	60.4	60.2
Western Mindanao	{ 51.2	{ 47.0	{ 55.2	40.1	76	65.6	67.4	65.0
Southern Mindanao				33.3	60	63.6	55.0	65.5
National	41.0	43.8	51.5	34.6[1]	55	58.9	52.0	63.2

NOTE Calculated from regional data presented in original source using 1980 populations as weights.

SOURCES Estimates for 1965, 1971 and 1975: Tan and Holazo (1979, pp. 473–4, 'Series B'). Estimates for 1983: World Bank (1985a, 'Series B'). Estimates for 1983: World Bank (1985a, p. 88) and Mangahas (1985a, pp. 84–6). Estimates for 1985: NEDA, Technical Working Group on Poverty (1988, Table 3).

With respect to time trends, the data in Table 2.13 generally show increasing poverty. Nationwide, the percentage of Filipino families living below the poverty line rises from 41 per cent in 1965 to 59 per cent in 1985. The regional data show the most rapid increases in southern Luzon, the Visayas, and metropolitan Manila. Although this picture of increasing poverty is consistent with the real wage evidence, the estimates in Table 2.13 cannot themselves be regarded as conclusive, owing to the problems of data quality and methodology mentioned above.

In particular, the poverty estimates are highly sensitive to assumptions as to the pattern of income understatement in the survey data, the definition of the poverty line, and the choice of price indexes for extending the line through time. This precariousness of the resulting estimates is strikingly illustrated by the disparate findings of the World Bank's three successive reports on poverty in the Philippines.

The World Bank's first Philippine poverty report (World Bank, 1980b) found a sharp drop in the percentage of families in poverty between 1961 and 1965, followed by a small increase between 1965 and 1971, and a large increase between 1971 and 1975 (see Table 2.14). The Bank concluded that poverty had risen since Marcos came to power. This provided ammunition to critics of the regime, and provoked considerable controversy when the report was leaked to the press.

The World Bank's second Philippine poverty report (World Bank, 1985a) extended the poverty estimates to the early 1980s using ISH data. The results purported to show that poverty had decreased substantially since 1971. The accuracy of the 1975 data, which had shown a rise in poverty in the early 1970s, was now questioned by the Bank, among other reasons because of the exceptionally low ratio of FIES to National Accounts income (see Table 2.10). The report concluded:

> [A] modest and plausible decline in rural and urban poverty incidence took place between 1971 and the early 1980s. There was thus some trickle down of growth to the lower income groups. (World Bank, 1985a, p. 9)

This finding was quite at odds with the conclusions one would draw from the real wage data, which were also examined in the World Bank report.

Noting this apparent contradiction, the World Bank (1985a, p. v) offered three explanations to reconcile the poverty and the real wage trends.

First, the Bank claimed that in both rural and urban areas, 'families headed by wage-earners generally had lower levels of poverty incidence'. Hence 'the decline in real wages still left most of the families with total family

TABLE 2.14 *World Bank Estimates of Poverty, 1961–1985*
(per cent of families living below poverty line nationwide)

Year	Source: World Bank poverty report issued in			
	1980	1985	1988	
			p. 2	p. 115
1961	57.9			
1965	43.3			
1971	44.9	50.7	52.0	36.1
1975	53.2	60.6		45.3
1980		40.8		
1981		41.4		
1982		36.6		
1983		39.0		
1985			51.9	51.7

SOURCES   World Bank (1980b, p. 160; 1985a, p. 10; 1988a, pp. 2, 115).

incomes above the poverty line'. This argument is quite unconvincing. The inference that real incomes of the non-wage earning poor were rising at the same time that real wages for unskilled urban labor and agricultural labor were falling is, to say the least, implausible. Moreover, there can be little doubt that agricultural wage laborers are generally among the poorest half of the rural population. And while there are no doubt some persons in the urban 'informal sector' who earn even less than unskilled urban wage laborers, the latter are arguably poor by any reasonable definition.

Second, the Bank stated that increased female labor force participation raised the average number of employed persons per household from 1.8 to 2, and that this, together with an ostensible decline in average household size, lowered the ratio of dependents to income-earners. Increased female labor force participation, however, was more likely a response to declining real incomes than a cause of rising real incomes, as discussed above.

Third, and more plausibly, the Bank noted that 'deficiencies in the data base, both in regard to wages and in respect of family incomes, may also be at the root of the apparent contradictory trends in wages and poverty'. In this regard it should be noted that, whatever their faults, the wage data are the product of collection procedures carried out annually over many years by the same agencies (BAEcon and the Central Bank), whereas the income data are the product of intermittent surveys using varying methodologies, the reliability and comparability of which are highly doubtful. Therefore, if data deficiencies are indeed the explanation, it would seem reasonable to place greater confidence in the wage trends. Moreover, even in the unlikely event that both data sources are flawed to the same extent but in opposite directions, the magnitude of the estimated real wage decline is much larger than that of the estimated poverty reduction, and hence one would conclude that real incomes of the rural and urban working classes did in fact decline.

Aside from the unreliability of the income data, part of the explanation for the ostensible reduction in poverty lies in the methodology the World Bank used to construct a price index to extend its 1983 poverty line to earlier years (World Bank, 1985a, pp. 69–75). As a price deflator, the Bank used a weighted average of the *rice* price index and the overall consumer price index (CPI). Their respective weights (0.7 and 0.3 for rural areas, 0.6 and 0.4 for urban areas) were based on the *food* and non-food shares of expenditure among low-income households. The stated rationale is the observation that rice prices rose more slowly than the overall CPI between 1975 and 1983. While this is true (see Table 4.1), prices of other food items rose more rapidly than the price of rice, and in some cases more rapidly than the general CPI.[57] Expenditure data from the 1985 FIES (NEDA, 1986b, p. 99) indicate that while food accounts for 67 per cent of expenditure by low-income households, cereals and cereal preparations account for only 32 per cent. Next in importance are fish and marine products (12 per cent) and fruits and vegetables (5 per cent), both of which showed price rises *above* the general rate of inflation in 1975–83.

The substitution of rice for 'food' in the World Bank's price deflator thus understates the rise in the cost of living for poor families.[58] The result is a downward bias in the reported poverty trend: as the real purchasing power represented by the poverty line diminishes over time, fewer and fewer households fall below it. The magnitude of the impact on poverty estimates cannot be precisely ascertained, since this would require the application of a corrected poverty line to the raw data on family income, which are not publicly available. In a footnote, however, the World Bank (1985a, p. 70, n. 4) notes that if the 1975 poverty line had been extrapolated using the CPI, rather than the Bank's 'food'-weighted price index, the 1983 poverty lines would have been 60 per cent higher in rural areas and 45 per cent higher in urban areas. It is readily conceivable, therefore, that the poverty reduction discovered in the World Bank's second poverty report is largely attributable to its peculiar construction of a price index.

The third and most recent of the World Bank's Philippine poverty reports (World Bank, 1988a) charts a middle course between the first two. Rather than showing increasing poverty, as in the first report, or decreasing poverty, as in the second, the third report shows no change over time. Confining the comparison to the years 1971 and 1985, on the grounds that data for other years are not comparable (p. 2), the report concludes that nationwide the percentage of families living in poverty remained constant at 52 per cent.[59] The fragility of this finding is apparent not only from our review of the data sources and a comparison with the World Bank's earlier reports, but also from the fact the statistical appendix of the same report presents, without comment, a different set of estimates (reproduced in the final column of Table 2.14) showing that poverty incidence *rose* from 36 per cent in 1971 to 52 per cent in 1985.

Other Welfare Indicators

Data on nutrition and infant mortality confirm that millions of Filipinos lack access to basic human needs.

A 1982 survey by the Food and Nutrition Research Institute found that two-thirds of Philippine families consumed less than the recommended minimum daily calorie intake, and that one-third consumed less than 80 per cent of the recommended level (see Table 2.15). These figures are likely to understate the prevalence of undernutrition, since two relatively impoverished regions in Mindanao were omitted from the survey for security reasons (Quisumbing, 1987a, p. 37).

A 1985 survey of preschool children by the Philippine Nutritional Surveillance System found that 22 per cent were moderately to severely underweight (less than 75% of the weight-for-age standard); 14 per cent were wasted (less than 85 per cent of the weight-for-height standard); and 25 per cent were stunted (less than 90 per cent of the height-for-age standard).[60]

In the absence of comparable data for earlier years, it is not possible to draw firm conclusions as to long-term trends in the extent of undernutrition.[61]

Official data on infant mortality in the Philippines show a decline from 85 deaths per 1,000 births in 1960 to 35 per 1,000 in 1986. The reliability of these data is an open question, since they refer only to deaths officially

TABLE 2.15   *Distribution of Households by Adequacy of Calorie Consumption, 1982 (percentage of households)*

Per cent of recommended calorie intake	Total households	Rural households	Urban households
Less than 70%	17.8	17.3	18.7
70–79%	15.8	17.0	13.4
80–89%	18.9	19.8	17.3
90–99%	14.5	13.8	15.9
100–109%	10.8	10.7	11.2
More than 109%	22.1	21.4	23.5

(Totals may not add to 100 per cent due to rounding.)

SOURCE   Food and Nutrition Research Institute (1984, p. 87), based on a survey of 2,880 households.

registered with government authorities.[62] The World Bank (1988a, p. 4), in its third Philippine poverty report, cites the official infant mortality figures as evidence that 'during the seventies some welfare indicators improved substantially on average, probably in correlation with the high growth of the period'. Yet the statistical appendix to the same World Bank report contains alternative estimates showing that between 1970 and 1983 infant mortality *increased* from 54 to 59 per 1,000 in rural areas and from 45 to 55 per 1,000 in urban areas (see Table 2.16). Even if we accept the lower figures, Philippine infant mortality ranks among the highest in East and Southeast Asia (see Table 1.1).

Many infant and child deaths in the Philippines can be traced to hunger and to lack of access to basic health care services. Dr. Rodolfo Florentino, deputy director of the Nutrition Center of the Philippines, stated in the late 1970s that more than half of child deaths were linked to inadequate food intake: 'Out of the ten leading causes of death at least five – probably the top five – are related to malnutrition.'[63] Undernourished children are less able to survive such common diseases as respiratory infections and measles. According to official data, 42 per cent of infant deaths in 1986 were caused by pneumonia or other respiratory problems, and a further 13 per cent by diarrhea, vitamin and nutrient deficiencies, or measles (National Statistical Coordination Board, 1989, p. 9/30).

The allocation of health care resources in the Philippines has mirrored the unequal distribution of wealth and power. UNICEF's Manila office (1988, pp. 207–8) reports that in the final two years of the Marcos regime, 1984 and

TABLE 2.16 *Infant Mortality Rates, 1970–1983*
(deaths per 1,000 live births)

Year	Total	Rural	Urban
1970	51.4	54.3	45.2
1973	57.0	61.0	49.0
1983	57.3	59.0	54.6

SOURCES Rural and urban estimates from World Bank (1988a, p. 169); total derived using population weights as reported by National Statistical Coordination Board (1989, p. 1/14).

1985, the government provided $229 million in subsidies to three specialized institutions – the Philippine Heart Center for Asia, the Kidney Foundation of the Philippines, and the Lung Center of the Philippines – all of which 'cater to upper income families', in the UN agency's words. This was *five times* more than total Philippine government funding for primary health care, only $45 million in the same period.

UNICEF terms this 'a serious misallocation of health resources'. The term 'misallocation' implies, in this case, a willingness to make interpersonal comparisons of well-being. Economists often shrink from such comparisons, despite the fact that they are an inescapable, if seldom explicit, feature of many policy decisions. The authors of the UNICEF study conclude that too little was spent on saving the lives of poor people, and too much on saving the lives of the rich. The preferences of the Philippine government revealed a different set of interpersonal weights.

CONCLUSIONS

The Philippines did not experience spectacular growth in national income in the Marcos era, but neither did the economy stagnate. In 1986, real per capita income was more than one-third higher than in 1962.

How was this larger income pie distributed? The answer cannot be found in the official family income and expenditure surveys. Comparisons with the National Accounts reveal that the survey data seriously understate aggregate income. The extent of understatement is not likely to be constant across income classes, nor is its pattern likely to have remained constant through time. There are reasons to suspect that understatement of incomes of the rich increased over time, while understatement of incomes of the poor decreased, but one can only guess as to the magnitudes involved. Any conclusions about distributional trends based on the survey data are quite tenuous, since results are highly sensitive to assumptions regarding these shifts.

Real wage data provide strong evidence, however, that Philippine income distribution, already highly inequitable in the early 1960s, became even more unequal in next two-and-one-half decades. By 1986, real agricultural wages were less than three-fourths of their 1962 level. In metropolitan Manila the decline was even greater, as real wages of unskilled and skilled workers fell to less than one-third of their 1962 level. Various survival strategies, including increased labor force participation, cushioned the impact of falling real wages on household incomes. But there can be little doubt that many poor families experienced drastic declines in real income.[64] Meanwhile, the incomes of the rich rose strongly enough to lift per capita national income. In other words, the country experienced immiserizing growth. The remaining chapters of this book examine the reasons for this outcome.

NOTES

1. Examining the history of industrialized countries, Kuznets (1955) tentatively concluded that inequality had increased in the early stages of industrialization and later decreased. For discussions of the subsequent literature, see Saith (1983) and Bigsten (1988).
2. Since national income adds individuals by adding their incomes, a person with an income of 50,000 pesos counts 10 times as much as a person with an income of 5,000 pesos. If the income of the richer person increases by 500 pesos, or one per cent, this counts the same as if the income of the poor person increased by the same 500 pesos, or 10 per cent. This is one solution to the problem of how to aggregate individuals to obtain an income-based measure of social welfare, but by no means the only one. One alternative would be to let a 10 per cent income gain for a rich person carry the same weight as a 10 per cent income gain for a poor person. An additional peso would thus have a greater impact on social welfare if it went to a poor person than if it went to a rich person. Another alternative would be to put a higher weight on a 10 per cent income gain for a poor person than on a 10 per cent income gain for a rich person. Ahluwalia and Chenery (1974) term these methods 'GNP weights', 'equal weights', and 'poverty weights', respectively.
3. Repetto notes that corrections for the depletion of other natural resource would probably result in an even larger downward adjustment. Moreover, Repetto's methodology may understate the cost of resource depletion since it relies on prevailing international market prices to value the resources in question. In the presence of excessively high rates of

resource extraction these prices will be too low to fully capture the social cost.

4. For a review of these and other deficiencies of national income estimates, see Eisner (1988).

5. Estimated by ordinary least squares. Owing to the sharp drop in GNP per capita in the 1980s, its *average* annual growth rate is lower than the fitted trend, at 1.3 per cent per year.

6. Subperiod growth rates estimated from a kinked exponential model; for method, see Boyce (1986).

7. The number of regions was increased from ten to thirteen (including the National Capital Region), and provinces were reallocated among regions.

8. This term was coined by Geertz (1963) with reference to agriculture in Java.

9. For discussion, see International Labour Office (1974, pp. 12–13, 177–90) and Tidalgo and Esguerra (1984, pp. 19–23).

10. For discussion of data collection procedures, see Balagot and Librero (1975, pp. 4–8) and Khan (1977, pp. 244–5).

11. Ideally, one should use price indices based on the basket of commodities consumed by agricultural laborer households in different regions. Price indexes for specific occupational groups in the Philippines are not available for this period, and hence the overall CPI is used here. We know, however, that between 1962 and 1974 food prices tended to rise more rapidly than non-food prices, while after 1974 the opposite was true (see NEDA, 1986, pp. 116–17). Since poor people, including agricultural laborers, tend to spend a larger-than-average fraction of their income on food, we can infer that real wages declined more rapidly than indicated in the table prior to 1974, and less rapidly thereafter.

12. Estimates for the years 1962–65 are derived by splicing these with the seven-crop averages reported by Balagot and Librero (1975) for the years 1957 to 1973. The average ratio of their annual wage to the rice and corn average from Table 2.7 in the overlapping years (1966 to 1973) is 1.035. In Table 2.7 the overall agricultural wage in 1962 to 1965 is hence derived by dividing the Balagot-Librero figure by 1.035.

13. In 1974 consumer prices in the Philippines rose by 34 per cent, a rate surpassed during the period under review only in 1984 when inflation reached 50 per cent. The smaller real wage drop in 1984 suggests that wage-price adjustment lags may have shortened over time.

14. Estimated from the series in Table 2.7 by ordinary least squares.

15. Based on 1986 exchange rate of 20.5 pesos/dollar.

16. World Bank (1979c, Table 4.19, p. 125A). These data are reproduced in Lal (1986, p. 188).

17. Other sources of urban wage data are of limited use, since they report legislated as opposed to actual wages, or include the remuneration of salaried employees, or are sporadic in their coverage. The *Philippine Statistical Yearbooks*, for example, only report legislated wage rates

(NEDA, 1986, pp. 482–3; NSCB, 1989, pp. 11, 20–1). For discussion of other data sources, see Reyes, Milan and Sanchez (1988, pp. 5–8).

18. Insofar as urban workers devote a higher-than-average percentage of their income to food, the use of the overall CPI again somewhat understates real wages declines prior to 1974 and somewhat overstates the decline thereafter (see note 11, above).

19. UNIDO (1985, p. 20), citing data from the government's National Economic and Development Authority, also reports a severe drop in real wages in the manufacturing sector in 1984: setting real wages in August 1983 equal to 100, real wages in August 1984 had fallen to 78.

20. In 1980 the ratio of the average wage for the nine occupations reported in the World Bank table to the average for all fifteen reported by the Central Bank (1980, pp. 269–70) was 0.997; hence only a slight upward scaling was needed to make the skilled labor series comparable. The growth rates reported by Montes do not distinguish between skilled and unskilled labor; hence the same rate is here applied to both.

21. Estimated from the data in Table 2.8 by ordinary least squares.

22. A World Bank report (1985a, p. 21) states, '[I]f anything, low open unemployment rates indicate the need for relatively more and more people to do some work and help families tide over an economic crisis'. This may overstate the case. The data in Table 2.9 indicate that open unemployment in the Philippines rose during the economic crisis in 1984.

23. For definitions and discussion of data sources, see Tidalgo and Esguerra (1984, pp. 88–90) and World Bank (1985a, pp. 21–3, 60–4). For a general discussion of the problem of defining employment, see Sen (1975, Ch. 1).

24. The conversion factors implicit in Tidalgo and Esguerra's Table 5.3 (p. 91) are 67.7 per cent in 1971–76 and 67.2 per cent in 1976–80. The authors do not elaborate on the basis for these ratios. Referring to an earlier paper by Tidalgo (1976), the World Bank (1979c, p. 112A) deduces that the full-time unemployment equivalent provides a 'rough measure of the surplus labor time (below a 'full-time' employment norm of 40 hours) available in the employed labor force', independent of desire for more work.

25. Lande and Hooley (1986, p. 1089). See also World Bank (1985a, pp. 20–1).

26. Comparative statistics on labor force participation presented by the World Bank (1985a, p. 63) for persons 15 and older in the third quarter of 1976, based on past-week and past-quarter reference periods, indicate that the change in reference period increased the LFPR by only one percentage point, from 59.5 per cent to 60.5 per cent. The change in the age cut-off may have had a larger effect.

27. In this case, however, women's participation in the labor force appears to date back several generations (Rutten, 1982, pp. 76–7). Reyes, Milan and Sanchez (1988, pp. 10–11) similarly remark, 'Generally, when real

incomes of families decline, women tend to join the labor force in order
to augment family income'.

28.   Employment grew at 3.3 per cent and population at 2.7 per cent (see
        Tables 2.1 and 2.4).

29.   The FIES methodology is discussed in World Bank (1979c, pp. 1–2);
        Mangahas and Barros (1980, pp. 65–8, 90–1); and World Bank (1988a,
        pp. 159–67). The ISH methodology is discussed in World Bank (1985a,
        Annex 1, pp. 38–50).

30.   For discussion of these discrepancies, see also World Bank (1980b,
        pp. 114–20), where slightly higher ratios for 1965, 1971 and 1975 are
        reported.

31.   For press accounts, see Bowring (1981) and Clad (1988). A draft of the
        Bank's first poverty report (World Bank, 1979c) was leaked prior to its
        final editing; see Bello *et al.* (1982) for discussion of its findings.

32.   For these reasons, the expenditure data generally indicate less inequality
        than the income data. In 1961 and 1971, for example, Gini coefficients
        for expenditure were 0.42 and 0.41, respectively, whereas the Gini
        coefficients for income were 0.46 and 0.45 (World Bank, 1979c, p. 18A;
        Dowling, 1984, p. 54).

33.   Ratios of FIES to National Account expenditure, as reported by the World
        Bank (1988a, p. 159) were:

1961	*1965*	*1971*	*1975*	*1985*
0.71	0.83	0.80	0.63	0.54

        These can be compared with the corresponding income ratios in
        Table 2.10.

34.   In addition, the income concept in the National Accounts is not identical
        to that in the surveys. For example, personal income in the National
        Accounts includes employer contributions to social security schemes,
        where as FIES income is likely to miss this form of remuneration. This
        and other differences are reviewed in detail by Mangahas, Quizon and
        Lim (1977, pp. 1751–7), who conclude that the definitional differences
        are 'slight'.

35.   Several sources report income distribution and poverty measures based
        on the 1975 FIES, but express strong doubts about the quality of the
        data (World Bank, 1979c, p. 18A; World Bank, 1985a, p. 16; Dowling,
        1984, p. 52). Mangahas and Barros (1980, p. 68) cite undersampling of
        wealthy households as a major flaw of the 1975 FIES.

36.   Thus the World Bank (1980b, pp. 116–17) remarks, 'It is well known
        that rich individuals tend to conceal their true income and expenditure'.
        Mangahas, Quizon and Lim (1977, p. 1749–50) report that in the 1975
        FIES non-cooperation of respondents was directly related to income size:
        among the wealthiest 'class AB' families 22 per cent of respondents were
        reported as 'Don't know/refused'; among the poorest 'class E' families
        the proportion was only 5 per cent.

37.   For example, Mangahas, Quizon and Lim (1977) state that upper-income
        households were under-sampled in the 1975 FIES. The World Bank
        (1980b, p. 117) questions this claim.
38.   Commenting on the 1971 FIES, the ILO (1974, p. 9) remarked: 'There
        is good reason to suspect that under-reporting was higher in 1971 than
        before. For instance, for the top 10 per cent of urban families, the data
        imply a fall of almost one-third in the real incomes from 1965 to 1971,
        which surely is implausible'.
39.   The two series differ slightly. In this book the IMF series is generally
        used in preference to the NEDA series. However, since the IMF does
        not provide disaggregated price indexes, the NEDA series is used
        when differences between the food and non-food price trends are
        considered.
40.   This is their overall share in family expenditure according to the 1985
        FIES (NCSO, 1986b, p. 99).
41.   According to the 1985 FIES, the poorest 30 per cent of families devote 72
        per cent of their expenditure to food, beverages, and tobacco, whereas the
        corresponding figure for richest 10 per cent is only 34 per cent (NCSO,
        1986b, p. 99).
42.   The World Bank (1988a, p. 11) reports that 'poor families are larger, with
        an average size of 6.0 persons versus 4.9 for the non-poor'. It is curious,
        therefore, that in revising the 1985 FIES data the Bank (1988a, p. 164)
        finds that ranking families from low to high *per capita* income yields a
        slightly lower Gini ratio than ranking families from low to high *family*
        income.
43.   For example, the World Bank (1988a, p. 5) reports on the basis of 1985
        FIES data that 24 per cent of families and 28 per cent of the population
        lived 'below subsistence conditions'.
44.   In presenting the table from which 'series A' is here drawn, the World
        Bank (1988a, pp. 5, 123) does not clearly state that the decile ranking
        of families is based on *per capita* income, but a close reading of the
        report's methodological appendix (pp. 159–67) indicates that this is the
        case. Using raw FIES data, the Bank constructs deciles based on per
        capita family income and reports their nominal average income (Table
        5.5, p. 166). These incomes correspond to those reported in 1978 pesos
        on pp. 5 and 123, when deflated by the CPI as reported in NEDA (1986,
        p. 116).
45.   Using the raw FIES data, the Bank not only converted the decile ranking
        to a per capita income basis, but also revised the 1985 distribution
        published by the government to correct for the NCSO's use of the same
        income levels to construct rural and urban income deciles. See World
        Bank (1988a, pp. 162–4).
46.   The NEDA CPI reported in Table 2.11.
47.   For the poorest 30%, the weight on food, beverages, and tobacco is 0.72,
        while that on non-food is 0.28. For the richest 10%, the weights are 0.34
        and 0.66, respectively.

48. Changes in understatement in the intervening deciles are here assumed to offset each other.
49. Khan (1977, pp. 242–3), examining rural incomes in the period 1956–71, similarly finds that average real income grew while the absolute incomes of the poorest 20 per cent declined.
50. According to the FIES data, the ratio of urban to rural average income declined from 2.5 in 1961 to 2.1 in 1971 and 1985 (calculated from data in World Bank, 1988a, p. 123).
51. Hence in Series C the same adjustment scalars are applied to both rural and urban households. Since incomes tend to be lower in rural areas, a combination of these revised rural and urban distributions would yield a slightly different total (or national) distribution than that reported in Table 2.12, which is derived by the application of the same scalars directly to the total household distribution. This inconsistency cannot be readily remedied in the absence of more detailed data.
52. For example, the World Bank (1988a, p. 1) derives a poverty line based on the least-cost consumption basket needed to purchase 2,016 calories and 50 grams of protein per day, plus non-food needs based on expenditures reported for the lowest income group in the FIES. The NEDA Technical Working Group on Poverty (1988) follows a similar methodology.
53. For discussion of methodological problems in poverty estimation, see Sen (1981).
54. The former yields national poverty estimates of 36.7 per cent, 42.1 per cent, and 45.1 per cent in 1965, 1971, and 1975, respectively.
55. Inter-regional rice price differences were used as a proxy for overall regional price variation; see World Bank (1988a, Table 13, notes b and c).
56. Economists tend to be skeptical of such 'subjective' or 'bottom-up' measures of poverty, but 'objective' income-based measures are not necessarily more reliable given data quality and methodological problems. For discussion of the self-rating approach, see Mangahas (1984, 1987).
57. Consider the following 1983 price index data for metro Manila (1975 = 100):

CPI	Rice	Meat	Fish	Dairy	Fruit & vegetables
237.3	164.4	206.7	250.0	202.5	277.8

    Source: calculated from NEDA (1986, pp. 117, 132–3). Less detailed data for prices outside metro Manila (p. 119) suggest similar trends.
58. The excessive weight on rice in the World Bank's price deflator is compounded by the fact that the overall CPI is apparently used as the proxy for the 'non-food' component of family expenditures, even though it includes cereals.
59. According to the report (World Bank, 1988a, p. 3), rural poverty incidence remained constant at 58 per cent, while urban poverty incidence rose from 38 per cent to 42 percent. At the national level

poverty incidence remained unchanged, however, due to rural-to-urban migration.

60. Florentino, Narciso, and Valerio (1986, pp. 6, 11), citing data from the National Nutrition Council.

61. For a review of the available evidence, see Quisumbing (1987a).

62. National Statistical Coordination Board (1989, pp. 9/9, 9/26).

63. Quoted by Dalton (1978, p. 35).

64. The conclusion that Philippine income distribution underwent strong polarization in this period is reinforced in Chapter 4, where we examine trends in rice consumption.

3 The Green Revolution

INTRODUCTION

Rice is the foundation of the Philippine economy. It is the country's single most important crop, and the staple food for much of the population. It is especially important to the country's poor majority, as both consumers and producers.

A central element of Philippine development strategy since the mid-1960s has been the introduction of new rice technology, popularly known as the 'green revolution'. The technological key in this strategy is the introduction of 'high-yielding varieties' (or HYVs). These could be more accurately labelled 'highly fertilizer-responsive' varieties, since they give higher yields only under a specific set of conditions, notably greater fertilizer use and adequate water control.

Asian rice agriculture has a long history of technological change. Long before the green revolution, cultivators in the Philippines and elsewhere bred tens of thousands of distinct rice varieties, and developed intricate water control systems, including the famous rice terraces of northern Luzon.

The green revolution marked a departure, however, in three respects. First, the strategy was conceived not by Asian rice cultivators, but by international agencies. Second, the new technology was developed not in the farmers' fields, but at scientific research institutions which these agencies established. Third, the objective of the green revolution was technological change not in a single region or even in a single country, but in rice-producing Asia as a whole. In its origins, methods, and scale, the green revolution thus was a historically unprecedented attempt to transform Asian rice agriculture through conscious intervention from 'above'.

The birthplace of the new rice technology was Los Banos, a small town 60 kilometers south of Manila, where the International Rice Research Institute (IRRI) was established in 1962 by the Rockefeller and Ford Foundations (Barker, Herdt and Rose, 1985, p. 62). Scientists were recruited from around the world, and the world's largest collection of rice varieties was assembled to provide the genetic raw material for IRRI's plant breeders. Their efforts focused on combining the genetic attributes of high fertilizer responsiveness and a short-statured plant type, so as to create a variety which could support

heavy ears of grain without toppling under their weight. The first such
variety, IR–8, was released in 1965.

The Philippines not only was the birthplace of the HYVs, but also led
the way in their adoption. By the 1970–71 crop year, half of the country's
rice acreage was planted with the new varieties, and this rose to 75 per cent
by 1979–80.[1] If IRRI was the green revolution's technical laboratory, the
Philippine countryside was its social laboratory.

The architects of the 'green revolution' had one overriding objective:
increased food production. National aggregate food output was the 'only
valid measure' of the new strategy's payoff, W. David Hopper, then a staff
economist at the Rockefeller Foundation, told a 1968 New York symposium
on the 'Strategy for the Conquest of Hunger'.[2] Philippine government
emissary Carlos Romulo, in the symposium's closing address, likewise
proclaimed that the success of the new strategy would be measured solely
in terms of 'its impact upon the productivity and profitability of our rice
farms – the only measure which really counts'.[3]

Proponents of the strategy expected, however, that the new rice technology
would also have a positive distributional impact on the poor. Three major
benefits were taken to be virtually axiomatic. First, increased rice output
would, *ceteris paribus*, lower the price of rice. Since the poor spend a
larger fraction of their income on food than do the rich, they would benefit
disproportionately. Second, poor farmers would share in the gains to rice
producers. The new technology was not only scale-neutral but also labor
intensive, a special advantage to smaller growers who have lower labor
costs. Third, landless agricultural workers would benefit too, thanks to the
increased demand for labor and the resulting increased employment and
higher wages.

This chapter begins an examination of the impact of the green revolution
strategy on the Philippine economy, focusing on the strategy's primary objective, the growth of output. Chapters 4 and 5 then investigate the strategy's
impact on the distribution of income.

AGRICULTURAL GROWTH: THE RECORD

Crop production can grow by increases in acreage and by increases in yield
per unit area. Prior to the 1960s, the former was the main source of growth
in the Philippines, as new lands were brought under the plough. To a lesser
extent, acreage growth also took place via increases in cropping intensity
(the number of crops cultivated per year on a given piece of land). With
the advent of the green revolution, the sources of growth in Philippine

agriculture bifurcated: non-rice crops continued to grow primarily via the extensive path, while rice output grew primarily via the intensive path of rising yields.

Philippine agriculture is more diversified than that of some Asian rice-producing countries. Rice accounted for 36 per cent of the total value of crop output in the early 1960s and for 28 per cent in the mid-1980s, compared, for example, to more than 80 per cent in Bangladesh.[4] Coconut and sugarcane, the main traditional export crops, each accounted for 15–20 per cent of the value of crop output throughout this period. Corn (or maize), the principal food grain in some regions, accounted for ten per cent of crop output value in the mid-1980s. In addition, root crops, bananas, pineapples, mangoes, and coffee each accounted for three to five per cent (see Table 3.1).

It is striking that, notwithstanding the green revolution, the growth rate of Philippine rice output between 1962 and 1985 was lower than that of any other major crop, with the exception of sugarcane (see Table 3.2). The reason lies in the virtual stagnation of rice acreage, which grew at an average annual rate of only 0.4 per cent in the period as a whole. Acreage here refers to gross area (that is, double-cropped land is counted twice), so this growth includes any gains from increased cropping intensity. At the same time, the area under all crops grew at 2.2 per cent per year. In this respect, rice lagged behind the rest of Philippine agriculture.

Looking at growth in yield per unit area, however, the picture is almost reversed. Rice yields rose at 3.4 per cent per year, faster than those of any other major crop except the fruits. Between 1962–64 and 1983–85 rice yields doubled from 1.24 to 2.48 metric tons of *palay* (unhusked rice) per hectare. The increase was fairly steady, broken only by the sharp declines in 1972 and 1973, which were due to the tungro virus epidemic in 1971 and exceptional typhoon and flood damages in 1972 (see Figure 3.1b).[5] The speed of this increase was without precedent in Asian rice agriculture. At comparable stages in their yield growth, it took Japan 70 years and Taiwan 30 years to increase their rice yields by 50 per cent (Ishikawa, 1970, pp. 24–5).

The green revolution in the Philippines was a rice revolution. Corn registered modest growth in yield, but this was largely due to increased input use of traditional varieties. As of 1986 less than 10 per cent of the country's corn acreage was sown to the improved varieties released in the last decade (Agricultural Policy and Strategy Team, 1986, p. 180). Growth in coconut and sugarcane was achieved almost entirely via acreage increase; indeed, both crops reportedly had lower yields in 1983–85 than in 1962–64.[6] Output of the two most important non-traditional export crops, bananas and pineapples, grew rapidly via both acreage extension and increased yields. The growth of export crops is further examined in the Chapter 6.

TABLE 3.1 *Area, Yield and Output of Major Crops, 1962–1964 and 1983–1985* (triennial averages)

Crop	Area ('000 ha)		Yield (mt/ha)		Output ('000 mt)		Share of total crop output value (%)[1]	
	1962–64	1983–85	1962–64	1983–85	1962–64	1983–85	1962–64	1983–85
Rice[2]	3143	3201	1.24	2.48	3907	7924	36.0	27.6
Corn	1955	3247	0.65	1.02	1277	3304	7.4	10.1
Rootcrops	262	422	5.22	5.41	1416	2281	4.5	4.0
Coconut	1386	3226	1.09	0.96	1508	3090	20.2	15.1
Sugarcane	261	437	7.73	7.22	2021	3148	16.9	15.8
Bananas	217	324	2.83	11.73	612	3801	1.6	5.4
Pineapples	235	564	0.64	2.88	149	1617	0.8	3.1
Mangoes	463	436	1.81	8.69	845	3783	0.7	4.0
Coffee	448	1410	0.86	0.94	384	1324	1.7	4.4

Key: ha = hectares; mt = metric tons.

NOTES
1. Total value includes crops not listed in this table.
2. Yield and output in terms of *palay* (unhusked rice); milled rice/*palay* conversion factor = 0.67.

SOURCES Calculated from data in NEDA (1976, pp. 134–55) and NEDA (1986, pp. 266–75).

TABLE 3.2 *Growth Rates of Output, Area and Yield of Major Crops, 1962–1985 and Subperiods (per cent per annum)* [1]

Crop	1962–1985			1962–1973			1974–1985		
	Output	Area	Yield	Output	Area	Yield	Output	Area	Yield
All crops[2]	3.64	2.22	1.42	8.18	2.65	5.53	-0.90	1.80	-2.70
Rice	3.81	0.42	3.39	3.82	1.20	2.61	3.80	-0.36	4.16
Corn	4.94	2.80	2.14	5.80	3.46	2.33	4.07	2.13	1.95
Rootcrops	4.15	3.27	0.88	1.72	2.00	-0.28	6.57	4.54	2.03
Coconut	5.12	4.17	0.94	5.70	4.68	1.02	4.53	3.67	0.86
Sugarcane	2.73	2.54	0.19	5.52	6.38	-0.86	-0.06	-1.30	1.24
Bananas	10.33	2.24	8.08	8.51	1.28	7.23	12.15	3.21	8.94
Pineapples	11.35	4.71	6.64	6.32	2.33	3.40	16.38	7.10	9.28
Mangoes	7.60	-0.73	8.33	8.22	-1.61	9.84	6.98	0.16	6.82
Coffee	7.03	5.70	1.34	5.01	2.87	2.13	9.06	8.53	0.54

NOTES
1. Exponential and kinked exponential growth rates estimated from annual data by ordinary least squares; for methodology, see Boyce (1986).
2. Value of output of all crops (including those not listed in the table) deflated by consumer price index.

SOURCES As Table 3.1; consumer price index from IMF (1987, pp. 560–1).

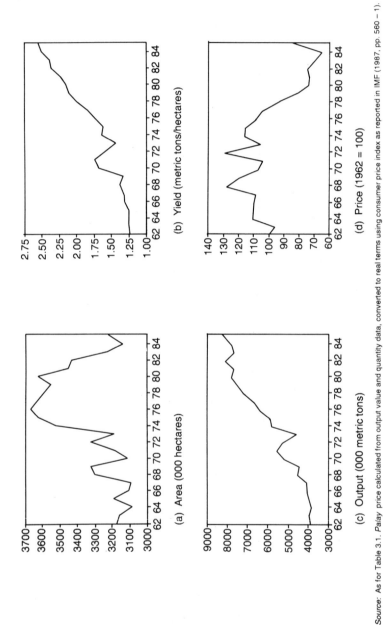

Source: As for Table 3.1. *Palay* price calculated from output value and quantity data, converted to real terms using consumer price index as reported in IMF (1987, pp. 560 – 1).

Figure 3.1: *Palay* **Area, Yield, Output, and Price, 1962 – 1985**

The accuracy of the official agricultural statistics on which these estimates are based is an open question.[7] Data collection is 'heavily oriented toward the survey of rice and corn at the expense of "lesser" food and commercial crops' (Rose, 1985, p. 252), and according to the World Bank (1979a, p. 1), 'statistics on rice are generally better than those on corn'.[8] Mears *et al.* (1974, p. 25) conclude that the rice statistics are probably more useful in comparing changes over time than for determining absolute yield levels. However, David (1989, p. 4), states that the technique for rice output estimation in use since the late 1960s is 'biased towards giving progressively higher estimates', in which case estimated growth rates are somewhat inflated. As so often in empirical analysis, one must steer a course between naive acceptance of official data and a nihilistic conclusion that they are completely worthless. The data are highly imperfect, but they do bear some relation to reality.

Regional data on rice yields, HYV use, and the share of rice in total crop acreage are reported in Table 3.3.[9] These permit several observations. First, the spread of the new varieties occurred throughout the country, albeit at an uneven pace. Second, the importance of rice in the agricultural economy varies greatly among regions, ranging from less than ten per cent of crop value in Central Visayas and Southern Mindanao to more than 60 per cent in Central Luzon and Cagayan Valley. Third, the Central Luzon 'rice bowl', which led in the adoption of HYVs with 93 per cent of its rice acreage sown to them by the early 1980s, registered the highest yields in the country even before the introduction of the new technology.

A comparison of these data with the regional poverty data reported in Table 2.13 indicates that regions with higher levels of rice yields tended to have had lower levels of poverty incidence in both the early 1960s and the early 1980s.[10] However, there is little correlation between the rates of change of the two variables.[11]

THE CLOSING OF THE LAND FRONTIER?

The supply of agricultural land is limited. Economists have long contemplated the implications of this fact. Two centuries ago, the Reverend Thomas Malthus put forward his famous 'principle of population', claiming that the pressure of human population growth on food supplies condemns the mass of humanity to live forever in a state of semi-starvation. 'The principal and most permanent cause of poverty', he wrote, 'has little or no *direct* relation to forms of government, or the unequal division of property'. Rather, poverty is the inevitable consequence of population growth. Hence, 'as the rich do not in reality possess the *power* of finding employment and maintenance for

TABLE 3.3 *Paddy Yields by Region, 1962–1964 and 1981–1983*

Region	Palay yield (mt/ha)[1]		Yield trend[2] (growth rate, % per annum)	Share of rice acreage sown to HYVs, 1981/83 (%)	Palay share of all crops' value, 1983 (%)
	1962/64	1981/83			
National	1.24	2.32	3.30	80.5	24.7
Ilocos	1.26	2.16	2.84	72.1	40.2
Cagayan Valley	1.21	2.28	3.33	76.0	62.4
Central Luzon	1.83	3.19	2.92	93.2	63.4
Southern Tagalog	1.14	1.99	2.93	73.6	23.4
Bicol	1.18	2.04	2.88	87.5	37.9
Western Visayas	1.20	2.09	2.92	89.3	18.1
Eastern Visayas	} 0.88	1.73	3.14	76.2	19.5
		(1.60)			
Central Visayas		1.41		75.2	6.8
Northern Mindanao	} 0.85	2.47	5.86	87.6	14.9
		(2.59)			
Central Mindanao		2.65		71.6	22.8
Western Mindanao	} 1.22	2.18	3.67	61.7	10.8
		(2.45)			
Southern Mindanao		2.64		80.2	9.1

NOTES

1. Numbers in parentheses are averages for regions subdivided after 1975, weighted by rice acreage.
2. Interpolated from 1962–64 and 1981–83 yields.

SOURCES Yields and HYV share calculated from unpublished Bureau of Agricultural Economics data provided to the author by Robert the poor, the poor cannot, in the nature of things, possess the *right* to demand them'.[12]

Malthus's exculpation of the rich for the misery of the poor has undoubtedly contributed to the enduring appeal of his analysis. Yet the timing of his prediction could not have been more ironic. His own country, Britain, and much of the world stood on the brink of an unprecedented increase in living standards. Technological and institutional changes brought dramatic gains in human productivity in agriculture and industry, a possibility which Malthus did not anticipate. He also failed to foresee that population growth could ultimately stabilize as individuals with improved living standards chose to have fewer children.[13]

In recent years, several economic historians have advanced a very different analysis of the economic impact of population growth. They contend that productivity-increasing technological and institutional changes are not exogenous events which just happen to occur, but rather are *induced* by demographic pressure. For example, population growth has been held to explain transitions from hunting-and-gathering to shifting cultivation and from the latter to permanent agriculture (Boserup, 1965); the development of irrigation systems (Simon, 1975; Kikuchi and Hayami, 1978); and, in perhaps the most grandiose formulation, 'the institutional innovations which account for the rise of the Western world' (North and Thomas, 1973, p. 8).

Neither variant of demographic determinism fits the experience of the Philippines in the twentieth century. Contrary to the Malthusian logic, agricultural output grew faster than population. Agricultural growth was not, however, simply a response to population pressure, for its pattern was profoundly shaped by the country's political economy.

Between the turn of the century and 1960, annual *palay* output *per person* rose from 80 to 140 kilograms, notwithstanding the fact that the country's population more than tripled. Between 1960 and 1985, annual output rose further to 170 kilograms per person, while population doubled.[14] In the entire 85-year period the population of the Philippines rose nearly eightfold, from 7 million to 55 million. At the same time rice output *per person* doubled. History again confounded the dismal predictions of the Reverend Malthus.

In the first half of the century, Philippine agriculture grew primarily by the extension of cultivation to new lands. The total area under cultivation rose from 1.3 million hectares at the turn of the century to 7.5 million in 1960 (Hooley and Ruttan, 1969, p. 224). Rice acreage increased from 600,000 hectares in 1903 to 3.2 million in 1960. Yields of *palay* rose from 0.8 to 1.2 metric tons per hectare between 1900 and 1930, but then remained virtually unchanged until the mid-1960s (Mears *et al.*, 1974, pp. 335–6).

After 1960, as documented above, rice output rose by yield growth rather than acreage increase. A number of observers maintain that this change reflected the 'closing of the land frontier' in the Philippines.[15] With little scope for further acreage extension, population pressure now induced rising yields per unit area. The construction of irrigation systems became more profitable than the opening of new land, as had happened in Japan after 1880 and in Taiwan and Korea earlier in the twentieth century.[16] This population-induced investment in irrigation in turn permitted the introduction of the new seed-fertilizer technology, which has also been described as a response to 'rapid shifts in rice demand due to population growth'.[17]

The interpretation of the green revolution in the Philippines as a case of population-driven land-use intensification leaves two questions unanswered:

— Why, as the country's land frontier began to close, did net additions to gross cropped area go exclusively to non-rice crops, rather than to the principal food grain?

— Why did the response come 'from above' via the intervention of international agencies and the state, rather than 'from below' via initiatives by the cultivators themselves?

The answers reveal much about the achievements and limitations of the strategy.

In export crops and corn, as noted above, acreage expansion continued to be the major source of output growth from 1962 to 1985. The area under the non-rice crops reported in Table 3.1 doubled from 5 million to 10 million hectares, while rice area was held to a little more than 3 million hectares. Some of the newly cultivated lands were not well suited to rice cultivation; as Barker (1978, p. 141) notes, within a country the 'turning point' from land-surplus to land-scarce agriculture may vary from region to region and among different crop environments. In particular, much of the growth of corn acreage occurred in traditional corn-growing regions of Mindanao, the Visayas, and the Cagayan Valley, where hilly terrain and lack of irrigation make rice cultivation difficult.

There is little doubt, however, that much land under other crops can (or could, with suitable improvements such as levelling and bunding) be sown to rice. Several studies have shown that Filipino farmers respond to changes in the price of rice relative to those of other crops by shifting acreage among them.[18]

Acreage extension was stimulated by the decontrol of foreign exchange in 1962, which brought windfall profits to agricultural exporters. The resulting 'shift in terms of trade between domestic food and commercial export crops', Hayami and Ruttan (1985, p.380) observe, 'was associated with a shift of resources into export production'. The distribution of the resulting profits is examined in Chapter 7.

The compression of rice acreage was an explicit element of the Philippine government's agricultural strategy. In 1976, Minister of Agriculture Arturo Tanco, Jr., set the long-run goal of reducing the country's net area under rice to 1.7 million hectares.[19] Hence the green revolution in Philippine rice agriculture can be viewed as a response not to the closing of the land frontier in an aggregate sense, but rather to the preemption of the remaining scope for acreage expansion by other crops, notably export crops.[20]

The second question is one of agency: if population pressure induced the development of the new seed-fertilizer technology, why did the initiative come from outside agencies rather than from the people whose numbers were growing? In Japan, for example, land-use intensification in the face of population pressure in the 19th and early 20th centuries came about via local land improvements, particularly in water control, and via the development and spread of new varieties originated by farmers themselves.[21] Kikuchi and Hayami (1978, p. 855) speculate that two factors facilitated this local-level response: first, the gradual growth of population provided 'sufficient time for village communities to develop an organizational capacity to mobilize communal labor to build and maintain irrigation facilities'; and second, 'the decentralized power structure of the feudal system might have contributed to the greater response of rulers to the local need'.

In much of the Philippines, however, such local-level responses have been weak. One result, discussed in more detail below, has been the underdevelopment of water control. The government has substituted its own investments for local water control initiatives, but these have been expensive and are beset by operational inefficiencies.

The green revolution represented a further substitution. Rather than following after the extension and improvement of water control, as in Ishikawa's (1967) account of the stages of Asian rice agriculture, the new seed-fertilizer technology emerged as an alternative to it. In a sense, it was born prematurely. It offered the possibility of quick and substantial yield increases at relatively low cost, without waiting for resolution of the messy institutional problems of water control. The dependence of the new technology on water control ensured, however, that eventually the hydraulic constraint would re-emerge.

The international agencies and the Philippine government had a number of motives for seizing the initiative. They faced political pressure from rice consumers, notably the urban middle classes. The price of rice in the Philippines is an intensely political issue; hence, the government's tendency to import large quantities of rice in election years in order to lower prices to consumers (Mangahas and Librero, 1973). Moreover, the goal of import substitution in rice was appealing on grounds of both nationalism and foreign exchange savings.[22] The government and its international allies were also anxious to prevent renewed discontent among rice cultivators, who had formed the backbone of the Huk insurgency in central Luzon (Kerkvliet, 1977), and it was hoped that the new technology, together with land colonization schemes and agrarian reform, would contribute to this end.

Some have argued that the green revolution also sprang from the desire of suppliers of chemical inputs to expand their markets.[23] The green revolution certainly increased demand for fertilizer and pesticides in the Philippines and other third world countries, but transnational corporate producers of these commodities had little direct involvement in the development of the new varieties.[24] Whether the technology was unduly biased towards agrochemicals is an open question. It is doubtful that comparable yield increases could have been achieved so rapidly without a increased reliance on agrochemicals. Whatever the degree of bias, one does not need a conspiracy theory to explain it, for the outlook of the new technology's inventors was strongly conditioned by the historical precedent of agriculture in the industrialized countries.

In sum, while demographic pressure may help to explain why Philippine rice agriculture embarked on a process of yield-led growth in the 1960s, the green revolution's origins also lie in the country's political economy. The priority given to export crops effectively precluded acreage extension as a route to increased rice output. In this rather special sense, the 'land frontier' for rice cultivation was closed. At the same time, yield increases through locally-initiated land improvements along the Japanese model were hindered by a lack of institutions for collective action, for reasons further investigated below. Government-financed investments in large-scale irrigation systems provided a costly and partial substitute. In this economic and political context, the green revolution offered a quick technological 'fix' to policy makers in search of a route to increase rice production.

THE NEW RICE TECHNOLOGY AND WATER CONTROL

The new rice technology has three essential elements: the 'high-yielding' or 'modern' rice varieties originated at the International Rice Research Institute; chemical fertilizers, to which these varieties are highly responsive; and water control, notably irrigation in the Philippine setting. In addition, chemical pesticides are often necessary to protect the new varieties from insects and diseases.[25] To encourage cultivators to incur the higher costs of these inputs, the Philippine government provided subsidized credit tied

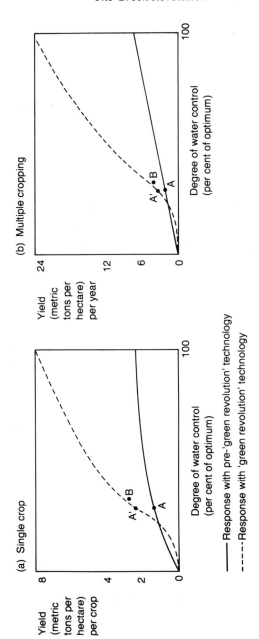

Figure 3.2:   **Impact of New Technology on Response of Rice Yield to Water Control**

to input purchases, particularly in the mid-1970s under the 'Masagana–99' credit program.[26]

The key inputs of the new technology – seeds, fertilizer, and water control – are highly complementary. In the absence of one, the productivity of the others is greatly reduced. Hence it is possible that one input, by constraining the production impact of the others, can act as the 'limiting factor' or 'leading input' in the growth process, in effect becoming the 'shift variable in the production function' (Ishikawa, 1967, pp. 85, 181).

The leading input in Asian rice agriculture is often water control – that is, irrigation, drainage, and flood control.[27] Water control differs from seed and fertilizer in two crucial respects. First, water control typically requires investment prior to the cropping season, unlike seed and fertilizer which can be purchased in the current period of production. In the language of microeconomic theory, water control is a fixed input while seeds and fertilizer are variable inputs. Second, water control is often 'lumpy'. That is, it must be provided to a number of cultivators for their joint use, rather than to individual farmers in isolation. Seeds and fertilizer, by constrast, are perfectly divisible. The twin needs for prior capital investment and for institutional solutions to the problems of joint use combine to make water control the binding constraint. While a cultivator with water control can obtain seeds and fertilizer fairly easily, the reverse is not true.

The advent of the new, short-statured rice varieties heightened the importance of water control in Asian rice agriculture, since they require continuous submergence from planting to maturity at depths within the fairly narrow band of 2–15 centimetres (1–6 inches). If the crop receives too little water or too much, the yield of the new varieties falls sharply.[28]

The degree of water control can vary from zero to the technical optimum. This range of variation underlies the four successive stages in Asian rice agriculture distinguished by Ishikawa (1967). In the first stage, yields are very low and susceptible to rainfall fluctuations. In the second, the introduction of modest water control permits the stabilization of yields. In the third, water control improvements permit multiple cropping, which increases land productivity by raising the number of crops per acre per year, rather than by increasing the yield per crop. In the fourth stage, the further perfection of water control allows increased fertilizer application, the introduction of higher-yielding varieties, and the use of improved techniques such as row transplantation of paddy. At this point water control ceases to be the leading input, and other complementary inputs – fertilizer, seeds, and improved techniques – assume this role.

This stylized scheme must be adapted to fit the historical experiences of specific countries. In Japan, for example, where only one rice crop per year can be grown, water control improvements permitted the cultivation of non-rice crops such as wheat, barley, and vegetables in the winter season (Hayami *et al.*, 1975, p. 58). In the Philippines, the introduction of the new seed-fertilizer technology did not wait on the perfection of water control. Instead, Ishikawa's stages have overlapped, water control playing its various roles simultaneously rather than in neat succession.[29]

The Philippine experience is depicted schematically in Figure 3.2(a). The introduction of the new varieties is represented as a shift in the response curve relating paddy yield to the degree of water control.[30] At low levels of water control, yields with the new technology are actually lower than those with the pre-existing technology. Once the degree of water control reaches a certain threshold, however, yields under the new technology exceed those under the old.

In the early 1960s Philippine rice agriculture was located at point A on the 'before' curve, with average paddy yields of about 1.25 metric tons per hectare (mt/ha). Point A′ on the 'after' curve represents the hypothetical gain from a 100 per cent shift to the new technology, with no improvement in the degree of water control. In the mid-1980s Philippine rice agriculture had moved to point B, with average rice yields of about 2.5 mt/ha. The yield gain arose partly from a shift toward the 'after' curve (with adoption of the new varieties on 85 per cent of the country's rice area) and partly from improvements in water control.

The preponderant role of irrigated lands in the green revolution is evident in Table 3.4. Philippine rice statistics distinguish among three classes of land – irrigated, rainfed, and upland – according to the degree of water control. Both rainfed and upland rice depend entirely on rainfall for soil moisture, but in the case of the former, the paddy fields are bunded so as to retain surface runoff.

The new rice technology led to a widening of differences in land productivity among the three types. Between 1962–64 and 1983–85, irrigated rice yields rose by 90 per cent to three metric tons of *palay* per hectare. Yields of 'rainfed' rice rose by 60 per cent to nearly two mt/ha. Yields of upland rice rose by 30 per cent to one mt/ha.

At the same time, the distribution of rice land among these three water regimes shifted: irrigated rice acreage climbed by nearly 80 per cent, while rainfed acreage slipped and upland acreage contracted sharply. In part, these shifts reflect improvements in water control: some upland fields were bunded, moving into the rainfed category, and some rainfed fields became irrigated. But the shifts also reflect the abandonment of rice cultivation by growers who were effectively driven out of rice farming by competition from areas with better water control. According to official data, for example,

TABLE 3.4 *Paddy Output, Area and Yield on Irrigated,*
Rainfed and Upland Lands, 1962/64–1983/85 (triennial averages)

	1962/64	1974/76	1983/85
Output ('000 metric tons) [1]			
Total	3914	6061	7924
Irrigated	1548	3339	5216
Rainfed [2]	1838	2356	2534
Upland [3]	528	365	174
Gross area ('000 hectares)			
Total	3143	3611	3201
Irrigated	977	1505	1742
Rainfed	1497	1678	1292
Upland	669	428	167
Yield (metric tons/hectare)			
Total	1.25	1.68	2.48
Irrigated	1.58	2.22	2.99
Rainfed	1.23	1.40	1.96
Upland	0.79	0.85	1.04

NOTES
1. Output of *palay* (unhusked rice); 1 kg *palay* = 0.67 kg milled rice.
2. 'Rainfed' lands are rice paddies which have been bunded but depend upon rainfall
   for moisture.
3. 'Upland' rice lands are unbunded fields.

SOURCES   Bureau of Agricultural Economics data as reported by Alix (1979, p.
A–6, Table 6) for 1962–64 and by Rosengrant *et al.* (1987, p. 2.69, Table 2.7) for
1974–76 and 1983–85.

total rice acreage in the Bicol region dropped from 367,000 hectares in 1970
to 275,000 hectares in 1983, with upland rice accounting for most of the
decline.[31]

    To obtain a rough indication of the relative importance of the new seed-
fertilizer technology and water control improvement in yield growth, we can
estimate what paddy yields would have been in 1983–85 had the distribution
of rice area among the irrigated, rainfed, and upland categories remained the
same as in 1962–64. Weighted by this area distribution, the average paddy
yield in 1983–85 (based on the yields reported in Table 3.4) would have been

2.08 metric tons per hectare, as opposed to the actual 2.48 metric tons. Taking the area distribution as a measure of water control, this represents the yield at point A' in Figure 3.2(a). The 'pure' shift effect from the new rice technology effect thus accounts for two-thirds of the yield increase in the period.[32]

What of multiple cropping? In year-round warm environments, such as that of the Philippines, a major potential role of water control is to allow increased cropping intensity, for example, by dry-season irrigation. This possibility is incorporated in Figure 3.2(b), where the before-and-after response curves are drawn with yield *per year* rather than yield per crop on the vertical axis. With optimal water control, maximum cropping intensity, and the new technology, paddy yields could reach (say) 24 metric tons per hectare, as opposed to 8 mt/ha in a single season.[33]

Multiple cropping of paddy in the Philippines remains at a fairly low level. Compared to a maximum potential, with adequate year-round water, of perhaps 3 crops per year, the actual average is probably in the vicinity of 1.3.[34] Trends cannot be precisely ascertained from the available data. Official statistics distinguish between the 'first' rice crop, grown in the 'wet' season and harvested from July to December, and the 'second' crop, grown in the 'dry' season and harvested from January to June. In some regions, however, the latter is actually the primary rice season owing to rainfall patterns.[35] The area under the 'second' crop thus cannot be taken as a measure of multiple cropping, since some of it did not bear a 'first' crop. A rough 'guesstimate', derived by comparing the share of 'dry' season rice in irrigated and rainfed acreage, indicates that double cropping increased only marginally between 1970 and 1983.[36]

The Philippines thus does not fit neatly into Ishikawa's stage scheme. Although the degree of water control was sufficient to allow wide-scale adoption of the new seed-fertilizer technology, it did not permit a substantial increase in multiple cropping. For two decades the new seed-fertilizer technology, rather than water control, provided the major source of yield increase. But the eclipse of water control's role as the binding technological constraint in Philippine rice agriculture was only temporary.

In the early 1980s, the yield gains from the green revolution in the Philippines 'began to be exhausted' (World Bank, 1989a, p. viii). By 1982, 84 per cent of total rice area (and 93 per cent of irrigated rice area) was sown to the new varieties. Hence, the World Bank (1989a, p. 65) concluded, 'sharp increases in paddy productivity through conversion of [to] Green Revolution technology were no longer possible'.

In a careful analysis of rice production trends at the regional level, Bouis (1989) similarly concludes that the technological 'pipeline' in Philippine rice agriculture has 'run dry'. Yields reached a plateau in Central Luzon and Southern Tagalog, where the initial impact of the green revolution was concentrated, in the early 1970s. Thereafter the spread of the new technology to the Visayas, Mindanao, and northern Luzon sustained yield growth rates at the national level. In the 1980s, however, the scope for further extension reached its limits.

THE RETURN OF THE HYDRAULIC CONSTRAINT

On retiring as the first director of the International Rice Research Institute, Robert Chandler, Jr. recorded his disappointment that 'rice scientists, who obtained yields of 5 to 10 metric tons per hectare on the IRRI farm, still could not explain why so many Filipino farmers (for example) obtained, on the average, less than one metric ton per hectare increase in yield after shifting from traditional to high-yielding varieties'.[37]

Nowhere is this yield gap more striking than in the Philippines, the birthplace of the new technology. Despite the substantial growth documented above, Philippine rice yields remain well below potential levels. The country's average of 2.5 metric tons of paddy per hectare in 1983–85 can be contrasted, for example, to 3.9 mt/ha in Indonesia, 5.3 mt/ha in China, and 6.3 mt/ha in Korea and Japan.[38]

IRRI researchers, investigating the reasons for the yield gap in the late 1970s, found that most of it was explained by factors 'beyond the farmers' control', which they defined to include not only natural conditions, such as the amount of sunshine and the frequency of typhoons, but also the adequacy of water control. Differences in the use of 'managed inputs', such as fertilizer and pesticides, made a rather modest contribution to the gap between potential and actual yields.[39]

Water control, however, occupies an intermediate terrain between privately manageable inputs and the raw forces of nature. While often beyond the *individual* farmer's control, it is not entirely beyond the control of the farmers *as a group*. This is where the major explanation for the gap between potential and actual rice yields in the Philippines lies.

Perfect water control – the 100 per cent optimum depicted in Figure 3.2 – is possible on experimental farms, but it is not an economically attainable objective for any rice-producing country. The difference between the technological optimum and the economic optimum is depicted in Figure 3.3. The upward-sloping curve, *MC*, represents the rising marginal cost of producing an additional ton of paddy per hectare via water control improvements. The horizontal line (*P*) represents the marginal benefit of growing another ton of paddy, approximated by its price. Point C depicts the

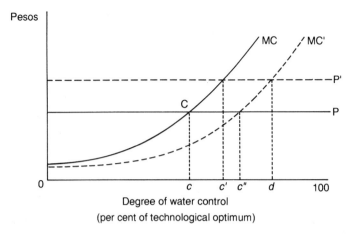

Figure 3.3: **Economically Optimal Water Control**

economic optimum, beyond which rising costs make further water control development unprofitable. The economically optimal level of water control is a fraction (c) of the technological optimum.

The position of the curves, and the extent to which further water control development is economically feasible, depends among other things on two crucial factors: (a) the demand for rice, and (b) the institutional framework for water control. An increase in demand for rice, arising, for example, from higher average incomes or a redistribution of income from rich to poor, would raise the price of rice to P', increasing the optimal degree of water control to c'. Cost-reducing institutional (or technological) change would shift the marginal cost of water control to MC', increasing the optimal degree of water control to c''. Together, increased demand and cost-reducing institutional change would increase the optimal degree of water control to d.

Cost-benefit studies indicate that irrigation investment was quite profitable in the Philippines from the 1950s to the 1970s. Kikuchi and Hayami (1978a, p. 859) report that the internal rate of return was more than 25 per cent in the early 1950s, and about 20 per cent in the early 1960s. The advent of the new seed-fertilizer technology boosted the profitability of irrigation, pushing internal rates of return above 30 per cent in the late 1960s and early 1970s.

Irrigated acreage reportedly rose from 0.5 million hectares in 1952 to 0.9 million in 1965, and to 1.4 million in 1985 (see Table 3.5).[40] This growth came after decades of virtual stagnation under US colonial rule. Hooley

The Philippines

TABLE 3.5 *Irrigated Area by Type of System, 1952–1985*[1]
('000 hectares)

Year	Type of System			
	NIA[2]	Communal	Pump & other	Total
1952	111	334	39	484
1955	138	369	45	553
1960	261	417	61	739
1965	319	527	89	935
1970	421	618	119	1158
1975(a)	561	808	256	1625
1975(b)	475	589		1064
1980	474	724		1198
1985	570	852		1422

NOTES
1. Data refer to 'irrigable' or 'service' area, not all of which necessarily received irrigation water. (See text note 40.)
2. National Irrigation Administration gravity flow systems.

SOURCES   Data for 1952 to 1975(a) are from Kikuchi and Hayami (1978b, p. 318). Data for 1975(b) to 1985 are from Rosengrant *et al.* (1987, p. 3.31). [Both cite the National Irrigation Administration as their original source.]

and Ruttan (1969, p. 224) report that between 1902 and 1948 the country's irrigated area rose by only 25 per cent, while total cultivated area almost tripled. As a result, the proportion of crop land irrigated fell from 25 per cent at the turn of the century to about 10 per cent at independence.

Historically, the main form of rice irrigation in the Philippines has been the impoundment and diversion of surface waters by autonomous local groups. Such initiatives, described as 'communal' irrigation in official statistics, today account for roughly half of the country's irrigated acreage (see Table 3.5). Since the early 1950s, large-scale canal projects initiated and operated by the government's National Irrigation Administration (NIA) with technical and financial support from the US government, the World Bank, and the Asian Development Bank, have been a major source of growth in irrigated acreage.[41] The third type of irrigation reported in Table 3.5, 'pump and other', primarily refers to smaller government schemes which draw water from rivers and reservoirs.

The Philippines 'still has a very large potential for profitable irrigation development', according to Hayami and Ruttan (1985, p. 320). World Bank estimates of extent of the country's unexploited irrigation potential are presented in Table 3.6. These err on the low side for several reasons. The estimates, culled from NIA studies, do not include the potential for non-NIA schemes. In particular, there is no estimate of the potential for further extension of communal irrigation. With respect to pump and other irrigation, the World Bank (1982, p. 28) reports that 'no reliable inventory exists . . . nor is there a clear indication of the areas truly served by these systems or the potential for future development'. In addition, the Philippines has a large and as yet virtually untapped potential for groundwater irrigation (that is, irrigation from underground aquifers). The National Water Resources Council has estimated that enough groundwater could be extracted to irrigate 1.5 million hectares annually during the dry season, without deterioration of water quality or groundwater reserve levels (World Bank, 1982, p. 43). Finally, the World Bank estimate omits possibilities for water control improvement on lands which are already classified as irrigated.

Despite these omissions, the World Bank (1982, p. ii) found that 'only about 40% of the technically irrigable area of the Philippines has been developed'. The authors of the Bank study concluded, however, that 'current plans for irrigation development should be scaled down' owing to inadequate projected future levels of demand for rice.

The Bank's reasoning illustrates the inseparability of questions of allocative efficiency from questions of distribution. The demand for rice in the Philippines greatly depends on the distribution of income, a point further explored in the next chapter. Hence future growth in demand will depend on how income gains (or losses) are distributed across the country's population. If the lion's share of income increments accrue to the rich, whose income elasticity of demand for rice is low, then demand will grow much less rapidly than if income gains accrued primarily to the poor.

In its rice demand forecasts, the World Bank (1982, p. 66) assumed a very low income elasticity of demand for rice, 0.1. That is, a ten per cent rise in national income was expected to generate only a one per cent increase in demand for rice. This elasticity may well be realistic given a continuation of the highly inegalitarian distributional trends documented in Chapter 2. Whether policy should be guided by the assumption that these trends will continue is, however, open to debate.

One solution to the demand constraint posed by the low purchasing power of many Filipinos would be government distribution of rice to the poor at subsidized prices. In 1981 the government's Ministry of Agriculture published a Food and Nutrition Plan which called for a large-scale program

TABLE 3.6 *Irrigated Area and Irrigation Potential by Region, 1980*
('000 hectares)

Region	Existing area[1]				Under construction[3]	Additional potential[4]
	NIA[2]	Communal	Pump & other	Total		
Northern Luzon	80	165	40	285	110	136
Central Luzon	200	115	45	360	20	460
Southern Luzon	55	80	40	175	75	70
Visayas	70	60	35	165	25	118
Mindanao	65	130	30	225	100	270
Total	470	550	190	1210	330	1054

NOTES
1. 'Service area', not all of which may actually receive water.
2. National Irrigation Administration gravity flow systems.
3. NIA gravity flow systems only.
4. NIA estimates (surface water only).

SOURCE World Bank (1982, pp. 27–32).

of this type. This proposal was rejected by the government as too costly, however, leading the World Bank (1982, p. iii) to conclude that 'a greatly scaled-down program is probably the most which can be anticipated'. The assumed distributional constraint on demand for rice thus persisted in the political arena.

'In the absence of a firm commitment by the Government to launch a major rice-based nutrition program aimed at the poorest groups in the country', the World Bank (1982, p. 44) concludes, 'and in the absence of a deliberate program of rice production for export, maintaining rice self-sufficiency to the end of the century does not require a major program of additional major gravity irrigation systems after the projects now under construction are completed'. Coming from the NIA's main international funding agency, this conclusion is not merely academic: it represents the making of policy.[42]

The second crucial constraint on development of the Philippines' irrigation potential is institutional. Since water control often requires joint resource use by a number of cultivators, its costs depend, among other things, on the degree of cooperation among cultivators in the construction, operation, and maintenance of facilities and in the allocation of water. When the degree of cooperation is low, the costs of water control are high. An inegalitarian and contested agrarian structure can pose a serious impediment to cooperation. This raises the marginal cost of water control development and reduces the economically optimal level depicted in Figure 3.3.

Communal and government irrigation systems provide illuminating contrasts in this respect. Traditional communal systems, ranging in size from a few hectares to 4,000 hectares, were initiated by the cultivators themselves. Some of them centuries old. They continue to rely on local resources – notably labor – for their operation and maintenance.

A number of institutional mechanisms have been developed by communal irrigators to foster cooperation and to discourage potential 'free riders' from attempting to appropriate benefits while shirking costs. In the *zanjera* irrigation systems of Ilocos, for example, individual land holdings are fragmented into a number of parcels dispersed in equal proportions across the different zones of the command area. Potential conflicts between 'head-enders' whose lands are close to the water source and 'tail-enders' whose lands are further away are thereby avoided.[43] Labor obligations for maintenance work are distributed among members in proportion to their irrigated acreage.

A recurrent theme in accounts of communal irrigation in the Philippines is the importance of moral consensus among the participants. Reviewing a number of case studies, Siy (1988, pp. 23–5) concludes:

Perhaps the most striking lesson was that the collective effort to build the irrigation system and subsequently to maintain it had resulted in a strong sense of ownership among those who had contributed. Their contributions earned them a socially recognized right to receive water from the system, a right which bound the group to fairness in water distribution.

The strongest of the communal irrigation systems demonstrate what Siy terms a 'fundamental concern for fairness and egalitarianism'.

In a study of a 90-hectare communal irrigation system in Central Luzon's Zambales Province, Kikuchi, Dozina and Hayami (1978, p. 225) conclude that success rested on the presence of 'good leaders' who 'managed to organize the program with the consent of the community members'. These leaders were share tenants, like their fellow irrigators, and this common class status made it 'easier for the community members to accept the proposal of the leaders . . . The same proposal might not have been accepted by the majority if it had been proposed by owner-operators or landlords'. Contrary to the efficiency-equity 'trade-off' so often assumed by economists, equity here promoted efficiency.

In other cases, communal irrigation systems include both rich and poor, and divergences of interest between them are contained by patron-client bonds. In an account of a 500-hectare system in Camarines Sur Province in southern Luzon, de los Reyes (1985, p. 12) reports that management was a 'collective endeavor of the *dakulang tao* [upper class landowner] leaders and their allies', who relied on 'personalistic, vertical ties as a means of mobilizing farmers' and used 'social pressure rather than formal sanctions as a means of imposing discipline'.[44]

The elite were in turn disciplined by the prevailing moral consensus. Association leaders shared the general 'folk view of water . . . that every farmer has a right to irrigation – because of his inherent right to farm or earn a living' (de los Reyes, 1985, p. 13). Patron-client bonds tempered the rough edges of inequality, subordinating property rights to a more basic 'right to live' or 'right to subsistence'.[45] However, the unity of the irrigation association was weakened by factional competition among different *dakulang tao*. Ordinary cultivators contributed to the necessary maintenance activities only when their own patrons were in charge, with the result that only half actively participated at any given time.

The fact that communal systems have emerged in some places but not in others may be partly due to differences in the degree of moral consensus. Where the rural society is sharply polarized between rich and poor, and where patron-client ties are too weak to suppress conflict between them, cooperative use of water resources can be problematic. In recent decades, as discussed in Chapter 5, traditional patron-client ties in Philippine rice agriculture have come under increasing stress. The new rice technology, government land reform policies, mechanization, and population growth in the absence of adequate non-agricultural employment have all contributed to a sharpening of class differences among rice producers. This may have tightened institutional constraints on locally-initiated irrigation development, making it more difficult to reach agreement as to how water should be allocated and how the costs of construction and maintenance should be shared.

The government can attempt to circumvent local institutional constraints by assuming the task of water control development itself. As Barker (1978, p. 152) remarks, 'Government investment in land infrastructure represents, to a large extent, a substitution for community investment'. The costs of government investment tend, however, to be relatively high. One reason is often the failure to mobilize relatively low-cost local resources. The per hectare cost of purchased materials and hired labor under communal irrigation systems is only one-tenth that under government National Irrigation Administration systems (Kikuchi, Dozina and Hayami, 1978, p. 212).

Another reason for the relatively high cost of government schemes is that the lack of local-level institutions for cooperation often undermines efficiency in water allocation. Forty years after the construction of an irrigation system on the Angat River in Central Luzon, Takahashi (1969, p. 120) reported that 'anarchy' prevailed over the use of irrigation water at the village level. Similarly, NIA and IRRI researchers report that in the World Bank-financed Upper Pampanga River irrigation project, 'illegal turnouts' or unauthorized water diversions account for 40 per cent of the irrigated area.[46]

In addition, farmers dependent on government irrigation systems often mistrust official assurances as to the timing of water deliveries, and hence do not begin land preparation until water has been flowing in the feeder channels for several days. The result, Barker *et al.* (1984, p. 42) report, is 'water wastage and a constriction of multiple cropping opportunities'.[47] These pervasive inefficiencies help to explain why estimated internal rates of return on NIA canal systems are only one-third as high as those on communal systems (Rosengrant *et al.*, 1987, p. 3.41).

While pressing ahead with large-scale canal schemes, the Philippine government began to provide financial and technical assistance to communal systems in the late 1950s. By 1975, systems accounting for some 40 per cent of the area under communal irrigation had received government aid.[48] This was a mixed blessing. Government officials often had little appreciation of the communal institutions which governed water allocation and maintenance activities. At the same time, the substitution of external resources for local resources lessened the erstwhile patrons' dependence on their clients, corroding the bonds which facilitate collective action in an inegalitarian society. As Barker *et al.* (1984, p. 30) observe, external assistance 'can not only encourage the demise of community investment and responsibility, but also attach the local system to the unpredictable future actions of the technical bureaucracy'.

The NIA began experimenting with an alternative 'participatory' approach in its assistance to communal systems in two pilot projects in Nueva Ecija in 1976. The agency sent community organizers to live in the project areas, and encouraged the formation of farmers' committees to design and monitor system improvements. The effort reportedly was fairly successful in one case, but in the other it was thwarted by 'pressure from a local politician who wanted his own men to control the association' (Bagadion, 1988, p. 13).

In the 1980s this alternative approach was pursued on a wider scale, and comparisons with conventional projects found the participatory systems to be less dominated by larger farmers (de los Reyes and Jopillo, 1988, p. 102). This experience suggests that there is some scope for the reorientation of government initiatives toward more 'bottom-up' approaches, but in the Philippines this has been the exception, rather than the rule.

In sum, water control remains a key constraint in Philippine rice agriculture. Underlying this technological constraint is an institutional one. Water control improvement often can be most efficiently achieved by the mobilization of community labor, but this poses public-good problems. How will labor commitments and other costs be apportioned among individuals? How will irrigation water be allocated so that everyone receives a fair share? In some places, communal irrigation systems have successfully resolved these problems, but elsewhere conflict and mistrust among individuals have impeded collective action.[49] Government initiatives provide a costly and imperfect substitute for local-level resource mobilization.[50]

The green revolution brought temporary relief from this impasse, allowing the country to achieve substantial rice yield increases via the shift to new seed-fertilizer technology. But while the degree of water control permitted adoption of the new technology on a wide scale, it did not permit the new varieties to attain their full potential yields, nor did it permit much increase in multiple cropping. It seems likely that further land productivity growth in Philippine rice agriculture will depend on progress in these areas. The hydraulic constraint in Philippine rice agriculture has returned.

ENVIRONMENTAL IMPLICATIONS OF THE NEW RICE
TECHNOLOGY

The 'green revolution' in Philippine rice agriculture has brought with it three
potentially serious environmental problems: (1) the risk of crop failure due
to genetic vulnerability; (2) the negative externalities of pesticide use; and
(3) dependence on inputs derived from non-renewable natural resources.
These 'social costs' reduce the net benefit of the rice production increases
documented above, and raise questions as to their long-run sustainability.

Genetic Vulnerability

Genetic vulnerability arises when a single plant variety or a set of varieties
with shared genes occupies a large proportion of cropped area. In traditional
rice agriculture, the severity of insect and plant disease outbreaks was limited
by genetic diversity, as cultivators grew many rice varieties which differed in
their susceptibilities to specific strains of pests. As the IRRI varieties spread
to large areas, this diversity was greatly reduced, creating an environment
in which natural selection favors the evolution of pests particularly suited to
the new varieties, and increasing the vulnerability of the country's rice crop
to epidemics.

The attendant risks became apparent in the Philippines in 1971, when
an outbreak of tungro virus resulted in the loss of one-third of the Central
Luzon rice crop. Plant breeders at IRRI responded quickly, releasing new
varieties with genes for resistance to the virus and its insect vector, the
green leafhopper (Barker, Herdt and Rose, 1985, pp. 63, 67). Philippine rice
agriculture embarked on the perpetual race between the pest and the plant
breeder which characterizes much of modern agriculture.[51]

The thousands of rice varieties bred over the centuries by the cultivators
themselves provide the raw material for plant breeding. This genetic base is
imperiled, however, as local rice varieties are displaced by the new varieties.
IRRI has devoted much effort to the collection and preservation of rice
germplasm, and more than 70,000 varieties are now stored and replicated
in the Institute's 'germplasm bank' (IRRI, 1989, p. 3). Some varieties undoubtedly slipped through the IRRI net, however, and became extinct. IRRI's
Annual Report for 1978 reported that displacement of traditional varieties
in irrigated areas of the Philippines had reached the point where 'canvassing
netted only few seed samples' (IRRI, 1979, p. 12).

The concentration of vital genetic resources in one or a few locations is
a poor substitute for a genetically diverse agriculture. Some commentators

have raised the spectre of the monopolization of genetic resources for commercial ends (see, for example, Farmer Assistance Board, 1982, p. 80). Rice germplasm stored at IRRI is made freely available to plant breeders throughout the world, and it can be hoped that public sector control will ensure that this practice continues. The eggs-in-one-basket syndrome poses serious risks, however, for a breakdown in the technical apparatus of the germplasm bank (due, for example, to accidents or war) could drastically reduce the genetic base for the world's most important food crop.[52]

Pesticide Externalities

A second set of external costs arises from the use of chemical pesticides to combat insects and diseases. The extent of pesticide use in Philippine rice cultivation is not well-documented. There is no doubt, however, that it rose sharply with the spread of the new seed-fertilizer technology, in part due to the greater susceptibility of the new varieties to pests, and in part to the greater potential losses with higher yields.

The government's National Food and Agriculture Council estimated in the late 1970s that at recommended input levels, pesticides accounted for 16 per cent of the variable cost of *palay* production, only slightly less than fertilizer at 20 per cent (World Bank, 1979a, Vol. II, p. 16). This may overstate the actual share of pesticides, since their use was 'generally well below recommended levels' (*ibid.*, p. 2). According to the World Bank (1980a, pp. 36–7), rice accounted for the 'major share' of the 225 million pesos ($30 million) in pesticide sales in the Philippines in 1977, but the average pesticide expenditure per hectare of rice was only 20 per cent of that set in the Masangana–99 credit package.

The hazards of chemical pesticides include health effects on workers, the loss or contamination of aquatic food resources, and the emergence of a 'pesticide treadmill' in which ever larger doses of more potent pesticides are needed to counteract the emergence of pesticide-resistant insects and plant diseases. A 1987 survey in Benguet Province in northern Luzon found that 45 per cent of workers did not use protective masks while spraying pesticides, 74 per cent did not use gloves, and 82 per cent did not wear boots.[53] Safety information provided by pesticide suppliers in the Philippines is often printed only in English, and local advertisements have depicted smiling farmers applying granulated pesticide by hand without gloves or other protective clothing.[54]

Many pesticides are highly toxic to fish and other aquatic life, which are an important element of the Filipino diet.[55] Small fish in flooded rice paddies are killed immediately by the application of common pesticides, and surface water runoff kills or contaminates species in rivers, ponds, lakes, and the sea. The impacts on the Philippine fishing industry and consumers have yet to be thoroughly studied, but press accounts indicate widespread concern about the problem.[56]

A further negative externality associated with pesticide use is the emergence of resistant pests by natural selection. This 'treadmill effect', extensively documented in countries with long histories of pesticide use (see, for example, Georghiou, 1986), imposes an additional social cost in the form of escalating pesticide expenditures to achieve the same level of pest control.

In light of these costs, a strong case can be made for an 'integrated pest management' strategy which stresses the development of host plant resistance, biological controls, and pest-reducing agronomic practices such as crop rotation, reserving 'chemical warfare' for use as a last resort. Such a strategy was endorsed in principle in the US Agency for International Development's \$5 million Philippine crop protection project launched in 1977 (USAID, 1977, pp. 27–9). The World Bank (1980a, p. 37) continued to advocate a chemical-intensive strategy, however, calling for 'a major development effort' by the Philippine government and private pesticides companies 'to promote a reasonable level of protection for the rice crop'. The Bank's notion of reasonable protection included prophylactic pesticide applications to prevent pest outbreaks.[57] This prescription for treatment before the disease is in sharp contrast to the selective role for pesticides in integrated pest management.

Non-renewable Resource Dependence

Dependence on the non-renewable natural resources used to produce chemical fertilizers has been a further environmental cost of the green revolution. In particular, most nitrogenous fertilizer (which accounts for the bulk of Philippine fertilizer imports) is produced using fossil fuels (see Sheldrick, 1987). This makes fertilizer prices susceptible to the instability of the world energy market, and to the possibility of a long-run rise in prices as fuel stocks are depleted. The world oil price increases of the 1970s caused a doubling of the price of nitrogen fertilizer relative to the price of rice in the Philippines (David and Balisacan, 1981, p. 25).

It is sometimes claimed that Filipino rice farmers have become 'hooked' on the new rice technology, so that when input prices rise, they have no choice but to pay. This claim rests on the questionable assumption that cultivators cannot switch back to traditional low-input rice varieties if it becomes profitable to do so. Rice seed can be replicated by the growers themselves, and as long as traditional varieties have not been completely eliminated, one can expect acreage to shift back to them if, for example, higher fertilizer prices make them become more profitable than the HYVs. In Malaysia, rice cultivators responded to a cost-price squeeze in the early 1970s by discontinuing the use of a popular IRRI variety (Herdt and Capule, 1983, pp. 38–9). Traditional rice varieties have virtually disappeared in parts of the Philippines, making it difficult for individual farmers to switch to them. Nationwide, however, hundreds of thousands of hectares remain under traditional varieties. The fact that rice farmers with adequate water control continue to grow the new varieties suggests that they have remained at least as profitable as the traditional varieties.[58]

Filipino rice cultivators have been subjected to a price squeeze, as documented in the next chapter. But falling rice prices since the mid-1970s have reduced the profitability of both traditional and 'modern' rice technology. The problem is not that Filipino farmers are 'hooked' on the new technology, but rather that relatively sluggish growth in demand has reduced the profitability of rice cultivation in general.

The environmental shortcomings of the new rice technology do not imply that scientific research in Philippine rice agriculture should play a diminished role in the future. On the contrary, they point to the need for further research to breed a continuing stream of pest-resistant varieties and to explore new areas such as biological nitrogen fixation and integrated pest management. The expansion and geographical diffusion of agricultural research would map new technologies more closely to local environments and reduce risks of crop loss by fostering greater genetic diversity. In coming years, therefore, the Philippines will need not just IRRI, but many mini-IRRI's.

CONCLUSIONS

The green revolution in the Philippines succeeded in fulfilling its architects' primary objective: more food production. In little more than two decades, the country's rice output doubled. This was achieved almost entirely through increased land productivity, leaving room for export agriculture to grow through acreage extension.

In pursuit of this goal, the planners chose what appeared to be the easiest route: the breeding of new varieties for high fertilizer response. This allowed them to circumvent temporarily the institutional constraints on water control development. The strategy brought the risks of genetic vulnerability, but the scientists generally managed to keep a step ahead in the race against insects and plant diseases. The fertilizer price rise sparked by the energy crises of the 1970s did not act as a serious brake on output growth.

Today, even if individual farmers could return to the cultivation of traditional rice varieties, the Philippine economy could not readily readjust to volume of the rice output of the early 1960s. Were yields to return to those earlier levels, with no change in rice acreage, the country would need massive food imports to avert disaster. In this sense, the green revolution in the Philippines is irreversible.

The country could divert land from export crops to rice production, permitting current rice output levels to be sustained with lower yields per acre. With high input prices, high environmental costs of the new rice technology, and low social benefits from export agriculture – not an implausible combination – such a trade-off would make sense. In the long-run, however, growth in rice production in the Philippines will require further increases in output per unit area.

Little scope remains for conversion of existing rice lands to the new varieties. Hence future yield growth is likely to hinge on improvements in water control, which would permit higher yields per crop and more crops per year. The need for collective action in irrigation, drainage, and flood control brings institutional issues to center stage. By reducing inequalities and the attendant conflicts in the countryside, a thoroughgoing land reform would facilitate cooperation and local resource mobilization in the construction, maintenance, and operation of water control facilities. The resulting potential for increased production is one element of the case for land reform in the Philippines. The other element, explored in the following chapters, is distributive justice.

NOTES

1. Barker, Herdt and Rose (1985, p. 63); Herdt and Capule (1983, p. 16). Herdt and Capule (pp. 14–15) attribute the rapidity of adoption in the Philippines to the fact that IRRI is located there, as a consequence of which 'IRRI research may be most relevant in the Philippines'.

2. Hopper (1968, p. 111). Hopper explicitly juxtaposed this production focus to other concerns (p. 105): 'National governments must clearly separate the goal of growth from the goals of social development and political participation. . . . [I]f the pursuit of production is made subordinate to other aims, the dismal record of the past will not be altered'. With respect to land tenure, Hopper offered the following 'passing comment' (p. 110): 'Insofar as these institutions act as determinants of the allocation of resources for production, they must be embraced in the strategy

for the conquest of hunger. Insofar as they operate only to establish social conditions in rural society, I place them outside our immediate narrow concern of mapping the road to abundance.'

3.   Romulo (1968, p. 119). Romulo was also a member of the International Rice Research Institute's Board of Directors.

4.   On Bangladesh, see Boyce (1987, p. 115).

5.   The official Philippine agricultural statistics designate dates by the year in which the crop year ends (contrary to the standard practice in many other countries): '1972' thus refers to the 1971–72 crop year. This practice is followed here.

6.   See Table 3.1. This reflects sharp yield declines in the 1980s. The positive yield growth rates reported for these crops in Table 3.2 result from fitting a trend line to annual data for the period as a whole.

7.   Rather than land use surveys and crop cuts, as carried out for example in India, the Philippine estimates are based on interviews with a sample of farmers, and are hence subject to recall bias. The raw data from farmer interviews are then revised upward by agricultural officials: 'Thus, the entire agricultural data base consists practically of subjective estimates' (David, 1989, p. 4). For discussion, see Mears *et al.* (1974, pp. 23–5, 350–3) and Rose (1985, pp. 250–4); on the Indian methodology, see Maitra and Lahiri (1975).

8.   Rice output estimates may be more reliable than those for acreage and yield: 'The statistics on extension of the irrigable area reported by the National Irrigation Authority is [sic] not reconcilable with the irrigated palay area harvested reported by the Bureau of Agricultural Economics although the major use of irrigation is for palay. This raises some question as to the reliability of the palay yields which are derived from production and area harvested'. (World Bank, 1979a, p. 1.) For an analysis of the reliability of the official data on corn, see David *et al.* (1990).

9.   Acreage growth data are not reported owing to boundary changes over time. The regional data are likely to have a higher margin of error than national estimates (see Mears *et al.*, 1974, p. 24). In particular, the reported 1981–83 yields for Northern Mindanao, Central Mindanao, and Southern Mindanao are substantially higher than their reported yields in preceding years and hence are open to question.

10. The correlation coefficient between average *palay* yields in 1962–64 as reported in Table 3.3 and 1965 poverty incidence as reported in Table 2.13 is – 0.35. That between average yields in 1981–83 and rural poverty incidence in 1985 is – 0.67.

11. The correlation between *palay* yield growth as reported in Table 3.3 and the growth rate of poverty incidence in 1965–83 calculated from the data in Table 2.13 (using the Mangahas estimates for 1983) is 0.13; using rural poverty incidence in 1985 as the end point the correlation is – 0.15. If, however, the Mindanao regions are dropped owing to the relatively low weight of rice in their crop value and their questionable yield data for the 1980s (see note 9), then a moderate association emerges between

higher yield growth and lower poverty growth ($r = -0.35$ and $r = -0.47$, respectively).

12. Malthus (1817, Vol. III, p. 318). 'If these truths were by degrees more generally known', Malthus (p. 319) continued, 'the lower classes of people, as a rule, would become more peaceable and orderly, would be less inclined to tumultuous proceedings in seasons of scarcity, and would at all times be less influenced by inflammatory and seditious publications, from knowing how little the price of labour and the means of supporting a family depend upon a revolution'.

13. For discussion of this 'demographic transition', see Hartmann (1987, pp. 271–85).

14. Calculated from population and output data in Mears *et al.* (1974, pp. 335, 343) and NEDA (1976, pp. 132, 48; 1986, pp. 63, 266). The 80-kilogram estimate is the average for 1902–3 and 1909–10, the earliest years for which Mears *et al.* present data.

15. Hooley and Ruttan (1969, p. 249), for example, write that 'the 1960–70 decade may represent the "closing of the land frontier" in Philippine agricultural development'. Barker (1978, p. 141) states that the Philippines reached the turning point from land-surplus to labor-surplus agriculture 'about 1960'. Similarly, Kikuchi and Hayami (1978, p. 852) date the 'exhaustion of unused land' and the consequent rise in the agricultural labor/land ratio from the late 1950s. See also Larkin (1982), who terms 1820–1920 the 'century of the frontier' in the Philippines.

16. See Hayami *et al.* (1976), Kikuchi and Hayami (1978), and Hayami and Kikuchi (1978).

17. Hayami (1971, p. 454). Hayami cited increased productivity in the fertilizer industry as a second factor which contributed to a decline in the fertilizer/rice price ratio.

18. See, for example, Mangahas, Recto and Ruttan (1966) and Bouis (1982).

19. Tanco (1976), quoted in Ofreneo (1980, p. 77). Tanco envisioned double-cropping on all rice lands, implying a gross cropped area of 3.4 million hectares.

20. Doubts about the 'closing of the land frontier' in the Philippines are also expressed by James (1978) and David, Barker and Palacpac (1984, pp. 33–4).

21. See Hayami, Akino, Shintani and Yamada (1975, especially pp. 50–61, 206). See also Hayami (1971) and Kelly (1982).

22. Hence the name of the first government program to promote the new technology, launched in 1966: the Rice and Corn Self-Sufficiency Program (Ishikawa, 1970, pp. 13–14).

23. See, for example, Feder (1983, pp. 14–15, 28, 103–4).

24. Corporate financial contributions to IRRI were quite small; see IRRI's annual reports and Farmers Assistance Board (1982, pp. 74–5). More-over, the green revolution was enthusiastically promoted in countries such as India, in which most fertilizer is produced by nationalized industries.

25. Mechanization is not an essential element of the new technology, but it made substantial inroads in Philippine rice agriculture in the wake of the green revolution, as discussed in Chapter 5.

26. Launched with much fanfare in 1973, the Masagana–99 program peaked in the 1974–75 crop year, when it provided subsidized credit to 529,000 rice cultivators in the wet season and to 356,000 in the dry season. Repayment problems soon crippled the program, and the numbers fell to less than 100,000 cultivators per season by 1980–81 (Lim, 1986, Table 4).

27. See Ishikawa (1967), Hsieh and Ruttan (1967), Kikuchi and Hayami (1978), Hayami and Ruttan (1985, pp. 304–20), and Boyce (1987, Ch. 6; 1988).

28. Chandler (1979, p. 42). In recent years this limitation has led to a new emphasis in rice research on the breeding of new varieties for less favorable environments, but recognition of this need has been slow (Barker, Herdt and Rose, 1985, pp. 211–12).

29. The same is true in Bengal; see Boyce (1987, pp. 36–7, 162–99).

30. Measurement of the degree of water control poses formidable practical problems. As Gopinath (1976) observes, a distribution of cultivated area according to its 'irrigation coefficient', defined as the ratio of the quantity of irrigation water to total requirements, would be preferable to the usual binary 'irrigated' and 'unirrigated' classification. The same applies to drainage and flood control, which together with irrigation determine the degree of water control. Herdt (1983, p. 119) presents empirical estimates of a water response function for the IR–8 variety, using millimeters of water applied per day as the water control measure. Wickham, Barker and Rosengrant (1978, p. 222) present empirical estimates of fertilizer response functions for 'modern' and 'traditional' varieties in the Philippines under irrigated and rainfed water regimes.

31. Calculated from unpublished BAEcon data provided to the author by Dr. Howarth E. Bouis. Upland rice area in Bicol reportedly fell from 87,000 hectares in 1970 to 5,600 in 1983.

32. That is, 0.83 mt/ha of the 1.23 mt/ha yield increase between 1962–64 and 1983–85. The average of 1962–64 yields, when weighted by the 1983–85 area distribution, is 1.40 mt/ha. The 'pure' water control improvement effect thus accounts for 12 per cent (0.15 mt/ha) of the total yield increase. The remaining 21 per cent of the yield increase came from the 'interaction effect' of the two. If, instead of area distribution, we used a more refined measure of water control improvement, its estimated contribution to yield growth probably would be larger, but the non-water technology shift would still be likely to account for more than half of the observed yield increase.

33. Multiple cropping experiments at IRRI, which enjoys near-perfect control, have given yields of 23.6 mt/ha, using either four crops per year or a year-round continuous cropping system with sequential weekly planting (Barker, Herdt, and Rose, 1985, p. 216). See also Bradfield (1970, p. 242, cited by Dalrymple, 1971, p. 89).

34. Rosengrant *et al.* (1987, p. 3.36) estimate cropping intensity on irrigated lands in 1984 at 152 to 165 per cent. Assuming little multiple cropping of rainfed and upland paddy, this implies an overall cropping intensity for rice of roughly 130 per cent.

35. The terms 'wet' and 'dry' most accurately reflect conditions in Central Luzon, where 98 per cent of rainfed rice is grown in the wet season. In Cagayan region, by contrast, 70 per cent of rainfed rice is grown in the 'dry' season. (Figures for 1983, calculated from unpublished BAEcon data.) Prior to 1968, the definition of the 'first' and 'second' crop in the official statistics varied among regions, depending on the cultivators' own definitions (Barker, Herdt and Rose, 1985, p. 106, n. 23).

36. In 1970 41 per cent of irrigated acreage was cultivated in the 'dry' season; this rose to 44 per cent in 1983. The corresponding figures for rainfed rice were 28 per cent and 29 per cent. If the latter figures are assumed to represent the seasonal distribution of single-cropped rice, with the higher percentages of 'dry season' rice on irrigated land indicating double cropping, then the estimated double-cropped rice area rises from 180,000 hectares (6% of total rice acreage) in 1970 to 264,000 hectares (9%) in 1983 (calculated from unpublished BAEcon data). The actual levels are somewhat higher since in some areas a fairly even seasonal distribution of rainfall permits double cropping without irrigation. Thus Dalrymple (1971, p. 88) estimated that two rice crops per year were grown on approximately 15 per cent of total Philippine rice area in the mid-1960s. Assuming no change in this respect, the conclusion that double cropped area rose by only a small amount (84,000 hectares) would nevertheless hold.

37. Chandler (1975), quoted by Barker, Herdt and Rose (1985, p. 157, n. 2).

38. Calculated from data in FAO (1987, Table 17, pp. 72–73).

39. The yield gap research is summarized by Barker, Herdt and Rose (1985, pp. 220–9). The conclusion that the yield gap under the farmers' control is rather modest is voiced by Herdt and Mandac (1981, p. 398).

40. The available data on Philippine irrigation are less than perfect. Figures on the area administered by the government's National Irrigation Administration (NIA) refer to hypothetically 'irrigable area' under existing projects rather than to area actually irrigated, and in the case of 'service area' also includes some land taken up by roads, canals, and ancillary buildings (for discussion, see World Bank, 1982, p. 34). This difference may help to explain the divergence between the two sets of estimates reported in Table 3.5. NIA estimates of area under communal and other non-NIA irrigation are probably subject to a substantial margin of error.

41. The United States Bureau of Reclamation undertook a study of the development potential of major Philippine river basins in the early 1960s for the newly-formed National Irrigation Administration. Numerous projects identified in this study were subsequently undertaken by the NIA

with World Bank and the Asian Development Bank financing (World Bank, 1982, pp. 25, 48–56).

42.   World Bank funding of NIA projects began in 1968 and amounted to $722 million in loans as of 1982; the second most important source of finance, the Asian Development Bank, had provided $180 million (World Bank, 1982, pp. 25, 48, 53).

43.   See Siy (1982), Coward (1979), and Lewis (1971, Ch. 12).

44.   De los Reyes (1985, pp. 12–13) contrasts this system with the *zanjeras* of Ilocos Norte, in which one finds the 'serious implementation of the rules which the farmers themselves have evolved . . . particularly with regard to labor and material obligations of members for system maintenance'.

45.   See Szanton (1972) and Scott (1976).

46.   Bagadion (1988, p. 5); see also Barker *et al.* (1984, p. 51).

47.   The myopic time horizons of policy makers further lowers the efficiency of government irrigation investments. Kikuchi and Hayami (1978b, p. 323) find that the level of Philippine government irrigation investment has been highly responsive to year-to-year fluctuations in the world price of rice. They term this behavior 'rational in the short run' but 'highly inefficient in the long run', since long-term investments should be guided by long-term planning. They ascribe this short-sightedness not only to the government but also to international agencies such as the World Bank. See also Hayami and Kikuchi (1978).

48.   Calculated from NIA data reported by Kikuchi and Hayami (1978b, p. 318), which indicate that government assistance had been extended to 321,000 hectares out of a total of 808,000 hectares under communal irrigation. The World Bank (1982, pp. 27–8) reports that the NIA had provided assistance to systems covering about 340,000 hectares, but estimates total area under communal irrigation at 550,000 hectares, in which case government-assisted systems would account for more than 60 per cent of total area. On NIA attempts to secure 'participation' of irrigators in such assistance projects, see Alfonso (1983).

49.   Barker (1978, p. 157) remarks, the 'social structure erects a formidable barrier to the investment of social-overhead capital at the optimal level'. Ruttan (1978, pp. 412–13) characterizes the Chinese revolution as an institutional change which enhanced the country's 'capacity to mobilize its labor resources', illustrating the potential linkage between land redistribution and water control. For further discussion, see Boyce (1988).

50.   This does not mean that there is no role for external technical and financial resources in a community-led strategy of water control development. But as Hayami *et al.* (1975, p. 191) conclude, outside resources 'can really be effective only when they are complemented by institutional innovations that contribute to increases in local initiatives'.

51.   The fact that all IRRI varieties carry a common gene for dwarfness is a particular concern. Although the US National Academy of Sciences (1972, p. 188) found 'no evidence of strong linkage between the

dwarfing gene and genes for resistance/susceptibility to any of the major diseases', the emergence of such a genetic linkage in the future cannot be ruled out. The southern corn leaf blight which struck the US maize crop in 1970–71 stands as a worrying precedent: the new pathogen strain was virulent on all maize carrying a genetic trait of male sterility common to most of the country's crop. See Wade (1974, p. 1186).

52. This is not just an academic possibility. At CIMMYT, the international wheat and maize research center in Mexico, irreplaceable maize collections from the 1940s were lost when the seed bank was reorganized in the mid-1960s. In Peru, one of the largest collections of maize germplasm in South America was lost when three refrigeration compressors failed (Wade, 1974, p. 1187). And at IRRI, a fire in December 1978 destroyed a laboratory from which seed stocks had been transferred a few months earlier; fortunately, it did not affect an adjacent room where 20,000 accessions were stored (IRRI, 1979, p. 14). Duplicate sets of the some rice seeds are deposited at the US National Seed Storage Laboratory in Ft. Collins, Colorado. In the early 1970s this facility was described as being 'overcrowded, understaffed, and sorely in need of funds' (Miller, 1973, p. 1231). Despite subsequent improvements, the protection afforded by this 'back-up copy' is less than 100 per cent.

53. Rola (1988, p. 14). These figures were derived from a survey of vegetable growers. A companion survey of rice cultivators in Iloilo also found that many did not wear any protective clothing while spraying (*ibid.*, p. 20). Loevinsohn (1987) presents epidemiological evidence linking insecticide exposure to increased mortality among rice farmers in Central Luzon.

54. Farmers Assistance Board (1982, p. 31). One such advertisement is reproduced on p. 25 of this reference. An example of a label infringing the International Code of Conduct on the Distribution and Use of Pesticides is reproduced by Goldenman and Rengam (1987, p. 43).

55. Porter and Ganapin (1988, p. 35) state that fish and other seafood provide 54 per cent of the total protein intake for the average Filipino household, a ratio exceeded only by the Japanese. The World Bank (1989c, p. 42) reports that fish and shellfish account for 55 per cent of the animal protein intake of the Philippine population.

56. For a compilation of accounts, see Farmers Assistance Board (1982). In Laguna de Bay, the country's largest lake, the total annual fish catch declined from 320,000 metric tons in 1964 to 128,000 metric tons in 1982, primarily owing to pollution from factories, sewage, and agricultural chemicals (Porter and Ganapin, 1988, p. 40). For a review of studies on pesticide residues in fish in the US and Canada, see McEwan and Stephenson (1979, pp. 332–42).

57. 'Farmers tend to wait for signs of infestation prior to treatment although by then', the World Bank (1980a, p. 37) asserts, 'it is too late to prevent major loss'. In 1984 the World Bank earmarked $15 million of a $150

million agricultural inputs loan to the Philippines for the import of pesticides.

58.   In NIA irrigation schemes, however, one constraint on the ability of farmers to revert to traditional varieties may be that the agency bases the timing of water deliveries on the growth cycle of the faster-maturing new varieties. See Kerkvliet (1990, pp. 42 ff.).

4 What Price Rice?

THE GREEN REVOLUTION AND INCOME DISTRIBUTION

The division of a pie can be as important as its size. Although the principal aim of the green revolution strategy was production, the distribution of gains and losses from the new rice technology soon emerged as a central concern.[1]

Proponents of the strategy advanced several *a priori* reasons to expect that the green revolution would benefit the poor. First, all else equal, more food production means lower food prices. Since the poor spend a larger fraction of their income on food than do the rich, the lower food prices lead to a more equal distribution of real income. Second, the new technology, being scale-neutral, is accessible to poor farmers as well as to rich ones. All can share in the gains to producers. Third, the new technology increases labor demand. Landless agricultural workers therefore gain from more employment, higher wages, or both. These gains to the poor were often taken to be virtually axiomatic – an agricultural variant of the trickle-down view that output growth will automatically benefit the poor.[2]

Others have been less sanguine about the distributional consequences of the green revolution. A popular line of criticism in the Philippines has centered on the movement of output and input prices. Once Filipino rice farmers had become dependent on the new technology, they were hit by a price squeeze: real rice prices fell while fertilizer and pesticide prices rose. This is said to have left producers with lower real incomes than before the introduction of the new technology.

As critique of the distributional impact of the green revolution, this is not entirely compelling. If rising input prices were the main problem, then farmers could respond by reverting to traditional, low-input technology. As noted in the preceding chapter, this has not occurred in the Philippines on an appreciable scale. If, on the other hand, falling output prices were a major factor in the price squeeze, then the adverse impact on producers must be weighed against the positive impact on consumers in general, and on poor consumers in particular.

Elsewhere in Asia, criticism of the distributional impact of the green revolution has focused on its differential effects on the rural population. Poor farmers are largely excluded from the new technology, according to these critics, since they cannot afford the necessary initial outlays, especially for water control, and lack the political clout to obtain input subsidies. Hence the new technology tends to benefit only the richer farmers, who are able to extract input and output subsidies from the government and profit from increased yields. The result is a polarization of rural incomes, in which the poor become poorer, not only relatively but also absolutely, due to forces set in motion by the green revolution itself. The higher output of rich farmers depresses prices for poor farmers. Tenants are displaced as rich landowners switch to direct cultivation with wage labor. Poor farmers lose access to water resources as these are appropriated by the rich.[3] In these cases the poor suffer not because they adopt the new technology, but because the rich do while the poor cannot.

This chapter and the next investigate the distributional impact of the green revolution in the Philippines. This chapter examines rice price movements and the distribution of gains between consumers and producers. Chapter 5 then disaggregates 'producers' into diverse groups and classes, and considers the differential effects of the strategy on them.

PRICE DETERMINATION FOR A POLITICAL COMMODITY

Like food staples throughout the world, rice in the Philippines is a 'political commodity'.[4] Consumers want low prices, producers want high prices. In balancing their competing interests, the Philippine government has historically favored the consumer.[5] The reasons are not hard to fathom. As Streeten (1987, p. 77) observes, urban consumers 'can cause a good deal of trouble by rioting and even overthrowing the government when food prices rise'.

At first glance the distributional impact of the green revolution via rice prices seems fairly straightforward. Increased supply causes the price to fall, thereby causing the real incomes of consumers to rise. The poor, who spend more of their income on necessities such as rice than do the rich, gain absolutely and relatively.

For producers, the net effect of the higher output and lower price in principle can be either positive or negative. Producer income may go up or down depending on how much output rises, how much its price falls, and how the costs of production change. In any given locality, the net result can vary not only over time, but also among individual producers, a point to which we return in Chapter 5. Rice producers in the Philippines are also rice consumers. When output goes up and prices fall, they gain as consumers even though they may lose as producers. The smaller the producer, the greater the relative weight of the positive consumer effect. Among producers too, therefore, a rice price decline tends to have an equalizing impact.[6]

Simple theory tells us, then, that when output increases lead to lower rice prices (a) the impact on consumer incomes is positive; (b) the impact on producer incomes is uncertain; and (c) within each group, positive income effects are proportionately larger for the poor than for the rich. Some of the consumers who benefit have higher incomes than the surplus rice producers, and if prices fall so steeply that incomes of the latter decline, then inequality between these two groups will widen. But the overall effect is likely to be a more equal distribution of real incomes.

In the wake of the green revolution, Philippine rice prices were strongly influenced not only by domestic output growth, but also by (1) government policy on the import and export of rice and (2) remarkably slow growth in domestic demand. As so often in the real world, *ceteris* was not *paribus*.

From the early 1960s to the mid-1970s, the real price of rice (that is, its price relative to the overall consumer price index) rose. The real wholesale price in Manila peaked in 1974 (see Table 4.1). Thereafter the price dropped sharply, and by 1980 it was lower than it had been in the early 1960s. In the initial years of the green revolution the price trend was thus quite favorable for producers, while in later years it turned in favor of consumers.

Rice price trends in the Philippines reflected trends on the world rice market. Throughout this period, the Philippine government exercised monopoly control over the import and export of rice. Government policy thus mediated the linkage between world and domestic prices.

The response of rice prices to increased domestic production depends on the extent to which the rice economy is integrated into the world market. The polar case of a closed economy, in which rice is neither exported nor imported, is depicted in Figure 4.1(a). Because rice is a basic necessity, demand for it is fairly inelastic with respect to price. When increased domestic production shifts the supply curve from S_0 to S_1, the price falls from P_0 to P_1. Consumers benefit: the increase in consumers' surplus (the area $P_0P_1E_1E_0$) is a measure of their welfare gain. Producers lose: the change in producers' surplus (the difference between area P_0E_0F and area P_1E_1F) is a measure of their loss. Although each individual producer is driven by competitive pressure to adopt the new technology, the collective result is lower producer incomes. Farmers are caught on the 'agricultural treadmill', producing more and earning less.[7]

TABLE 4.1 *Rice Prices, 1962–1985*

Year	Manila wholesale price (Pesos/kg)	Consumer price index (1980=100)	Real wholesale price (1980 P/kg)	Manila wholesale price ($/ton)	World price[1] ($/ton)	Domestic/ world price ratio	Farmgate palay price[2] (1980 P/kg)	Farmgate/ wholesale price ratio (rice equivalent)
1962	0.41	15.91	2.58	110	153	0.72	1.45	0.84
1963	0.47	17.20	2.73	120	143	0.84	1.39	0.76
1964	0.57	18.72	3.04	146	138	1.06	1.60	0.78
1965	0.55	19.29	2.85	141	136	1.03	1.59	0.83
1966	0.67	20.23	3.31	172	163	1.05	1.59	0.72
1967	0.68	21.38	3.18	174	206	0.85	1.58	0.74
1968	0.64	21.81	2.93	164	202	0.81	1.87	0.95
1969	0.60	22.10	2.71	154	187	0.82	1.75	0.96
1970	0.72	25.48	2.83	122	144	0.85	1.56	0.82
1971	0.91	30.93	2.94	142	129	1.10	1.52	0.77
1972	1.15	33.47	3.44	172	147	1.17	1.89	0.82
1973	1.31	39.01	3.36	194	350	0.55	1.54	0.68
1974	1.97	52.34	3.76	290	542	0.54	1.69	0.67
1975	2.08	55.88	3.72	287	363	0.79	1.69	0.68
1976	1.99	61.02	3.26	267	254	1.05	1.58	0.72
1977	2.05	67.08	3.06	277	272	1.02	1.52	0.74
1978	1.96	71.98	2.72	266	368	0.72	1.37	0.75
1979	2.14	84.60	2.53	290	334	0.87	1.19	0.70
1980	2.29	100.00	2.29	305	434	0.70	1.07	0.70

Year	Manila wholesale price (Pesos/kg)	Consumer price index (1980=100)	Real wholesale price (1980 P/kg)	Manila wholesale price ($/ton)	World price[1] ($/ton)	Domestic/ world price ratio	Farmgate palay price[2] (1980 P/kg)	Farmgate/ wholesale price ratio (rice equivalent)
1981	2.61	113.08	2.31	330	483	0.68	1.07	0.69
1982	2.92	124.64	2.34	342	293	1.17	1.08	0.69
1983	3.09	137.14	2.25	278	277	1.00	1.01	0.67
1984	4.79	206.18	2.32	287	255	1.12	0.95	0.61
1985	6.63	253.81	2.61	356	217	1.64	1.20	0.69

NOTES

1. 5% broken, f.o.b. Bangkok.
2. Exclusive of milling costs. Rice/*palay* conversion factor = 0.67.

SOURCES Manila wholesale price: Unnevehr (1983, p. 30) for the years 1962–82. Data for 1983–85 calculated from NEDA (1986, p. 132) on assumption that the ratio of the wholesale price to the ceiling retail price remains 0.98 as in 1982. Dollar conversion using average annual exchange rates from IMF (1987, pp. 558–9).

Consumer price index: IMF (1987, pp. 560–1).

World price: IRRI (1986, p. 214); FAO (1987b, p. 289).

Farmgate price: *Palay* price calculated from value and quantity data reported in NEDA (1976, p. 134; 1986, p. 266).

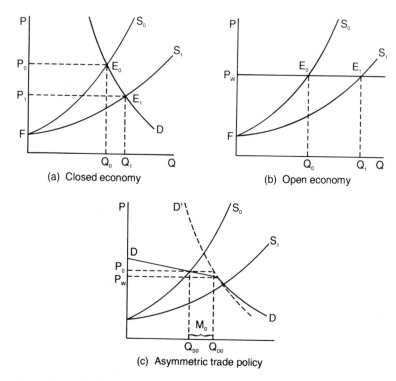

Figure 4.1:   **Rice Prices: Effect of Output Supply Shifts**

The opposite polar case of a completely open rice economy is depicted in Figure 4.1(b). The price is set exogenously in the world market. The domestic supply shift has no effect on domestic prices (assuming that it is too small to affect world prices). Instead it causes a reduction in rice imports or an increase in rice exports. In this case, consumers are not affected by domestic output growth, while producers benefit by the increase in producers' surplus (the area E_0E_1F).

The Philippine rice economy is between these extremes, neither fully closed nor fully open. In the mid-1960s, on the eve of the green revolution, the country imported on average 300,000 metric tons annually, equivalent to more than ten per cent of domestic supply (see Table 4.2). As domestic production increased, imports were reduced, and in the late 1970s and early 1980s the country exported rice.[8] Import substitution and exports thus dampened the price effects of the new rice technology.

TABLE 4.2 Rice and Food Supply per Capita, 1962–1985

Year	Rice supply ('000 metric tons)				Population (millions)	Net rice supply per capita (kg/year)	Calorie supply per capita from all food sources (kcal/day)
	Gross output[1]	Net imports	Seed & wastage[2]	Net supply[3]			
1962	2620	0	242	2377	28.8	82.5	1597
1963	2658	256	244	2670	29.7	89.9	1791
1964	2575	300	237	2638	30.6	86.2	1769
1965	2675	569	246	2998	31.6	94.9	1851
1966	2729	108	247	2590	32.5	79.7	1753
1967	2743	239	248	2734	33.5	81.6	1843
1968	3056	-40	272	2744	34.6	79.3	1765
1969	2978	0	268	2710	35.7	75.9	1834
1970	3506	0	294	3212	36.7	87.5	1845
1971	3737	369	310	3796	37.9	100.2	1868
1972	3568	633	303	3897	38.9	100.2	1801
1973	3088	238	271	3055	40.0	76.4	1838
1974	3913	311	329	3895	41.1	94.8	1924
1975	3960	238	335	3863	42.1	91.8	2077
1976	4309	71	357	4023	43.4	92.7	2112
1977	4516	24	369	4172	44.6	93.5	2187
1978	4823	-39	386	4398	45.8	96.0	2208
1979	5035	-38	398	4600	47.0	97.9	2256

Year	Rice supply ('000 metric tons)				Population (millions)	Net rice supply per capita (kg/year)	Calorie supply per capita from all food sources (kcal/day)
	Gross output[1]	Net imports	Seed & wastage[2]	Net supply[3]			
1980	5250	−236	412	4602	48.3	95.3	2373
1981	5174	−175	403	4596	49.5	92.9	2374
1982	5442	−10	419	5013	50.8	98.7	2442
1983	5180	−11	398	4771	52.1	91.6	2321
1984	5253	−30	399	4824	53.3	90.5	2374
1985	5494	389	416	5467	54.7	99.9	2248

NOTES

1. Milled rice. Rice/*palay* conversion factor = 0.67.
2. Assuming 6% wastage and 40 kg *palay*/hectare seed (as assumed in World Bank, 1979a, Vol. II, p. 40).
3. Net availability = gross production + net imports − seed and wastage.

SOURCES   Output: As for Table 3.1. Net imports: Mears *et al.* (1974, p. 331) for years through 1971; World Bank (1986b, p. 58) for subsequent years. Population: NEDA (1976, p. 47; 1986, pp. 33, 72). Calorie supply per capita from all food source: *Food Balance Sheet* data, as reported by National Statistical Coordination Board (1988, p. 30) for years 1973 through 1985; and by Quisumbing (1987a, p. 12) for earlier years. The estimates reported by Quisumbing are here scaled down to accord with revised Food Balance Sheet methodology, using an adjustment factor of 0.88 (the average ratio of two sets of estimates in the years 1973–75).

The country's rice economy was by no means perfectly open, however. Table 4.1 reports the ratio of domestic to world rice prices. With complete openness, this ratio would have been fairly constant and close to 1.0.[9] In practice it varied considerably over time.

The world rice market is highly unstable, as a glance at the world price data in Table 4.1 reveals. In part this is due to the preponderance in world production of South and Southeast Asia and the importance of monsoon rainfall for these crops. In addition, the international rice market is rather thin. The ratio of traded to total production is low, and much trade takes place through government-to-government agreements.[10] Faced with volatile world prices, 'almost all national governments insulate their domestic rice economy from the international market by enacting licensing arrangements for importing or exporting, or frequently by reserving such trade solely for government account' (Timmer and Falcon, 1975, pp. 381–2). Philippine government policy has been no exception.

As one might expect, then, domestic rice prices in the Philippines tend to move in the same direction as world prices, but with smaller fluctuations. Philippine insulation from the world rice market has been asymmetric, however. Between 1962 and 1984, the domestic price was not permitted to rise much above the world price, even when the latter was low.[11] It was held well below the world price, however, when the latter was high. In 1974, with world rice prices at their historic peak, the domestic-to-world price ratio fell to 0.54. It again fell below 0.7 during the high world prices of 1980–81. This reflects the Philippine government's political priorities: consumers were more protected from high world prices than were producers from low world prices.

The kinked demand curve in Figure 4.1(c) depicts the resulting situation. When the domestic price exceeds the world market price, P_w, the government imports rice. The demand curve faced by Filipino producers, D, is therefore highly elastic above the world price (though not perfectly elastic insofar as the government permits domestic prices to rise somewhat above world prices). If the domestic supply curve is S_0, the resulting domestic price is P_0; domestic output is Q_{S0}; demand, read from the consumer demand curve D', is Q_{DO}; and the difference, M_0 is the quantity imported. The government is willing, however, to let domestic prices fall far below world prices, particularly when the latter are high. Hence the demand curve faced by Filipino producers is far less elastic below P_w (being more elastic than the closed-economy demand curve D' only insofar as the government chooses to export rice). In such a setting, an increase in domestic output causes only a small decline in price as long as there is scope for import substitution, but beyond this point output growth causes a sharp decline in price.[12]

Under this asymmetric trade policy, the kinked demand curve faced by domestic producers shifts up and down with the world price. Hence the distribution of gains from the new rice technology depends on the world price level. When world rice prices are high, such that the supply shift occurs along the lower segment of the demand curve, we approach the closed-economy result: consumers gain, while producer incomes decline. When world rice prices are low, such that the shift occurs along the upper segment of the demand curve, we approach the open-economy result: consumers gain little, while producers gain a lot. If the shift pushes the supply curve across the kink point, the outcome lies in between.

Of course, to say that producers reap larger gains from domestic output growth when world prices are low is not to say that they benefit from lower world prices *per se*. On the contrary, a drop in world prices leads to lower producer incomes whenever price determination occurs along the upper segment of the demand curve, that is, whenever the country is importing rice. Such a situation is depicted in Figure 4.2(a). When the world price falls from P_{w0} to P_{w1}, the demand curve faced by Filipino producers shifts from D_0 to D_1. At the high world price the country exported a little rice; at the new low price it imports a lot. The shaded area shows the resulting decline in producers' surplus.

This schematic account of rice price determination complicates our analysis of the price effects of the green revolution in several ways. First, the political basis of rice price determination means that domestic production shifts play a more limited role than in the conventional supply-and-demand analysis. In principle, the government can set the domestic rice price at any level it chooses through its control over international trade. In such a context it is problematic to ascribe price movements to the green revolution in the Philippines; rather, increased domestic production eases the financial constraint on the government's pursuit of its target price.

Second, insofar as domestic output shifts do influence prices, the distribution of gains between consumers and producers depends on the world price. The latter varies over time, sometimes with dramatic impacts on consumers and producers in the Philippines.

Third, while world prices are exogenous from the standpoint of the Philippines, they are not exogenous in a larger analysis of the green revolution. The spread of the new rice technology throughout South and Southeast Asia affected international supply, putting downward pressure on world prices. Examining the distribution of gains between producers and consumers in developing countries as a whole, in a model akin to that of Figure 4.1(a), Evenson and Flores (1978) estimate that in the early 1970s consumers derived annual benefits of $529–590 million, while producers

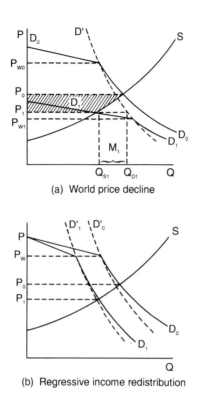

(a) World price decline

(b) Regressive income redistribution

Figure 4.2:   Rice Prices: Effects of Demand Shifts

incurred net losses of \$251–491 million. Insofar as world rice prices influenced domestic prices – as in the Philippines – these international impacts translate into corresponding gains and losses at the national level.

Finally, the position of the kink in the demand curve faced by Filipino producers depends on the exchange rate at which world prices are converted into pesos. A stronger peso has the same effect as the world price decline shown in Figure 4.2(a), lowering P_w (in peso terms) to the benefit of consumers and to the detriment of rice producers. A number of economists focused on this issue in the 1980s, and some went so far as to argue that overvaluation of the peso constituted the 'single most powerful disincentive' to Philippine agriculture.[13] Exchange rate policy was merely one element, however, in the broader political economy of rice price determination.

INCOME DISTRIBUTION AND EFFECTIVE DEMAND

The movement of rice prices in the Philippines was also influenced by changes in domestic demand.

As population grows, the demand for food can be expected to increase; that is, at any given price the total quantity demanded will be higher. In a market economy, however, people do not exercise effective demand by virtue of their mere existence: they exercise it by virtue of their purchasing power. Hence it is not population growth *per se* which shifts the demand curve for rice, but rather the growth of income. The extent to which growth in national income translates into greater demand for rice crucially depends on how the extra income is distributed across the population.

In 1985, sixteen per cent of family income in the Philippines was spent on cereals, mainly rice and corn (see Table 4.3). The share spent on cereals varied greatly across family income classes, however. The poorest households, with incomes of less than 6,000 pesos per year, devoted more than 40 per cent of their income to cereals. Among the richest households, with incomes above 100,000 pesos per year, the corresponding figure was less than five per cent.

Comparing the two lowest income classes in Table 4.3, we find that a 10 per cent increase in income per family is associated with a 6.9 per cent increase in cereals expenditure; that is, the income elasticity of cereals expenditure is 0.69. Among the highest income classes the elasticity is only 0.17. The estimated elasticity for the Philippine population as a whole is 0.40, a figure reasonably consistent with cross-sectional evidence from other countries.[14] In other words, a ten per cent rise in income per family can be expected to lead to a four per cent rise in cereals expenditures, *provided that the distribution of income remains unchanged*.

In practice, the distribution of income often changes over time. In the Philippines, as documented in Chapter 2, there is reason to believe that income inequality rose from the early 1960s to the mid-1980s, and that real incomes of the poor declined absolutely even as average real income increased. Income redistribution from the poor to the rich reduces demand for rice, since the rich spend a much smaller fraction of their income on rice than do the poor. This is depicted in Figure 4.2(b) as a shift in the demand curve from D_0 to D_1. This pushes down the price of rice, particularly at times when the domestic price is below the world price.

By examining trends in rice consumption, population, prices, and income, we can derive a measure of the extent to which such a redistribution of income did in fact occur. The rate of growth of rice consumption can be partitioned into three components: the population effect, attributable to a

TABLE 4.3 *Grain Expenditures by Family Income Class, 1985*

Income class ('000 pesos/family)	Per cent of total families	Per cent of total income	Income per family ('000 pesos)	Share of income spent on cereals (%)	Cereals expenditure per family ('000 pesos)	Income elasticity of cereals expenditure[1]
<6	3.8	0.6	4.5	41.6	1.9	
6–10	11.3	3.0	8.2	35.8	2.9	0.69
10–15	18.1	7.3	12.5	30.5	3.8	0.57
15–20	15.6	8.8	17.4	26.5	4.6	0.52
20–30	19.7	15.5	24.5	21.7	5.3	0.38
30–40	11.0	12.2	34.5	17.2	5.9	0.29
40–60	10.6	16.5	48.4	13.5	6.5	0.25
60–100	6.4	15.4	75.5	9.4	7.1	0.16
>100	3.5	20.7	183.4	4.8	8.8	0.17
All	(100)	(100)	31.1	16.0	5.0	0.40

NOTES

1. Elasticity for the ith income group $= [(C_i-C_{i-1})/C_{i-1}]/[(Y_i-Y_{i-1})/Y_{i-1}]$, where C_i = cereals expenditure per family and Y_i = total income per family in the ith income group. Overall elasticity = $\hat{e}$ estimated from the equation $\ln C = a + e \ln Y$ by ordinary least squares.

SOURCE Calculated from Family Income and Expenditure Survey data reported in NCSO (1986b, pp. 1, 99).

growing population with per capita income held constant; the price effect, derived by multiplying the real rice price trend by the price elasticity of demand; and the *ex post* income effect, attributable to the growth *and redistribution* of per capita income. The latter differs from the usual definition of the 'income effect' as the growth of per capita income times some *ex ante* income elasticity of demand.[15] Instead, the income effect is here calculated as a residual: it is the change in consumption not attributable to the population and price effects.[16] The *ex post* income elasticity of demand can then be calculated as the ratio of the income effect to the rate of growth of per capita income.[17]

If per capita income growth were proportionally distributed across the population such that everyone's income grew at the same rate, then the *ex post* income elasticity of demand would approximately equal the cross-sectional elasticity, estimated as 0.4 in Table 4.3. In other words, a ten per cent rise in per capita income would lead to a four per cent increase in rice consumption. If income growth were accompanied by a progressive shift in distribution, the incomes of the poor rising more rapidly than those of the rich, then the *ex post* income elasticity would be greater than 0.4. With a regressive shift it would be less than 0.4. If, for example, the entire growth in income in the Philippines accrued to the richest ten per cent of families, while the incomes of the remaining 90 per cent remained unchanged, the expected income elasticity would be in the 0.1–0.2 range. In a situation of growth with impoverishment, in which the absolute incomes of the poor declined, the *ex post* income elasticity might even turn negative: rising per capita incomes could be accompanied by less rice consumption per person.

Table 4.4 presents the relevant data to calculate the *ex post* income elasticity of demand for rice in the Philippines. Between 1961 and 1980, rice consumption grew at 2.9 per cent per annum, slightly ahead of population growth at 2.8 per cent. The declining real price of rice yielded a positive price effect of 0.5 per cent per annum. In the same period per capita income rose at 2.8 per cent per annum. The resulting *ex post* income elasticity of demand is *minus* 0.15. This implies that growth in income per capita was accompanied by strong polarization, in which the incomes of the poor declined absolutely. This finding reinforces the central conclusion reached in Chapter 2: in this period the Philippines experienced growth with impoverishment.[18]

The impact of this regressive shift in income distribution on the demand for rice can be more fully appreciated if we compare actual consumption growth to that which would have resulted in a counterfactual situation of unchanged income distribution and hence an income elasticity of 0.4. With income per capita growing at 2.8 per cent per annum, the resulting income effect would have contributed 1.1 per cent per annum to the growth of rice

TABLE 4.4 *Rice Consumption Growth and the Ex Post Income Elasticity of Demand, 1961–1980*

Years	Rates of growth (% per annum)					Ex post income elasticity[3]
	Rice Consumption	Population	Price Effect[1]	Income effect[2]	GNP per capita	
1961–80	2.86	2.77	0.50	−0.41	2.78	−0.15
1961–67	2.30	3.00	−0.23	−0.47	1.89	−0.25
1967–73	3.59	2.90	−0.70	1.39	2.87	0.48
1973–80	2.83	2.57	2.17	−1.91	3.35	−0.57

NOTES

1. Price trend times price elasticity of demand.
2. *Ex post* income effect = consumption growth minus population growth minus price effect (see text).
3. Calculated as *ex post* income effect divided by growth rate of per capita GNP.

SOURCES Rice consumption, population growth and price effect from Siamwalla and Haykin (1983, Table 10, pp. 27–9). GNP at constant prices from IMF (1987, pp. 562–3).

consumption (0.4 x 2.8). Adding the population and price effects, this would have generated a rice consumption growth rate of 4.4 per cent per year, as opposed to the actual 2.9 per cent.[19]

The pattern of income redistribution appears to have varied over time. The years 1961–67 saw strong polarization, with an *ex post* income elasticity of demand of –0.25. The middle period, 1967–73, showed an *ex post* elasticity of 0.48, similar to our cross-sectional estimate of 0.40, indicating little polarization or perhaps even a slight decrease in inequality in this subperiod. In 1973–80 the *ex post* elasticity plummets to –0.57, implying that income polarization greatly intensified during the martial law years.

The impact of impoverishment on demand for rice in the Philippines was recognized by the World Bank. In a 1979 review of Philippine grain production policy, the World Bank noted that total rice consumption in the 1970s had grown at only 2.9 per cent per year, barely above the rate of population increase. 'There is some evidence', the review observed, 'that real incomes of the low income group have declined during the 1970s, thus inhibiting their consumption of rice' (World Bank, 1979a, Vol. I, p. 5).

Assuming an income elasticity of demand for rice of only 0.1, the World Bank (1982, pp. ii, 66) concluded that new irrigation development in the Philippines 'should be considerably delayed' given the sluggish projected growth in demand.[20] In a November 1986 report titled 'The Philippines: A Framework for Economic Recovery', the World Bank advised the Aquino government to de-emphasize rice production: 'With export prospects for rice being very questionable and *self-sufficiency in rice in place*, a considerable amount of rice lands – mainly rainfed lowland and upland areas – may have to be released for other crops' (World Bank, 1986b, Vol. II, p. 122; emphasis added).

Of what does this 'self-sufficiency in rice' consist? Not of full stomachs. In 1982, after two decades of rising per capita supply of rice and total calories (see Table 4.2), a nationwide survey by the Food and Nutrition Research Institute found that 67 per cent of Filipino families had less than adequate calorie intake; more than half consumed less than 90 per cent of the adequate level (see Table 2.15). Sixty-nine per cent of the country's pre-school children were found to be underweight; one in six were less than 75 per cent of the weight-for-age standard (Quisumbing, 1987a, p. 44). This deprivation was recorded *before* the economic crisis began in 1983, triggering a collapse in real incomes.

Philippine rice 'self-sufficiency' arose, then, not only from the output growth achieved by the green revolution, but also from the inadequate purchasing power of the mass of the population, whose hunger could not be translated into effective demand. Quisumbing (1987a, p. 17) concludes:

[O]ne cannot explain the prevalence of malnutrition in a period of increasing food and agricultural production and so-called aggregate food 'sufficiency' as *primarily* a supply problem. Rather, it is a case of the uneven distribution of the available food within the population.

Declining rice prices in the Philippines thus reflected not only supply shifts, but also a lack of effective demand due to a highly inequitable and worsening distribution of purchasing power. Lower rice prices can be a cause of rising real incomes for poor consumers, but they can also be a *result* of their declining real incomes. Hence the declining rice price trend reported in Table 4.1 is not an unambiguous indicator of good news for the poor, whether as consumers or as producers.

While impoverishment slowed the growth of demand for cereals for direct consumption, demand for cereals for use as animal feed grew strongly. This reflected increased demand for meat among families at the top of the scale, where real incomes were rising. In 1985, the richest ten per cent of Filipino families spent on average 6,225 pesos per year on meat; the poorest fifteen per cent spent on average only 400 pesos per year.[21] The utilization of corn (maize), the country's second most important grain crop, as animal feed rose from 32 per cent of total supply in 1969–70 to more than 50 per cent in 1985 (Agricultural Policy and Strategy Team, 1986, p. 157). In the Philippines white corn is used primarily for direct consumption and yellow corn for animal feed. 'Since demand is expected to increase faster for feed use than for human consumption', the World Bank (1979a, Vol. I, p. 17) concluded, 'yellow corn should be given priority in future research'. Buoyant demand for yellow corn and slack demand for white corn and rice represent two sides of the coin of rising income inequality.

TRENDS IN PRODUCER INCOME

For Filipino rice producers, the green revolution began well and ended badly. In the early years, up to the mid-1970s, aggregate producer income (though not the incomes of all producers) rose, but thereafter it declined. Trends in the gross and net producer revenue are depicted in Figure 4.3. Gross revenue in constant pesos peaked in 1977, and then fell as output growth was outweighed by the real price decline.[22] Net revenue peaked earlier, reflecting rising production costs.

The reasons for declining real rice prices have been discussed above: domestic output growth, declining world rice prices, government rice import

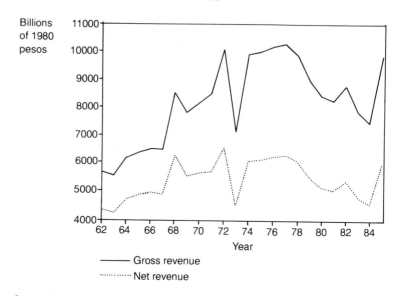

Sources: Gross revenue = value of *palay* output as reported in NEDA (1976, pp. 134 – 155) and NEDA (1986, pp. 266 – 275), converted into 1980 pesos using consumer price index as reported in IMF (1987, pp. 560 – 1).

Net revenue = gross revenue minus the total cost. Calculated on assumption that total cost rises from 24% of total revenue in 1962 – 66 to 39% in 1974 – 85 (see text for details).

Figure 4.3:   Gross and Net Revenue of Rice Producers, 1962 – 1985

and export policy, and sluggish growth of domestic demand all contributed to the trend. In addition, producers' revenue could have been affected by changes in their share of the consumer price.

The foregoing discussion has assumed that consumers and producers face the same rice price. In reality, the prices differ by a marketing margin, representing the costs of milling, transport and storage and the profit of rice traders. This margin can change through time. A comparison of the farmgate producer price to the Manila wholesale price from 1962 to 1985 reveals that the margin widened (see the last column of Table 4.1). Farmgate prices averaged 82 per cent of the wholesale price in 1962–69, whereas they slipped to 69 per cent in 1978–85.

Unnevehr (1983) cites two reasons for widening margins in the 1970s. First, the reduction in net imports and shift to net exports at the end of the decade is expected to raise the margin, since a higher proportion of the Manila supply became subject to domestic transport and storage costs.[23] Second, the 'official margin' – that is, the margin between the nominal floor price for producers and ceiling price for consumers administered by the government – rose through time (Unnevehr, 1983, pp. 8–11).

Whether these adequately explain the trend is open to question. In the 1962–85 period as a whole, the correlation between net imports and trader margins is approximately zero.[24] The impact of the official margin is diminished by the fact that the vast majority of rice producers are unable to sell at the official price to the government procurement agency, the National Food Authority; instead they sell to private traders, often at lower prices.[25] And the trend in the official margin itself needs to be explained.

An alternative, but complementary, hypothesis is that the higher marketing margins – both unofficial and official – reflected increased market power and political influence on the part of rice traders. In part this could have been a result of the diminished importance of imports in domestic supply. More-over, the political relationship between rice traders and the Marcos regime may have changed over time, as traders exchanged a share of their profits for official and unofficial favors, including greater tolerance of market power.[26]

At first glance, official policy appears to have been rather inimical to trader interests. According to Unnevehr's (1983, p. 11) calculations, official margins were so small that they covered costs of milling, transport and stor-age only in two of the nine years from 1972–73 to 1980–81. His calculations are based on market interest rates, but at the same time the government provided subsidized credit to private traders, 'presumably to lower private marketing costs'.[27] Evidently some traders exercised effective demand for government resources.

The claim that rice traders reap above-normal profits through local monopsony or oligopsony has considerable political appeal, for it allows one to advocate both higher prices for producers and lower prices for consumers. Opinion as to whether there is any basis for this claim in the Philippines has been sharply divided. Cernohous (1966, p. 70) asserted that 'even in the absence of any credit obligations or tenancy relationship, the buyer usually possesses enough monopsony power to be able to pay the farmer less than the competitive price'. Dismissing this observation as 'little more than a repetition of the conventional wisdom regarding middleman behavior with little or no empirical content', Ruttan (1969, p. 516) argues that storage and marketing are quite competitive, since they require little specialization and involve few economies of scale.[28] Similarly, Bouis (1983, p. 92) concludes that the Philippine rice market 'operates efficiently in the absence of government controls'.[29]

Nevertheless, detailed reports of local-level oligopsony continue to appear in the Philippine press.[30] In Manila, the 'big seven' rice traders are said to act as a cartel, controlling some 35 per cent of the national rice market

(Philippine Peasant Institute, 1989). In 1989, the Aquino government's Secretary of Agriculture characterized the National Food Authority's role as follows: 'We play with the traders. If the traders know we don't have enough stock and we cannot fight them in the market, they will raise the price'.[31] In other words, the Secretary claimed that in the absence of government intervention the rice traders act as price makers.

The extent of market power in the rice trade varies from locality to locality, which may help to account for the diversity of views on the subject. Research by the Philippine Peasant Institute (1989) indicates that rice markets are less competitive further from Manila: for example, the market share of the top three traders decreases as one approaches the capital region. Traders may exercise market power as buyers, driving the producer price down, or as sellers, driving the consumer price up, or both. Moreover, local-level market power may co-exist with more competitive regional or national markets, and vice-versa. These variations make it difficult to assess the overall extent of market power in the Philippine rice trade. However, the diminishing farmgate-to-wholesale price ratio reported in Table 4.1 is consistent with the hypothesis that market power increased between the 1960s and the 1980s.

Filipino rice producers have been hit not only by falling output prices, but also by rising input prices, particularly for fertilizers. These were driven by oil price increases, but here too oligopolistic pricing may have played a role. Fertilizer imports were in the hands of only six firms. Their activities were coordinated by the government's Fertilizer and Pesticide Authority, which acted as 'the sole arbiter on products, quantities, prices and delivery schedules' (World Bank, 1980a, p. 31). Domestic fertilizer manufacture was in the hands of three of the same firms. The largest, Planters Products, Inc., which took over the transnational firm Esso's Philippine operations in 1970, was described in the Marcos era as 'a good example of the workings of bureaucrat capitalism – the use of public agencies for the accumulation of private wealth'.[32] At the same time, three companies – Shell, Bayer, and Planters Products – accounted for 60 per cent of total pesticide sales in the country (World Bank, 1980a, p. 37).

A study of rice farms in Central Luzon found that the costs of production rose from 24 per cent of gross revenue in 1966 to 38–40 per cent in the late 1970s.[33] On this basis, we can derive rough estimates of net revenue, or aggregate producer income. These estimates, depicted by the broken line in Figure 4.3, indicate that the net revenue of Filipino rice farmers peaked in 1972.[34]

Estimates of the growth rates of gross and net producer revenue (adjusted for inflation using the consumer price index) are reported in Table 4.5. Since gross revenue is the product of output and price, its growth rate is the sum

TABLE 4.5 *Growth Rates of Gross and Net Revenue of Rice Producers,*
1962–1985 and Subperiods
(per cent per annum; constant pesos)[1]

	1962–85	*1962–73*	*1974–85*
Gross revenue	1.80	4.97	−1.37
Output	3.81	3.82	3.80
Price	−2.01	1.16	−5.17
Total cost	4.47	9.80	−0.85
Net revenue	0.56	2.85	−1.72

NOTE

1. Exponential and kinked exponential growth rates estimated by ordinary least squares; for methodology, see Boyce (1986).

SOURCES   As Figure 4.3.

of theirs. Between 1962 and 1985, output grew at 3.8 per cent per annum and the real producer price (the farmgate price reported in Table 4.1) fell at 2.0 per cent; hence gross revenue rose at an annual rate of 1.8 per cent. Subtracting production costs, however, net revenue rose at only 0.6 per cent. In the 24-year period as a whole, then, aggregate producer income rose very modestly.

This overall trend conceals quite different experiences in the two 12-year subperiods, however. Between 1962 and 1973, net revenue rose at an annual rate of 2.8 per cent, but between 1974 and 1985 it declined at a rate of 1.7 per cent. This temporal break had an important effect on the distribution of gains and losses among individual producers, some of whom adopted the new technology earlier than others, a point to which we return in the next chapter.

CONCLUSIONS

Economic theory tells us that consumers in general, and poor consumers in particular, will benefit from increased food output and the resulting price declines. Depending on how sharply prices fall, producers may win or lose, but any losses are partially offset by their gains as consumers, an effect which is strongest for the poorest producers. In theory, then, more food production leads to absolute income gains for many poor people and less inequality within both urban and rural areas. A sharp price decline will increase inequality between average rural and urban incomes, but the overall impact of more food production is likely to be more equal income distribution, thanks to lower inequality within both groups.

Reality is more complicated. In the Philippines, as elsewhere, rice prices are strongly influenced by government policy, rather than being determined simply by the free play of market forces. The underlying cause of declining real rice prices in the Philippines therefore was government policy, rather than output growth *per se*. The same policy objective could have been achieved by increasing rice imports; domestic output growth simply eased the budgetary constraints on achieving it.

Whether it results from domestic output growth, world price movements, or government policy, a supply-driven rice price decline benefits consumers and lessens intra-consumer and intra-producer inequality. In the Philippines, however, rice price declines were driven by shifts in demand as well as supply. Regressive income redistribution curtailed the growth in rice demand, leading to a *negative ex post* 'income effect' in the 1962–85 period as a whole. This finding puts a rather different light on the relationship between rice price movements and the welfare of poor consumers: falling rice prices were, in part, an *effect* of their declining real incomes, rather than entirely a *cause* of rising real incomes.

On the producer side, aggregate income rose in the early years of the green revolution and subsequently declined. In the end, producers' income was little higher than at the outset of the green revolution, notwithstanding the doubling of their output. Output growth, government rice price policy, sluggish demand growth, widening trader margins, and rising input costs all contributed to this result.

The fundamental conflict between the interests of consumers and producers over food prices poses an inescapable dilemma for any government. It is politically convenient to champion simultaneously higher prices for producers and lower prices for consumers, blaming oligopsonistic traders for inflating the margin between the two. The exercise of market power in the Philippine rice trade may have increased during the green revolution. Even if all rice markets in the country were perfect, however, the basic rice price dilemma would remain.

If we simply, and perhaps naively, define the green revolution strategy to mean the pursuit of more rice output, with all else taken to be exogenous (including changes in world prices, government trade policy, and domestic demand), then the strategy probably had an equalizing effect on income distribution insofar as it lowered the price of rice. The sole qualification is that consumers benefitted more than producers, particularly after the mid-

1970s, contributing to widening rural-urban inequality. For millions of the poorest Filipinos, in both the cities and the countryside, cheaper rice means more to eat.

If, however, the strategy is defined more broadly, then the distributional impact of the green revolution is less clear-cut. Despite the positive impact of lower rice prices on poor consumers, absolute poverty increased. Among the country's poor majority, effective demand was limited not by full stomachs, but by empty pockets. Cheaper rice mitigated, but did not reverse, the trend towards impoverishment. Widening income disparities were not exogenous to government policy. Nor were they entirely exogenous to the green revolution itself, as we shall see in the next chapter.

NOTES

1. See, for example, Falcon (1970) and Griffin (1974).
2. For this reason, Griffin and Ghose (1979, p. 370) term it the 'trickle-down modified' doctrine.
3. These and other mechanisms of impoverishment attributable to the green revolution are enumerated by Bardhan (1987) and Boyce (1991).
4. The phrase is used by Mangahas (1975, p. 295) and by Timmer and Falcon (1975, p. 373).
5. Timmer and Falcon (1975, p. 401) assign the following weights to the objectives of Philippine rice policy: consumer welfare, 0.4; price stability, 0.2; self-sufficiency, 0.2; and farm income, 0.2. Mangahas (1975, p. 296) assigns similar weights: urban consumer welfare, 0.2; political stability, 0.3; anti-inflation, 0.2; self-sufficiency, 0.1; and farm income, 0.2. Political stability, price stability, and anti-inflation objectives of course overlap considerably with urban consumer welfare. Mangahas (p. 297) considers the weight on urban consumers to have been even stronger prior to Marcos's declaration of martial law.
6. For an elaboration of this point, see Hayami and Herdt (1977).
7. See Cochrane (1958, Chapter 5) for the classic exposition of the agricultural treadmill.
8. The government exported rice in the late 1970s at a loss. Agriculture Minister Arturo Tanco (cited by Luzon Secretariat of Social Action, 1982, p. 12) explained that the National Food Authority had to sell, even though the world market price was below the cost of production, because its mounting inventory could no longer be accommodated by existing warehouses. Floresca (1980) reports a net loss of 75 million pesos on nine rice export contracts signed from November 1977 to August 1979. Unnevehr (1983, p. 14) reports losses of 90 million pesos between 1977 and 1979. Unnevehr (1983) and Unnevehr and Balisacan (1983) nevertheless maintain that the Philippines held a comparative advantage

in rice production, attributing the losses to the lack of high-quality rice processing facilities and the failure of government policies to transmit world price premiums for higher quality rice.

9. The expected price ratio is not exactly one, among other reasons because of (a) freight and insurance costs and (b) quality differences. The world price reported in Table 4.1 is f.o.b. Bangkok for 5% broken milled Thai rice, which commands a substantial premium on world markets over 'low-quality' (more broken) Philippine rice (see Unnevehr, 1983, pp. 14–16). The exclusion of shipping costs and the use of a higher priced grade have opposing effects on the expected domestic-to-world price ratio.

10. Thus Timmer and Falcon (1975, p. 373) remark, the 'trade is so conditioned by special deals and constraints that "the international price of rice" has little meaning'. For discussions of world rice price instability, see also FAO (1975; 1985) and Siamwalla and Haykin (1983).

11. The year 1985 appears to have been an exception. The wholesale price estimates for 1983–85 reported in Table 4.1 are rough estimates, derived as follows. NEDA (1986, p. 132) reports a consumer price index for rice; a comparison with data in Unnevehr (1983, p. 30) indicates that this series approximates the retail *ceiling* price. Unnevehr reports unpublished Central Bank data on wholesale prices to 1982. Wholesale prices for 1983–85 are here estimated from the NEDA data by applying the ratio of wholesale to retail ceiling prices which obtained in 1982: 0.98. In the preceding ten years, this ratio varied from 0.91 to 1.09. Estimating lower and upper bounds on the wholesale price by means of these ratios, the domestic/world price ratio in 1985 would range from 1.52 to 1.82.

12. Alternatively, one could assume that the kink occurs at a target price set by the government below the world price so as to favor consumers. The kinked demand curve in Figure 4.1(c) resembles that in the oligopoly theory. Note, however, that it results not from the actions of private firms preoccupied with market shares, but rather from the actions of a government preoccupied with consumer constituencies. Whereas in oligopoly theory the kinked demand curve is often associated with sticky prices, here it is associated with considerable price instability.

13. Bale (1985), quoted by Streeten (1987, p. 88). See also David (1983), Bale (1983), and Bautista (1987).

14. Yotopoulos (1985, p. 481, n. 1) reports that typical values range from 0.4 to 0.8. Goldman and Ranade (1977) derive similar estimates of the expenditure elasticity of demand for cereals in the Philippines from 1971 Family Income Expenditure Survey data.

15. See, for example, the 'income effects' reported by Siamwalla and Haykin (1983, p. 27) and FAO (1985, p. 9).

16. This assumes no change in tastes, other than changes arising from changes in income. In the Philippine case this assumption seems reasonable.

17.	The term '*ex post* elasticity' is used by Yotopoulos (1985, p. 469), whose own calculations omit the price effect. The elasticity, e, is here calculated as e = (C-N-P)/Y, where C = the rate of growth of consumption, N = the rate of growth of population, P = the price effect, and Y = the rate of growth of per capita income.

18.	In a time-series analysis of rice demand in the Philippines, Nasol (1971) also estimates negative income elasticities. He refers to this as an 'illogical' sign, but shifts in income distribution offer a logical explanation.

19.	Similar discrepancies are reported by Siamwalla and Haykin (1983) for a number of other Asian countries. They suggest (p. 29) that 'world-wide economic changes that have taken place since 1973 may have shifted income distribution away from high rice consumers in all these countries'.

20.	See Chapter 3, pp. 81–83.

21.	Calculated from Family Income and Expenditure Survey data reported in NCSO (1986b, pp. 1, 99).

22.	The 1985 recovery proved short-lived; see NEDA (1989, p. 5:7).

23.	Unnevehr (1983, pp. 27–9), following Timmer (1974).

24.	The simple correlation between the net imports as a percentage of supply and the farmgate/wholesale price ratio is 0.12 (calculated from data in Tables 4.1 and 4.2).

25.	A 1981–82 survey of 72 Central Luzon rice cultivators by the International Rice Research Institute found that only 14 per cent were able to sell to the NFA, and that the amount sold was 9 per cent of total sales volume. Opportunities to sell at the floor price were rationed, among other means, by administrative procedures including the requirement that the seller hold a passbook issued by the NFA, quality restrictions, and payment by checks that forced the seller to travel to certain banks to obtain payment (Unnevehr, 1983, pp. 18–20). Similar obstacles are cited in the case studies of the Foodwatch Research Team of the Philippine Peasant Institute (1988).

26.	The linkage between market power and political power was demonstrated vividly in the sugar and coconut trade, as documented in Chapter 7.

27.	Unnevehr (1983, p. 23). Unnevehr mentions that the Grains Quedan program, which made loans with stocks bonded by the National Food Authority as security, disbursed P516 million in 1978–82, and that another P297 million was disbursed in 1971–80 under a joint program of the Development Bank of the Philippines and the World Bank. The former carried annual interest rates of 10 per cent, the latter of 14–18 per cent. Unregulated interest rates on long-term bank loans, by contrast, were 21–25 per cent.

28.	Ruttan (1969, p. 504). As empirical support for his view that Philippine rice and corn markets are competitive, Ruttan reports linear regressions of the wholesale price on the farmgate price. A slope coefficient not significantly different from 1.0 is taken to mean that 'the marketing margin is independent of price' and to be 'inconsistent with the hypothesis that middlemen profit by widening the margin between farmers and consumers during periods when retail prices are relatively high'. This is a curious formulation of the market power hypothesis. The test does not indicate whether excess profit exists at any point in time, but rather whether the excess profit, if any, goes up when prices go up, say as a result of weather or world price changes. Why this should be expected is not entirely clear. In any event, Ruttan reports coefficients which *are* significantly greater than one for a number of regions.

29. Bouis notes that Philippine politicians and the Philippine press often blamed abnormal seasonal rice price increases on monopolistic traders, and presents a model which explains such rises in the period 1961–73 in terms of uncertainty about government rice-import and buffer-stock operations. In concluding that rice markets are competitive, he assumes (a) that market power would necessarily manifest itself in abnormal seasonal price increases, and (b) that the two explanations of seasonal price increases are mutually exclusive. Neither assumption is self-evidently true.

30. See, for example, Joson (1989) and Guieb (1990).

31. Secretary Carlos Dominguez, in an interview with Manlogon and Lacaba (1989, p. 15).

32. Bello *et al.* (1982, p. 81). PPI received large subsidies from the government, and Agriculture Minister Arturo Tanco, Jr., sat on its board. The degree of government control over PPI became a legal and political issue during debt rescheduling negotiations between the Philippine government and commercial bank creditors in 1985 and 1987, when the latter successfully pressed the government to assume PPI liabilities.

33. Most of the increase was due to costs of agricultural chemicals – fertilizer, pesticides, and herbicides – which rose from 3% of gross revenue to 15%. Cordova, Mandac, and Gascon (1980), cited by Barker, Herdt, and Rose (1985, p. 90).

34. Total cost is here derived by applying the Central Luzon ratios to total producer revenues, assuming that it rises from 24% of total revenue in 1962–66 to 25% in 1967, and thereafter by annual increments of 2% up to 39% in 1974–85. In reality, of course, this percentage varies from year to year, rising, for example, in years of unfavorable weather. Hence Figure 4.3 probably understates the fluctuations in net revenue. This would have little effect, however, on the trend estimates reported in Table 4.5.

5 The New Rice Technology and Rural Inequality

INCOME, POWER, AND DISTRIBUTION

In the course of the green revolution, the aggregate income of rice producers in the Philippines first rose and later declined, as documented in Chapter 4. 'Producers' are not a homogeneous group, however, and the gains and losses were not evenly distributed among them. This chapter examines the impact of the new rice technology on the diverse groups and classes involved in rice production. These include producers in the strict sense of people who actually perform labor in the fields, and in the much looser sense of people who supervise, collect rent, provide credit, and trade in inputs and in rice.

When producer incomes increase due to technological change, not all producers benefit equally. Initially, they 'benefit in proportion to their ownership of resources and the earnings of the resources' (Barker, Herdt, and Rose, 1985, p. 157). Economists often ignore the effects of this unequal distribution of benefits on the distribution of power. Yet changes in the balance of power can profoundly affect resource ownership and earnings, with further impacts on income distribution.

The existence of linkages between income and power is quite evident to the person on the street or in the rice field. Relative income and power tend to be mutually reinforcing. If the income of A rises relative to the income of B, the power A can exercise over B is likely to increase. This may in turn have 'second generation' effects on the distribution of income. For example, A's increased power may enable him to redefine or reallocate property rights so as to further redistribute income in his favor.

In theory, the income pie can grow such that everyone receives a bigger slice. Power, however, is a zero-sum game. An increase in A's power over B implies, by most definitions, a decrease in B's power over A.[1] Insofar as power rests on income disparities, a decline in B's *relative* income means a decline in B's power, even if B's *absolute* income increases.

When the absolute incomes of the poor rise, their welfare improves in an important respect, even if the incomes of the rich rise faster, shifting the balance of power against the poor.[2] If interactions between income and power are sufficiently strong, however, over time the redistribution of power

125

may lead to a further redistribution of income from the poor to the rich. Mild polarization, in which inequality increases as incomes of the rich and poor move in the same direction, can beget strong polarization, in which the rich become richer while the poor become poorer.

The impact of power on income distribution arises from four 'institutional' phenomena swept under the *ceteris paribus* rug in much economic analysis:

— *Initial endowments*, such as property rights, do not fall from the sky: they are socially constructed. Once constructed, these rights are neither fixed nor inviolable, but rather the objects of contests among individuals, groups, and classes, the outcomes of which hinge upon the distribution of power. A shift in the balance of power can precipitate a redistribution of endowments.

— *Externalities and public goods* are further sources of conflict. Who can impose 'external costs' on whom? Who bears the costs of public goods? Who enjoys preferential access to impure public goods with a degree of rivalry in consumption, such as irrigation water? The answers again hinge on the distribution of power. A shift in the balance of power can hence lead to a redistribution of the costs and benefits arising from these 'market failures'.

— *Market power* allows individual economic agents to force up the market price of a commodity they sell, or force down the price of a commodity they buy, thereby transferring income from others to themselves. The extent of such 'market imperfections' as oligopoly and oligopsony is partly determined by struggles between their beneficiaries and victims. Political power can be wielded to secure market power, or to subdue it.

— *Government policies* affect the distribution of income directly, through taxes and transfers, and indirectly, among other ways by affecting the outcomes of conflicts over endowments, market failures, and market imperfections. Nowhere in political economy is the decisive role of the distribution of power more evident.

Some economists have recognized the importance of the resulting linkages between relative income and power. Simon Kuznets (1963, p. 49), for example, suggested that 'the *power equivalents* of the same relative income spread show a much wider range when the underlying average income is low than when it is high' [emphasis added]. He noted the possible feedback effect, whereby 'as time goes on, the spread in economic power will perpetuate and widen still further the underlying income differentials'. Most economists, however, have been reluctant to lift their gaze beyond the artificial boundary separating 'economics' from 'political science'.[3]

Much of the literature on the distributional impact of the green revolution has suffered from this defective vision. Proponents of the strategy have readily conceded that it may widen relative inequality in rural areas. Large farmers may benefit more than small farmers, landlords more than tenants, employers more than laborers. All ostensibly receive higher real incomes, however, and hence all are better off. Missing from this analysis is any consideration of the 'power equivalents' of widening inequality, and their consequences for such ostensibly exogenous variables as the nature and distribution of property rights, the competitiveness of the market structure, and the formation of government policy.

These linkages are often hard to trace, but that does not make them unimportant. All too often, economists have resembled Sen's (1988, p. 555) 'rigorous searcher looking methodically for his lost car keys under the lamp-post, not because he lost his keys there, but because the light is better on that spot, making scientific search easier'. The following analysis will venture into the shadowy terrain of anthropology and politics.

AGRARIAN STRUCTURE

The distributional impact of a new agricultural technology is invariably shaped by the agrarian structure into which it is introduced, that is, by the institutions governing the distribution of rights in the agricultural means of production, notably land. In the case of Philippine rice agriculture, any discussion of agrarian structure must open with a note of caution. Reliable countrywide data on land ownership distribution and tenancy do not exist. Village-level studies reveal a wide variety of institutional arrangements, making it risky to generalize from specific cases. Moreover, the agrarian structure has changed over time, and did so with particular speed during the green revolution years. What follows is a broad-brush sketch, the details of which would vary from one setting to another. It is drawn from interviews and from a reading of the available literature, much of which is based on village studies in the Central Luzon 'rice bowl'.[4] More information from other regions would no doubt modify the picture.

Tenants and Landlords

Until the 1970s, most rice in the Philippines was produced by share tenants, who turned over a percentage of the crop to the landlord at harvest time. A 50–50 split between them was not unusual, but shares varied considerably within and among localities.[5] Tenants could, and often did, augment their share by concealing part of the harvest from the landowner.[6] Landlords ranged from petty proprietors to *hacenderos* owning 1,000 hectares or more, while tenants generally cultivated one to three hectares per household.

Tenants often borrowed money or grain from their landlords, and many were perpetually indebted. Cash loans at 10 per cent monthly interest and rice loans at 50 per cent per season were not unusual, but terms could vary widely even within a single village. For example, Fegan (1979, p. 323) mentions a landlord who charged anywhere from zero to more than 50 per cent interest on consumption loans 'to reward or punish individual dependents'. Debt payments often 'mopped up the tenants' share', leaving just enough for subsistence.[7]

Economic transactions between landlord and tenant were underpinned by a social web of reciprocal obligations. In times of need, the tenant expected the landlord to provide assistance in the form of loans, intervention in disputes, and so on. The landlord in turn could call on the tenant for occasional unpaid labor services and political support. More than an interlocking set of market exchanges, their relationship was 'based on mutual moral obligations which were asymmetrical in character'.[8]

'In extending credit to his tenants', McLennan (1982, p. 73) remarks, 'the *hacendero* was more interested in power than profits'. The two were, of course, complementary. By rationing scarce resources to favored clients, the patron ensures that his or her dependents regard access as a privilege rather than a right. This in turn forces the poor to pay what Fegan (1979, pp. 6–7, 368) terms a 'second price' in the form of 'social deference and/or subordination' for access to resources controlled by the rich. 'As in all power situations', Fegan notes, 'the overt warmth of the dependents' regard for superiors may be solely the obligatorily affable mask worn by a courtier or ambassador that hides resentment and the desire for revenge'. Were the client to drop this mask, however, the personal consequences would be severe.

Power, being rooted in contests among people, is seldom either absolute or absolutely secure. The patron is not a scaled-down version of Wittfogel's (1957) mythic 'oriental despot'. Consider the case of a small farmer who borrowed 300 pesos from a moneylender, recounted in the 1930s by Governor-General Theodore Roosevelt, Jr.:

> Each year, when the time came to pay his interest, the usurer offered him remission if he would sign a new document substituted for the original one and written in a language he did not understand. At the end of the fourth year he owed 3,000 pesos.[9]

The usurer had the power to inflate the initial debt, but he could not simply force the farmer to accept a bogus debt of 3,000 pesos at the time of the original loan. Instead, he had to incur the transaction costs of the annual ritual of debt enhancement. Social norms, reflecting the balance of power between creditor and borrower, had to be observed.[10]

Patron-client relationships differ markedly from the impersonal market exchanges of the standard economics textbook, in which commodities trade at a single market price. They also differ from the more sophisticated model of 'interlocking factor markets', in which the economic value of one resource, such as credit, is incorporated in the nominal price of another, such as land rent.[11] In demanding the 'second price' of deference, rather than letting the first price rise to market-clearing levels, the patron attempts to purchase legitimacy and to prevent challenges to his control over resources. In other words, the enforcement of property rights is embedded in the process of exchange.

Property Rights

Until the twentieth century, land rights in the Philippines were generally unrecorded. Neither landlord nor tenant depended on a piece of paper backed by a formal legal apparatus to define and enforce their respective claims to the land. Their positions instead rested on precedent and power. The local landowning elites relied for their support primarily on 'a loyal following of "little people", mainly peasants' (Kerkvliet, 1977, p. 22).

The Spanish government introduced formal land titles in Central Luzon in the late nineteenth century, initiating a shift in the political basis of property rights from local society to the state. McLennan (1969, p. 673) depicts this as an effort at social reform, intended to 'rectify the plight of the peasantry' who were vulnerable to dispossession by local elites. In practice, he concludes, it had the opposite effect:

> The *principalia* [landowning elite] used the opportunity of registering their land to claim extensive areas occupied by smallholder neighbors. Illiterate and ignorant of the processes of the law, the peasants were helpless to protect themselves.

By providing a new basis for the enforcement of property rights, state intervention altered the balance of power – and, as a result, the distribution of wealth – in favor of the rich.

Landgrabbing continued unabated under US rule. In 1913, the new colonial government launched a cadastral survey, officially registering land ownership rights (but not tenancy rights). The competition for land titles was intense. Local elites often managed 'to overpower weaker claimants', Kerkvliet (1977, p. 22) recounts, 'by "fixing" the titles in assessors' offices and winning court cases against peasant landowners who did not understand the law and lacked "connections" in government agencies'.[12] Jose (1959, pp. 102–3) describes the plight of settlers in Pangasinan in southern Ilocos:

> [T]o them, to their neighbors, the only markers that identified their farms were the mounds, the old trees which they spared, the turn of a creek, a clump of bamboo, an old dike . . . But some learned men, who knew that the cadastral surveys could bring them new wealth, ignored these landmarks. In the survey plans which they submitted, they gobbled up the farms of the settlers, and when the titles were ready, the old landmarks – the trees, the mounds, the creeks – were abolished and the immigrants found themselves tenants.[13]

Land registration thus did not simply formalize a pre-existing order, but rather initiated a scramble in which the competitive edge went to those with a comparative advantage in greasing the wheels of officialdom.

Landlord-tenant relations entered a new era, in which the traditional social bonds of reciprocity began to become unglued. The intervention of the colonial state 'inflated the landlords' power, reduced their need for a loyal following, and as a consequence whittled away their incentives to serve the community' (Kerkvliet, 1977, p. 22). Many landlords moved to provincial towns or Manila, leaving the supervision of their properties to overseers. As land titles passed to a new generation without personal ties to the tenants, physical absenteeism was compounded by 'psychological absenteeism'.[14]

The overseers who acted as intermediaries between absentee landlords and their tenants sometimes emerged as powerful figures in their own right. Some were employed by the landlord on commission, while others paid a fixed rent to the landlord in return for the right to collect share rents from the tenants.[15] In the mid-1960s, Takahashi (1969, p. 117) found that many tenants, especially those who dealt with overseers, did not know the full names of their landlords.

Meanwhile, the growth of population and the lack of alternative employment increased the supply of prospective tenants, reducing the pressure on landlords and overseers to fulfill their side of the customary patron-client bargain. Loans became less frequent, and loan terms less generous. Landlords and overseers demanded larger shares of the crop. Tenant stratagems for concealment of part of the harvest were less readily tolerated, and evictions of less profitable or insufficiently compliant tenants increased.[16]

The formalization of land titles in the colonial era thus did not enhance security of property rights across the board. More secure property rights for the rich went hand-in-hand with less secure rights for the poor. This divergence, though perhaps unanticipated by some colonial administrators, was hardly surprising, for it was rooted in the zero-sum nature of power.

Today, the property rights of poor Filipinos remain highly insecure. For example, Fegan (1979, pp. 87–9) reports that in a rice-farming village in Central Luzon's Bulacan province, the *kalabaw* (water buffalo) of small farmers are routinely seized by 'village political entrepreneurs who are adept at the use of armed violence'. The rustlers target political enemies or wavering supporters, for their object 'is not simply profit, but to drive home a lesson'. Fegan explains the typical course of events:

> If his *kalabaw* disappears . . . the owner approaches that politico who he feels arranged the rustling, or an ally or superior politician of the same coalition, to ask him to undertake recovery of the beast – promising future loyalty. It is not realistic to expect municipal police to want or be able to help, unless the owner has a direct personal connection with the Mayor. After a few days the politico reports that he has located the beast, but that it is being held in an enemy area where he cannot recover it by force but must ransom it. Usually he will suggest that the rustlers have arranged sale for slaughter, but will take a little less than the meat price to avoid risks in transit, and out of 'respect' for him. The owner has no recourse but to hand over *tubos*, ransom to the leader, often in the certainty that the same leader arranged the rustling to punish him.

The fact that property rights are inevitably conditional on the balance of power is evident to the peasant who pays a little less than the market price to recover his own water buffalo.

The land frontier has offered the poor a safety valve in only a limited sense. By migrating, tenants could escape a particular landlord, but not landlordism. *De facto* land ownership was established, often by force, in areas of new settlement: 'Whenever a road was to be constructed through an undeveloped section, homesteaders flocked in rapidly, to find only too often that influential persons who had been privately informed of the construction even before it was begun had taken up the choice land on both sides of the road' (Pelzer, 1945, p. 112). Even today, share tenancy remains widespread in upland areas, where 90 per cent of the land is nominally under public ownership. Peasants pay rent to 'non-cultivating claimants', who 'are generally absentees and acting as virtual landowners' (Cornista, 1985, p. 3).

In response to their deteriorating economic positions, tenants at times joined together to challenge the landlords' power. The most famous such movement arose in Central Luzon in the 1930s and gave birth to the Hukbalahap (People's Anti-Japanese Army) in World War Two. The Huks won control of much of Central Luzon during the war, supplanting landlord authority and slashing rents.[17] After the war, the government moved against the Huks and landlords reasserted control. 'Civil guard' units, financed jointly by the government and landowners' associations, policed the rice harvest. In a Bulacan village, for example, tenants recall that the guard erected a tower in which they installed an army-surplus searchlight to watch the standing crops at night (Fegan, 1979, p. 76).

With the end of the World War Two, the United States government made the fateful choice in the Philippines, as elsewhere in Asia, to support established elites in their struggle with 'subversive' peasant movements. The fact that many members of the elite had collaborated with the enemy during the war was generously forgiven. The US and the newly independent Philippine government responded to the Huk challenge with the stick of military repression and the carrot of agrarian reform. The latter was more appearance than substance, being candidly described by President Magsaysay's defense secretary as 'psych war aimed at the soft core of the Huk movement'.[18] The combination proved effective, however, and the threat of peasant insurgency in the Philippines was temporarily defeated.

Landlessness and Wage Labor

By the early 1960s, Philippine rice agriculture was witnessing the emergence of a new class: landless wage laborers. The origins of this class remain somewhat obscure. Although landless wage labor dates from Spanish times, it only recently became a large-scale phenomenon in rice cultivation. No aggregate data exist on the growth of landlessness and wage labor, and village studies reveal considerable diversity among localities. While these difficulties also apply to other aspects of the agrarian structure, landlessness and wage labor are particularly problematic, for in the Philippine setting their very definition proves slippery.

Consider the boundary between family labor and hired labor. If, upon marriage, a son establishes a separate household and then works for his father for a 'wage', is this hired labor or family labor?[19] What if, upon the death of the father, the formal land title passes to one child, who then 'hires' his or her brothers and sisters to work on it for a 'wage'?[20] What if, a generation later, the same relationship exists among cousins? Does the distinction between family and hired labor here hinge on whether the relatives consider the 'owner' to hold the land in name only on behalf of the family as a whole? Does it depend on whether family members are hired in preference to others, or receive higher wages, or have other *de facto* claims on the farm income such as free vegetables, interest-free loans, or outright gifts? 'In a village where many are kin, but non-household labor is paid', Fegan (1972b, p. 139) remarks, 'the term "family" labor may make for confusion'. Likewise the terms 'landless' and 'wage labor'.

The boundary between wage labor and sharecropping can be fuzzy, too. Consider the arrangement whereby a group of laborers cuts and threshes the paddy in return for one-sixth or one-seventh of the harvest. In its traditional form, in which anyone could join the group and share in the crop, this arrangement was called *hunusan* in Laguna province.[21] In the late 1960s and early 1970s a new variant emerged, in which harvesting is limited to those who have earlier weeded the crop without receiving wages. This arrangement, still more akin to sharecropping, is called *gama* in Laguna. It has also been reported in Ilo-ilo, where it is termed *sagod*; in Bicol, where it is termed *agui-agui* or *hilani*; in Leyte, where it is termed *prendes*, and may entail either transplanting or weeding as a condition for sharing in the harvest; and in Central Luzon, where the weeding variant is termed *damo-gapas* and the transplanting variant *tamin-gapas*.[22] In such cases the workers are neither tenants nor wage laborers, but something in between.

Not all 'wage laborers' in Philippine rice agriculture, however defined, are landless. In fact, the same individual may work for others and hire those others to work for him. Such mutual 'wage' employment has been reported, for example, in Mindanao (Castillo, 1975, pp. 242–7). Takahashi (1969, pp. 141–2) found two variants of this practice among tenants in a Central Luzon village in the 1960s. When labor costs were shared with the landlord, the tenants paid each other wages. When labor costs were borne by the tenants alone, they engaged in non-wage labor exchanges. Takahashi attributed this difference to the tenants' desire to reduce rental payments to their landlords. Labor-pooling arrangements, with or without cash payments, could also be explained by the need for rapid completion of certain tasks, or by cultural preferences for working in groups.[23] It would seem rather arbitrary to describe these arrangements as 'wage labor' in one instance and not in the other.

Furthermore, many individuals and households in rural areas engage in both agricultural and non-agricultural labor. The latter includes work in transport, construction, light manufacturing, personal services, and petty trading. Here, too, the mode of employment often is not straightforward wage labor. Many work as what Fegan (1972b, p. 135) terms 'dependent petty entrepreneurs', obtaining equipment, raw materials, or credit from 'small capitalists' on a piece-rate, contract, or loan basis.[24]

A number of accounts agree, however, that a distinct class of landless wage laborers has emerged in Philippine rice agriculture in recent decades. In Central Luzon, Wolters (1984, p. 187) reports 'a rapidly increasing number of landless and underemployed laborers'. Fegan (1979, pp. 92, 418) similarly describes landless laborers as 'the most numerous and fastest increasing class' in the countryside. In the Bulacan village he studied, for example, 58 per cent of the households were landless in the early 1970s, whereas none had been landless in the 1930s. In a Laguna village which has been repeatedly surveyed over the years, 31 per cent of households were headed by landless laborers in 1966. The proportion rose to 43 per cent in 1974, and to 63 per cent in 1980.[25]

Linguistic evidence supports the hypothesis that landless laborers are a fairly recent phenomenon in Luzon's rice agriculture. The Tagalog term *magbubukid* refers to anyone who works in the fields, encompassing small owner-cultivators, tenants, and hired laborers. There is no traditional term for hired laborers as a distinct category, though in recent years a term for them has emerged, *manggagawang bukid*. In the western Visayas, by contrast, where landlessness may have a longer history, the language has separate and mutually exclusive terms for peasants (*mag-uuma*) and laborers (*mamumugon*).[26]

The growth of landlessness in the Philippines is sometimes attributed to population growth.[27] There is no inherent reason, however, why population growth would alter the *composition* of the agricultural labor force, even when the land frontier is closed and non-agricultural employment does not accommodate the growing numbers. An alternative outcome, with partible inheritance, is the subdivision of farms into smaller and more numerous holdings. Some of these farms may not be 'viable' in the sense of providing sufficient income to support a family, but farming can be supplemented by off-farm work, and owning a little land is often more viable than owning none at all.

Both partible and impartible inheritance have been reported in Philippine rice agriculture.[28] In the latter case, in which land passes to a single heir, population growth can help to explain landlessness. In many cases, however, landlessness can be traced to an entire family's loss of its land rights. Many in the Laguna village, for example, reported that they had become landless 'through selling or pawning their tenancy titles' (Kikuchi, 1983, p. 61).

LAND REFORM

Ironically, the growth of landless wage labor in the Philippines was accelerated by government land reform programs. The 1963 agrarian reform law of the Macapagal government, for example, contained a 'self-cultivation' clause, exempting landowners from reform provisions if they ejected their tenants and switched to wage labor.[29] Wage labor farms were likewise exempted from the Marcos government's land reform program of the 1970s. Insofar as this this exemption reflected anything other than political expediency, the guiding principle behind it seems to have been a belief that wage labor was socially desirable, whereas tenancy was not.

In October 1972, one month after his declaration of Martial Law, Marcos issued Presidential Decree No. 27, under which ownership of tenanted rice and corn lands was to be gradually transferred to the tenants. The decree went a step beyond the 1971 Amendment to the Land Reform Code, which had aimed for conversion from share tenancy to fixed-rent leasehold. Under P.D. 27's 'Operation Land Transfer', landlord holdings in excess of seven hectares were to be expropriated. The landlord would receive compensation equal to two and one-half years' normal harvest, 10 per cent of it in cash and the remainder in Land Bank bonds. The erstwhile tenant would become an 'amortizing owner', making annual payments to the government Land Bank for 15 years. The amortizing owner would initially receive a Certificate of Land Transfer (CLT) and then, after completing the payments, an 'Emancipation Patent'. These new land rights were to be transferable only by inheritance. On landlord holdings below the seven-hectare limit, tenants would become leaseholders with secure tenancy rights and fixed rents.[30]

Although P.D. 27 was accompanied by much fanfare – Marcos proclaimed it 'the only gauge for the success or failure of the New Society'[31] – it was riddled with loopholes. The reform applied only to land sown to rice and corn, so landlords could evade it by switching to other crops. It applied only to tenanted land, so landlords could evade it by converting to wage labor. In addition, tenanted rice and corn lands could be registered in the names of different family members to evade the seven-hectare ceiling.[32]

Many landlords sought to discourage their tenants from asserting their rights under the law. One important threat, given the importance of water control in rice agriculture, was denial of access to irrigation sources.[33] Other pressures the landlords brought to bear included the filing of spurious civil and criminal cases against the tenant, eviction of kinsmen's houses from the tenant's houselot, refusal to produce accurate harvest records, forbidding the tenant to cut bamboo outside his houselot, forcing the tenant to move his house to a new location, and outright physical intimidation.[34]

Not surprisingly, there is little official documentation of the extent of these practices. Within months of the issuance of P.D. 27, however, the Department of Agrarian Reform (DAR) reported that 'many landowners' were ejecting their tenants. Some tenants, the DAR reported, were forced to declare themselves to be farm laborers, while others were driven off the land through 'physical acts of dispossession like bulldozing of farms, demolition and/or burning of houses, manhandling, intimidation, etc.'.[35] In other cases, landlords paid some compensation to the tenant to secure his removal. A DAR official interviewed in 1989 voiced the belief that wage labor in rice agriculture grew rapidly in the 1970s in response to P.D. 27.[36]

By 1986, CLTs had been issued for less than 800,000 of the 6 million hectares under rice and corn in the Philippines. Tenants on another 550,000 hectares had been converted, at least on paper, to permanent leaseholders.[37] For the CLT holders, there was often less to the distinction between amortization payments and rent than met the eye. Some paid 'amortization' directly to their 'former' landlord, who in theory forwarded it to the Land Bank. In some cases, *de facto* share tenancy persisted. Notwithstanding legal prohibitions, a market in CLTs emerged. In addition to outright sales, land alienation has often occurred through mortgage arrangements.[38]

Government publicists nevertheless portrayed the Marcos land reform program as a resounding success. A 1980 Philippine News Agency release claimed that '359,000 farmers now own the land they till via the issuance of 501,364 certificates of land title'.[39] As Wurfel (1983, p. 9) remarks, '[t]he previously subtle attempt to equate CLTs with titles had lost its subtlety'. This enthusiasm extended to Washington, where a senior US Agency for International Development official informed a Congressional subcommittee in 1981 that '88 per cent of eligible families had received land titles' under the Marcos reform.[40]

This claim was nonsense, but it would be an exaggeration to conclude that the Marcos land reform accomplished nothing. Some tenants did benefit, particularly better-off ones with the political leverage to secure CLTs on favorable payment terms. 'The primary beneficiaries of the land reform', write Barker, Herdt, and Rose (1985, p. 255), 'were the larger tenants (2 to 3 hectares) who held political power in the villages'. Returning to the Bulacan village he first studied in the early 1970s, Fegan (1982b) found that the Marcos land reform had effectively broken up the large rice haciendas. Mangahas (1986, pp. 18–19) concludes that Operation Land Transfer was 'a moderate, somewhat long-drawn-out beginning at land reform'.

The most glaring shortcoming of Philippine land reform has been its utter neglect of the poorest and possibly most numerous stratum of Philippine rural society, the landless. Reforms have promoted land-to-the-tenant, not land-to-the-laborer. Indeed, insofar as share tenancy previously offered some landless households a chance for upward mobility, land reform may have worsened their plight.[41]

DIFFERENTIATION AMONG RICE FARMERS

In the Philippines, the green revolution did not take place in an agricultural economy of independent small farmers. Rather the new rice technology was introduced into a differentiated agrarian structure, in which tenants and laborers worked the land, and non-working landlords extracted most of the surplus above their subsistence needs. By the time IRRI's 'miracle seeds' appeared on the scene in the 1960s, the traditional patron-client ties which had legitimized this fundamental inequality and softened its rough edges were coming undone. The reallocation of property rights during US colonial rule had tilted the balance of power further in favor of the rich, and lessened their dependence on clients. Peasant rebellion had ruptured landlord-tenant relations in much of Central Luzon. The emergence of a distinct class of landless wage laborers marked a new stage in economic polarization. The government's top-down land reform program was a further source of conflict and change.

This agrarian structure shaped the distribution of gains and losses from the green revolution. And the resulting shifts in relative incomes in turn sparked further differentiation of the agrarian structure.

Early Adopters vs. Late Adopters

The vast majority of Filipino rice cultivators had adopted the new rice technology by the mid-1980s, but some did so sooner than others. As a new technology spreads, producers who lag in its adoption are not simply left behind with unchanged incomes. Rather, their incomes decline, owing to what can be termed 'price effects' and 'power effects'.

Price effects are familiar to economists. When a profitable new technology is introduced, those who adopt it first reap above-normal profits. Over time, as the output price falls due to increased supply, and input prices possibly rise due to increased demand, the profit margin is squeezed until it returns to normal. In the meantime, producers who lag in adoption of the new technology see their incomes *decline*, as they receive lower prices for their output (and perhaps pay higher prices for inputs) while continuing to use the old technology.

Power effects are less familiar to economists, but possibly more evident to Filipino rice producers. As income distribution shifts in favor of early adopters, so does their power *vis-à-vis* late adopters. This gives the earlier adopters a new advantage in contests over endowments, externalities, public goods, market power, and government policy.

'Even where one group of farmers lags behind in adoption', write Barker, Herdt and Rose (1985, p. 148), 'the logical consequence of a continuation of the process is for the lagging group to eventually catch up with the leaders'. If 'catching up' simply means adopting the new technology, this is a truism unless some are blocked from access to the new technology, for example by inadequate water control. However, if it means something more – a restoration of the *status quo ante* in the distribution of income between early and late adopters – then the statement is false, for it neglects the cumulative impact of both price and power effects in the course of technological change.

A key question, therefore, is whether there are systematic prior differences between early adopters and late adopters. If, for example, small farmers adopt earlier than large farmers, the effect will be a more equal income distribution. If, on the other hand, large farmers lead, the effect will be polarization. Similarly, if some regions lead and others lag, the direction of the distributional impact depends on their initial relative positions.

In the case of the new rice technology in the Philippines, there is considerable evidence that the benefits of early adoption accrued primarily to landlords as opposed to tenants, to larger owners and tenants as opposed to smaller ones, and to more prosperous regions as opposed to poorer ones. In other words, timing differences in the diffusion of the new rice technology led to strong polarization in the distribution of income among producers.

The leading role of landlords in the green revolution was noted by early observers. In 1966, the first batch of IRRI seed to reach a Nueva Ecija barrio was distributed to 'landlords who possessed ten hectares of paddy or more'.[42] No seed was distributed directly to their tenants, or to smaller landowners. Touring Central Luzon on behalf of the Asian Development Bank, Ishikawa (1970, pp. 13) reported that his 'vivid impression was that thus far the major agents responding to this dynamic force were non-cultivating as well as partly cultivating landlords, who are converting themselves into new commercial farmers'. Ishikawa attributed non-adoption of the new rice technology by poorer cultivators to their lack of access to credit for the purchase of inputs, and to their lower ability to bear risk and uncertainty.

With respect to differences among tenants, Herdt (1987, p. 335) reports that in 1970 the average farm size of adopters in Central Luzon was 50 per cent larger than that of non-adopters. By 1982, the smaller farms had 'caught up' in the sense that virtually all their land was now sown to HYVs,

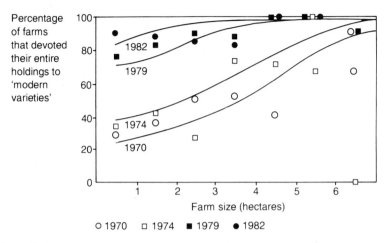

Source: Herdt (1987, p. 337).

Figure 5.1:   Adoption of HYVs in Central Luzon by Farm Size, 1970 – 1982

too.[43] The diffusion pattern is shown in Figure 5.1, in which the curves depict the relationship between farm size and adoption of the new varieties at successive dates.

Among the regions, a clear pattern emerged in which relatively high-income regions led in adoption of the new rice technology, and lower-income regions lagged. In the early 1980s, the share of rice acreage sown to HYVs ranged from 62 per cent in Western Mindanao to 93 per cent in Central Luzon (see Table 3.3). The regional adoption pattern from 1970 to 1983 is depicted in Figure 5.2. Central Luzon, the region with the lowest poverty incidence outside the capital area (see Table 2.13), led in HYV adoption. Poorer regions such as Cagayan Valley, Eastern and Central Visayas, and Western Mindanao lagged. Within regions, moreover, irrigated lands were favored over unirrigated lands, and lowlands over uplands. The impact of the new technology on those who could not adopt it is reflected in the abandonment of rice cultivation on thousands of hectares in less favorable environments.[44] The Philippine experience thus conforms to the general finding elsewhere in Asia that the new varieties 'tend to confirm the regional bias that existed previously'.[45]

The price effects of differential adoption rates were complicated in the Philippine case by the trends reviewed in the previous chapter. In the early years of the green revolution, real rice prices in the Philippines rose

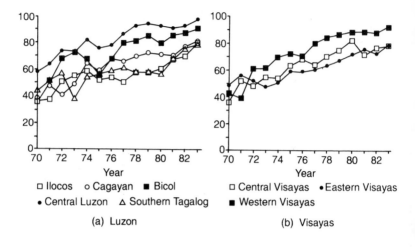

(a) Luzon   (b) Visayas

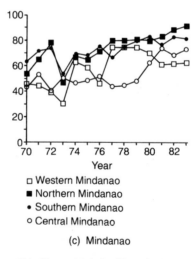

(c) Mindanao

Source: Calculated from unpublished Bureau of Agricultural Economics data.

**Figure 5.2:   Adoption of HYVs by Region, 1970 – 1983
(percentage of total rice acreage sown to HYVs)**

under the impact of world price movements. All rice producers benefitted, but early adopters of the new technology benefitted most, accentuating inequalities between landowners and tenants, large farms and small farms, rich regions and poor regions. The latter gradually 'caught up' in terms of technology adoption, but as they did so the profitability of rice farming was sharply diminished by falling real output prices and rising input prices. Economically, there was no catching up.

The New Producer Elite

Under the combined impact of the new rice technology, government price policies, and agrarian reform, the distribution of income and the balance of power in the Philippine rice economy changed. Two new rural elites emerged, one primarily engaged in production, the other in commerce.

The new producer elite includes former landlords and former tenants who now cultivate wholly or primarily by means of hired labor. In the early years of the green revolution, Ishikawa (1970, pp. 13, 29–30) found that such 'new commercial farmers' were emerging from the ranks of the landlords, and termed this 'the most important event in the institutional aspect of the spread of the modern inputs in Central Luzon'. Ledesma (1982, pp. 114–16) reports that in Iloilo 'landlords-turned-entrepreneurs', many of whom commute from nearby cities, now manage their rice farms 'no longer in terms of maintaining patron-client relations with their tenants, but as business ventures subject to profit or loss'. Hayami and Kikuchi (1982, p. 132) similarly report a transition from the 'old elite' to a 'new power elite' in Laguna, citing as an example a landlord who consolidated 73 hectares under his direct administration in the 1970s.

In some places, the new producer elite includes many ex-tenants, who became amortizing owners or fixed-rent leaseholders under the land reform. In particular, those tenants who managed to fix their amortization payments or leasehold rents on the basis of pre-HYV yields could reap substantial gains when they then adopted the new technology.[46] The ability of tenants to capture some of the land productivity gains was reflected in shifts in the relative prices of ownership titles and (nominally non-saleable) tenancy rights. In a Laguna village, for example, the real price of ownership titles fell sharply from 1968 to 1975, while that of tenancy rights rose.[47]

Fegan (1982b, p. 9) remarks on obvious signs of increased prosperity among ex-tenants in irrigated villages in Central Luzon:

Many farmers have built or have enlarged and improved their houses. They have new furniture, electrical appliances like TVs, fans, record players plus other consumer goods like motorcycles, bicycles and watches. Many have also been able to buy or pay off loans on hand tractors and pumps, put their children through elementary and high school, and make new investments on small-scale commercial pig and poultry-raising.

These signs of prosperity were absent in rainfed and flood-prone areas less suited to the new rice technology.

Among the more prosperous amortizing owners and leaseholders, many have ceased to work on the land themselves, instead relying on the labor of others. Some have become 'intermediate landlords', subletting their holdings to the landless despite the fact that subtenancy is prohibited by law.[48] Others employ wage labor in its many variants. In irrigated areas of Central Luzon, landless laborers are sometimes hired under long-term *kasugpong* contracts:

> A typical example was found in the case of a large farmer, holding three hectares of leasehold land and two hectares of amortizing land in the Municipality of Munoz, Nueva Ecija. While he operated a small rice mill and a grocery store (*sari-sari*), he left almost all the farm tasks including land preparation except transplanting, weeding, and harvesting to a family with three working males. . . . For their service, this *kasugpong* family received 10 per cent of gross paddy output from this farm. They lived in a shanty in the farmer's residential quarter but neither food nor clothing was provided from the master.[49]

Such arrangements combine features of sharecropping and wage labor.

The rising incomes of the new producer elite were derived not only from the profits of the new rice technology itself, but also from their access to government-subsidized credit. The Masagana–99 credit program, which peaked in 1974–75, provided cheap institutional credit tied to the adoption of the new rice technology. Weak collection mechanisms enabled many farmers 'to take the credit and run'.[50] The program exacerbated rural inequalities in four ways. First, loans were made to farmers, but not to the landless. Second, loans were purposely directed towards farmers with irrigated land rather than to those with rainfed land.[51] Third, among the eligible farmers, better-off individuals with political and banking connections were favored.[52] Finally, the rural bankers themselves profited handsomely: it has been estimated that two-thirds of the total subsidies were pocketed by the local banks, and only one-third by the borrowers.[53]

Members of the new producer elite sought to expand their agricultural operations, particularly in the 1970s when rice cultivation remained profitable. Unlike earlier decades, land accumulation appears to have come about primarily through intra-village transfers, as individuals acquired additional farms via moneylending and then cultivated them by means of hired labor and illegal subtenancies. The rise of this new class, sometimes described as 'kulaks',[54] coincided with the eclipse of the old landlords, a pattern reminiscent of previous transitions in other Asian rice-producing countries.[55]

Land transfers often took place covertly owing to legal restrictions, and hence data on their extent are not readily available. However, village studies contain illuminating examples. Fegan (1989b, p. 165) reports the sale of CLTs in a Bulacan village, often after an initial usufructuary mortgage: 'Then with the collusion of the outgoing tenant, village headman, landowner, and ministry officials, the legal farm right was transferred'. Hayami and Kikuchi (1982, pp. 129–32) document land accumulation by large tenant operators in a Laguna village, via purchases of rights from other tenants and rentals from landowners. The largest single transfer, of 60 hectares formerly under direct landlord administration, was disguised as a management contract, but in practice it was 'nothing but a leasehold contract' under which the operator paid a fixed rent.

Banzon-Bautista (1989, p. 152) reports that in a Pampangan village, where one in three farmer households 'experienced significant reductions in landholdings' between 1977 and 1984, in most cases the land had been sold covertly to buyers with 'Saudi money', labor earnings from the Middle East. Many of the sellers were themselves attempting to obtain Middle East work contracts, underscoring the fact that the rice sector is not isolated from the national and international economy.

Members of the new producer elite have sought to diversify their household income sources. They invest in their children's education so as to give them access to urban salaried jobs, often saving to put the first child through school, who then finances the education of the second, and so on.[56] With the declining profitability of rice production in the 1980s, many have also diversified into local services and trading activities, blurring the line between them and the other segment of the new rural elite.

The New Commercial Elite

The new commercial elite includes farm input suppliers, contractors for mechanized farm services, bankers, moneylenders, and rice traders. Umehara (1983, p. 37) considers this group to have been the 'real beneficiaries' of the green revolution in the Philippines. Between 1970 and 1978, he finds that the farm operator's share in paddy output in a Central Luzon village fell from 39 to 16 per cent and the landlord's share from 30 to 15 per cent, while the share of the 'dealer/contractor/moneylender' rose from 15 to 42 per cent.[57]

Umehara (1983, p. 40) describes a typical member of the commercial elite, the owner and general manager of a rural bank, who channelled government loans to farmers while diverting some of the money to finance his 'side business of retailing fertilizer, chemicals, contracting farm workers and rendering such service as plowing and threshing with the use of machinery'.

Faced, on the one hand, with the well-padded stick of agrarian reform and, on the other, with the income opportunities opened by the new rice technology on the other, landlords led the shift into these newly expanding lines of commercial activity. Noting that many Central Luzon landlords now trade in agricultural inputs, rice, and consumer goods, Fegan (1982b, p. 24) remarks, 'Those totally dependent on land seem to be like the institution of the rice hacienda, due to fade from history'. Umehara (1983, p. 38) observes that 'smart landlords' who perceived the new opportunities 'quickly responded and joined the ranks of the commercial elite'.

Some ex-tenants also diversified into services and trading. As an example, Fegan (1989b, pp. 166–7) describes a long-time champion of tenant rights who by 1980 controlled nine irrigated farms, averaging three hectares each, which he had acquired via moneylending. The borrowers continued to work the farms under covert tenancy arrangements, while the moneylender 'supplied certified seed from his own licensed seed-producer's farm (at double the ordinary price), fertilizer, chemicals, and services of his hand tractor, plus cash for transplanting expenses, all at retail rates plus 10% per month interest'. The borrower also contracted to use the moneylender's thresher.

Fegan (1989b, p. 168) dates the 'take off' of such 'integrated services capitalist enterprises' from the late 1970s, when institutional credit dried up and the light axial-flow threshing machine was introduced. The latter was important in that it provided a reliable collection mechanism for the moneylender-trader. Just as rice hacienda owners once used *tilyadoras*, big threshing machines, as a means of control in the division of the crop at harvest time, the new rural elite uses small mobile threshers as a means for tightened control over the harvest.[58]

On the 'producer' side of the Philippine rice economy, then, the primary beneficiaries of the green revolution were the new rural elites, drawn from the old landlord class and an upwardly mobile segment of the tenantry. Some remained involved in rice production in a managerial role, some devoted themselves to related commercial activities, and some engaged in both. But the green revolution also created losers, whose real incomes declined. These included poorer farmers who lagged in adoption of the new technology and lacked access to government subsidies; farmers who lost their land rights, often to moneylenders; and above all, the landless laborers.

THE NEW RICE TECHNOLOGY AND LABOR ABSORPTION

In theory, the new rice technology was to be labor-absorbing. The application of additional inputs – fertilizer, irrigation, pesticides – would require additional labor. Since fertilizers stimulate growth of weeds which compete with the short-statured new varieties, more labor would be required for weeding and for line-transplantation of paddy, which facilitates weed control. Larger harvests would require more labor to reap, thresh, and winnow. For landless laborers, the green revolution thus promised more employment, higher wages, or both.

Mechanization of rice production was not part of the green revolution technology package. The new varieties did not require that human labor be replaced by tractors, power tillers, herbicides, or threshing machines. Yet this is precisely what happened in the Philippines. In practice, the green revolution and mechanization were bound together, not by technology, but by political economy.

In the two decades following the introduction of the new rice varieties, the average real wage in Philippine rice agriculture fell by almost 25 per cent (see Tables 2.7 and 5.1). The regional wage variations reported in Table 5.1 are reasonably consistent with the poverty estimates reported in Table 2.13: regions with lower agricultural wages tended to have a higher percentage of households in poverty in both the mid-1960s and the mid-1980s.[59]

The regional data do not provide clear-cut evidence on the relationship between the new rice technology and wage trends. Comparing the wage data in Table 5.1 with the rice yield data in Table 3.3, we find that wage levels tend to be higher in regions with higher yields, but the correlation is rather weak.[60] However, the correlation between *trends* in yields and wages is negative: regions with more rapid yield growth tended to have more rapid wage declines.[61] On the other hand, regions with a higher share of their rice area sown to HYVs tended to experience slower wage declines.[62]

The wage trends reported in Table 5.1 may partly reflect the impact of inter-regional migration of agricultural laborers, which has been common in recent decades.[63] In particular, laborers have migrated from relatively low-wage regions, such as the Visayas, to higher-wage regions, such as Central Luzon. In Bulacan, for example, Fegan (1989b, p. 174) reports the recent appearance of a very poor stratum of landless laborers, known locally as

TABLE 5.1   *Real Agricultural Wage by Region, 1966–1986*
(average daily wage, palay *production; constant 1986 pesos)*

Region	Average wage [1]		Trend [2] (% per annum)
	1966–68	1984–86	
National	39.85	30.41	−1.30
Ilocos	42.39	31.13	−1.40
Cagayan Valley	36.43	27.61	−1.21
Central Luzon	43.30	37.31	−0.98
Southern Tagalog	60.14	37.42	−1.99
Bicol	34.45	28.74	−0.58
Western Visayas	30.51	26.10	−0.47
Eastern Visayas	} 33.41	23.48 (23.20)	−1.25
Central Visayas		22.92	
Northern Mindanao	} 40.54	25.66 (26.53)	−2.51
Central Mindanao		27.40	
Western Mindanao	} 46.97	27.60 (27.03)	−2.75
Southern Mindanao		26.46	

NOTES
1. Numbers in parentheses are simple averages for regions subdivided after 1975.
2. Exponential growth rate estimated from annual data by ordinary least squares. Trend for subdivided regions is estimated using simple averages.

SOURCES   Unpublished nominal wage data provided by the Bureau of Agricultural Economics. Converted to 1986 pesos using consumer price index as reported in IMF (1987, pp. 560–1).

'Bisaya', from Cebu, Bohol, Samar, and Bicol. This may help to explain why inter-regional wage differentials narrowed over time. A multiple regression analysis of wage trend variations confirms the contradictory effects of yield trends and HYV adoption, and indicates that regions with higher wages in the mid-1960s experienced more rapid wage declines in subsequent years.[64]

The role of the new technology in the decline of real agricultural wages in the Philippines has been a matter of controversy. A number of observers contend that the blame for falling wages and increasing rural poverty lies not with the green revolution, but with population growth. '[T]he shift in the supply of labor caused by rapid population growth', Hayami and Ruttan

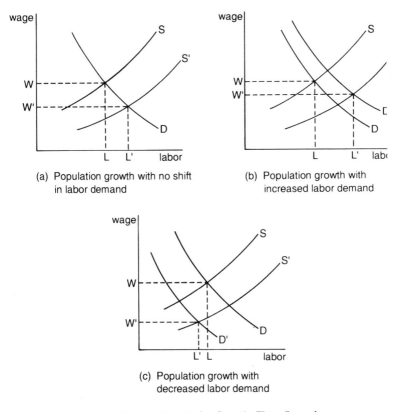

(a) Population growth with no shift
in labor demand

(b) Population growth with
increased labor demand

(c) Population growth with
decreased labor demand

Figure 5.3:   **Wage Declines and Population Growth: Three Scenarios**

(1985, p. 336) write, 'has outpaced the shift in demand for labor caused by technological progress'. Similarly, David and Otsuka (1987, p. 11) blame continuing rural poverty on 'high population growth and the failure of industrialization strategies' rather than on technological change in the food grain sector.

Increased labor supply, arising from population growth coupled with in-adequate non-agricultural employment growth, can help to explain declining wages, but not declining employment. In a context of increased labor supply, the latter can only be explained by contraction in labor demand. Three alternative scenarios are shown in Figure 5.3. Figure 5.3(a) depicts the effect of population growth alone, with no shift in demand for labor: the wage falls from *w* to *w'* and employment increases from *L* to *L'*. Figure 5.3(b) shows the Hayami-Ruttan scenario, in which labor demand grows too slowly to prevent a wage decline. Compared to the stagnant-demand situation, the wage decline is smaller and the employment increase larger. Figure 5.3(c) depicts the combined effect of increased labor supply and decreased labor demand. In this case, the wage decline is larger and the employment increase smaller than in the first two scenarios. If the contraction in demand for labor is strong enough, it is even possible that total employment will *decline*, despite the increase in labor supply, as shown in the figure.

In Philippine rice agriculture, employment increased in the early years of the green revolution, but then it declined. By the mid-1980s, employment per hectare fell to mid-1960s levels, and in some places it may have fallen even lower. The employment growth in the early years is consistent with the population-driven wage declines depicted in Figures 5.3(a) and 5.3(b). However, the employment declines in the later years *can only be explained by a reduction in labor demand*, as depicted in Figure 5.3(c), a reduction so sharp as to more than offset the employment-increasing effect of supply-driven wage declines.

Beginning in 1966, researchers from the International Rice Research Institute surveyed a number of rice-producing households in Central Luzon and in Laguna province on a regular basis. The resulting panel data provide the most detailed information available on employment trends in Philippine rice agriculture. The data indicate that total employment per hectare of wet-season rice rose until the mid-1970s. Thereafter, employment declined. By 1986, labor use in Central Luzon had fallen to almost the 1966 level; in Laguna, labor use fell below the 1966 level as early as 1978.[65] In both cases, employment displayed an inverted U-shaped trend, as depicted in Figure 5.4. The IRRI data also reveal the increasing substitution of hired labor for family labor discussed above: family labor declined steadily, while hired labor rose and then declined. Other data sources indicate that the decline in employment was more pronounced for women than for men.[66]

In some places, these bleak employment trends were partially offset by increased cropping intensity. In the Central Luzon sample, for example, double-cropping of rice rose from 19 per cent of rice area in 1966 to more than 50 per cent after 1979, an increase which Cordova, Otsuka, and Gascon (1988, p. 4) attribute to the opening of the Pantabangan irrigation system in Nueva Ecija and to the introduction of non-photosensitive, quick-maturing varieties. In the country as a whole, however, gross rice acreage also displayed an inverted-U trend as shown in Figure 3.1(a). By the mid-1980s, Philippine rice acreage was about the same as the early 1960s. Declines in employment per hectare thus were not offset by increases in cultivated area.

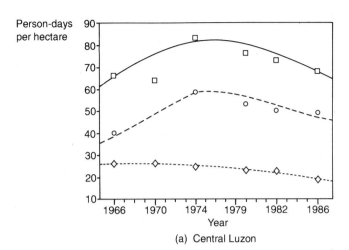

(a) Central Luzon

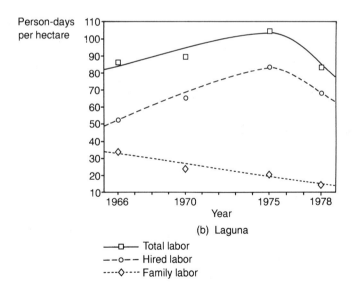

(b) Laguna

———□——— Total labor
——o—— Hired labor
----◇---- Family labor

Source: Based upon data reported by Cordova (1979) and Cordova, Otsuka, and Gascon (1988).

Figure 5.4:   Trends in Labor Use in Rice Production, 1966 – 1986

The employment trends reported in Figure 5.4 were not unique to the Philippines. Reviewing evidence from many Asian countries, Jayasuriya and Shand (1986) distinguish two phases of the green revolution. During the first, employment rose due to greater crop care activity and bigger harvests. During the second phase, however, initial employment gains were eroded by labor-displacing technological change.

Three technological changes contributed to labor displacement in Philippine rice agriculture in the 1970s and 1980s. The first was the mechanization of land preparation, in which water buffalos were replaced by tractors and two-wheeled power tillers. The second was the shift from manual weeding to the use of chemical herbicides and the associated shift from transplanting to direct seeding, which had especially serious impacts on female employment.[67] The third was the introduction of light threshing machines.

When such labor-saving technological changes occur in response to rising real wages, they can be viewed as a sign of progress. In Philippine rice agriculture, however, labor displacement occurred not at time of rising wages, but in a period of falling wages. Labor was not pulled from rice agriculture by more remunerative employment in other sectors. It was pushed out.

Why did labor-saving technological change occur in a setting of low and declining real wages? One possibility is that the new technology was simply more efficient, allowing producers to cut costs by substituting machines and chemicals for labor. The fact that farmers adopted the labor-displacing technologies suggests that this was true insofar as their *private* costs were concerned, but this does not mean that the labor-displacing technologies were efficient from a *social* standpoint. Three factors contributed to a divergence between private and social costs: (1) the enforcement problems inherent in the wage mode of employment; (2) capital subsidies from the government and international agencies; and (3) the external costs of pollution.

Labor control problems arise from the opposing interests of wage laborers and their employers. If the employer pays by the day or hour, he purchases time but not effort. The extraction of labor from the laborer requires supervision, which is costly. The profit-maximizing employer spends time or money on supervision up to the point where the resulting marginal gain in worker effort is worth the marginal cost.[68] If the employer pays on a piece-rate basis, he must guard against malfeasance, such as the pilfering of grain at harvest time, again incurring the associated enforcement costs. In addition to these problems of control of the individual laborer, the employer faces the problem of controlling the laborers as a group, since they may band together to bargain, to strike, or even to challenge the existing distribution of property rights.

Such problems became increasingly prevalent in Philippine rice agriculture as hired labor replaced family labor. Under the impact of the green revolution and land reform, as discussed above, some landlords ejected their tenants and shifted to wage-based cultivation, and leaseholders and amortizing owners increasingly relied on hired labor. Fegan (1979, p. 87) remarks, 'The tenant farmer today is, in most households, the only member to do farm work, and that is reduced to plowing, harrowing and supervising'. In some ways, the new employer-laborer relations resemble the patron-client ties between landlord and sharecropper in earlier generations. For example, the ability of landless laborers to bargain over wages is often limited by their dependence on employers for access to houselots.[69] Tensions between them, and the associated problems of labor control, are by no means absent, however, any more than they were absent from landlord-tenant relations in the old days.

The labor-control rationale helps to explain why larger rice farms in the Philippines tend to mechanize more than smaller farms.[70] The larger the farm, the more serious the labor control problem, not only because more laborers require more supervision, but also because the willingness of the laborer to expend effort in the absence of supervision may diminish as the social distance between the laborer and employer increases.[71] In addition, smaller farms rely more on family labor, which may 'cost' less than hired labor for various reasons, including the fact that people prefer to work on their own land.[72]

It is possible, then, for mechanization to be profitable on wage-labor farms and, at the same time, unprofitable on family-labor farms. The 'efficiency' of mechanization can thus hinge upon the mode of employment. Compared to cultivation by means of family labor – that is, to a situation in which there is no dichotomy between ownership of land and labor on it – wage labor and mechanization *both* may be costlier, less efficient ways to produce rice.

The use of threshing machines as a debt collection mechanism by the new commercial elite represents a variant on this labor-control rationale. Here, too, mechanization arises from the enforcement problems inherent in a dichotomy between ownership of the means of agricultural production (here broadened to include inputs and credit) and the tiller of the soil.

Capital subsidies have also encouraged labor-displacing technological change in Philippine agriculture. The private cost of farm machinery has been cheapened through government policies, including subsidized credit, overvalued exchange rates, and direct subsidies on the equipment itself. These price distortions have been encouraged in no small measure by the credit, foreign exchange, and imports provided by international agencies. For example, Barker (1978, p. 145) notes that, 'Despite the questionable social benefits of tractorization, the World Bank has loaned over half a billion dollars to Asian countries in the past decade for mechanization, and has done so at well below the interest rate for investment loans from local sources'.[73] Insofar as larger farms have preferential access to government subsidies, these too contribute to the positive correlation between farm size and mechanization.

Negative externalities drive a further wedge between private and social costs, one especially relevant to the increasing use of chemical herbicides in Philippine rice farming. Herbicides not only displace labor previously employed in manual weeding, but also allow direct seeding to replace much more labor-intensive transplantation, since manual weed control is difficult in direct-seeded fields (Cordova, Otsuka, and Gascon, 1988). The extent of the resulting contamination of fish and other aquatic life, which form an important part of the Filipino diet, has not been documented, but this a matter for serious concern.[74]

Labor control problems, capital subsidies, and the neglect of negative externalities combined to bias technological change in a labor-displacing direction. An additional source of bias came from abroad, where some of the labor-displacing technologies originated. The very large investments required for herbicide research and development, for example, would not have been profitable in labor-abundant countries such as the Philippines (Jayasuriya and Shand, 1986, p. 424). Such investments were profitable, however, in the United States and Japan, not only because labor is relatively scarce there, but also because rice is grown in these countries with substantial government subsidies and tariff protection, and the external costs of pollution are again neglected by private producers. The introduction of these herbicides into Philippine rice agriculture represents an international transfer not only of technology, but also of the impact of other countries' price distortions on the direction of technological change.

Was the green revolution in Philippine rice agriculture labor displacing, contrary to the expectations of its architects? The answer depends on whether or not we define the new rice technology to include mechanization and herbicides. If restricted by definition to the new varieties, water control, fertilizer, and pesticides for insect and disease control, then there can be little doubt that the new rice technology was labor-absorbing, as borne out by Philippine experience up to the mid-1970s. If, however, the new technology is defined to include tractors, power tillers, herbicides, and mechanical threshers, then its net effect was labor-displacing. In some places, such as Laguna, this labor displacement was so great that per-hectare employment declined even in the face of increased labor supply which, *ceteris paribus*, would have increased employment as depicted in Figure 5.3(a).

There is no inherent *technological* linkage between the new fertilizer-responsive varieties on the one hand and mechanization and herbicides on the other. Yet in Philippine rice agriculture, both arrived together or in quick succession, bearing out Griffin's (1978b, p. 140) observation that 'modernization in the Philippines and the rest of contemporary Asia is a seamless web; tractors and modern varieties are politically linked'. The political linkage operates at both the macro level of government policy and the micro level of agrarian relations. Insofar as the Philippine government responded to the interests of rice producers, as opposed to consumers, it responded to the interests of the new rural elites, who were the primary beneficiaries of both the new rice technology narrowly defined and the labor-displacing technologies. At the same time, given the initial context of a very inegalitarian agrarian structure, the income streams generated by the new varieties predictably sharpened the dichotomy between ownership of the means of agricultural production and agricultural labor, enhancing the private attractions of labor-saving technologies.

In short, labor displacement in Philippine rice agriculture was an outcome not of the new seed-fertilizer technology itself, but rather of the political and economic setting into which it was introduced.

CONCLUSIONS

'It took both time and experience', Karl Marx wrote more than a century ago, 'before the workpeople learnt to distinguish between machinery and its employment by capital, and to direct their attacks, not against the material instruments of production, but against the mode in which they are used'.[75]

Something similar could be said of the new seed-fertilizer technology in Philippine rice agriculture. Almost since its inception in the mid-1960s, the 'green revolution' has been assailed by critics in the Philippines and elsewhere not only for failing to improve the living standards of the poor, but for actually contributing to their further decline. The technology itself can be criticized on the grounds that it provides only temporary escape from the hydraulic constraint on rice output, and that it does so at the cost of significant environmental risks. The distributional impact of the green revolution hinges, however, not upon inherent features of the technology itself, but rather upon the social 'mode' in which it is used. If rice farmers receive declining real incomes owing to falling rice prices, the explanation must be sought in the inadequate growth of effective demand for food, and in the political objectives of government price policies. If those gains which do accrue to producers are captured by a new rural elite, while the real incomes of those who labor in the fields decline, the reason lies in the social relations which govern production and exchange. If wages and employment for agricultural laborers fall, as the increased labor requirements of the new seed-fertilizer technology are offset by labor-displacing machines and herbicides, the blame lies with the constellation of circumstances which make the latter privately profitable.

The green revolution went through two distinct stages in the Philippines. In the first stage, aggregate producer income rose. In the second, rice prices fell, chemical input prices rose, and aggregate producer income declined. In the first stage, the new rural elite pursued rice production by means of hired labor. In the second, their focus shifted to commercial activities. In the first stage, employment per hectare rose. In the second, it declined. The watershed between these two stages came roughly in the mid-1970s.

In the absence of reliable data on income distribution, we can venture only an informed hypothesis as to the net effect of the two stages of the green revolution in rice-producing areas. Average incomes in the rice sector probably rose in the first stage and fell in the second. In both stages, income distribution probably underwent a process of weak polarization: in the first stage, the income gains of the rich exceeded those of the poor; in the second, the losses of the poor exceeded those of the rich. The overall effect of these successive periods of weak polarization was probably strong polarization, such that in the mid-1980s the rural rich wound up absolutely richer than in the early 1960s, and the rural poor absolutely poorer.

Linkages between income and power played an important role in this outcome. The rising relative incomes of the rich in the first period translated into increased power. This made them better able to prevail in contests over rights to land, water, and other endowments; to impose negative externalities on others; to exercise price-making power in credit, inputs, and rice markets; and to influence government policies and their implementation. These advantages in turn helped to cushion the rural elite from declining producer incomes in the second period, enabling them to push the losses on to the poor.

Although technological change contributed to this outcome, it did so only in combination with the initial distribution of wealth and power, population pressure against the means of employment, and the government's agrarian reform program. In warning against 'single-factor explanations' of changes in income distribution, Hayami and Ruttan (1985, pp. 330, 344) observe that the impact of technological change 'is a function both of the character of the technology and of the economic and institutional environment into which it is introduced'.

In the Philippine case, the net result was that the rural poor became poorer. This in turn had negative demand-side effects on both agricultural and industrial growth. The declining purchasing power of the rural poor helps to explain the negative *ex post* income elasticity of demand for rice. At the same time, their lack of purchasing power limited the home market for basic consumer goods.[76]

As a *technology*, the green revolution had much to recommend it. The highly fertilizer-responsive varieties increased production of a basic food staple which forms an important part of the diet of the poor. In the absence of mechanization and herbicides, which were not *necessary* components of the new technology, the green revolution would have increased demand for labor. Perhaps these gains could have been achieved with less reduction in genetic diversity, and with less reliance on agrochemicals. Clearly there is scope for further agricultural research oriented to the enhancement of biological nitrogen fixation, the breeding of pest-resistant varieties, and diversification of the varietal mix. It is doubtful, however, that comparable output growth could have been achieved at the time without some of these costs. The seed-fertilizer technology was not perfect, but the claim that its potential benefits outweighed its costs cannot be dismissed lightly.

As a *development strategy*, however, the green revolution in the Philippines was deeply flawed. The insistence that aggregate food output was the 'only valid measure' of the strategy's success revealed the limitations of the technocratic vision of development. Growth in rice production may have been a necessary condition for improvement in the well-being of the country's poor majority, but clearly it was not sufficient. In the Philippines, the new technology was introduced into a setting marked by profound inequalities of wealth and power at both the national and village levels. That it produced inegalitarian results in this setting is not surprising.

In retrospect, the new rice technology bought valuable time for the Philippines. For two decades, it eased the constraints on rice production, providing a breathing space during which the country could have addressed the crucial underlying issues of water control development, land reform, and the redistribution of wealth so as to create a basis for sustained and equitable growth. The tragedy is that the opportunity was squandered.

NOTES

1.   Much ink has been spilled in attempts to define 'power'. For present purposes, Bartlett's (1989, p. 30) definition is useful: power is 'the ability of one actor to alter the decisions made and/or welfare experienced by

another actor relative to the choices that would have been made and/or the welfare that would have been experienced had the first actor not existed or acted'. This definition is broad enough to encompass the three dimensions of power discussed by Lukes (1974): the power to affect choice, to set the agenda, and to shape values.

2.   Of course, welfare is not simply a matter of absolute income, and if our definition of welfare puts enough weight on power it is possible that the welfare of the poor will decline despite their income gain. Absolute income is, however, an indisputably important factor in well-being, particularly when the people in question lack basic necessities of life and live in an exchange economy. For a discussion of broader notions of individual welfare, see Sen (1984) and Sen *et al.* (1987).

3.   For a lucid discussion of resulting impoverishment of economic analysis, see Bartlett (1989).

4.   In 1981–83, Central Luzon accounted for 14 per cent of the country's rice area and 20 per cent of rice output (calculated from Bureau of Agricultural Economics data).

5.   A 1954 law set legal shares at 70–30 in favor of the tenant on first class land and 75–25 on second class land, with all expenses born by the tenant (Fegan, 1979, pp. 297, 319–20). Pahilanga-de los Reyes and Lynch (1972, p. 16) report that landlords in Nueva Ecija in 1971 stated that more than half of share tenancies were on a 50–50 basis, with the remainder according a larger share to the tenant. Traditional 50–50 divisions are also mentioned by Kerkvliet (1977, pp. 12–13), Wolters (1984, pp. 24, 86), and Fegan (1982a, p. 105). Within a single Central Luzon village in the early 1970s, Fegan (1979, p. 311) found divisions ranging from 50–50 through 60–40 to 70–30 in favor of the tenant on irrigated land and 75–25 on non-irrigated land. Divisions in which more than half the crop went to the landlord are reported by Kerkvliet (1977, p. 15).

6.   For a detailed account of tenant stratagems for understatement of harvests, see Fegan (1979, pp. 259–73). The margin of understatement depended, among other things, on the degree of landlord supervision. Fegan (1979, p. 306) mentions instances in which nominal shares were 60–40 but real shares, allowing for concealment, were about 70–30. See also Pahilanga-de los Reyes and Lynch (1972, p. 21) and Fegan (1972b, p. 140).

7.   Fegan (1979, p. 3). Fegan (p. 302) cites the case of an exceptionally production-oriented hacienda manager who made a policy of leaving 15 per cent of the net harvest to the tenant, whatever the debt outstanding, so as to leave some incentive for the tenant to work hard.

8.   Wolters (1984, p. 25). See also Lewis (1971, Chapter 11) and Pahilanga-de los Reyes and Lynch (1972).

9.   Roosevelt (1934, p. 200) cited by Pelzer (1945, p. 95).

10. In posing the question, 'Why do we not try to walk off without paying after a taxi ride?', Basu (1984, pp. 5–8) similarly identifies the fundamental importance of norms in shaping economic behavior. If, in the

absence of norms, the 'rational' rider pays only for fear that the driver would otherwise assault him, then why does the driver not threaten to assault the rider even when he pays, so as to extract double the fare? Basu answers that the proper fare is offered and accepted because both parties act according to social norms.

11. See Bardhan (1984, Ch. 12) and Basu (1984, Ch. 12).
12. For further details, see sources cited by Kerkvliet (1977, p. 22). Hayami and Kikuchi (1982, p. 74) state that such land grabbing was more pervasive in the frontier areas of inner Central Luzon than in the coastal region around Manila Bay, since power was more unevenly distributed and indigenous property rights were less clearly established in the frontier areas. See also McLennan (1982, pp. 71–7).
13. Quoted by McLennan (1969, p. 674).
14. Kerkvliet (1977, p. 25). In some provinces absenteeism in both senses was not new; see McLennan (1982, p. 75).
15. Takahashi (1969, p. 71) reports that in central Luzon such overseers were termed *katiwala* and *namumuisan*, respectively.
16. See, for example, Kerkvliet (1977, Ch. 1); Fegan (1979, 1982); McLennan (1982); and Wolters (1984).
17. For an account of the rise and fall of the Huks, see Kerkvliet (1977).
18. Jose Crisol in a 1969 interview with Kerkvliet (1974, p. 289). The reform package included resettlement of Huks on 'unsettled' lands in Mindanao. Although this program was highly publicized, Kerkvliet (1977, p. 239) reports that only 950 families, most of whom in fact had not been active in the Huk movement, received land under the program. For discussion of other reforms, see Kerkvliet (1977, pp. 198–9, 238–40) and references therein.
19. This situation is described by Fegan (1972b, p. 139).
20. The situation described here is reportedly common, for example, among amortizing owners (ex-tenants under the Marcos land reform discussed below) in some rice areas (interview with Corazon Soliman, director of the Agency for Community Educational Services, Manila, June 1987).
21. Fegan (1979, pp. 251–2) points out that while the farmer is obliged by convention to open the harvest to all teams and individuals who appear at the starting time, he can turn away those who arrive late: 'Thus a farmer can reward allies, punish enemies, and turn aside strangers by advising secretly only the heads of favored harvest teams of the day and time reaping is to begin'.
22. See Kikuchi and Hayami (1980, pp. 32–5); Ledesma (1982, p. 7); Bautista, Thiesenhusen, and King (1983, p. 78); and Fegan (1979, p. 87).
23. Fegan (1972b, p. 136). Takahashi's explanation in terms of reduction of landlord shares is not wholly convincing. Fegan (p. 140) notes that the same goal can be accomplished by alternative means, such as the *kikbak* (kickback) system in which the tenant and overseer 'collude to understate the harvest to the owner in such a way that the tenant is guaranteed some retained rice not seizable for debt'. Moreover, Hayami and Kikuchi

(1982, p. 119) report that 'labor exchange with wage payments' has persisted after the conversion from share tenancy to fixed-rent leasehold. They attribute this to 'social inertia' and to a desire to circumvent the 'social compulsion within the community to employ landless members', an explanation rather inconsistent with their discussion of the rapid transition from *hunusan* to *gama* harvesting arrangements.

24. Fegan here is referring to off-farm work by tenant farmers, but elsewhere he remarks that the landless likewise 'exploit diversified and essentially incentive-paid personal niches' (Fegan, 1979, p. 360).

25. Kikuchi (1983, p. 61). For reviews of the growth of landlessness, see also Makil and Fermin (1978), Rosenberg and Rosenberg (1980), Aguilar (1981), and Ledesma (1982).

26. Interview with Francisco Lara and Cynthia Hallare, Philippine Peasant Institute, Quezon City, January 1989.

27. See, for example, Hayami and Kikuchi (1982, p. 122) and Kikuchi (1983, p. 60).

28. Hayami and Kikuchi (1982, pp. 110, 129) report subdivision in the Laguna village. Fegan (1979, pp. 380–1) reports that the prevailing pattern among tenants in a Bulacan village is ultimogeniture, in which the farm is passed to the youngest child. On gender differences in inheritance customs, see Quisumbing (1991).

29. In theory, ejected leaseholding tenants were entitled to a 'disturbance allowance' equivalent to five years' rent. See Ishikawa (1970, p. 29) and Kerkvliet (1974, p. 293).

30. For details, see Kerkvliet (1974), Overholt (1976), Rocamora and O'Connor (1977) Po (1981), Wurfel (1983), Mangahas (1985), and Hayami, Quisumbing, and Adriano (1987).

31. *Daily Express* (Manila), 23 October 1973, quoted by Kerkvliet (1974, p. 187).

32. Fegan (1979, p. 287) comments: 'This evasion is made easy by the chaotic, partial, and out of date land title records in the Bureau of Lands in Manila, and in each municipality, and by venal officials who allow landowners to tamper with land records to back-date fake division among heirs. In some cases the records continue to show hacienda lands as belonging to individuals who have been dead for a generation or more'.

33. See Fegan (1979, pp. 244, 324) for an example. Banzon-Bautista (1989, p. 146) reports a case in Pampanga in which a hacienda owner responded to demands for an end to share tenancy by removing a pump which had drawn water from a reservoir. The villagers countered by making the reservoir into a communal fishpond.

34. These and other stratagems are enumerated by Fegan (1979, pp. 243–4, 323–9; 1982b, pp. 4–5).

35. Department of Agrarian Reform Memorandum from Secretary Conrado F. Estrella to All Regional Directors, 9 January 1973, and Circulars No. 2 and 2-A from Secretary Estrella to All Regional Directors *et al.*, 14 and 15 February 1973; quoted by Kerkvliet (1974, p. 293).

36. Interview with Geraldo Bulatao, Assistant Secretary, Department of Agrarian Reform, Quezon City, January 1989.
37. CLT coverage from NEDA (1986b, p. 96). Mangahas (1985, p. 219) reports leasehold coverage of 526,000 hectares in December 1979. As of September 1988, according to data furnished to the author by the Department of Agrarian Reform, 562,030 hectares had been covered by Operation Leasehold. These may be overestimates, however. Other DAR data indicate that CLTs had been issued for only 470,639 hectares as of 30 June 1986, and that Certificates of Agricultural Leasehold had been issued for only 260,465 hectares as of 1988 (James Putzel, private communication). On regional variations in the implementation of land reform, see Kerkvliet (1990, pp. 31 ff. and Appendix Table B. 1).
38. These include cases in which land rights are used as collateral for a loan and seized on default, and usufructuary mortgages (called *prenda* in parts of Luzon and *alili* in the Visayas and Mindanao) in which lender acquires cultivation rights from the time of the loan until it is repaid (interview with Francisco Lara and Cynthia Hallare, Philippine Peasant Institute, Quezon City, January 1989). In a Bataan barrio in January 1989, cultivators told me that the going rate for usufructuary mortgages was 20,000 pesos/hectare. The acquisition of land via mortgages has long historical roots in the Philippines; see Umehara (1974, p. 6) and Hayami and Kikuchi (1982, pp. 71–2). For a discussion of recent mortgage arrangements in Central Luzon, see Fegan (1982b, p. 10). Floro (1986, pp. 257–71) presents evidence that 'farmer-lenders' in Nueva Ecija, Iloilo, and Cagayan, deliberately seek to 'maximize default' rather than interest returns, so as to accumulate land put up as collateral.
39. *Bulletin Today* (Manila), 19 October 1980; quoted by Wurfel (1983, p. 9).
40. Statement of Frederick Schieck, Acting Assistant Administrator, Bureau of Asia, Agency for International Development, before the House Foreign Affairs Subcommittee on Asia and Pacific Affairs, 31 March 1981; quoted by Wurfel (1983, p. 10).
41. Hayami (1987) makes this argument, adding that 'While the possibility has been lost to climb up the agricultural ladder, the possibility to drop down has been left open'.
42. Griffin (1974, p. 54), citing Huke and Duncan (1969).
43. 'Farms' here meant operational holdings of tenants and owner-cultivators. Roughly 90 per cent were non-owners; over time, the predominant form of tenure shifted from share tenancy to leaseholds. For details, see Herdt (1987, pp. 332–3).
44. See pp. 75–6, above.
45. Lipton and Longhurst (1989, p. 158). Ruttan (1977, p. 19) concludes that in general, 'The contribution of the new seed-fertilizer technology to the widening of regional income disparities has apparently been greater than its impact on disparities in income within communities and regions'. See also David and Otsuka (1987).

46. See Otsuka (1987); Hayami (1987, p. 9); and Fegan (1989a, p. 134).
47. Hayami and Kikuchi (1982, pp. 116–17). In 1975 pesos (using regional rice prices as a deflator) ownership titles fell from 60,000 to 15,600 pesos/hectare, while the real price of tenancy titles more than doubled from 1,852 to 4,068 pesos/hectare. The existence of markets in informal tenancy rights was reported prior to the Marcos land reform by Takahashi (1969, pp. 79–81).
48. The phrase 'intermediate landlords' is used by Hayami and Kikuchi (1982, p. 122). Similarly, Fegan (1979, p. 184) describes the tenant who cultivates by means of hired labor as 'an entrepreneurial farmer, or a sort of intermediary landlord'.
49. Hayami (1987, p. 11). In addition to this 'semi-tenant' type of *kasugpong* contract, Hayami describes two others: a 'permanent laborer' type in which the worker is typically a young single male who receives room and board from the employer, and a 'semi-attached laborer' type in which the laborer lives separately and can engage in casual labor outside the employer's farm.
50. Fegan (1989a, p. 135). See also David (1979), Esguerra (1981), and Lim (1986). For a somewhat more sanguine view, see Grace (1978).
51. See Lynch (1976) and David (1983, pp. 40–8).
52. Government data on formal agricultural credit (including non-rice crops) indicate that in 1967, farms smaller than three hectares, which accounted for 73 per cent of all Philippine farms, received only two per cent of the credit; farms three hectares and larger, which accounted for 27 per cent of all farms, received 98 per cent. In 1974, at the height of Masagana 99, farms 3 hectares and larger continued to receive 80 per cent of the credit (David, 1979, pp. 26–9).
53. Esguerra (1981), cited by David (1983, p. 48).
54. See, for example, Fegan (1982b) and Bello *et al.* (1982, p. 75).
55. See, for example, Abdullah (1980). Hayami and Kikuchi (1982, p. 78) compare the former rice haciendas of Central Luzon to the erstwhile *zamindaris* of Bengal.
56. See Fegan (1979, pp. 476–84; 1989b, pp. 165–6), who refers to this as an 'establishment fund'. Caldwell (1982, p. 69) describes similar 'sibling assistance chains' in Africa.
57. Umehara (1983, Table 9, p. 36). The remainder represented the shares of laborers and banks.
58. On the enforcement rationale behind *tilyadoras*, see Hayami and Kikuchi (1982, pp. 83–91). On the enforcement rationale behind the light axial-flow thresher, see Fegan (1989b, pp. 165–9). See also Fegan (1982b, pp. 19–23) for a similar analysis of the possibility of mechanized reaping.
59. The correlation coefficient between 1966/68 wages reported in Table 5.1 and the 1965 percentage of (rural and urban) households living in poverty reported in Table 2.13 was $r = -0.27$. The correlation between 1984–86 wages and 1985 rural poverty was $r = -0.71$.

60. The correlation between wage and yield levels is $r = 0.16$ in the mid-1960s and $r = 0.48$ in the mid-1980s.
61. The correlation between the wage and yield trends reported in Tables 3.3 and 5.1 is $r = -0.64$. If the Mindanao regions are excluded grounds that the accuracy of their reported rice yields in the 1980s is questionable (see p. 92, note 9), the trend correlation remains negative but not significantly different from zero: $r = -0.13$.
62. The correlation between the HYV share reported in Table 3.3 and the 1984–86 wage levels reported in Table 5.1 is $r = 0.37$; the correlation between the HYV share and the wage trend is $r = 0.67$.
63. See, for example, Kikuchi and Hayami (1983), Wolters (1984, p. 138), Orden (1987), and Otsuka, Cordova and David (1987).
64. Multiple regression analysis of inter-regional variation in wage trends, using the data reported in Tables 3.3 and 5.1, gives the following result (t-ratios in parentheses):

$$DW = -1.3 - 0.039 \ W67 - 0.048 \ DY + 3.9 \ HYV$$
$$ (0.8) \ (2.8) (4.1) (2.5)$$
$$\bar{R}^2 = 0.84; \ F(3,5) = 15.2; \ n=9$$

where DW = the 1966–86 trend in real wages for agricultural laborers in *palay* production; $W67$ = the average 1966/68 wage; DY = the 1962–83 rice yield trend; and HYV = the percentage of rice area sown to HYVs in 1981/83. Dropping either DY or HYV from the equation does not dramatically alter the estimated coefficients on the remaining variables, nor does the exclusion of the two (consolidated) Mindanao regions.
65. The data are reported by Cordova (1979) and Cordova, Otsuka, and Gascon (1988). The decline in employment per hectare in Laguna continued in subsequent years; see Kikuchi, Huysman, and Res (1983, p. 8), who also report an inverted-U employment trend in an Iloilo village.
66. See Res (1985), who reports gender differences in employment trends in rice farming in a village in Iloilo; see also Fegan (1989b, pp. 171–3).
67. On gender differences in employment in rice production activities, see Res (1985) and Fegan (1979, pp. 218–23, 457–9).
68. The labor extraction problem is generally neglected in economic theory. For attempts to redress this neglect, see Bowles (1985) and Bowles and Edwards (1985, pp. 155–73).
69. See Fegan (1979, pp. 89, 370, 424–6).
70. For statistical findings based on a sample of Central Luzon farms, see Cordova, Otsuka, and Gascon (1988, p. 13 and Table 5).
71. For discussion, see Boyce (1987, pp. 39–40, 213).
72. For example, a person may prefer to work on his or her own land for a marginal product of 20 pesos/day, even though the going wage is 30 pesos/day. For discussion, see Sen (1975, pp. 17–28, 146–53).
73. For a review of credit programs supporting agricultural mechanization in the Philippines, see Reyes and Agabin (1985). World Bank loans for

agricultural credit in the Philippines primarily supported tractorization in sugar lands, as discussed below in Chapter 7. In a study of rice threshing machines, Duff (1986, p. 22) notes that 'policy instruments have tended to subsidize threshers in the Philippines to a considerably greater extent than in Thailand'. He concludes, however, that the net social benefit was positive. This of course raises the question of why subsidies were necessary.

74. Herbicides registered for use on rice in the Philippines include 2,4-D, bentazon, butachlor, hexazinone, MCPA, molinate, MSMA, nitrofen, propanil, thiobencarb, and trifluralin (registered with the Fertilizer and Pesticide Authority as of 1980, as reported in Farmers Assistance Board, 1982, Annex A). For studies of bioaccumulation of herbicides in Japanese rice agriculture, see Lee *et al.* (1976) and Ishibashi *et al.* (1983). In addition, herbicides are sometimes contaminated with toxic by-products of their manufacture; see, for example, Henig (1979).

75. Marx (1867: 1967 edn, Vol. 1, p. 429).

76. An extra peso of income can be divided among savings (s), consumption of imports (m), consumption of domestically-produced food (f), and consumption of domestically-produced non-food items (n). Denoting the rural rich by the subscript 'r' and the rural poor by the subscript 'p', the following relations are likely: $s_r > s_p$; $m_r > m_p$; $f_r < f_p$. If the poor's higher marginal propensity to consume food is outweighed by their lower propensities to save and to consume imports, then the poor have a higher marginal propensity to spend on domestically-produced non-food items: n_r $(= 1 - s_r - m_r - f_r) < n_p$ $(= 1 - s_p - m_p - f_p)$. For discussion, see Ranis and Stewart (1987, pp. 149–151). Whether the latter relation holds in the Philippines is an empirical question which does not yet appear to have been answered.

6 Farming for the World Market

INTRODUCTION

In the Philippines, as in many Asian, African, and Latin American countries, export agriculture historically has been the single most important locus of interaction with the world economy. In the mid-1960s, sugar, coconuts, and forestry accounted for 80 per cent of Philippine export earnings. Further growth in agro-forestry exports was to be a central element of the country's economic development strategy under Marcos. Agriculture Secretary Arturo R. Tanco, Jr., enumerated three principal goals for the 1970s: 'the further development of our traditional exports, the discovery and promotion of new agricultural exports, and the substitution of imports by local production'.[1] Similarly, the World Bank (1973, Vol. 1, p. 19) placed 'expansion of agricultural exports' alongside foodgrain self-sufficiency as major goals for Philippine agriculture.

In the simplified world of economics textbooks, international trade has an unambiguously positive impact on both trading partners. By specializing in the production of commodities in which it has a comparative advantage, each country attains a higher national income than would prevail in the absence of trade. Certain individuals or groups, with skills or assets tied to the production of uncompetitive commodities, may lose from trade, but the winners could compensate the losers and still reap a net gain. In the language of welfare economics, international trade provides a 'potential Pareto improvement'.

The experience of Philippine export agriculture reveals the shortcomings of this textbook picture. The country undoubtedly has a comparative advantage in the production of several export crops. However, three major issues absent from the comparative advantage parable emerge forcefully in the Philippine case.

First, world markets are neither perfectly competitive nor static. Prices for Philippine agricultural exports reflect the protectionist policies of various governments, the preferential trade agreements among them, and the exercise of market power by transnational firms. Prices change through time due to changes in these institutions and other shifts in supply and demand.

The terms of trade for Philippine agricultural and forestry exports – that is, the ratio of their prices to those of the commodities the country imported – declined markedly between the early 1960s and the late 1980s. At the same time, prices of several key exports were highly unstable, transmitting gyrations in world markets to the domestic economy.

Second, the textbook parable neglects the interactions between income and power which shape the distributional impact of export agriculture. If all the relevant transactions were voluntary – the textbook ideal – then one might presume that decisions to grow crops or cut trees for export could only improve the well-being of the parties involved. If, for example, individual Filipino farmers freely chose to grow export crops, or freely chose to lease or sell their land to others to do so, then one might infer that they thereby became better-off. Likewise, if workers freely chose to sell their labor to agro-exporters, then one might infer that they found this preferable to the alternatives. The assumption, of course, is that the alternatives are set exogenously: export agriculture merely expands the range of choice, and never constricts it. In practice, the pursuit of self-interest often is not confined to the benign forms assumed in the fairy tale of perfect competition. Many crucial transactions in the history of Philippine export agriculture have been far from voluntary: examples include the forcible appropriation of land, debt bondage of cultivators and laborers, and political seizure of control over marketing channels. Moreover, export agriculture channelled the country's political economy along a particular historical path: past choices, whether voluntary or not, constrained the range of subsequent alternatives.

A third issue emerges most vividly in the forestry sector. Exports of logs and lumber have given rise to large 'external costs' in soil erosion, watershed degradation, climate disruption, the reduction of biological diversity, and the loss of future income in the forestry sector itself. In a textbook world, such negative externalities are efficiently minimized by government intervention: unlike self-interested individuals, the government weighs the full social costs against the benefits to be gained by cutting the forest. In practice, the government's scales are frequently tipped by the balance of political power. The costs and benefits of activities which cause environmental degradation generally are distributed unevenly, both across individuals and over time, creating winners as well as losers. In the Philippines, as elsewhere, govern- ment policy has often accorded disproportionate weight to the interests of the winners.

This chapter begins an examination of these issues, by introducing the main agro-forestry exports of the Philippines and situating them within the context of their world markets. Chapter 7 describes the relations of pro- duction and exchange which govern the distribution of income from export agriculture. Chapter 8 then explores the political economy of Philippine deforestation.

AGRICULTURAL AND FORESTRY EXPORTS

The year 1962 was an auspicious one for Philippine export agriculture. Devaluation and decontrol of foreign exchange brought windfall profits to agro-exporters and were widely seen as a political triumph for the 'sugar bloc' whose economic fortunes had been compressed by the import substitution policies of the 1950s. The Philippines, the world's second largest sugar exporter at the time, received a substantial increase in its US sugar import quota after that country banned imports from the world's top sugar exporter, Cuba (Pineda-Ofreneo, 1985, p. 6). In addition, the year 1962 saw the introduction of large ocean tankers which could carry coconut oil, a technological breakthrough which cut shipping costs and set the stage for the Philippines, the world's leading coconut exporter, to move up the processing ladder from the export of copra (dried coconut meat from which oil is extracted) to the export of oil.[2]

These developments, coupled with the green revolution which saved the land frontier for non-rice uses, sparked rapid growth in the area under export crops. The acreage devoted to the two main traditional export crops, coconut and sugarcane, doubled by the mid-1970s. At the same time, bananas and pineapples emerged as important 'non-traditional' export crops.[3] Together, these four crops accounted for roughly two-fifths of the total value of agricultural output in the Philippines throughout the Marcos era (see Table 6.1). Along with forestry products, they accounted on average for 60 per cent of the country's total export earnings between 1962 and 1985, their share falling from 80 per cent in the early 1960s to 30 per cent in the early 1980s as a result of declining prices and export diversification (see Table 6.2).[4]

Coconut products were the single largest export of the Philippines in the Marcos era. Reflecting the importance of the crop in the minds of Philippine policy makers, Defense Minister Juan Ponce Enrile, a senior coconut industry official, predicted in 1980 that '25 per cent of Philippine growth in the next twenty to thirty years will come from coconuts'.[5] The Philippines accounts for more than half of world coconut exports. The country is sometimes termed the 'Saudi Arabia of coconut oil', a phrase which understates its share of the market, but at the same time overstates its market power, since this is severely constrained by the existence of natural and synthetic substitutes.

TABLE 6.1 *Area, Yield, Output, and Value of Major Export Crops, 1962–1985* [1]

Crop Variable	1962–66	1967–71	1972–76	1977–81	1982–85
Coconut [2]					
Area ('000 ha)	1475	1880	2253	2996	3210
Yield (mt/ha)	1.0	0.9	1.1	1.4	1.0
Output ('000 mt)	1523	1704	2461	4244	3264
Value (m pesos)	626	1053	2367	6513	8512
All-crop share (%) [3]	20.4	16.8	14.9	19.0	14.4
Sugarcane					
Area ('000 ha)	290	356	499	478	445
Yield (mt/ha)	7.0	6.7	6.6	6.9	7.2
Output ('000 mt)	1985	2386	3311	3267	3212
Value (m pesos)	497	1360	2716	5277	8632
All-crop share (%)	16.4	20.4	17.6	15.6	16.1
Bananas					
Area ('000 ha)	216	226	247	305	326
Yield (mt/ha)	3.0	3.7	5.8	11.3	11.9
Output ('000 mt)	641	845	1437	3447	3870
Value (m pesos)	49	409	999	1724	3062
All-crop share (%)	1.6	5.6	6.4	5.0	5.5
Pineapples					
Area ('000 ha)	25	28	30	53	60
Yield (mt/ha)	6.5	8.2	11.6	14.6	25.5
Output ('000 mt)	162	228	351	813	1523
Value (m pesos)	23	84	325	751	1634
All-crop share (%)	0.8	1.3	1.9	2.2	3.0

Abbreviations: ha = hectares, mt = metric tons, m = million

NOTES
1. Quinquennial averages.
2. Output in raw nuts.
3. Share in value of output of all crops.

SOURCES   NEDA (1976, pp. 134–53; 1986, pp. 266–75).

TABLE 6.2 *Exports of Major Agricultural and Forestry Products, 1962–1985* [1]
(US $ million f.o.b. value)

Product	1962–66	1967–71	1972–76	1977–81	1982–85
Coconut products:	240	216	443	851	614
Copra	153	107	148	101	13
Coconut oil	56	78	230	575	461
Other [2]	30	32	66	174	140
Sugar and sugar products	150	175	470	451	320
Bananas	0	5	49	98	122
Pineapple products	11	18	34	86	113
Forestry products	184	267	317	426	316
Logs	148	218	197	118	70
Lumber, plywood, & other	36	49	120	308	246
Total exports	724	973	2120	4537	5012
Share in total exports (%)					
Coconut	33.0	22.6	20.7	20.0	12.2
Sugar	21.0	18.0	21.5	10.1	6.4
Bananas	0.0	0.4	2.3	2.2	2.4
Pineapples	1.6	1.9	1.6	1.9	2.3
Forestry	25.2	27.9	16.0	9.6	6.3
Total share	80.8	70.8	62.1	43.8	29.5

NOTES
1. Quinquennial averages.
2. Desiccated coconut and copra meal or cake.

SOURCES NEDA (1976, p. 423; 1986, pp. 362–3)

Coconut production in the Philippines beyond domestic needs dates from 1642, when a Spanish edict required each 'indio' to plant 100–200 coconut trees to provide caulk and rigging for the colonizers' galleons. Large-scale copra exports began in the late nineteenth century, in response to demand from European and North American manufacturers of margarine and soap. The first mills for extraction of coconut oil in the Philippines were established early in the twentieth century. The United States became the largest market for Philippine coconut oil, and gave it preferential tariff treatment until 1974. Copra continued to predominate in trade with European countries, owing to tariffs on oil which were imposed to protect European millers.[6] After World War II, the primary uses of coconut oil in the world economy shifted from edible to non-edible industrial products, such as soap, detergents, cosmetics, explosives, and pharmaceuticals.[7]

The 1962 devaluation and consequent increase in the profitability of coconut exports stimulated rapid acreage growth. From one million hectares in the 1950s, the area planted to coconut rose to 2 million hectares by 1971, and to 3 million by 1979. Much of this growth occurred on the land frontier, notably on logged-over virgin lands in Mindanao (Tiglao, 1981, p. 58). Coconut yields stagnated, however, at about one metric ton per hectare (see Table 6.1), reflecting low input use and a lack of investment in the replanting of aging trees.[8]

Coconut yield stagnation is sometimes attributed to the low prices received by growers, but the fact that farmgate prices were attractive enough to stimulate acreage expansion suggests that the explanation lies elsewhere. One possible factor is inadequate investment in coconut research and extension. Hicks and McNicoll (1971, pp. 205–6) state that 'practically no basic research has been directed toward developing a higher yielding coconut palm'. They attribute this to the fact that, unlike other tree crops in tropical agriculture, coconuts 'have always been a smallholders' crop, and few growing interests are large enough to justify expensive research'. Precisely for this reason, however, most crop improvement research throughout the world is conducted by public sector institutions rather than by private growers. Relatively low investment in coconut research and extension in the Philippines may reflect the political weakness of small growers and other political priorities among the larger growers.[9]

The primary coconut crop improvement initiative under the Marcos government was a program to replace older trees with the new 'Mawa' (Malayan x West African) hybrid, touted as the coconut equivalent of IRRI rice. The program failed for both agronomic and political reasons. The Mawa hybrid, although shorter than traditional varieties, also has a shorter root system which makes it unable to withstand typhoons. The traditional tall varieties bend with the high winds, but Mawa topples and dies, a shortcoming which greatly limits its potential geographic range in the Philippines.

The program was widely perceived as a vehicle for private gain rather than for the public good. A special tax levied on coconut growers (further described in Chapter 7) was used to finance the purchase of Mawa seed from a farm owned by 'coconut king' Eduardo Cojuangco, a close associate of President Marcos.[10] The seedlings were then distributed to the growers, who received subsidies (financed by the levy) for replanting costs. 'In many cases', according to Jose V. Romero, Jr., chairman of the Philippine Coconut Authority under the Aquino government, 'the growers just banked the money and threw away the seedlings'. Romero questions whether the scheme was really expected to succeed: 'Cojuangco's aim was just to get the government to buy his production, and then let the government dump it'.[11] In marked contrast to the spread of IRRI rice, the Mawa variety remains a rare sight in the Philippine countryside.[12] The Agricultural Policy and Strategy Team (1986, p. 249) states that government funding for coconut breeding research was 'abruptly discontinued by the Philippine Coconut Authority when the MAWA variety was first earmarked for exclusive use in the replanting program, for now obvious reasons'.

The 1970s saw a boom in coconut oil milling in the Philippines, and a shift from copra to oil in the composition of the country's coconut exports (see Table 6.2). The milling boom was encouraged not only by reduced shipping costs, as mentioned above, but also by government policies. These included higher export tariffs on copra (Tiglao, 1981, p. 30), and investment incentives which in the end led to the creation of substantial excess capacity in the milling industry.[13]

Sugar was the Philippines' second most important agricultural export in the Marcos years. Sugar exports date from the eighteenth century (Huke, 1963, p. 310), but the commanding role of sugar in the Philippine political economy began in the latter half of the nineteenth century, when large plantations were established in Negros. 'Within the space of a half-century', writes historian Alfred McCoy (1982, p. 311), 'the fertile coastal plain of Negros Occidental was transformed from a sparsely populated rain forest into the most productive agricultural area in the archipelago'. In 1980, Negros accounted for two-thirds of Philippine sugar output. The provinces stretching from Tarlac to Batangas, in central and southern Luzon, are the country's second most important sugar region.[14]

The sugar plantation owners and millers formed the single most powerful political bloc in the Philippines during and immediately after US colonial rule. In the 1950s, the sugar bloc chafed under the foreign exchange controls which compelled them to convert their export proceeds to pesos at a below-market rate. At the same time, however, the bloc continued to benefit from its preferential access to the protected US sugar market.

The lifting of foreign exchange controls in 1962, and the increase in the US quota for Philippine sugar after the Cuban revolution, brought renewed prosperity to the sugar bloc. Sugarcane acreage doubled from 250,000 hectares in 1962 to more than 500,000 in the mid-1970s. However, yields per hectare registered little change (see Table 6.1).[15] In sugarcane, as in coconuts, the post-1962 growth in output thus was achieved through acreage extension rather than yield intensification. In this case, however, yield stagnation cannot be blamed on a lack of sufficient political clout to secure public investment in agricultural research and extension.[16]

In the mid-1970s the Philippine sugar industry went into decline, ultimately reaching the point in 1987 where the country had to import sugar in order to meet domestic needs and fill the US quota (Doronila, 1987). Three main factors in this decline were the softening of world prices, the loss of preferential access to the US market, and the creation of a monopsonistic sugar trading apparatus under the Marcos regime. The first two are discussed in this chapter, the third in Chapter 7.

Bananas have long been grown for domestic consumption in the Philippines, but their export began only when Japanese tariff barriers were lowered in the 1960s and the transnational banana firms sought a source of supply near the Japanese market. The Philippines became Asia's 'banana king', the only one of the world's top six banana exporters outside Latin America. Japan is its primary export market, and the Philippines is that country's main supplier.

The banana acreage expansion reported in Table 6.1 includes crops for both export and domestic consumption. There is a sharp divide between the two crops, however, with distinct export varieties characterized by higher yields, greater need for disease control, and greater durability of the fruit for long-distance transport (FAO, 1986, pp. 1, 7). Total export banana acreage was restricted to 21,000 hectares (subsequently increased to 25,500 hectares) by a 1973 Presidential Letter of Instruction, with the stated aim of avoiding a supply glut. The transnational firms obtain the bananas mostly from local agro-corporations under long-term production and marketing contracts.

The development of the banana export industry has been accompanied by dramatic yield increases. Official data indicate that in the early 1960s, prior to the advent of the export industry, banana yields averaged only 3 metric tons per hectare (mt/ha; see Table 6.1). The FAO (1986, p. 62) reports that yields in the export sector were 24 mt/ha in 1973 and rose to 39 mt/ha in the early 1980s.[17]

Pineapples are the other leading 'non-traditional' agricultural export of the Philippines. Their cultivation for export dates from the 1920s, when US producers began to shift to new production sites in response to plant disease problems in Hawaii (Hawes, 1987, pp. 104–5). Further relocation from Hawaii occurred in the 1960s and 1970s in response to rising land and labor prices there. In the mid-1980s, the Philippines ranked as the world's second largest exporter of both canned and fresh pineapple (after Thailand in the case of canned pineapple, and after the Ivory Coast in the case of fresh pineapple), with canned pineapple accounting for three-fourths of the country's pineapple exports (FAO, 1987a, pp. 171, 175).

Like bananas, pineapples are exported from the Philippines by transnational firms. In this case, however, the transnationals directly manage the plantations, on lands in Mindanao leased from the government's National Development Company (NDC) and private landowners. These are among the largest pineapple plantations in the world.[18] Philippine pineapple output grew quite rapidly from the early 1960s to the mid-1980s. According to the official statistics, pineapple acreage more than doubled, and yields per hectare quadrupled (see Table 6.1).

Forestry products, including raw logs, cut lumber, plywood, and veneer, have been comparable to sugar as a source of Philippine export earnings since the early 1960s (see Table 6.2). From less than ten per cent of total exports in the early 1950s, forestry products grew to more than 25 per cent in the 1960s. After 1970, however, export volume began to decline as the country's forest resources were depleted.

The composition of forestry exports shifted over this period, as in the case of coconut, towards greater domestic processing. The share of raw logs in total forestry export value fell from more than 80 per cent in the early 1960s to less than 25 per cent in the 1980s; the share of cut lumber and other products (primarily plywood and veneer) increased correspondingly, notwithstanding the tariff barriers on processed wood products maintained by importing countries.[19]

THE TERMS OF TRADE

Movement in the external terms of trade – the prices of exports relative to the prices of imports – is a crucial aspect of any nation's interactions with the world economy. For the major Philippine agricultural exports, this trend has been quite adverse, as shown in Figure 6.1. Power (1983, p. 9) remarks, 'Few countries in the world have suffered as much from the movements of international prices'.[20] In 1985, each barrel of coconut oil, each bag of sugar, each bunch of bananas, each carton of canned pineapples, and each board foot of lumber exported by the Philippines bought fewer imports than in 1962. The decline in the terms of trade was by no means smooth, however, as prices for coconut, sugar, and logs and lumber fluctuated greatly, transmitting instability from the world economy to the Philippine economy.

To a certain extent, the decline and instability of agricultural and forestry export prices can be understood as an outcome of market forces. An overabundance of agricultural commodities on the world market and intense competition among producing countries have been general features of the post-war era. Moreover, agricultural commodities have long served as the textbook examples of the boom-and-bust price cycles which competitive markets can engender. The markets for Philippine agricultural exports are

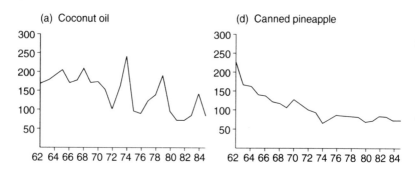

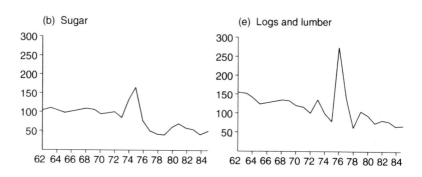

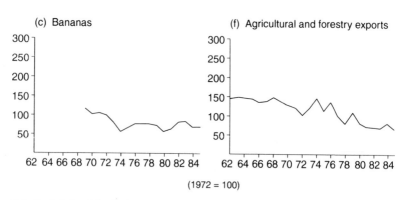

(1972 = 100)

Note: Nominal prices deflated by import prices
Source: Table 6.3

Figure 6.1:   Terms of Trade for Agricultural and Forestry Exports, 1962 – 1985

also characterized, however, by pervasive 'imperfections' arising from government interventions and oligopolistic market structures. The unfavorable price movements of Philippine agricultural exports thus reflect the interplay of economics and politics on a world scale.

Table 6.3 reports the price indices for the major Philippine agricultural and forestry exports and for Philippine imports. The overall terms of trade – the ratio of a weighted average of agro-forestry export prices to import prices – is reported in the final column. This index fell by more than half between 1962 and 1985: *in 1985 the Philippines had to sell 2.25 times as much agricultural and forestry products to purchase the same quantity of imports as in 1962.*

The terms of trade were relatively stable in the mid-1960s, declined from 1968 to 1972, and then rose sharply in 1973 and 1974, notwithstanding the petroleum import price increase of those years, thanks to booms in the coconut, sugar, and timber markets. This initiated several years of extraordinary price instability. Nominal coconut prices dropped to less than half the 1974 level in 1976, then doubled by 1979, and then collapsed again. Nominal sugar prices, after more than tripling between 1972 and 1975, dropped back to the 1972 level in 1978, then doubled in the next three years, and then tumbled again. The nominal price index for logs and lumber shot up nearly six-fold between 1972 and 1976, and then fell to a quarter of its 1976 level in two years, before stabilizing in the 1980s.[21] Meanwhile the Philippines faced an inexorable rise in nominal import prices. Hence, after several ups and downs in the 1970s, the terms of trade resumed their downward slide in the 1980s.

This deterioration in the terms of trade continued an earlier trend. Coconut prices moved 'generally downward' after World War II: the world price of coconut oil had fallen from 26 US cents per pound in 1948 to 11 cents in 1962 (UNECAFE, 1969, p. 86). Between 1950 and 1962, the ratio of Philippine export prices to Philippine import prices had declined by 24 per cent.[22] Price instability is also a longstanding feature of the Philippine experience with world markets. The price of coconut oil fell an astonishing 90 per cent in the post-war depression of 1921–22, and again by 70 per cent between 1928 and 1934 with the onset of the Great Depression (Tiglao, 1981, pp. 3, 6). Notwithstanding the cushion of preferential access to the US market, the average price of Philippine sugar exports similarly dropped by 74 per cent between 1920 and 1922, and by 37 per cent between 1927 and 1934 (calculated from data in Hawes, 1987, p. 175).

The overall impact of deteriorating terms of trade on agricultural export earnings from 1962 to 1985 is summarized in Table 6.4, which partitions export value growth rates into their quantity and price components. Each of

TABLE 6.3 *Agricultural Export Price Indices and Terms of Trade, 1962–1985 (1972 = 100)*

Year	Copra	Coconut oil	Sugar	Bananas	Canned pineapple	Logs & lumber	Agri-cultural exports[1]	Imports	Terms of trade[2]
1962	122.1	119.9	73.7	NA	158.8	110.4	102.7	71.4	143.8
1963	136.9	133.7	82.8	NA	124.3	114.9	110.7	76.2	145.4
1964	144.3	145.4	78.7	NA	123.5	106.8	109.8	76.8	143.1
1965	162.1	159.8	75.6	NA	108.3	95.5	110.4	78.1	141.3
1966	140.6	134.2	78.8	NA	108.6	100.7	105.4	79.4	132.8
1967	140.1	142.3	84.5	NA	98.6	106.2	109.7	81.2	135.2
1968	161.8	166.9	86.7	NA	93.7	107.5	118.2	80.7	146.5
1969	143.9	140.1	88.1	97.0	86.9	109.6	111.4	82.7	134.7
1970	152.5	160.4	88.3	96.0	118.0	111.6	117.3	93.5	125.4
1971	138.7	143.9	91.6	100.2	108.1	110.1	113.1	95.5	118.4
1972	100.0	100.0	100.0	100.0	100.0	100.0	100.0	100.0	100.0
1973	190.4	198.8	108.2	103.7	119.5	173.4	153.6	128.8	119.2
1974	439.8	508.1	277.6	119.3	134.7	207.0	307.2	211.6	145.2
1975	190.3	208.7	363.7	144.0	164.4	167.8	242.0	219.6	110.2
1976	153.4	192.4	170.1	165.1	186.2	598.2	290.5	217.2	133.8
1977	266.5	296.8	122.8	181.7	199.7	336.0	236.5	241.2	98.0
1978	313.7	338.7	101.7	188.3	204.1	146.9	190.8	245.8	77.6
1979	516.7	512.6	106.8	195.8	215.8	281.5	290.6	270.1	107.6

Year	Copra	Coconut oil	Sugar	Bananas	Canned pineapple	Logs & lumber	Agri-cultural exports[1]	Imports	Terms of trade[2]
1980	327.0	342.6	208.8	200.0	242.1	333.3	283.6	358.6	79.1
1981	265.0	284.3	269.2	248.2	281.0	286.5	274.9	398.6	69.0
1982	231.7	241.5	193.5	274.1	282.7	267.5	233.5	340.5	68.6
1983	210.5	286.8	180.6	282.9	278.6	261.4	230.1	342.4	67.2
1984	NA	547.2	154.2	265.9	281.1	249.6	304.7	386.7	78.8
1985	NA	295.7	171.2	250.0	264.6	239.7	231.3	363.8	63.6

NA = not available

NOTES
1. Weighted index of prices of the commodities reported in this table, with weights derived from 1972 export values. Banana excluded prior to 1969; copra prices for 1984 and 1985 inferred from coconut oil prices.
2. Net terms of trade for agricultural exports reported in this table.

SOURCES   Calculated from data in NEDA (1976, pp. 426–8, 434; 1986, pp. 364–6, 377).

TABLE 6.4 *Growth Rates of Agricultural and Forestry Exports: Value, Quantity, and Price, 1962–1985*[1] *(per cent per annum)*

Commodity	Quantity	Price[2]	Value
Copra[3]	−11.9	−4.8	−16.7
Coconut oil	7.9	−3.6	4.3
Sugar	0.4	−4.2	−3.8
Bananas[4]	13.5	−2.6	10.9
Canned pineapple	7.4	−4.1	3.4
Logs & lumber	−4.4	−3.3	−7.6
Agricultural exports[5]	0.3	−3.7	−3.3

NOTES
1. Exponential growth rates estimated by ordinary least squares.
2. Ratio of nominal price index to import price index.
3. 1962–83.
4. 1969–85.
5. Aggregate of the individual commodities reported above.

SOURCES   As for Table 6.3.

the commodities showed a downward real price trend in the period, ranging from −2.6 per cent per year in the case of bananas to −4.8 per cent in the case of copra. Coconut oil, banana, and pineapple exports grew substantially in volume, but considerably less in value due to the adverse price trends. The quantity of sugar exports showed a near-zero trend, and their value fell due to the price decline. The quantity of copra exports declined with the shift towards exports of pressed oil, and exports of logs and lumber declined due to resource depletion. The overall result was that while the total volume of these leading agro-forestry exports grew at 0.3 per cent per year, the quantity of imports the Philippines could purchase from the proceeds declined at 3.3 per cent per year.

This outcome was not simply the result of the free play of market forces, as will be evident from an examination of the world markets for the Philippines' principal agricultural exports.

Coconut: Competition from Substitutes

Although it is by far the world's largest coconut exporter, the Philippines exercises little market power owing to the availability of close substitutes.

'Coconut oil is a minor oil locked in a competitive battle', Hicks (1967, p. 212) observed, 'not so much with other producers of coconut oil but with other sources of oil'. Soybean oil, groundnut oil, cottonseed oil, lard, and tallow are among the major competitors in edible uses such as margarine and cooking oil. Petroleum-based synthetics are the major competitors in non-edible uses such as the manufacture of detergents. Demand for coconut oil, and for the copra from which it is extracted, is therefore highly price-elastic.

The downward trend and instability of coconut prices can explained primarily in terms of the world supply of competing substitutes. Producers of edible oils in the industrialized countries receive subsidies and other protection from their respective governments. The effect of these policies is to increase the world supply of edible fats and oils, eroding the competitive position of Philippine coconut oil, and depressing world prices for all freely traded fats and oils.

The introduction of petroleum derivatives as substitutes for coconut oil in industrial uses began on a large scale in the late 1960s. In this case, an important constraint on the competitiveness of coconut oil has been the failure of market prices to capture the negative externalities in the production and use of the synthetics. Even within the Philippines, there are complaints that coconut oil-based soap 'is being replaced by petro-based detergent which is polluting our waterways' (Abadilla, 1987, p. 4). Here, as in a number of other sectors of the world economy, neglect of the social costs of pollution confers an illusion of efficiency upon the products of the petrochemical industry.[23] In addition, Hicks (1967, p. 201) noted 'an alarming contrast between the resources, research, and investment applied to the problem of reducing the cost of synthetic oils and the general neglect of the really substantial cost-reducing potential of natural oil'. This contrast reflects profound differences in the size and power of their respective producers. Large firms in the petroleum sector have the capacity not only to finance research and development, but also to internalize much of the resulting benefit streams. Natural oil producers must rely on public sector research, which often has been minimal.[24]

Preferential trading arrangements with the United States played a key historical role in the growth of Philippine coconut exports in the face of the competitive and politicized world market for edible oils. The terms of Philippine access to the US market have reflected the balance among the competing interests of US edible oil producers, US firms engaged in the milling and export of coconut oil in the Philippines, and US industrial consumers of coconut oil, which generated 'conflicting demands to penalize and protect the Philippine product' (Hicks, 1967, p. 135). The resulting tariff policies protected US edible oil producers from foreign competition, but applied substantially lower duties to Philippine oils than to those of other countries.[25]

US tariff and commercial policy is described by Hawes (1987, p. 61) as 'the most important factor in stimulating the expansion of the Philippine coconut industry' in the colonial period. The Philippines continued to receive preferential access to the US market after independence under the United States-Philippine Trade Agreement of 1946 and the Laurel-Langley Agreement of 1955. These preferences were gradually reduced, however, and finally terminated in 1974 with the expiration of the Laurel-Langley Agreement. Stripped of the political armor which had protected it, the Philippine coconut industry became fully exposed to competition from producers of substitutes in the world market.

Sugar: Politics in Command

The world market for sugar, the Philippines' second most important agricultural export, is also characterized by stiff international competition and widespread government interventions designed primarily to favor domestic producers, particularly in Europe and North America. In addition, preferential trading arrangements have long played a crucial role in the international political economy of sugar.

The two main sources of sugar on the world market are sugarcane, grown in sub-tropical locations such as the Philippines, and sugar beet, grown in temperate locations in Europe and North America. In addition, high-fructose corn syrup (HFCS) derived from maize has become an important substitute in recent years, particularly in the United States.

It is often claimed that the Philippine sugar industry is 'inefficient' by international standards.[26] The persistence of labor-intensive cultivation in the Philippines in the face of mechanization by other producers is sometimes considered *prima facie* evidence of this inefficiency. Yet cross-country comparisons of sugar production costs reveal that the Philippines is among the world's lowest-cost producers. In 1986, production costs for cane sugar varied worldwide from 11 to 16 US cents per pound, free on board (FOB), while production costs for beet sugar ranged from 13 to 38 cents per pound. The average cost of production in the Philippines was 13 cents per pound, towards the bottom end of the worldwide range.[27]

Remarkably, the world market price for sugar at the time was *eight* US cents per pound. That is, it was below the average production costs of any major sugar-producing country. What is more, this was a favorable price compared to the previous year, 1985, when the average world price was only four cents per pound (Reinah, 1987, p. 141). The Philippines clearly faces a rather peculiar market for this traditional agricultural export.

Two key features of the international sugar market help to explain the apparent anomaly of a world price below the average cost of production of the lowest-cost producers: (1) the existence of massive subsidies for sugar producers in the industrialized countries, and (2) the prevalence of preferential trading agreements among importers and exporters. These political deals together do much to determine the distribution of the income from the world sugar cake. In the late 1970s and early 1980s, the Philippines saw its share pared to a few crumbs.

In the mid-1980s, roughly three-fourths of the world's 100 million ton annual sugar crop was produced for domestic consumption, often insulated from the world market by government price-support policies. Only 10–12 per cent of world output was traded on the 'free' international market, the remainder being traded under long-term agreements.[28] As the dumping ground for the surplus production encouraged by various price supports around the world, the free market is the least favorable arena for a sugar-exporting country to engage in the global trade. It has been estimated that under a free-trade regime the world price of sugar would have been 12 cents per pound in 1985, as opposed to the actual price of four cents.[29] At the same time, the residual character of the free market exacerbates its price instability.

Roughly half the sugar traded internationally is sold at prices negotiated under long-term trade agreements and preferential arrangements. Examples include the one-time barter agreements between Cuba and the Soviet Union; the sugar protocol of the Lome Convention under which the EEC imports sugar from 17 African, Caribbean and Pacific nations at above-market prices; and the US sugar quota allocation systems in force prior to 1974 and reinstated in 1982.

United States import quotas and duties generally hold domestic sugar prices above those prevailing on the world market.[30] In 1985, for example, the average duty-paid sugar price in New York was 20 cents per pound, five times the world price.[31] The European Economic Community (EEC), a net importer of sugar as late as 1976, became the largest exporter to the world free market by 1979 thanks to subsidies to domestic producers approaching $1 billion per year (Pineda-Ofreneo, 1985, p. 22).

For Philippine sugar, which is effectively shut out of the EEC, preferential access to the US market has long been crucial. The suspension of US imports from Cuba in 1960 led to an increase in the Philippine sugar quota from 700,000 to 1 million tons, the largest assigned to any nation (Hawes, 1987, p. 91). The failure of other countries to meet their quotas gave the Philippines further opportunities to sell sugar to the US, facilitated by the lower duties on Philippine sugar under the Laurel-Langley Agreement. The resulting expansion of US demand was the primary stimulus for the growth of Philippine sugar acreage in the 1960s. In no small measure, the Philippine sugar industry was 'a ward of the protected US market' (McCoy, 1984, p. 57).

Preferential access to the US market ended in 1974, however, when the US scrapped its sugar quota system and the Laurel-Langley Agreement expired. Philippine sugar was suddenly thrust onto the world 'free' market, a blow disguised, but only temporarily, by the unprecedented high price prevailing at that time. From a peak of 59 US cents per pound in 1974, the world free market price slid below four cents in 1985 (Commodity Research Bureau, 1982, p. 332; 1988, p. 257). In a total world market of roughly 25 million tons (including trade under preferential agreements), US sugar imports declined by nearly 3 million tons, primarily owing to a shift to greater use of high-fructose corn syrup.[32] At the same time, Europe switched from being a net importer of 3 million tons to a net exporter of 2 million tons.[33]

Forced onto the free market, the Philippines diversified the destinations of its sugar exports. Whereas virtually all Philippine sugar exports had gone to the United States prior to 1974, the US share had fallen to 25 per cent by 1980. New buyers included Japan and the then centrally planned economies.[34] Philippine sugar exports nevertheless dropped from 1.5 million tons in 1974 to 570,000 tons in 1985. With the accompanying decline in sugar prices, real earnings (deflated by the import price index) plummeted by 87 per cent.[35] The Philippine sugar industry was plunged into the worst crisis in its history, and reports of starvation among sugar plantation workers on the island of Negros began to reach the world press.

The reintroduction of sugar quotas in the US in 1982 brought little relief. Quotas were allocated among exporting countries on the basis of their shares of the US market from 1975 to 1981, and the Philippine quota, which ranked third after those of the Dominican Republic and Brazil, was roughly one-fourth of what it had been prior to 1974.[36] Nevertheless this market was, as the US embassy in Manila cabled to Washington in 1984, 'very important' to Philippine producers, 'being the only export market in which they can sell their sugar for more than their cost of production'.[37]

The allocation of the US sugar quota is a political battleground. The US State and Defense Departments sought larger allocations for Caribbean and Central American countries in 1984, for example, on the grounds that 'the US must financially support the governments of this region and help them build a shield against communism'.[38] Although the Philippines retains considerable political importance in Washington, this provides only a limited buffer against the competing strategic and domestic political forces which shape the world market. In this international environment, the profitability of the Philippine sugar export industry rests on precarious foundations.

Bananas and Pineapples: The Non-traditional Exports

In the case of bananas, the Philippines' number three export crop after coconut and sugar in the 1970s and 1980s, the country's engagement with the world market is mediated by the three transnational firms – United Brands, Castle & Cooke, and Del Monte – which together account for two-thirds of the world banana trade and for 80 per cent of Philippine banana exports (FAO, 1986, pp. 8, 37).

The exercise of market power by these firms is examined in Chapter 7. In 1974, the major banana-producing countries formed the Union de Paises Exportadores del Banano (Union of Banana Exporting Countries, or UPEB), in an attempt to improve their leverage *vis-à-vis* the transnational firms. This effort foundered on insufficient coordination among member countries (FAO, 1986, pp. 67–68). The Philippines was the only major exporting country which did not join.[39]

In the 1950s and 1960s, the volume of world banana imports grew by nearly 5 per cent annually, while the real price of bananas underwent a long-term decline, falling at roughly 2 per cent per annum between 1950 and 1974. Since the early 1970s, both volume and real price trends have flattened out.[40] In 1986, the United Nations Food and Agriculture Organization (FAO, 1986, pp. 5, 76) predicted 'low or zero growth in world banana imports' in coming years.

In Japan, the primary market for Philippine exports, banana consumption rose phenomenally from the 1950s to the early 1970s. The Philippine banana export industry grew largely in response to this demand, its share of the Japanese market rising from 3 per cent in 1969 to 31 per cent in 1972 and to 90 per cent in 1982. After the mid-1970s, however, the size of the Japanese market began to contract. This partly reflected a shift in tastes, as bananas 'lost their exotic appeal', but it also resulted from Japanese government efforts to encourage domestic farmers to grow competing fruits, while import duties remained a 'significant cost item' for bananas (FAO, 1986, p. 57). This combination led to a 'virtual collapse of the market for bananas in Japan', in response to which the Philippine exporters adopted voluntary quantity restrictions in 1983, based on agreed shares of the Japanese market.[41]

Philippine involvement in the world pineapple market has been mediated by two of the same transnational firms – Del Monte and Castle & Cooke (through its Dole subsidiary). The World Bank (1985d, p. 23) remarks:

'Through their aggressive market building and distribution network, and backed by sustained advertising investments over many years, these firms have contributed much to the Philippines becoming a world leader in canned pineapple and juice.'

By the early 1970s, the Philippines had become the world's top exporter of canned pineapple, holding a 'dominant position in the world market' (FAO, 1976a, p. 24). As in Thailand, which subsequently surpassed the Philippines in canned pineapple exports, the growth of the industry in the Philippines reflected the decision of the transnationals to relocate production from Hawaii, where land and labor costs were rising (FAO, 1976a, pp. 25–6).

Compared with many food items, canned pineapple is a luxury good, and demand in the industrialized countries absorbs 90 per cent of world imports (FAO, 1987a, p. 175). Demand is quite sensitive to macroeconomic conditions, and the World Bank (1985d, p. 24) blames recession in the industrialized countries for the 23 per cent decline in Philippine exports of canned pineapples between 1979 and 1983.[42] The United States accounted for 60 per cent of Philippine exports in the mid-1980s.[43] Philippine sales to western Europe, the country's second most important market, are handicapped by the preferential access given by the EEC to the Ivory Coast and Kenya (FAO, 1976a, pp. 25, 27). Quotas and high import duties have also seriously limited sales in Japan (FAO, 1972, pp. 16–17).

CONCLUSIONS

Comparative advantage is not entirely an economist's pipe-dream. The Philippines' position as the world's top coconut exporter reflects not only its colonial past, but also its natural endowments. Philippine sugar production would be highly competitive in world markets in the absence of the government interventions which support higher-cost producers elsewhere. If the Japanese want to eat bananas, they must import them, and the Philippines is favorably placed to meet this demand.

But the parable of comparative advantage misses crucial parts of the story of Philippine agricultural exports. The international trade in coconut oil, sugar, and tropical fruit is far removed from the textbook world of perfect competition. The key comparative advantages in these markets are to be found in the realm of political influence, not in differences in production costs.

Coconut oil competes with other edible oils protected by industrialized-country price supports, and with synthetic substitutes whose prices do not include the external costs of pollution. The Philippine coconut industry's competitiveness thus suffers from the actions of other governments in the first case, and from their inaction in the other. The world market for sugar is a political artifact, bearing minimal relation to the market of the microeconomics textbook. In understanding the world sugar trade, the model of comparative advantage is about as useful as a rowboat in the desert. The market for tropical fruits is shaped not only by government policies, such as tariff barriers against imported fruit in Japan, but also by the oligopsonistic market structures.

The Philippines experienced severely declining terms of trade and great price instability for its agricultural exports from 1962 to 1985. Despite an upward trend in their volume, the total value of the country's leading agro-forestry exports fell at a annual rate of more than 3 per cent. Although price movements for the Philippines were particularly adverse, declining terms of trade and price instability have been common for many Third World primary-commodity exporters in recent decades.[44]

These price movements were the result of external political and economic forces over which the Philippines could exercise little, if any, control. They underscore a major limitation of the doctrine of comparative advantage as a guide to trade strategy, and cast doubt on the reliability of export agriculture as an engine of economic growth.

NOTES

1. 'Agriculture: A Strategy for the 70s', cited by Ofreneo (1980, p. 97).
2. The freight rate for Philippine coconut oil to the US Pacific coast, for example, dropped from $26 per ton to $9 (Hicks, 1967, pp. 160–1; see also Tiglao, 1981, p. 24).
3. Crops of less importance include coffee, tobacco, and abaca (Manila hemp, the fiber which was a leading Philippine export in the nineteenth century).
4. Data on Philippine exports are subject to substantial errors (see discussion of false trade invoicing in Chapter 10), but the figures reported here provide a reasonable picture of overall trends in export composition.
5. 'Enrile Cites Scheme for Coconut Industry', *Business Day*, 14 April, 1980, p. 3, cited by Tadem (1980, p. 43).
6. Canlas and Alburo (1989, p. 84) report that copra is allowed to enter Europe duty free, while coconut oil is subject to tariffs ranging from 5 to 15 per cent. Hicks (1967, p. 89) reported a very similar situation in the 1960s.
7. This paragraph draws on Tiglao (1981) and Hawes (1987, pp. 59–68), to which the reader is referred for further details. On uses of coconut oil, see also Woodruff (1979, pp. 112–23).

8. The reliability of the official data on coconut yields is open to question. Alternative estimates by the Philippine Coconut Authority indicate that average yields fell from 1.2 mt/ha in the 1960s to 0.7 mt/ha in the 1980s (Galang, 1988b, p. 72).

9. In a review of Philippine agricultural research, Evenson, Waggoner, and Bloom (1980, p. 26) remark that in the case of coconuts, 'Few varietal advances appear to have been made over the past 50 years or so'. In its 'green paper', the Agricultural Policy and Strategy Team (1986, p. 249) reports that 'no more than two agronomists with a doctorate degree are working on coconut plant breeding in the country'. The Team also reports (p. 499) that research expenditures on coconut from 1974 to 1984 were, on average, only 28 per cent of those on sugarcane. This may overstate the effective investment in coconut research, since much of the expenditures were channelled through the Philippine Coconut Authority, which tended to devote its research to 'buildings, public relations and funds' (Evenson, Waggoner, and Bloom, 1980, p. 27). Hicks's observation (1967, p. 202) that 'compared with the amount of work that has been done on rice, coconuts are a virgin field' thus appears to have stood the test of time.

10. The farm was on Bugsuk island, off the southern tip of Palawan. Cojuangco acquired most of the island in a trade with the Philippine government, giving up one hectare in Tarlac province for every three in Bugsuk. 'In retrospect', a US State Department cable remarks, 'the trade appears particularly attractive, since most of the rice land in Tarlac subsequently came under the President's land reform program'. ('Concentration of Power in the Philippine Coconut Industry: Implications for Investment and Trade', Cable No. A–47 from US Embassy, Manila, to Department of State, 9 May 1980, pp. 5–6.)

11. Interview with Jose V. Romero, Jr., Philippine Coconut Authority, Manila, 25 January 1989.

12. This may be fortunate, as the prospect of widespread adoption raised serious concerns about genetic vulnerability to crop disease epidemics (Banzon and Velasco, 1982, pp. 43–4; Sangalang, 1987, pp. 226–7). For further discussion of the hybrid replanting program, see Tiglao (1981, pp. 61, 85, 95–6), Sangalang (1987) and Habito (1987a, pp. 195–202).

13. Hawes (1987, pp. 63–8) attributes this overcapacity to 'faulty planning by technocrats in government', and notes that a number of the new mills ultimately 'reneged on their loan payments and closed down'. An additional reason, however, may have been the opportunities for profit and capital flight afforded by the procurement of milling equipment; see the discussion of sugar mills on pp. 320–1, below.

14. NCSO (1985, Table D3, p. 17). Huke (1963, p. 300) remarks that 'few internationally important crops show such marked concentration' in relatively small geographical areas.

15. Alternative data from the Philippine Sugar Commission, reported by the World Bank (1986a, p. 65), indicate that yields actually fell from 6.4

mt/ha in 1960/61–62/63 to 4.9 mt/ha during the peak acreage years of 1974/75–76/77. A decline in average yields is plausible insofar as some of the new lands brought under sugarcane were only marginally suited to the crop.

16. Information on research expenditure on sugarcane is contradictory. The Agricultural Policy and Strategy Team (1986, p. 499) reports that it exceeded research expenditure on any other crop in the 1974–84 period. Evenson, Waggoner and Bloom (1980, pp. 14, 25) report, however, that sugarcane research expenditures were relatively low, and conclude that public sector research stations 'have apparently been unable to maintain the steady programs required to be major contributors to new technology'.

17. The reliability of official yield estimates for the domestic (non-export) banana industry is open to doubt. Given the small share of the export crop in total banana acreage, the official figures reported in Table 6.1 imply that domestic banana yields tripled to nearly 10 mt/ha by 1982–85. Developments in banana production for domestic consumption are not well documented, making it difficult to judge the plausibility of this increase.

18. Krinks (1983a, p. 111) states that the pineapple plantation of Dole Philippines (a subsidiary of the US firm Castle & Cooke) is the world's largest.

19. In the mid-1970s, for example, Japan, the United States and the European Economic Community allowed duty-free importation of raw material but imposed 13–20 per cent tariffs on plywood (FAO, 1976b, pp. 46–7).

20. Measures of changes in terms of trade are notoriously sensitive to choice of the time period. Josling (1984, p. 10) reports that in the period 1970–79, the decline in the purchasing power of Philippine agricultural exports was about average for 79 developing countries.

21. These fluctuations are even more dramatic in the monthly price data. Between January 1973 and December 1976, for example, coconut oil soared from $168 per metric ton to a peak of $1,138 (in April 1974), and then dropped to $305 (Hawes, 1987, p. 70).

22. Calculated from data in NEDA (1976, Table 12.8, p. 434); see also Tryon (1967). This figure refers to all Philippine exports, but as noted above these were predominantly agricultural and forestry products.

23. Commoner (1990, p. 53) remarks, 'Nearly all the products of the petrochemical industry are substitutes for perfectly serviceable preexisting ones'.

24. See note 9, above.

25. For details, see Hicks (1967, pp. 52–80) and UNECAFE (1969, pp. 56–7).

26. See, for example, McCoy (1983, p. 143; 1984, p. 57); Hawes (1987, p. 125).

27. Reinah (1987, pp. 141, 152). The World Bank (1986a, p. 79) likewise reports the Philippines to be among the world's lowest-cost producers at

12.0 cents/pound. According to the World Bank data, Brazil had slightly lower costs at 11.5 cent/pound, while costs were higher in Australia (14.3 cents), Cuba (15.3 cents), Thailand (15.8 cents), and Mexico (18.3 cents). Harris (1987, p. 144) reports an index of the average sugar production costs in 24 countries in 1979/80–82/83, which ranged from 57 to 229 (with the weighted world average equal to 100). The Philippines ranked among the lowest-cost producers with an index value of 75, that is, 25% below the world average.

28. Reinah (1987, p. 142). See also Harris (1987) and Krueger (1990, pp. 176–8).
29. Krueger (1990, p. 178), citing Lee and Knutson (1987).
30. In 1981, US President Reagan, an ardent advocate of free trade, bowed to domestic political realities and expressed his 'regret' at the 'necessity' of signing the relevant orders (quoted by Reinah (1987, p. 146). For a history and analysis of US sugar policy, see Krueger (1990).
31. This was an exceptionally high ratio. In the 10-year period from 1978 to 1987, the average US-to-world price ratio was 2.63 (calculated from data in Krueger, 1990, p. 179).
32. The best-known example of this shift is the decision of US soft drink producers Coca Cola and Pepsi to approve 100 per cent use of HFCS in late 1984. In the previous decade, however, US sugar consumption had already declined by 17 per cent, while HFCS consumption had risen by 150 per cent (Pineda-Ofreneo, 1985, p. 17).
33. Data from *FAO Trade Yearbook*, various issues.
34. Nelson (1988, p. 284); see also Pineda-Ofreneo (1985, pp. 20–1).
35. Calculated from data in NEDA (1986, pp. 364–5, 377).
36. Pineda-Ofreneo (1985, p. 14). From 1986 to 1989, the average quota allocation for the Philippines was 222,000 metric tons per year (calculated from various issues of the US Department of Agriculture's Foreign Agricultural Service 'Report on the Status of US Sugar Import Quota for the Week Ending . . .').
37. Telegram Manila 05373, 29 February 1984, from Ambassador Michael Armacost to the Secretary of State, confidential (released under the Freedom of Information Act, and obtained by the author from the National Security Archive, Washington, D.C.).
38. US Defense Secretary Casper Weinberger, quoted by Pineda-Ofreneo (1985, p. 19).
39. The original UPEB members were Colombia, Costa Rica, Guatemala, Honduras and Panama. The Dominican Republic, Nicaragua, and Venezuela joined subsequently, and Ecuador participated in policy discussions as an 'observer'.
40. See FAO (1986, pp. 8, 71).
41. FAO (1986, p. 38). The shares were 27 per cent each for Standard Fruit (a subsidiary of Castle & Cooke), Del Monte, and TADECO (an affiliate of United Brands), and 19 per cent for DAHITRI (a group of independent corporate producers).

42. The depression of the 1930s similarly caused pineapple sales in the United States to plunge, prompting Del Monte to temporarily convert its newly established cannery in Mindanao to tuna production (Burbach and Flynn, 1980, p. 198).
43. This refers to Philippine exports of canned pineapple, juice and concentrate, which totalled $109 million (f.o.b.) in 1985; in addition, the country exported $18 million worth of fresh pineapples in that year, 97 per cent of which went to Japan (NCSO, 1986a, pp. 445–52).
44. For discussions, see Payer, ed. (1975), Spraos (1980), FAO (1982), Adams and Behrman (1982), Josling (1984), and Scandizzo and Diakosawas (1987).

7 Export Agriculture: Whose Advantage?

INTRODUCTION

The income generated by exports accrues not to countries, but to specific individuals within them. The institutional arrangements for the production and marketing of export crops determine how the income from export agriculture is distributed. In the Philippines, these arrangements typically have led to a highly inequitable result: the peasants and laborers who produce the crops have received minimal reward for their efforts, while those who control land, markets, and the state have profited greatly.

The institutions which govern the distribution of income do not fall from the sky. They emerge from struggles among individuals, groups, and classes. Interactions between income and power, discussed above in Chapter 5, play a central role in these struggles. The distribution of income in Philippine export agriculture has shaped, and in turn has been shaped by, the outcomes of contests over endowments, public goods and externalities, market power, and government policies.

The overt aim of the Marcos regime's development strategy for export agriculture was growth in output and export earnings. Behind the scenes, however, the regime aggressively pursued another agenda: the redistribution of income to favored individuals. Most notably, Marcos deployed state power to put control of the country's top agricultural exports, coconut and sugar, securely in the hands of presidential 'cronies'. The result was a dramatic re-division of the agro-export income pie, with bigger slices for the privileged few and smaller slices for the rest.

RELATIONS OF PRODUCTION

Production of the Philippines' four leading export crops – coconuts, sugarcane, bananas, and pineapples – takes place under a diverse set of institutional arrangements. In the Philippines, as in other major producing countries, coconut is 'essentially a small holder's crop' (UNECAFE, 1969, p. 11), yet tenancy and the use of wage labor in coconut farming are

189

widespread. Sugarcane is grown mainly on 'traditional' plantations, but patron-client ties between workers and plantation owners became increasingly strained in the Marcos era. Pineapples and most export bananas are grown on 'modern' plantations, by domestic corporations under long-term contracts with transnational firms in the case of bananas, and by the transnationals on land leased from the state in the case of pineapples. This section explores the nature of these production arrangements and their impact on income distribution.

Coconut: The 'Smallholder's' Crop

'Coconut farms' are a distinct entity in Philippine agriculture, since coconut is often a farm's primary or sole crop, rather than simply one component of a quite diversified crop mix. A 1978 survey of coconut farms by the Ministry of Agriculture found that their average total cropped area was 4.9 hectares, of which 4.0 hectares were under coconuts.[1] In recent years the intercropping of coconut with other crops, such as coffee, abaca, and lanzones, has been increasing, but monoculture remains the rule.

The four-hectare average conceals significant farm-size disparities among coconut farms. The 1971 census of agriculture found that the largest ten per cent of coconut farms, with ten hectares or more, accounted for 42 per cent of total coconut area.[2] The expansion of coconut acreage sparked by the 1962 decontrol of foreign exchange occurred primarily in the larger farm-size classes. A survey conducted by Nyberg (1968, pp. 51–2) found that 84 per cent of new plantings were on farms of ten or more hectares, and that 'essentially no new plantings were being made on farms smaller than two hectares'.

The census data on farm size distribution understate the degree of concentration in coconut lands, since they refer to operational holdings rather than to ownership. For example, in an upland coconut village in Quezon where Hayami, Quisumbing and Adriano (1990, p.118) report that a single landlord owned all the land and cultivated it by means of share tenants, the agricultural censuses would record each tenant's holding as a separate farm.

Estimates of the extent of tenancy vary widely, from 22 to 68 per cent of all coconut farms (Cornista and Escueta, 1983, pp. 4–5). Tenancy is reportedly more widespread in the coconut regions of southern Luzon than in the newer, and typically larger, coconut farms of Mindanao. Coconut landlords include middle class teachers, managers, military officers, and professionals, many of whom are absentees (Putzel and Cunnington, 1989, pp. 13, 15). Share tenancy is most common, with considerable variation in both the share and the responsibilities of the tenant. Variants include a 50–50 division of the copra with the tenant bearing all expenses in Quezon, or a 60–40 split in favor of landowner if the latter bears certain expenses; a 2/3–1/3 division in favor of the landowner in Albay, again with the tenant bearing all expenses; and, in Laguna, a one-seventh share of the green nuts to the tenant whose job is simply to protect the trees and to clear the land between them.[3]

Although family and exchange labor remain important on the smaller coconut farms, Cornista and Escueta (1983, p. 2) report that 'the emerging pattern is the use of hired labor in all production activities'. Government surveys conducted in 1974–78 indicate that hired labor accounted for 61 per cent of total labor inputs on coconut farms (Tiglao, 1981, pp. 38–40). David (1977) similarly estimates that in 1976 hired laborers accounted for 65 per cent of the 1,550,000 persons 'engaged in the actual act of farming on a coconut farm', and that of the remainder, 32 per cent were tenants and 3 per cent were owner-operators.[4]

Hired laborers are paid mainly on a piece-rate basis, which reduces the need for supervision and facilitates the use of family helpers by the hired worker (Tiglao, 1981, p. 44). Official data indicate that their daily wages tend to be slightly higher than those for agricultural laborers in rice, corn, and sugarcane cultivation (see Table 2.7). This may reflect longer working days, the use of family helpers by coconut workers, and perhaps higher daily earnings to compensate for fewer days of employment. The average annual earnings of coconut laborers are among the lowest of any occupational group in the country (Cornista and Escueta, 1983, pp. 10–11).

Unlike hired laborers in the other major export crops, coconut workers are generally unorganized, with 'no channel for the articulation of their interests and needs'. Nevertheless some coconut laborers have developed 'means of sharing poverty' at the local level, including the rotation of limited employment, the formation of work groups in which remuneration is shared equally among members, and the inclusion in such groups of non-members in dire need of employment (Cornista and Escueta, 1983, pp. 12–13). In addition, Hawes (1990) reports that in some areas the coconut workers have been organized by the National Democratic Front.

Tiglao (1981, p. 51) estimates that gross farm income from copra production is, on average, partitioned as follows: 50 per cent to the owner of the land as ground rent; 11 per cent to the farm operator as profit; 37 per cent to wage and family labor; and 2 per cent to cover non-labor production costs. These must be regarded as rough approximations, which would vary from farm to farm and from year to year depending, for example, on the farmgate price of copra.[5] There is little doubt, however, that returns to land typically exceed returns to labor in coconut production. The pattern of ownership of coconut land is therefore a critical determinant of income distribution in the sector.

There is no evidence of economies of scale in coconut cultivation. Agricultural census data reveal no correlation between farm size and the number of nuts per tree.[6] Data published by the Philippine Coconut Authority (1988, p. 102) indicate that yields in Mindanao, where average holdings are larger, tend to be higher than in Luzon, where average holdings are smaller, but Habito (1987b, p. 2) points out that environmental conditions are more favorable in Mindanao, and that the trees there are generally younger and hence more productive.

On the basis of interviews in coconut-growing areas of Luzon, Hayami, Quisumbing and Adriano (1990, p.117) report that intercropping is more common and more intensive on small family farms than on larger wage-labor farms. This may reflect lower costs of labor and supervision on smaller farms.[7] One constraint on the spread of intercropping, however, has been the fear of landlords 'that if they allow farmworkers to inter-crop these areas with vegetables and other food crops, they may lose control of the land' (Putzel and Cunnington, 1989, p. 35). In some cases, according to Habito (1987a, pp. 206), 'landlords actually prohibit their tenants from intercropping'. Because of these tensions over property rights, as well as the more widely recognized incentive problems, share tenancy poses 'a barrier to increased productivity on coconut farms'.[8]

Notwithstanding its image as a smallholder's crop, then, coconut production in the Philippines typically is characterized by a dichotomy between ownership of land and labor on it. Land ownership in the coconut sector is more widely dispersed than in other major export crops, but most coconut laborers do not own the land on which they work. The result is not only inequitable, but also possibly inefficient.

Sugarcane: The Traditional Plantation

Sugarcane is mainly, but not exclusively, a plantation crop in the Philippines. In 1983–84, the five hundred largest sugarcane plantations, with more than 100 hectares each, accounted for 25 per cent of the country's total sugarcane acreage. Smaller plantations in the 25-to-100 hectare size class accounted for a further 35 per cent of total acreage. Together, these plantations represented only ten per cent of the country's sugarcane farms. At the other end of the spectrum were farms of 10 hectares or less, which accounted for 78 per cent of sugarcane farms but only 23 per cent of total acreage (Bravo, Cornista and Ramos, 1986, Table 5).

As sugarcane acreage grew, the number of sugarcane farms increased from 17,800 in 1960 to 30,100 in 1982. At the same time, their average size remained virtually unchanged (declining from 14 to 13 hectares), suggesting that acreage extension was not confined to the largest or smallest size classes.[9] Expansion of the large estates occurred, at least in part, through expropriation of peasant lands. In the Negros highlands, for example, individuals 'versed in the legal formalities and ready with a bribe obtained titles to land long tilled by others' (Kamm, 1981). In so doing, the plantation owners followed in the footsteps of their forebears.

The establishment of sugar plantations in Negros in the latter half of the nineteenth century was sparked by the opening of the port city of Iloilo, on neighboring Panay, to foreign commerce in 1855. The following year saw the arrival of British vice-consul Nicholas Loney, who would one day be memorialized as the 'father of the Philippine sugar industry'. Loney's initial mission was to promote imports of British cloth, which eventually led to the demise of Iloilo's highly developed textile industry. Loney encouraged sugar production on Negros in order to provide a cargo for the return voyage to Britain, so as lower shipping costs and thereby enhance the competitiveness of British cloth. He encouraged the Iloilo textile traders to shift their capital into the establishment of sugarcane plantations on Negros.[10]

This required the forcible displacement and repression of the tribespeople living there, to whom the logic of comparative advantage was evidently obscure. McCoy (1984, p. 81) remarks, 'The conquest of Negros was more rape than seduction'. Assisted by Spanish military forces, who committed what a Spanish historian termed 'outrages, even abominable crimes',[11] the planters' armed gangs slaughtered the tribespeople and pushed them deep into the highlands. 'Landed property in agricultural export sectors', Paige (1975, p. 19) observes, 'seems a literal illustration of Proudhon's dictum that property is theft'. The history of sugarcane in Negros amply supports this proposition.

Having appropriated the land, the planters needed a labor force. A contemporary observer wrote in 1894 that labor shortages were 'the greatest problem' in Negros.[12] To obtain laborers from other islands, the planters offered cash advances, and they then bonded the immigrants to the plantation by means of high-interest debts, which were passed from generation to generation. The result was in some respects similar to slavery:

Lacking any other incentive to motivate their debt-bonded work gangs, plantation foremen made regular use of corporal punishment. Workers often absconded from their debts and fled the plantations, compelling planters to devise a complex system of security patrols and passes to return runaways to their home plantations. (McCoy, 1982, p. 320)

To supplement this permanent labor force, at harvest time the planters employed seasonal contract laborers recruited mainly in neighboring Panay.

The stark inequalities of wealth and power on the sugar plantations of Negros are the legacy of this agrarian history. The planters, or *hacenderos*, are today mostly absentee landlords living in Manila or in Bacolod, the provincial capital of Negros Occidental.[13] The lifestyle of the *hacendero* elite was more than comfortable, at least until the economic collapse of the 1980s; 'mansions, servants, luxury cars, and round-the-world trips were commonplace' (Hawes, 1987, p. 83). Their involvement in production is often minimal. 'Sugar is easy', explained one plantation owner. 'You just plant it and then go off to Manila or Europe'.[14]

A hierarchy of salaried administrators, overseers, and foremen supervises the plantation work force, which consists of a small number of skilled mechanics and tractor drivers, and a much larger number of unskilled laborers. The latter include (a) permanent workers (*dumaan*), who reside year-round on the hacienda and account for roughly two-thirds of the plantation labor force; (b) temporary or casual workers (*pangayaw*), who generally live nearby and make up a further 20–25 per cent of the labor force; and (c) migratory laborers (*sacadas*), who come only for the harvest and represent 10–15 per cent of the labor force at that time (Aguilar, 1984, pp. 10–11). The number of unskilled laborers in sugarcane production in the Philippines, excluding the *sacadas*, is estimated to exceed 400,000; they outnumber sugar landowners (including small owner-operators as well as *hacenderos*) by a ratio of more than ten to one.[15]

A 1982 survey found that 56 per cent of the permanent sugar plantation workers have lived on the same hacienda all their lives, and that 34 per cent had at least one parent who had been born on the same hacienda (Gonzaga, 1983, p. 9). In addition to the wage, the permanent workers receive housing. Rutten (1982, p. 22) describes the *dumaan* housing on one Negros hacienda:

Most houses consist of two rooms and a separate area for cooking, and cover not more than 25 square meters in all. They lack electricity, running water, and toilet facilities. Some are in bad shape, with leaking roofs and damaged walls.

Sometimes permanent workers are allowed to grow vegetables and fruit trees and keep some small animals in a small garden plot near the house. In a few cases, they also are permitted to grow rice on hacienda lands not well suited for sugarcane.

During the slack season, most permanent workers take loans from the hacienda for household expenses. Rutten (1982, p. 23) reports 'constant friction between workers and the planter over the amount of credit asked or given and the amount withheld from wages as debt repayment'. However, debt bondage appears to be largely a thing of the past, perhaps reflecting the transition from a labor-scarce economy to a labor-abundant one. When worker households move away, leaving their debts behind, the planter reportedly has 'no means to force them to repay' (*ibid.*).

The temporary workers and the migrant *sacadas* are employed only when labor requirements exceed the capacity of the plantation's permanent work force. The daily wages of temporary workers who live nearby are comparable to those of permanent workers, but they do not receive the fringe benefits of housing, garden plots, and access to credit. The *sacadas* receive lower wages, however, since their payment is channelled through a contractor who deducts a commission and interest on cash advances. In addition, the contractor often requires the *sacadas* to purchase all their food from him at prices he dictates.[16]

Even the permanent plantation workers suffer prolonged seasonal unemployment. Roughly 85 per cent of total labor requirements are concentrated in the seven-month period from October through April, during which cane is harvested and replanted. From early July through mid-September labor demand is virtually nil. Only 10 per cent of the labor force, consisting primarily of skilled workers, has full-time, year-round employment in the Negros sugar areas; the average amount of employment for unskilled workers is estimated to be 7.4 months per year (Aguilar, 1984, pp. 15–16).

Sugar-worker households typically spend 75–80 per cent of their income on food, an indication of their extreme poverty. In the late 1970s the daily wage of male laborers was equivalent to 3.9 kilos of second-class rice, roughly the same level recorded in a 1938 survey (Rutten, 1982, p. 39). Official data indicate that the real wage of sugarcane workers – when they have work – fell 10 per cent between 1970 and 1982 (see Table 2.7).

In the mid-1980s, the crisis of the Philippine sugar industry led to rising unemployment, further real wage declines, and a drying up of consumption credit. The result was starvation. Nutritional surveys in 1986 found that 74 per cent of pre-school children in Negros Occidental were malnourished, and that 35 per cent suffered from second and third-degree malnutrition, with body weights more than 25 per cent below normal.[17] The deprivation finally reached the threshold at which international agencies and the press take notice.[18] Declaring a 'hunger emergency' in Negros in September 1985, the United Nations Children's Fund (UNICEF) launched a feeding program, which was later supplemented by relief efforts of other agencies.

The plantation mode of sugarcane cultivation is not dictated by considerations of productive efficiency, as demonstrated by the viability of small-scale sugarcane cultivation in countries such as India, and in Central Luzon's Pampanga province, where sugarcane is typically grown on 4–10 hectare farms by share tenants using family labor.[19] Some Negros planters claim that large estates have 'economies of scale' since they can afford to own tractors for deep plowing, but rental markets in tractor services can eliminate this scale economy, and have done so in parts of Luzon and Mindanao where small and large sugarcane farms coexist.[20]

The limited evidence available on the relationship between farm size and productivity in Philippine sugarcane indicates that smaller farms tend to have (a) lower output per hectare and (b) considerably lower costs per hectare, such that (c) their cost of production per ton of sugar is lower. Moreover, smaller farms tend to use more labor-intensive techniques, raising employment and conserving 'high opportunity cost' resources such as machinery and chemicals.[21] But as Paige (1975, pp. 18–19) remarks, 'No matter how efficient a small holder's production, he cannot grow crops on lands that have been stolen from under him'.

During US colonial rule, the sugar bloc of wealthy planters and traders constituted 'the most powerful element in the Philippine economy' (Friend, 1963, p. 179). This dominance was challenged in the 1950s by the rising class of industrialists who prospered from import substitution. A sharp political cleavage arose over the issue of foreign exchange controls, with the sugar bloc leading the opposition to the controls (Doronila, 1985, pp. 104–5). The 1962 decontrol represented a political triumph for the bloc, and brought dramatic increases in their real income.[22] Together with the expansion of the US sugar quota, this windfall allowed the sugar bloc to 'reassert their political and economic authority' (Hawes, 1987, p. 92).

In the Marcos era, however, the Philippine sugar planters ultimately suffered not only reverses on the world market, as recounted in Chapter 6, but also political setbacks at home. After initially playing segments of the sugar bloc against each other, Marcos moved to emasculate the bloc's political and economic power so as to consolidate his own position. He struck politically by declaring martial law and dissolving Congress in 1972. He struck economically by the state takeover of sugar trading described in the next section. The power of the sugar bloc was not entirely uprooted by these measures, however, as it would have been by a definitive land reform. The bloc would re-emerge as a strong political force in 1986, when

Marcos was toppled and replaced by the daughter of a leading *hacendero* family.[23]

While the political fortunes of the sugar bloc fluctuated between 1962 and 1986, the relations of production on Philippine sugarcane plantations underwent subtle but important shifts. The patron-client ties between worker and planter gradually weakened. One symptom was the sugarcane workers' loss of usufructuary rights to plots of land. As planters sought to extend sugarcane acreage in the 1960s, many abandoned the traditional practice of allowing permanent plantation workers to cultivate rice on a tenancy basis on part of the hacienda lands.[24] Other symptoms of the erosion of patron-client ties included a contraction in consumption loans (see, for example, Gonzaga, 1986, pp. 69–70), the elimination of traditional Christmas gifts (e.g. Gonzaga, 1983, p. 76), the 'rationalization' of the work process by conversion from daily wages to piece rates, and the lowering of existing piece rates (see Rutten, 1982, pp.151–3).

The most far-reaching change was a trend towards the mechanization of sugarcane cultivation, which some analysts predicted would ultimately displace as much as 90 per cent of the labor force in sugarcane cultivation (McCoy, 1983, p. 166). Elsewhere in the world, the mechanization of sugarcane cultivation typically has occurred in response to rising labor costs sparked by the growth of alternative employment opportunities. Hawaii mechanized under the pressure of labor shortages during World War Two. In Australia, sugarcane was harvested by hand as late as 1960; thereafter, rising labor costs and technological innovations led to mechanization. Puerto Rico similarly mechanized in the 1970s in the face of rising wages.[25] Cuba began to mechanize after the 1959 revolution, when 'thanks to the expansion of other sectors of the economy, and to the social security system, the fear of unemployment and hunger no longer forced the rural workers to cut cane' (Edquist, 1985, p. 83).

This stimulus to mechanization has been absent in the Philippines. Real wages of sugarcane workers remained low and, if anything, displayed a downward trend in the Marcos years. Instead the primary stimulus came from the cheap credit policies of the government and international agencies, which reduced the cost of capital and tilted the relative advantages of labor and machines in favor of the latter. In 1966, the World Bank launched its first rural credit program in the Philippines. The loans, channelled through the Central Bank, led to a burst of tractor purchases, many of them by sugarcane planters. The key role of the credit program is indicated by the fact that 'the demand for machines fell off sharply with the exhaustion of the World Bank funds in 1968' (ILO, 1974, p. 523). The 1974 ILO mission (p. 526) asserted that the use of tractors in sugarcane production 'is probably justifiable whether labour and capital are measured at market prices or at their true social or opportunity costs'. If so, one must ask why subsidized credit was necessary to induce tractor purchases.

Sugarcane planters continued to be among the prime beneficiaries of subsequent rural credit programs, financed in part by further World Bank loans.[26] As of 1980, agricultural credit extended to sugarcane producers was equivalent to 474 per cent of gross value added in sugarcane production, a figure which can be contrasted to 58 per cent in rice and 9 per cent in corn.[27] As sugar prices dropped after 1975, the government suspended import duties on agricultural equipment, further encouraging mechanization (McCoy, 1983, p. 158). In addition, the influx of foreign lending to the Philippines in the late 1970s pushed up the real effective exchange rate, further lowering the cost to producers of imported equipment (see Chapter 11).

'Through its massive infusion of relatively cheap capital', writes McCoy (1985, p. 184), 'the World Bank had created a sufficient pool of heavy tractors to power any new system of mechanized cultivation'. This was the first step in the mechanization of Philippine sugarcane production. The second was the introduction in the late 1970s of an affordable set of matched implements developed in Australia, which could extend the tractors' uses beyond plowing to such operations as planting, fertilization, and weeding (for details, see McCoy, 1983, and Lacson, 1981). The final step, which has yet to be taken, is the mechanization of harvesting.

Some observers regarded mechanization as the *sine qua non* of efficiency and international competitiveness for the Philippine sugar industry. In 1979, Philippine Sugar Commission chairman Roberto Benedicto termed it 'the only option for raising the profitability of the industry'. In 1982, Labor Minister Blas Ople stated that 'while mechanization may cause labor displacement, it is inevitable if our sugar must remain competitive in the world market'.[28] The very limited role of 'market forces' in the world sugar trade was described in Chapter 6. It is by no means evident that labor-intensive sugarcane production in the Philippines would be uncompetitive with European or North American sugar production in the absence of massive subsidies to the latter. It is also far from clear that mechanization would be profitable in the low-wage Philippine context in the absence of direct and indirect subsidies on capital.

While mechanization has hastened the erosion of traditional patron-client ties between sugarcane workers and planters, the concomitant rise in labor militancy provides a further impetus for mechanization. 'After five years of paying for a machine', McCoy (1984, p. 71) remarks, 'a planter has acquired a capital asset, not a social responsibility'; moreover, machines are 'not inclined to disruptive industrial action'.The relations of production in the Philippine sugarcane sector thus have begun a transition from the personalized community of the traditional hacienda to the more impersonal world of the modern plantation.[29]

Bananas and Pineapples: The Modern Plantation

Philippine government strategy for the development of the country's two main non-traditional agricultural export crops, bananas and pineapples, has accorded a major role to transnational corporations (TNCs). 'To attract companies like yours', read a 1975 government advertisement in *Fortune* magazine, 'we have felled mountains, razed jungles, filled swamps, moved rivers, relocated towns, and in their place built power plants, dams, roads'.[30] Government efforts to attract TNCs went well beyond the provision of infrastructure. The government assisted in the acquisition of lands, imposed acreage restrictions to limit competition, and scrupulously refrained from imposing bothersome rules and regulations. In the words of the Agricultural Policy and Strategy Team's 1986 'green paper' (p. 287), the government policy was one of 'almost indiscriminate encouragement of foreign capital'.

Three motivations animated this policy. One was explicit: a belief that the TNCs would serve as agents of development, generating employment, foreign exchange, and technical progress, and providing the country with crucial access to overseas markets. The other two motives were unstated, but not unimportant: the creation of new vehicles for enrichment of political favorites, and the further cementing of the ties between the government and its foreign patrons.

The Philippine government's open door to transnational agribusiness dates from the US colonial era. The first TNC to invest in Philippine fruit exports was the California Packing Corporation (later to become Del Monte, a subsidiary of R. J. Reynolds), which commenced pineapple production in Mindanao in the late 1920s in response to pest problems in Hawaii. Through its local subsidiary, the Philippine Packing Corporation (Philpak), the firm initially circumvented the 1,024-hectare constitutional ceiling on individual landholdings 'by setting up homesteaders who claimed the land and then in turn leased the land to the corporation' (Hawes, 1987, p. 105). In the late 1930s the Philippine government devised a less cumbersome arrangement, with the creation of a public corporation known as the National Development Company (NDC). The NDC, permitted by law to 'hold public agricultural lands . . . in excess of areas permitted to private corporations, associations, and persons by the Constitution', entered into a 25-year contract with Philpak in 1938, granting the company exclusive use of 8,195 hectares of 'public' lands in Mindanao. This agreement, subsequently renewed for another 25 years, has been a source of political controversy in the Philippines, in part due to the very low rent.[31]

In 1963 a similar agreement paved the way for the second major agribusiness investment in Philippine fruit exports. The NDC entered into a 25-year contract with Dole, the fruit products subsidiary of the transnational Castle & Cooke (Hawes, 1987, pp. 109–10). The Agricultural Policy and Strategy Team (1986, p. 286) estimated that as of 1980 total rental and tax payments of Philpak and Dole amounted to 'a measly 1.7%' of their f.o.b. pineapple earnings. The Philippine pineapple export industry was entirely in the hands of these two TNCs until two smaller domestic firms entered the industry in the early 1980s (Hayami, Adriano and Quisumbing, 1987, p. 11).

In addition to 'public' lands, the pineapple transnationals acquired lands from individual smallholders through lease agreements.[32] In some cases, local officials are reported to have facilitated this process by refusing to process land title claims unless the farmer agreed to lease the land to the company (Broad, 1980, pp. 4–5). Nominal subcontracting agreements, in which the company supplies finance and inputs, and the farmer sells pineapples to the firm, have in practice entailed the surrender of 'absolute authority' over the land to the firm; according to Burbach and Flynn (1980, pp. 202–3), 'these contractees often wind up as hired laborers on their own lands'.

In the banana export industry, which began in the late 1960s, land acquisition was complicated by the fact that much of the most suitable land, also in Mindanao, was already heavily settled. Rather than engaging in direct cultivation, the transnational banana firms mostly entered into long-term agreements with local producers, under which the TNCs provide technical assistance, inputs and credit, and purchase bananas.

For the TNCs, the delegation of production to domestic partners has several advantages: production risks are shifted to the local corporation; adjustments of supply to demand fluctuations can be achieved via variations in quality control standards enforced by the TNC; and the tasks of acquiring land, dealing with the government, and controlling the agricultural laborers are left to local partners. The TNCs retain control over shipping and marketing, and this, together with the provision of production loans, ensures that 'their local partners will not think of going independent and directly selling their fruit to the market' (David *et al.*, 1983, p. 99). The prices in the transactions between the TNCs and their local partners are often a source of friction between them, as discussed in the next section.

In total, some 20,000 hectares are devoted to the cultivation of bananas for export in the Philippines – a statutory limit imposed by the government in order to restrict competition and protect profitability.[33] The largest of the domestic banana corporations is the Tagum Agricultural Development Corporation (TADECO), operating under a long-term marketing contract with the transnational United Fruit Company (later United Brands). In addition to the 1,024 hectares it owns outright (the legal limit), TADECO operates more than 4,000 hectares in the Davao Penal Colony. TADECO owner Antonio Floirendo, the 'warlord' of the Davao region in southern Mindanao, was a close political associate of Presidents Macapagal and Marcos (Hawes, 1987, p. 114). In addition to 7,500 resident banana workers, the firm employs prison labor for the most strenuous tasks on the plantation as part of the penal colony's 'rehabilitation program'. The 22-kilometer paved 'TADECO road', linking the plantation to the wharf, was 'built with government funds through the openly acknowledged intercession of Antonio Floirendo' (David *et al.*, 1983, pp. 31–5).

Other Philippine banana plantations, operated by domestic agro-corporations under marketing contracts with Del Monte's Philpak, Castle and Cooke's Dole affiliate, and several Japanese firms, generally range from 100 to 1,000 hectares. Much of this acreage is not owned outright by the domestic corporations, but rather is cultivated under two types of agreements with the landowners: lease agreements in which the owner formally rents the land to the corporation (or a corporate dummy), and farm management contracts in which the owner appoints the corporation to 'manage' the land in return for quasi-rent in the form of a fixed sum or a percentage of gross sales (David *et al.*, 1983, pp. 12–17).

In addition to the usual contracts with corporate farms, one TNC subsidiary (Stanfilco-Dole) entered into contracts with small banana growers, on average cultivating less than 6 hectares each. The difference from a wage-labor plantation is, however, less than meets the eye. According to the Agricultural Policy and Strategy Team (1986, p. 280), 'the provisions in the contracts regarding the production process are so rigid that the domestic producers become essentially disguised farm laborers'.[34]

In the export banana industry as a whole, wage laborers account for 85 per cent of the work force (Opena and Pahm, 1987, p. 7). The percentage is probably higher in the case of the pineapple industry. Wage workers on the corporate plantations are generally unionized. They are said to receive 'relatively more benefits' than wage laborers on small contract farms, and to be 'generally better off than those in other agricultural ventures'.[35] Nevertheless, a survey of twenty plantations by the Banana Export Foundation in the 1970s found that 70 per cent of the children of plantation workers suffered from moderate to severe malnutrition.[36]

Not all banana and pineapple plantation workers receive the legal minimum wage (Hawes, 1987, p. 123). One technique by which wages are minimized on some plantations is the *kabit* system, in which one worker (the *kabit*) is hired officially, and a second shadow worker performs an equal amount of work and shares the *kabit*'s wages. Similarly, male laborers hired by small growers are often expected to provide the unpaid labor of other family members. David (1982, pp. 459–60), who reports these phenomena, remarks that 'workers accept such onerous arrangements because if they do not agree to the terms, there are plenty of others to take their place'.

Labor costs represented less than 20 per cent of the gross banana price received by corporate growers from the TNCs in 1986. Non-labor costs, primarily for inputs and services provided by the TNCs, accounted for a further 40 per cent, leaving the growers a 40 per cent gross margin.[37] Within the Philippines, then, the lion's share of the income from export bananas goes to the corporate growers.

As in sugarcane, the dominance of the plantation mode of production in export bananas and pineapples cannot be attributed to agronomic imperatives. Small farmers can successfully grow bananas, as demonstrated by their dominance in production for the domestic market, which accounts for more than 90 per cent of the country's total banana acreage according to official statistics.[38] In the case of pineapples, the World Bank (1985d, p. 18) writes that the mechanized operations of the TNC plantations 'appear to be highly efficient'. The predominance of smallholder pineapple production in neighboring Malaysia suggests, however, that this is a viable alternative.[39]

As in the case of the Negros sugarcane plantations in an earlier era, the appropriation of land for non-traditional export crop plantations in Mindanao has been marked by protracted, and at times violent, struggles. Plantation area expansion has occurred, in the words of the Agricultural Policy and Strategy Team (1986, p. 283), 'at the expense of domestic tillers and minority groups'. Expansion was 'relatively easy' in the 1960s, as landholders 'were attracted by lump sum payments of several years' lease rentals or promises of easy money from contract growing', but in the 1970s:

> These landholders saw that earlier promises had not been completely true. In response, the military powers of the martial law government, subterfuge by government officials in the Bureau of Land cooperating with absentee landlords, harassment, and intimidation by corporate officials have all been used to get rid of the smallholders and acquire land needed for expansion. (Hawes, 1987, p. 123)

Reported pressure tactics have included threatening farmers with encirclement and loss of access to their lands if they do not sign lease agreements; the driving of cattle into cultivated fields by company employees protected by armed guards; the use of aerial sprays harming people and farm animals; and bulldozing people 'right off the land' (Burbach and Flynn, 1980, pp. 202–3). In the early 1980s, the deployment of the paramilitary 'lost command' to forcibly relocate settlers for the establishment of a large, NDC-backed palm-oil plantation in southern Mindanao extended this pattern to a new export crop (Sacerdoti and Ocampo, 1982).

Working as a wage laborer, remarks Hawes (1987, p. 121), 'is not very attractive to settlers who can make a free choice'. The relations of production in much of Philippine export agriculture represent the historic outcome of efforts by the wealthy and powerful to appropriate land. Their success has constrained the choices open to the poor, and has done much to channel the flow of income from export agriculture to a narrow elite.

RELATIONS OF EXCHANGE

The distribution of the income generated in Philippine export agriculture is shaped not only by the relations of production outlined in the previous section, but also by relations of exchange. In a world of perfect competition, income distribution would be determined solely by the distribution of endowments such as land, the tastes of consumers, and the technology of production. In the real world, however, where 'imperfect' competition is the rule, income distribution is also affected by market power, that is, by the ability of individual economic agents to affect prices.

Philippine export agriculture is not an exception. In coconut, the ability of buyers to depress the price of copra has long been a major avenue by which 'surplus' is extracted from producers. In sugar, the conflicts of interest among planters, millers, and exporters have long been a feature of the Philippine political scene. In both of these traditional export crops, the Marcos era saw far-reaching transformations of the market structure, with the consolidation of *de facto* monopsonies at the top of the marketing pyramid. In the non-traditional export crops, bananas and pineapples, the 'comparative advantage' of transnational corporations lies precisely in their control over worldwide marketing channels. In all these crops, market power has been deployed to redistribute income from producers to traders.

Coconut: From Oligopsony to Monopsony

Most copra in the Philippines is purchased from the growers by barrio (village) traders, who then sell it to town-based buyers, who in turn sell to the coconut mills and copra exporters. In the 1960s, according to Cernohous (1966, p. 74), there were more than 250,000 producers, roughly 10,000 barrio buyers, 3,400 town buyers, and fewer than 50 exporters and oil crushers.

Superimposed on this pyramid was a network of credit ties, binding individuals at each layer to those above them. 'The trade is financed from the top of the channel down', Cernohous explained, 'with many a town buyer actually being a mere agent of either an exporter or crusher, and most barrio buyers being sub-agents of town buyers'. The result was a pattern of market power whereby 'middlemen are essentially price takers *vis-à-vis* the group immediately above them, while at the same time being price makers *vis-à-vis* the group immediately below them'.

The mass of producers, of course, are simply price takers. Nyberg (1968, p. 52) reported that large coconut plantations often received prices 10–20 per cent higher than those received by small growers, perhaps by virtue of scale economies in marketing and their ability to bypass the lowest link in the marketing chain. In addition, small coconut farmers often have relatively little bargaining power owing to their lack of storage facilities, their need for cash, and their indebtedness to the buyer. The growers' lack of timely price information also enhances the monopsony power of the buyer, though Cernohous (p. 76) noted, 'even where the information reaches the farmer, in the absence of an actual competitive bid, it probably does not significantly alter his relative bargaining position'.

In some barrios there is only one buyer. Where there are several, the ability of growers to choose freely among them is often constrained by *suki* relationships, personalized ties between the grower and the barrio trader-creditor which are social as well as economic. These ties do not completely subordinate the grower to the buyer, but neither is the grower completely free. Cornista (1981, p. 350) reports, on the basis of field work in two Laguna villages, that a grower is obliged to sell to the *suki* buyer once the latter has extended credit.[40] If the buyer consistently offers an unfavorable price, however, the grower 'would seek out new buyers after paying his loan'. The extent of market power hence would hinge on the grower's ability to repay any accumulated debts to the copra buyer.

The sharp increase in coconut acreage in the 1960s and 1970s brought new buyers into the market, perhaps resulting in a diminution of local-level market power. Improved price information reduced the buyer's advantage in bargaining with individual growers. In some cases, a new practice emerged in which several potential buyers submit sealed bids to the grower who then can select the highest offer. Cornista (1981, p. 339) reports that this practice, known in Laguna as *subasta*, is confined to big coconut growers and remains less prevalent than individual bargaining. Moreover:

> To counteract the effects of *subasta* the buyers agreed to allow one of them (usually the biggest *kapitalista*) to outbid the rest. The profits which accrued from the transaction were divided equally among them. In a way, a monopsonistic situation resulted.   (Cornista, 1981, p. 340)

In the two villages studies by Cornista, this collusion eventually broke down as 'a number of coconut buyers started to act independently'.

The major change in coconut marketing during the Marcos era, however, was a dramatic concentration of market power at the top. This was achieved by the open exercise of political muscle, vividly illustrating one of the linkages between income and power discussed in Chapter 5. In the name of 'vertical integration' and 'rationalization', the Philippine coconut industry was consolidated under a single entity with effective control over virtually all copra purchases and over the production and sale of coconut oil on the domestic and export markets.

The takeover was engineered by a series of Presidential Decrees.[41] The three key steps were the imposition of levies on all coconut production, the creation of a bank in which these monies were deposited interest-free, and the purchase by that bank of the bulk of the country's oil-milling capacity. In theory, all of this was done for the benefit of the coconut growers, the nominal 'owners' of the assets purchased with the levies. In practice, the primary beneficiaries were a few close political associates of President Marcos, notably 'coconut king' Eduardo Cojuangco and Defense Minister Juan Ponce Enrile.

The first levy, imposed by legislative action in 1971, was to be used to provide credit to growers, to invest in the industry, and to finance the Philippine Coconut Producers' Federation, known as COCOFED, an association of large coconut landowners which had lobbied for passage of the law. A second, much larger levy was imposed by Presidential Decree in 1973. Known as the Coconut Consumers Stabilization Fund (CCSF) levy, its initial rationale was to subsidize domestic consumption of coconut products at a time of unprecedented high prices. In the next two years further decrees expanded the uses of the CCSF levy to include to include the establishment of Cojuangco's hybrid coconut seed farm and the acquisition of a commercial bank 'for the benefit of the coconut farmers'.

The United Coconut Planters' Bank (UCPB), with Cojuangco as president and Enrile as chairman of the board, soon became one of the largest commercial banks in the Philippines.[42] The interest-free deposit base provided by levy funds gave the bank a unique advantage. In January 1979, UCPB acquired Legaspi Oil Company, which milled a quarter of all Philippine coconut oil exports, in 'one of the largest corporate takeovers in Philippine history' (Tiglao, 1981, p. 88). Later in the same year UCPB bought Granexport Corporation from the US firm Cargill. These and other mills were placed under the control of the newly formed United Coconut Oil Mills (UNICOM), which by 1980 had cornered more than 80 per cent of the country's entire oil-milling capacity.[43]

Overcapacity in coconut milling, which had been stimulated by government Board of Investment incentives in the 1970s, contributed to the willingness of firms to sell out to UNICOM. An added push came from a 1978 Presidential Decree, which provided that subsidies funded by the CCSF levy would be provided only to mills owned and controlled by 'the coconut farmers', that is, by the UCPB and UNICOM. According to a US Embassy cable, the Filipino owners of relatively small mills were told, 'It was sell or else!' Large foreign mills were not subjected to 'direct pressure', but 'were simply put in a position where the owners believed that it was in their best interest to sell'.[44]

President Marcos characterized these developments as a historic triumph for the coconut growers: 'For half a century, the coconut farmers were the forgotten men of the country. Now you are no longer just coconut planters, you are bankers, owners of a coco mill complex'.[45]

A rather different picture emerges from other sources, among them US government cables obtained under the Freedom of Information Act. A May 1980 cable, marked 'confidential', offered the following candid assessment:

> Since martial law was declared in September 1972, the coconut industry has been steadily brought under the influence of a small group of people, chief among whom are [name deleted] and Eduardo "Danding" Cojuangco, both men long and close political associates of President Marcos. The prime motivation appears to be near total control of the coconut industry. There are four reasons which might explain why President Marcos would implicitly support, and even aid and encourage [names deleted], men whom he trusts in this effort.
> — First, control of the coconut industry provides President Marcos [deleted] with additional political and financial leverage to remain in power.
> — Second, control of the industry by men close to the President denies that control to anyone else.
> — Third, Marcos appears to use this method to reward his associates in the business community, the military and the bureaucracy.

— Finally, control of the industry has allowed the Philippines to attempt to better its terms of trade for coconut oil sold on the world
market.[46]

The total 'surplus' extracted from coconut producers by the Marcos-
Cojuangco-Enrile combine was substantial indeed. A 1984 US Embassy
cable reported that total collections levied on coconut producers since 1973
amounted to 9.26 billion pesos, equivalent to more than $1.1 billion at pre-
vailing rates of exchange. In addition, UNICOM used its control over prices
to establish profit margins of two or three pesos per kilo of copra, compared
to a 'good' normal margin of fifty centavos; the Embassy calculated that in
1983 alone, each peso of margin netted UNICOM an extra $214 million. At
the same time, the Embassy reported that UNICOM officially undervalued
its coconut oil exports, the difference between the actual and stated value
being 'deposited in dollar accounts abroad or used to fund various Cojuangco
projects'. The cable reported that, on top of these exactions, 'Cojuangco has
found many indirect methods of profiting from the monopoly'. For example,
equipment and materials purchases by UNICOM were routed through a
company operated by Cojuangco's son, who 'takes a ten per cent commission
on all purchases'.[47]

The Embassy estimated that the income personally accumulated by
Cojuangco through the coconut industry ranged 'from several hundred
million dollars to over a billion'.[48] It also reported that:

> Cojuangco supports the President in many different ways. It is generally
> believed that Cojuangco shares the spoils of the coconut monopoly with
> the President, although details of amounts and methods of payment are
> lacking. It is rumored that he handles some of the President's own
> investments. As a regional KBL chairman [Marcos's political party] in
> Central Luzon, Cojuangco is responsible for keeping the party faithful in
> line and for promoting KBL victories at the polls. . . . On a more personal
> level, Cojuangco offered Leer [*sic*] jets as wedding presents for Irene
> Marcos [the President's daughter] and her spouse when they were married
> last year. President and Mrs. Marcos eventually received the gifts when
> the newlyweds declined them'.[49]

Some of the wealth extracted from the coconut sector was used to enter
other industries via takeovers of existing firms. For example, Cojuangco
purchased large blocks of stock in the San Miguel Corporation, the largest
private corporation in the Philippines and the largest food and beverage
firm in Asia, and became its vice chairman.[50] A substantial fraction was

undoubtedly transferred abroad, a component of the capital flight examined in Chapter 10.

The coconut cabal was much less successful in wielding market power to secure higher prices for coconut oil abroad, owing to the ease of substitution among competing oils. An attempt to establish a 'COCOPEC' cartel failed completely; in the words of the US Embassy cable, 'All UNICOM got for its efforts was anti-trust suits in the US'.[51] The takeover of the coconut industry thus did nothing to enlarge the Philippine economic pie, but only changed the way it was sliced.

Within the Philippines, there was little organized resistance to the takeover. In part this was due to the poverty and geographic dispersal of the coconut growers, but outright intimidation also played a role. In July 1982, former Vice President Emmanuel Pelaez, the leading critic of the coconut monopoly in the Philippine legislature, was seriously wounded and his driver killed in an ambush.[52]

The most influential opposition instead came from the World Bank, which pressed for a 'return of market forces' to the coconut industry.[53] The International Monetary Fund likewise is reported to have demanded the dismantling of UNICOM as a condition for a standby credit. In response, a January 1985 Presidential Decree abolished UNICOM and replaced it by a 'cooperative endeavor' with sole legal authority to export coconut oil (Espiritu, 1987). The very limited nature of this reform is evident from an August 1985 US Embassy memorandum, also released under the Freedom of Information Act, which reported that 'current members of the coconut exporters cooperative have agreed to give Danding Cojuangco 32 centavos per kilogram of coconut oil exported and 20 centavos per kilogram of other coconut product exports', and that the money 'will be used for the coming elections'.[54]

In sum, the market structure of the Philippine coconut industry underwent a major concentration at the top in the 1970s and early 1980s. The primary motive for this transformation, and its primary effect, was redistribution of the income generated by the country's leading agricultural export. The beneficiaries were a handful of politically powerful individuals. The losers included millers and traders driven out of the industry, and above all the coconut growers, who experienced an intensification of the monopsonistic environment in which they sold their product.[55]

Sugar: Take from the Rich, Give to the Richer

Sugarcane planters have long been among the wealthiest and most powerful segments of Philippine society. In this respect, they differ greatly from most of the country's coconut growers. Yet the sugarcane planters, too, were victims of a similarly dramatic concentration of market power in the Marcos era, through which income was reallocated from the planters to a parastatal monopsony controlled by a presidential crony.

Prior to the advent of centrifugal sugar mills in the period 1909–29, each plantation had its own small steam-driven mill. The establishment of much larger centrifugal mills, or 'sugar centrals', created natural monopsonies at the local level. The centrals were 'linked to the individual haciendas by a network of steel rails and iron clad milling contracts' (McCoy, 1988, p. 19). The mills were financed by foreign investors and by the Philippine National Bank (PNB), which was created in 1916 in large part for this purpose (Hawes, 1987, p. 87). The PNB selectively distributed capital for mill construction to 'the most powerful family in each Negros sugar district', and in so doing it 'split the once homogeneous planter elite into contending sectors', with the division of profits between planters and millers as the focus of contention (McCoy, 1988, p. 19).

The ensuing conflict between millers and other planters was fought in the political arena. The initial 30-year contracts gave 45 per cent of the milled sugar to the planters and 55 per cent to the centrals, an arrangement highly advantageous to the latter (McCoy, 1988, p. 19).[56] By the late 1930s the planters' confederation in Negros had succeeded in raising the planters' share to 60 per cent in a number of centrals (Friend, 1963, p. 192). In 1953 the planters won passage of congressional legislation mandating a 70–30 split in their favor.

Limited access to the US market under that country's sugar quota created a further arena for intra-producer conflict and state intervention. The Sugar Limitation Law of 1934, passed in response to the imposition of the US quota, established individual quotas for each mill and grower for both the US export market and the domestic market. These quotas allocated the 'rents' created by the divergence between politically determined producer prices and the lower world market price. It has been estimated that the annual resource transfer from the US to the Philippines under the sugar quota system averaged $190 million per year (in 1980 dollars) in the period 1963–73.[57] Over time, the allocation of this income came to be viewed as 'similar to a property right', and tended to become institutionalized due to political inertia and to the fact that 'the additional resources available to rent recipients make it difficult to revise public policy' (Nelson, 1988, p. 291). Income and power again proved mutually reinforcing.

The Marcos regime successfully undermined these *de facto* property rights, however, and diverted a large fraction of the income generated by sugar exports into a few politically favored hands. The two key events came in 1974: the US abandonment of the sugar quota system, and a Marcos presidential decree which created the Philippine Exchange Company, Inc. (Philex) as the sole purchaser and exporter of Philippine sugar. The decree's unstated objective was 'to reduce the financial power of the owners of the large sugar estates' (Nelson, 1988, p. 288), and it has been characterized as 'every bit as important as the abolition of Congress two years earlier in President Marcos's continuing effort to reshape the Philippine political economy' (Hawes, 1987, pp. 94–5).

It may not have been coincidental that the US quota abandonment and the establishment of Philex occurred in the same year. The termination of the US quota increased Philex's room for manoeuvre, since the final market price was no longer stable and known to the planters. Former Ambassador Ramon Nolan was instructed by Marcos to 'get ready' to go to Washington to lobby for extension of the US Sugar Act, but to Nolan's astonishment the order to go never came. 'The country's premium market was at stake', he recalls, 'but we didn't send anyone!'[58] The lure of the high world market price prevailing at the time may also have contributed to the Philippine government's apparent complacence.

Philex initially reaped extraordinary profits, selling sugar on world markets for more than three times what it paid to the planters.[59] But when world prices bottomed out Philex began to incur losses. Marcos then transferred control of sugar trading to the Philippine Sugar Commission (Philsucom), with the National Sugar Trading Corporation (Nasutra) as its trading arm. Under its chairman, Roberto Benedicto, Philsucom was empowered to buy and sell all Philippine sugar, to set purchase prices, to buy transport and milling companies, and to take over mills deemed to be operating inefficiently. Like Eduardo Cojuangco, his counterpart in the coconut sector, Benedicto set up a bank, the Republic Planter's Bank, which soon became the sugar industry's second major source of finance after the PNB (McCoy, 1983, p. 146).

A 1984 US embassy cable released under the Freedom of Information Act reported that Benedicto 'has used his position to great advantage over the past several years to forge an economic fiefdom, to amass great wealth and to develop considerable political influence in sugar growing areas'. Among the profit mechanisms enumerated in the cable were the following:

— the collection of payoffs by traders seeking allocations of sugar for sale at guaranteed profit margins in the domestic market;
— the withdrawal of sugar from Nasutra warehouses, for sale domestically or abroad, without any record of the transaction: 'in all, some 600,000

metric tons of raw sugar is reportedly unaccountably missing from Nasutra warehouses';

— withholding of taxes from payments to producers, which were not turned over to the government;

— excessive withholding of money from payments to producers for repayment of PNB loans incurred during the period of low prices from 1977–80;

— withholding of 3 US cents per pound for 'export trading costs' when actual costs 'should be 1 to 1.5 cents per pound'; and

— 'inefficient and redundant shipping patterns' designed to benefit Benedicto and other Nasutra officials with shipping company interests.

The cable concluded that 'the operations of this one-man fiefdom amount to a significant and growing drain on the economy of the country'.[60]

Discrepancies between the reported and actual prices received by Nasutra's marketing offices in New York, London and elsewhere provided a further avenue for the siphoning of profits, according to the late MP Fermin Caram, Jr., a prominent Benedicto opponent.[61] It unlikely that the magnitude of such discrepancies will ever be known. Caram also charged that the non-enforcement of favorable long-term sugar contracts signed by Nasutra in 1980, 'for reasons known only to Benedicto and his cohorts', deprived the country of $1.1 billion in foreign exchange earnings (Santos, 1985).

Whereas the years prior to 1974 had seen steady transfers of 'rents' to Philippine sugar producers, subsequent years saw the reverse: resources were extracted from them. Nelson (1988, pp. 290–1) estimates that from 1974 to 1980 producers lost an average $406 million per year in 1980 dollars, and speculates that the largest illegal diversions of funds took place after that, from 1980 to 1985.

Where did the money go? No firm answer can be given to this question, but it seems that little was invested productively in the Philippines. Some was recycled by the Marcos regime into patronage and election campaigns, providing what the US embassy termed 'additional political and financial leverage to remain in power'.[62] But a number of observers concluded that much of the money was spirited out of the country.[63]

Although sugar planters and millers were more powerful than the small coconut growers, under martial law their political leverage was reduced to a historic low. Planter organizations campaigned for reforms, but many were reluctant to oppose the monopsony publicly because they were 'deeply in debt to banks controlled by Benedicto' and feared retaliation 'in the form of foreclosures or other economic measures'.[64] Labor unions staged work stoppages and picketed Nasutra's offices. Miller associations submitted appeals to Marcos. After the restoration of parliament, opposition MP's raised questions in subcommittee hearings.

As in the coconut industry, powerful opposition to the monopsony came from the World Bank, the International Monetary Fund, and the US government.[65] As always, however, their pressure was tempered by a desire to maintain friendly relations with the Marcos regime. Their aim was to rein in the worst economic piracy of the regime, not to topple the pirates. Finally, in December 1985, in response to the overall privatization guidelines established by the International Monetary Fund, a new trading firm, the Philippine Sugar Marketing Corporation (Philsuma), was created with representatives from the planters, the millers, and the government, to replace Nasutra (Reinah, 1987, p. 151). History did not provide adequate time to assess the efficacy of this belated reform, as Marcos fled the country two months later.

In sum, the distribution of income from Philippine sugar exports shifted dramatically in the Marcos era. The earlier system for the allocation of profits, notably those gained from access to the protected US market, was supplanted by a state-sponsored monopsony. Under the new order, Roberto Benedicto and his subordinates 'profited immensely', in the words of a US embassy cable, 'at the expense of planters, sugar workers, millers, and the economy of the country'.[66]

By the end of the Marcos era, the Philippine sugar industry was in a state of near-collapse. Most planters were deeply in debt, and sugarcane acreage had fallen to its lowest level since 1970.[67] The planters blamed the Benedicto monopsony and the slump in the world sugar market, but their indebtedness can also be attributed at least in part to their lavish lifestyles. 'Even when prices were low', one planter explained, 'we always made some profit because wages were so low'.[68] Others claimed that sugarcane growing became a losing proposition.[69] In either case the planters attempted to pass part of the adjustment burden to their workers: 'When the planters are squeezed', said one, 'we squeeze our labor' (Jones, 1980, p. 312). Under the stress of the crisis, traditions of paternalism on the sugar plantations further eroded. The transformation of exchange relations thus accelerated the changes in production relations in the sugar sector described above.

Bananas and Pineapples: The Fruits of Market Power

In the case of bananas and pineapples, the non-traditional agricultural exports which grew dramatically in the 1960–86 period, exchange relations again had a major influence on the distribution of income. Here market power was wielded not by a pseudo-public agency, but rather by three transnational corporations. And it was exercised not only *vis-à-vis* producers in the Philippines, but also *vis-à-vis* consumers in importing countries.

Del Monte and Castle & Cooke (Dole) marketed virtually all Philippine exports of canned pineapples. Together with United Brands, they also marketed four-fifths of the country's banana exports. Control over shipping facilities and marketing channels is the heart of the TNCs' operations, as evidenced by their willingness to leave production to nominally independent producers in many countries, as in the Philippine banana sector.

As noted above, there is often little difference between the case in which the TNC produces directly with wage labor and that in which it enters into subcontracting agreements with small growers. The latter effectively become hired laborers with their 'wage' (and any compensation for their rights to the land) set by TNC control over the prices of credit, inputs, and output. In this case, exchange relations are practically inseparable from production relations.

In the case of agreements with corporate banana growers, exchange relations govern the distribution of profit between the domestic producer and the TNC. The attendant conflict over the purchase price became particularly acute when the Japanese market for bananas began to shrink in the late 1970s. The bargaining strategies of the TNCs varied. The head of the bargaining team for Del Monte growers stated that Del Monte 'drives a hard bargain and transfers any losses to its growers', precipitating several bankruptcies by 1980, whereas Dole 'gives out loans to its growers, keeps the plantations going and perpetually in debt'.[70]

Data on gross margins indicate that the free-on-board price of Philippine bananas in 1984 was only 16 per cent of the retail price in Japan (FAO, 1986, p. 230). As noted in the previous section, 20 per cent of the growers' price represented labor costs, 40 per cent non-labor costs, and 40 per cent growers' profit; banana production labor thus accounted for about 3 per cent of the ultimate retail price, and growers' profit for 6 per cent. The extent to which the market power of the banana TNCs brings them higher net returns on investment cannot be gauged in the absence of data on profit rates from particular activities, a problem compounded by transfer pricing.[71]

A curious feature of the world banana trade, noted by the FAO (1986, p. 9), is that 'the percentage relationship between prices at different stages of the marketing system tends to remain highly stable in the long run, even when the system is subjected to great shocks'. In 1974, for example, when Latin American countries imposed banana export taxes, the resulting increase in the f.o.b. price was not passed on to consumers on a cent-for-cent basis, but instead was amplified via 'a succession of percentage adjustments in all margins of the system'. Two interpretations can be placed on this phenomenon, both of which suggest that the three banana TNCs, which together account for 70 per cent of total world trade, use their market power to reap above-normal profits. One possibility is that prices can be altered without regard to value added along the marketing chain. The other is that the f.o.b. price (including any export tax) in fact represents the main investment of working capital by the TNC, with relatively little value added thereafter, in which case the 84 per cent of the retail price absorbed by the marketing agents would seem excessive.

The Marcos regime attempted to channel a share of the profits generated by non-traditional agricultural exports to domestic political allies, the most famous of whom was Antonio Floirendo, the 'banana king' of the Davao region in southern Mindanao. The regime's room for manoeuvre was far more constrained, however, than in the coconut and sugar sectors. Hawes (1987, p. 103) observes: 'The foreign investor, at least in the case of fruit products, was too powerful a member of the "pact of domination" which makes up the Philippine state to be directly attacked by Marcos'. The government's response to the Davao banana growers' complaints about the TNCs' pricing policies is revealing: the top agro-export official of the Board of Investments 'hastened to remind the growers that while the banana multinationals are supposedly reaping high profits from the banana business in Davao, they established the banana industry in the country by way of capital infusion, technical assistance and marketing, and they are subject to the usual business risks'.[72]

In the non-traditional crops, then, as in coconut and sugar, exchange relations profoundly influenced the distribution of income from Philippine export agriculture. The main difference has been the dominant role of transnational corporations in the non-traditional crops, which limits the scope for surplus appropriation by domestic power brokers.

CONCLUSIONS

The prevailing relations of production and exchange together have meant that in export agriculture, as in other sectors of the Philippine economy, income is distributed in an extremely unequal fashion. The United States Agency for International Development (1980, p. 26) summarizes the result: 'Export expansion favors plantation agriculture and ties up substantial land assets in the hands of the few to the detriment of the landless agricultural workers, who receive a small share of the returns while suffering prolonged unemployment during periods of over-supply and periodically depressed prices'.

The core of the export agriculture development strategy in the Marcos era was the pursuit of self-interest. 'Marcos based his political coalition more on the pursuit of individual interest', Hawes (1987, p. 129) remarks, 'than on commitment to an ideology or even a shared vision of how agricultural exports could lead to national development'. Government policies aimed not to promote short-run efficiency, nor to foster long-run growth, nor to improve the well-being of the poor, but rather 'to transfer income to groups with the most political power' (Nelson, 1988, p. 283).

Success, like beauty, lies in the eye of the beholder. For Marcos and his cronies, who extracted billions of pesos from Philippine export agriculture, the strategy was a smashing success, the sole regret being that it could not continue longer. For the sugar planters, the verdict was mixed: the exactions of Marcos *et al.* were a serious burden, but some alternatives, such as genuine land reform, would have been worse. For the country's poor majority – among them the small farmers fleeced by the coconut monopsony, the sugar workers facing starvation in Negros, and the peasants displaced by the expansion of fruit plantations, the strategy was calamitous. Judgments as to the overall success or failure of the strategy would vary according to the weights one assigns to the welfare of these different groups. The implicit weights assigned by those who guided the country's policies are clear enough.

One limitation of comparative advantage as a guide to trade strategy was examined in Chapter 6: the phenomena of declining terms of trade and price instability. The distributional dynamics analyzed in this chapter bring out a second limitation: within a country, one person's advantage can be another's disadvantage. This happens not merely because some domestic products would be uncompetitive in a world of free trade – a point recognized in conventional trade theory – but also because interactions between wealth and power can set in motion a process of cumulative income polarization. Such interactions have long been a feature of both production relations and exchange relations in Philippine export agriculture.

The distributional outcome recounted in this chapter is not inherent in export agriculture. It could be greatly altered by Philippine government policy. Land reform and the systematic reduction of market power could redirect income to those whose labor produces the crops. The external constraints imposed by the political economy of world commodity markets would remain, however. Hence a case can be made not only for redistribution, but also for some diversification away from the leading agricultural exports, via allocation of land and labor to other uses.[73]

Redistribution and diversification would be complementary policies, when the latter is understood to include a shift to the cultivation of crops for domestic consumption, including rice and corn. Back in the 1890s, when the Negros sugarcane workers rose in revolt against the plantation owners, their aim was to 'destroy the haciendas and return to small-scale rice farming' (McCoy, 1984, p. 90). Nearly a century later, banana workers in Mindanao 'dreamed of the day when they could take their machetes and chop down the banana plants and begin growing corn' (Hawes, 1987, p. 124). The National Federation of Sugar Workers pioneered a program in the 1980s under which sugarlands were sown to rice and other crops.[74]

The link between land reform and crop diversification arises not only from the laborers' immediate desire for food security, but also from the cost advantages of family as opposed to hired labor, which open possibilities for more labor-intensive crops.[75] This was illustrated on a Negros sugarcane plantation which converted to rice cultivation in the wake of the 1980s crisis. Part of the land was cultivated directly by the workers, who paid a low rent in exchange for agreeing to work for the landlord at below-market wages on the remainder. The average rice yield in the workers' fields was nearly double that in the landlord's. Reporting this case, Hayami, Quisumbing and Adriano (1987, p. 18) conclude that it demonstrates that 'wage workers can become efficient farmers and that small family farms are the more efficient production organization than large estates based on wage labor, especially for labor-intensive crops such as irrigated rice'.[76]

Although the Marcos regime has passed into history, the entrenched interests in Philippine export agriculture continue to oppose alternative policies of land reform, market reform, and crop diversification. Shortly after taking power, President Corazon Aquino, the daughter of one of the most prominent sugar landowning families in the country, announced that she was 'not inclined to include sugarlands under land reform as studies show that the peculiarity of sugar production is such that it would not be economically feasible to cut up such lands into small parcels'.[77] Del Monte, the transnational fruit exporter, meanwhile 'threatened to relocate its operations to Thailand or Indonesia should the land-reform programme lead to drastic reductions in its land area' (Galang, 1988). Five years after Marcos's downfall, export agriculture remained untouched by land reform.

In future years, as in the past, the sector will provide a window through which central features of the Philippine political economy are transparently clear. The view it offers remains one of external vulnerability, internal inequity, and profound conflict over the control of resources and the exercise of market power.

NOTES

1. Cited by Hawes (1987, p. 57). In sandy, coastal zones this tendency towards monoculture reflects the special characteristics of soils, but in other places food crops such as rainfed rice or white corn would be among the feasible alternatives.
2. Data reported by Cornista and Pahm (1987, p. 23).
3. Cornista and Escueta (1983, pp. 5–6) and interview with Luzviminda B. Cornista, Manila, 24 January 1989.
4. Cited by Guerrero (1985, pp. 23–5). Mangahas (1985, Table 340.1, pp. 212–13) presents unpublished national sample survey data indicating that hired laborers accounted for a somewhat lower proportion, 48 per cent of the labor force in coconut farming in 1975.
5. Tiglao's estimates are derived from data for the mid-1970s. Annual data on real wages of coconut laborers presented by the World Bank (1985a, p. 29) for the years 1970–82 show a near-zero growth trend and much less instability than copra prices. The short-run elasticity of the real wage with respect to the real price of copra for these years is −0.01 (estimated using the ratio of the nominal copra price index to import price index as reported in Table 6.3). There is thus little evidence that copra price movements 'trickle down' to coconut laborers.
6. For 1980 data, see Hayami, Quisumbing, and Adriano (1990, p.117).
7. See Chapter 5, notes 71 and 72 (p. 161), above. Ofreneo (1980, p. 104) remarks that many small owner-operators in the Philippines continue to grow coconuts even though they 'would be registering net losses if their unpaid labor and that of their families were included in the computation' of farm income when valued at the market wage. The same finding in Indian farm management studies in the 1950s sparked the development of the theoretical literature on the inverse relation between farm size and land productivity (Sen, 1962).
8. Habito (1987a, p. 220). However, in Laguna and Cavite, where proximity to the Manila market opens profitable opportunities for intercropping with fruit trees, landowners have planted lanzones using hired labor, often with no involvement of the coconut tenant (interview with Luzviminda B. Cornista, Manila, 24 January 1989).
9. In 1982 as in 1960, roughly 80 per cent of sugarcane acreage was in farms 10 hectares and larger. The share of farms 50 hectares and larger declined, however, from 71 to 44 per cent of total acreage, owing to some 'fragmentation of these landholdings into mini-haciendas' (Bravo, Cornista and Ramos, 1986, Table 4 and p. 6). Schul (1967, pp. 164–6) gives several examples of plantation subdivision through inheritance, but

notes that in some cases the heirs create family corporations to keep large holdings intact.

10.   For an illuminating account of these events, see McCoy (1982).

11.   Quoted by McCoy (1984, p. 82). 'One of the most spectacular of these land grabbers', McCoy writes, was Teodoro Benedicto, the ancestor of Marcos's 'sugar czar' Roberto Benedicto.

12.   Echauz (1978, p. 61). He explained: 'There are sufficient laborers on the Island, but they do not like daily work in the fields. They prefer to enjoy the bounties of the plains and mountains laden with fruit or the resources of the rivers and seas that, with little effort, provide them with their daily bread. The need for able hands in Negros can only be answered by seeking them in other provinces'.

13.   In the Victorias milling district in Negros, for example, Schul (1967, p. 168) reported that '82 per cent of the land is owned by persons living outside the political boundary of the district'. For a social profile of the planter class, see Gonzaga (1986, pp. 38–44).

14.   Quoted by Chapman (1987, p. 26).

15.   Bravo, Cornista, and Ramos (1986, p. 10 and Table 9). Estimates of the number of sugar workers vary; see Aguilar (1984, pp. 10–11) for a comparison of several estimates for Negros.

16.   These practices were documented by Jesena (1969), a priest and professor at Ateneo de Manila University who lived and worked among the *sacadas*.

17.   Operation Timbang survey, cited by Japan Committee for the Negros Campaign (1987, pp. 16–17). Although this represented an increase in malnutrition over the immediately preceding years, a 1976 survey by the same group had found an even higher percentage of second and third degree malnutrition (42%), suggesting that widespread hunger is a longstanding feature of the Negros sugar economy.

18.   See, for example, McGill (1986) and Coote (1987, pp. 34–8).

19.   McCoy (1982, p. 325; 1985, p. 179). In neighboring Tarlac province, however, sugarcane is grown primarily on large haciendas.

20.   Hayami, Quisumbing and Adriano (1987, p. 15). A second ostensible scale economy is sometimes claimed to lie in the scheduling of cane deliveries to sugar mills. Yet Hayami, Quisumbing and Adriano (1987, pp. 15–16) report that most mills practice no effective scheduling of cane deliveries. The one exception they found was a large mill in Luzon's Batangas province. The average sugarcane farm supplying the mill was only one hectare in size, yet the mill had successfully reduced the interval between harvesting and milling to 1.5 days, compared to a 7-day average elsewhere in the country.

21.   A 1985 Philippine Sugar Commission study cited by the World Bank (1986a, Table 15, p. 80) reported that production costs were 108 pesos/picul of sugar on small farms of ten hectares and less, compared to 124 pesos on medium (10–50 hectare) farms, and 120 pesos on large (above 50 hectare) plantations. The World Bank concludes (p. 22) that

higher yields on large farms 'in general do not fully compensate for the increased costs per hectare resulting from a much higher level of mechanization, fertilizers and other inputs, overhead costs and finance charges'. However, the data appear to be based on a sample of only nine farms, so any conclusions must be tentative. The World Bank also estimated (pp. 76–7) that labor use per hectare was 30 per cent higher on low input/output sugarcane farms than on high input/output ones for the first (planted) crop, and the same for the second (ratoon) crop. Similar conclusions were reached in an intensive study of four sugarcane farms by the Ministry of Agrarian Reform (1984, Part II, p. 138).

22. Treadgold and Hooley (1967, p. 116) estimated that real incomes of exporters 'probably at least doubled' after decontrol. This was anticipated by Legarda (1962).

23. Corazon Cojuangco Aquino's family owns the 6,500-hectare Hacienda Luisita in Tarlac and a sugar mill there which accounted for 4% of total Philippine sugar production in 1974–83 (Galang, 1987).

24. See Rutten (1982, pp. 13, 27); see also her account (p. 156) of a violent 1978 confrontation which resulted from a planter's decision to evict workers from the small plots of rice land they tenanted.

25. These examples are mentioned by McCoy (1983, pp. 148–50, 155–6).

26. Between 1965 and 1978, the World Bank extended four rural credit loans to the Philippines, totalling $76 million. For an account of how 'the Philippine sugar industry succeeded in transforming the World Bank's third rural credit programme into a tractor finance scheme for large plantations', see McCoy (1985, pp. 180–2).

27. World Bank (1983, p. 139). The corresponding figures reported for sugarcane, rice and corn in 1975 were 369, 38, and 10 per cent, respectively.

28. Both Benedicto and Ople are quoted by Gonzaga (1983, p. 1). Even writers keenly aware of the social consequences of sugar mechanization in the Philippine setting have concluded that mechanization is 'dictated by world market forces', and that 'the sugar industry's choice remains one between mechanization or bankruptcy' (McCoy, 1985, p. 192).

29. See also Rutten (1982, pp. 10, 178). This usage of terms *hacienda* and *plantation* differs somewhat from that of Paige (1975, pp. 4–11), who defines the 'commercial hacienda' as an enterprise on which both owners and workers derive their income primarily from land (the latter via subsistence tenancies), and a 'plantation' as one on which owners derive income primarily from capital, and workers from wages. Contemporary Philippine sugar plantations do not fit neatly into Paige's typology; like Malaysian rubber estates (described by Paige, pp. 51–7), they seem closer to the land/wage category of owner/worker income sources, a combination he identifies with migratory labor, sharecropping, and a propensity for revolutionary change.

30. 'Remember Bataan?' *Fortune*, October 1975, p. 47. The advertisement was for the Bataan Export Processing Zone, but the comments are equally applicable to agribusiness investment.

31. In the early 1960s Senator Lorenzo Tanada, a leading opponent of the agreement, estimated the yearly rental paid by Philpak to the NDC at 8–10 pesos per hectare, versus a market rate of at least 500 pesos/hectare. See Hawes (1987, p. 106).

32. Estimates of the transnationals' pineapple acreage vary: Tadem (1980, p. 50) reports that Castle & Cooke and Del Monte cultivate 30,000 hectares and 24,000 hectares, respectively, while Hayami, Adriano and Quisumbing (1987, pp. 17–18) report corresponding figures of 10,000 and 11,400 hectares. Hayami, Adriano and Quisumbing (1987, p. 18) report that land leased from private owners represents half of Philpak's pineapple acreage and 20 per cent of Dole's.

33. Presidential Letter of Instruction (LOI) No. 58, issued in 1973, set a 21,000-hectare limit; this was increased to 25,500 hectares by LOI No. 790 in 1979 (FAO, 1986, pp. 35–6; David *et al.*, 1983, pp. 21–5). According to Krinks (1983a, p. 121), LOI No. 58 was 'drafted by corporate executives' in the banana industry. The Agricultural Policy and Strategy Team (1986, p. 283) remarks that these decrees assured 'oligopolistic control of the industry'. FAO (1986, p. 35) data indicate that net area remained below the statutory limit in the early 1980s, reflecting the depressed state of the country's export market. This does not mean that acreage limitation is superfluous as a barrier to entry, however, since (a) in theory, the profit-maximizing level of output would be higher under competition than under oligopoly, and (b) other potential entrants might be able to produce at lower cost, for example owing to the labor and supervision cost advantages of family farms.

34. The Stanfilco 'independent growers program' is discussed in detail by David *et al.* (1983, pp. 53–76), who highlight the chronic indebtedness of the small growers to the firm. The firm's general manager characterized the grower accounts as 'a pain in the neck' (Friesen and Stoltzfus, 1978, p. 7), and the company reportedly decided to phase out the program in 1985 (Agricultural Policy and Strategy Team, 1986, p. 282). The FAO (1986, p. 38) states that rising production costs in excess of output price increases had already led most small independent growers 'to sell out to the exporters and become lessors of their land'.

35. Opena and Pahm (1987, pp. 8, 15). Hayami, Adriano and Quisumbing (1987, pp. 32–3) similarly conclude that the wage rates of regular plantation workers are 'quite high', generating average incomes comparable to those of an owner-cultivator with one to three hectares of land.

36. Cited by Lappe and McCallie (1978, p. 12).

37. Calculated from data presented by Opena and Pahm (1987, Table 3, p. 21).

38. Little has been written about the domestic banana sector. However, the dichotomy between banana production for export and for the domestic

market appears to bear a striking correspondence to that between the plantation and small-producer modes of organization. The Philippines is not unusual in this respect (Courtenay, 1980, p. 87).

39. Malaysia is Southeast Asia's number three pineapple exporter, after Thailand and the Philippines. Exports of canned pineapple from Malaysia and Singapore declined in the early 1970s and then levelled off. The FAO (1976a, p. 25) attributes this to the loss of preference on the United Kingdom market and to Malaysia's inability to produce the popular smooth Cayenne variety, rather than to any inherent inefficiencies of smallholder production. See also FAO (1972, pp. 3–4).

40. Similarly, in a 1977–78 survey of coconut marketing in southern Mindanao, the Ministry of Agriculture found that 50 per cent of producers obtained cash advances from copra buyers, 'thereby depriving them of the opportunity to sell at higher prices offered by other buyers' (Valiente *et al.*, 1979, p. 2). See also Tiglao (1981, p. 67).

41. For more detailed accounts, see Tiglao (1981, pp. 80–92), Sacerdoti (1982), Clarete and Roumasset (1983, pp. 14–21), and Hawes (1987, pp. 68–80).

42. A 1980 US Embassy cable ranked UCPB fourth among domestic private banks in liquid assets, third in deposits, fourth in net worth, and first in total investment ('Concentration of Power in the Philippine Coconut Industry: Implications for Investment and Trade', Cable A–47 from US Embassy, Manila, to Department of State, Washington, D.C., 9 May 1980, p. 7).

43. This control was subsequently consolidated further. A 1984 US Embassy cable reported: 'UNICOM mills, those which have toll [oil?] crushing contracts with UNICOM, and those which "cooperate" with UNICOM, account for more than 85 per cent of the country's crushing capacity. Even the "independent mills" are constrained by PCA [Philippine Coconut Authority] regulations to course their coconut oil exports through UNICOM. Copra exports are prohibited completely'. ('The Philippine Coconut Monopoly', Cable No. 05607 from US Embassy, Manila, to Secretary of State, Washington, D.C., March 1984, p. 4.) Canlas and Alburo (1989, p. 93) report that by 1983 UNICOM directly controlled 93 per cent of milling capacity.

44. 'Concentration of Power in the Philippine Coconut Industry', p. 11.

45. Quoted by Tiglao (1981, p. 92).

46. *Ibid.*, pp. 1–2. The deleted name evidently is former Defense Minister Juan Ponce Enrile (whose name inadvertently was not blacked out on page 6 of the same document).

47. 'The Philippine Coconut Monopoly', pp. 11, 14, 15.

48. *Ibid.*, p. 16.

49. *Ibid.*, p. 20.

50. *Ibid.*, p. 17. With annual sales of $653 million, San Miguel ranked 125th among Third World public and private corporations in 1984 ('South 500', *South* magazine, July 1984, pp. 50–64).

51. *Ibid.*, pp. 13–14. For details, see Bonner (1987, pp. 326–30).
52. The US Embassy reported to Washington, 'It was universally assumed that Cojuangco was behind the attempt on Pelaez's life' (*Ibid.*, p. 23).
53. *Ibid.*, p. 25.
54. The memorandum added that 'Cojuangco has sole control of the money and no audit is made'. 'Confidential Memorandum of Conversation, Subject: Meeting with [deleted], Participants: [deleted], John H. Penfold, Economic Counselor, AmEmbassy, Manila, John H. Andre II, Economic Officer, AmEmbassy, Manila', 8 August 1985, p. 2.
55. After the collapse of the Marcos regime, the spread between farmgate and mill-gate copra prices dropped, suggesting that by the mid-1980s monopsony had intensified at the local level, too. Philippine Coconut Authority (1988, p. 138) data indicate that the average spread declined from 1.70 pesos per kilogram in 1983–85 to 58 centavos in 1987. With total annual production of 2 million metric tons, this difference would amount to 2.25 billion pesos, or more than $100 million, per year. See also Lopez (1987).
56. In 1939, for example, a survey found the average return on investment on haciendas in one Negros sugar district to be 3.5 per cent, compared to a 61.7 per cent return for the mill (cited by McCoy, 1988, p. 20).
57. Nelson (1988, p. 290) derives this estimate by comparing the quota price to the world market price. Note, however, that while the former is, in general, artificially high, the latter is often artificially low, for reasons discussed in Chapter 6. Hawes (1987, p. 94) cites a similar estimate (when adjusted for inflation) by the office of the US Comptroller General: $97 million in the year 1967.
58. Interview with Ramon Nolan, Manila, 24 January 1989. By contrast, the Philippines sent a large delegation, including Nolan, to the much less important international sugar meeting in Switzerland in 1973. 'My heart was not in it', Nolan recalls, 'because the world market is not really a market: it is a dumping ground'.
59. See McCoy (1983, pp. 144–5) and Bonner (1987, pp. 260–1).
60. 'Philippine Sugar Industry Monopoly', Cable No. 01905 from US Embassy, Manila, to Secretary of State, Washington, D.C., 21 January 1984, pp. 2–8.
61. Letter from Fermin Caram, Jr. to President Corazon C. Aquino, dated 25 July 1988. A copy of this letter was furnished to the author.
62. 'Concentration of Power in the Philippine Coconut Industry', p. 9.
63. See, for example, Jones (1980, p. 312); Hawes (1987, p. 128); 'Philippine Sugar Industry Monopoly', p. 5.
64. 'Momentum Builds for Changes in the Philippine Sugar Monopoly', Cable No. 03901 from US Embassy to Secretary of State, Washington, D.C., 14 February 1984, p. 2.
65. *Ibid.*, p. 2; 'US Sugar Quota and the Philippine Sugar Monopoly', Cable No. 05373 from US Embassy, Manila to Secretary of State, Washington, D.C., 29 February 1984; and Reinah (1987, p. 151).

66. 'Philippine Sugar Industry Monopoly', p. 11.
67. Total sugarcane acreage in 1985 was 407,100 hectares, 29 per cent below its 1977 peak of 573,200 hectares (NEDA, 1986, p. 275).
68. Interview with Ramon Nolan, Manila, 24 January 1989.
69. See, for example, McCoy (1983). Given variations among producers in the costs of production and transport, it is possible that some growers were making a profit while others were not.
70. Roberto Sebastian, quoted by Hawes (1987, p. 117).
71. Friesen and Stoltzfus (1978, p. 10) report that TNC officials told them that transfer pricing was common. The problem is also noted by the FAO (1986, p. 60).
72. Reported in 'The Philippine Banana Industry', *Philippine Development* (fortnightly journal of the National Economic and Development Authority), Vol. 7, No. 16, 15 January 1980, pp. 12–13.
73. In its 'green paper' for the Aquino government, the Agricultural Policy and Strategy Team (1986, p. 263) concluded: 'Now is the time to introduce diversification in the Philippine agricultural sector to correct the overdependence on a few export crops and to avoid a position of vulnerability'. In particular, the Team recommended that new areas brought under sugar cultivation in the 1970s be converted to other crops.
74. See Jagan (1987) and Putzel and Cunnington (1989, pp. 94–6).
75. Rice is generally assumed to be more labor-intensive than sugarcane (see, for example, Hayami and Ruttan, 1985, p. 360). However, Crisostomo *et al.* (1971, p. 158) report contrary data based on an estimate of labor use on sugarcane farms in one milling district.
76. Similarly, the World Bank (1986a, pp. 3–4), in a study of sugarland diversification possibilities, observed that 'many good sugarcane lands, which could be used for other crops, are still lying idle and because of this it is estimated that over 100,000 sugarcane workers are either unemployed or seriously underemployed'. This problem 'has been aggravated by the highly skewed land distribution', the Bank acknowledged; 'crop substitution and the provision of alternative employment opportunities would have occurred much faster on smaller farms since, unlike large planters who usually have other sources of income, small farmers cannot afford to leave their lands idle for long'.
77. *Business Day*, 6 June 1986, quoted in Hawes (1987, p. 160). A more primordial objection was voiced by sugar planter Congresswoman Hortensia Starke: 'Your land is like your most beautiful dress, the one that gives you good luck. If someone takes it from you, he only wants to destabilize you, to undress you' (*The Manila Chronicle*, 19 July 1987, quoted in Anderson, 1988, p. 8).

8 Forestry: A Squandered Inheritance

INTRODUCTION

The trees in a forest, like the crops in a field, are products of the soil. However, they differ not only in botanical respects, such as the longer growing period, but also in two important institutional respects. First, unlike crop lands, forests are often in the public domain, posing open access problems. Second, deforestation, a widespread but not inevitable consequence of timber extraction, gives rise to distinctive external costs, including soil erosion, watershed and climate modifications, and losses of biological diversity, which are not taken into account by the timber extractor. The two are interlinked: insecure and contested rights of access to public resources promote a 'cut-and-run' ethos in forest management, and the severity of negative externalities increases as a result.

During the Marcos era, Philippine export earnings from forestry at times surpassed those from either of the country's leading export crops, coconut and sugarcane (see Table 6.2). As in export agriculture, the distribution of gains and losses reflected and reinforced profound inequalities of wealth and power. A small number of powerful individuals appropriated the benefits of public resources, while imposing the costs of negative externalities on others, including future generations of Filipinos. This chapter reviews the extent and consequences of the resulting deforestation, and examines the interaction between distributional conflict and environmental degradation.

Nominally, 90 per cent of the Philippines' 18.7 million hectares (ha) of uplands, including more than 11 million ha officially classified as timberlands, is publicly owned (Cornista, 1985, p. 1). In practice, however, fewer than 200 individuals controlled a large fraction of the country's forests during the Marcos era. A senior Aquino government official summarized their degree of control in the following statement: 'Some five million hectares are owned by 114 individuals'.[1] Forest lands were not 'owned' *de jure*, but rather were leased from the government by logging concessionaires. In practice, however, the *de facto* rights of the loggers were constrained more by political uncertainty than by effective social controls over land use.[2]

Prior to martial law, logging leases were granted for periods of one to ten years. In some cases, logging companies placed influential politicians on their boards of directors so as to obtain and renew leases. In other cases, politicians obtained the licenses themselves, and then rented them to logging firms. Given political uncertainties, most firms 'had no assurance that their lease would be renewed for another year, let alone that they would still be in the logging business many years hence' (Porter and Ganapin, 1988, p. 26).

In the 1970s, timber leases were extended to a 25-year term, but this was still too short to provide an incentive for sustainable yield management or forest replanting. The 25-year leases could, in theory, be renewed, but few logging companies were sanguine enough to plan on the basis of a 50-year time horizon. Hence in the Philippines, as in many other countries, concession holders preferred 'to take their quotas as quickly as possible rather than establish long-term operations in a climate of political and economic uncertainty' (Caufield, 1985a, p. 99). Logging firms acted as if their first cut was their last, initiating the process of deforestation.

THE COSTS OF DEFORESTATION

At the turn of the century, forests covered more than 20 million of the Philippines' 30 million hectares. Since then the country has witnessed some of the most rapid deforestation in the world. In 1981 the Food and Agriculture Organization of the United Nations estimated that, of the remaining 9.5 million ha officially classified as 'closed forest', only 3 million ha were undisturbed, and 2 million ha had been so severely degraded as to be incapable of regeneration (cited by Anderson, 1987, p. 250). Reviewing a variety of estimates, Revilla (1984, pp. 7–10) concluded that, as of 1983, 'forested forest lands' in the Philippines totalled 7.8 to 8.3 million ha, of which only 2.0–2.5 million ha represented old-growth forests. The US Agency for International Development (1985, p. 21) estimated the rate of net deforestation in the 1980s at 225,000 ha/year – an annual cut of 300,000 ha of mature stands as against annual reforestation of 75,000 ha – and predicted that the country's primary forests would 'virtually disappear' in the next 25 years.[3]

The Philippines led its Southeast Asian neighbors in a regional plunge into export logging and deforestation, beginning with an 'intensive marketing effort' for Philippine hardwoods in the early years of US colonial rule (Laarman, 1988, p. 155). Tropical hardwood log exports from the 'big three' supplier countries – the Philippines, Malaysia and Indonesia – grew at an 'astonishing pace' after World War Two, accelerating to 15 per cent per year in the 1965–70 period (Takeuchi, 1974, p. 4). The Philippines remained the region's biggest exporter until being overtaken by Malaysia and Indonesia in the early 1970s (FAO, 1977, p. 304).

Southeast Asia in turn led the tropical world. In the decade after World War Two, technological improvements led to a sharp decline in production costs for plywood and veneer made from lauan ('Philippine mahogany'), opening large new wood product markets (Laarman, 1988, p. 151). The big three Southeast Asian exporters together accounted for three-quarters of all log exports from the Third World in the early 1970s (Takeuchi, 1974, p. 5). As late as 1980, the Asia-Pacific region as a whole accounted for more than 80 per cent of Third World exports of logs and processed wood. But with the depletion of Southeast Asia's forests, the logging industry is shifting to Latin America and Africa, and the Asia-Pacific share is forecast to fall sharply in the coming years (Scott, 1989, p. 38).

The social costs which deforestation has imposed on present and future generations of Filipinos include: (1) the loss of future income opportunities in the forestry sector; (2) the climatic impacts of watershed modification; and (3) the loss of biological diversity and depletion of genetic resources.

Loss of Future Income Opportunities

In effect, the forests of Southeast Asia have been treated as free goods. As Guppy (1984, p. 954) remarks, 'the price of tropical trees *in the forest* is negligible' (emphasis in original). Log supply prices have been based almost entirely on the costs of resource extraction, that is, felling and transportation, without including the cost of reproduction.

On the demand side of the tropical hardwood market, the most explosive growth in the postwar period occurred in Japan, whose share of world consumption grew from 4 per cent in 1950 to roughly 50 per cent in the 1980s (Laarman, 1988, p.160). Japan has been the single largest market for Philippine forestry exports.[4] Evidently the 'social discount rate' applied to Philippine forests has been rather different from that applied to Japan's own extensive domestic forest reserves. In the Philippines it has been quite high – the potential benefits of conserving forests for future generations have counted for little – while in Japan it has been much lower. According to one forestry expert, 'Japan has a very clear strategy: to protect its forests for as long as possible, although it means overexploitation of Southeast Asia and the Pacific region'.[5] The Organization for Economic Cooperation and Development (1991, p. 37) estimates that in the early 1980s Japan's domestic timber harvest extracted only 53 per cent of the annual growth in its stock of trees. In other words, while the forest resources of Southeast Asia are being rapidly depleted, those of Japan are being augmented.

Tropical forests are in the intermediate area between renewable and non-renewable resources. Using techniques of 'sustainable yield management', in which only fully mature trees are cut and damage to adjacent trees is minimized, it is theoretically possible to extract a stable harvest of mature hardwoods every three to five decades. Worldwide, less than one per cent of tropical forests are currently managed in this way (Scott, 1989, p. 35). If less careful (and, in the short run, less costly) logging techniques are employed, it is possible to plant new trees, either some of the original long-maturing hardwoods or faster-growing species, preserving tree cover and soil if not the diversity of the original ecosystem.

Philippine forestry practices, however, have pushed the country's forests towards the non-renewable pole of the resource continuum. The typical pattern begins with intensive logging, in which immediately profitable trees are extracted with no concern for the surrounding vegetation. The Asian Development Bank (1987, p. 117) estimates that 'extracted volume may represent only 20 to 40 per cent of the total volume by which the growing stock is reduced in a logging operation', the remainder being attributable to the opening of roads and skid trails, damages to adjacent trees, and discarded residues.[6]

The roads built by the logging industry not only carry the logs out, but also carry settlers in. Logged-over areas are slashed and burnt to clear the land for agricultural use. Initially, rice, corn, and other annual crops are grown. But the fertility of the upland soils is rapidly depleted once the forest cover is removed due to soil erosion, the loss of organic matter, and the leaching of nutrients. Within as little as four years, the land becomes unable to support annual cropping, and the settlers either move to newly cleared lands or switch to less demanding tree crops. The abandoned land is often overgrown by coarse grasses. This in turn attracts cattle ranchers, who periodically burn the grass to provide tender young shoots for grazing. The fires further reduce the humus content of the soil, and kill any tree seedlings which might have sprouted. Finally the land becomes too poor even for cattle.[7]

When mistreated in this fashion, the tropical rainforest becomes a non-renewable resource. The constraint of non-renewability began to bind in the 1970s. After more than doubling in the 1960s, exports of logs and lumber fell from 4 billion board feet in 1970 to less than 1 billion in 1985 (see Table 8.1).[8] At the same time, the terms of trade for forestry exports declined sharply, reflecting increasing supplies from other Third World countries, often accompanied by similar deforestation. As a result, by 1985 the purchasing power of total Philippine earnings from exports of logs and

TABLE 8.1 *Exports of Logs and Lumber, 1962–1985*

Year	Quantity (billion board-feet)	Indexes (1962 = 100)		
		Quantity	Terms of Trade[1]	Value
1962	1.82	100.0	100.0	100.0
1963	2.36	130.2	97.6	127.1
1964	2.38	131.2	89.9	118.0
1965	3.01	166.0	79.0	131.3
1966	3.61	198.9	82.1	163.3
1967	3.55	195.6	84.6	165.5
1968	3.58	197.2	86.2	169.9
1969	3.66	201.9	85.6	172.9
1970	4.07	224.1	77.2	173.1
1971	3.65	200.8	74.6	149.7
1972	3.10	170.7	64.7	110.4
1973	3.47	191.1	87.1	166.5
1974	2.11	116.2	63.3	73.5
1975	2.06	113.2	49.4	56.0
1976	1.20	66.0	178.1	117.6
1977	1.06	58.4	90.1	52.6
1978	2.78	153.3	38.7	59.3
1979	2.16	119.2	67.4	80.3
1980	1.46	80.2	60.2	48.2
1981	1.25	69.0	46.5	32.1
1982	1.34	74.0	50.8	37.6
1983	1.51	83.4	49.4	41.2
1984	1.38	76.2	41.7	31.8
1985	0.96	52.9	42.6	22.6

NOTE
1. Ratio of nominal price of logs and lumber to import price index.

SOURCES   Calculated from data in NEDA (1976, pp. 427, 434; 1986, pp. 365, 377).

lumber was less than a quarter of its 1962 level, and only 13 per cent of the 1970 peak.

Herein lies the first social cost of the Philippine forestry 'development' strategy: the contraction of current and future income opportunities in the forestry sector itself. The full magnitude of this cost will be multiplied in coming decades when, as a result of worldwide deforestation, the prices of tropical hardwoods rise 'until eventually they reach the cost of replacement' (Guppy, 1984, p. 953).[9] A cruel irony is that by the time world prices rise to a sustainable-yield level, the Philippines is likely to have become a net importer of wood, its own resources having been depleted to the point at which they no longer suffice to meet domestic needs.[10]

Watershed Modification and Climatic Effects

Hydrological and climatic changes caused by deforestation give rise to a second set of social costs. In the Philippines, as in many countries, the forest acts as a sponge, absorbing water in the rainy season and gradually releasing it in the dry season. The forest vegetation and soil catch and hold the rainfall, returning about 60 per cent of it to the atmosphere via evaporation and plant transpiration, and letting about 40 per cent drain into rivers. The beneficial results include a smoothing of the time distribution of water discharge, the minimization of soil erosion, and the enhancement of runoff water quality (W. David, 1984, pp. 5, 10).

Deforestation destroys this 'sponge effect'. In the rainy months, rapid runoff leads to floods downstream. Soil erosion leads to the siltation of waterways and reservoirs, exacerbating floods and reducing water storage capacities. And in the dry months, reduced river flow leads to water shortage and drought.

Flying over the deforested uplands of the Philippines, one can see whole mountainsides being washed away. In the watershed of the Agno River in central Luzon, for example, by the mid-1970s all of the topsoil and half of the subsoil had been eroded from nearly 60,000 ha, and 75 per cent of the topsoil had been lost from another 125,000 ha; downstream, meanwhile, the river was so heavily silted that in some places it flowed higher than the surrounding rice fields, so that a break in its banks could cause severe floods (Porter and Ganapin, 1988, p. 24). A study of river sediment loads in 1978 revealed soil losses of 45 metric tons (mt) per hectare per year. In the still-forested Marbel basin of Mindanao, by contrast, the sediment yield was less than one mt/ha/year.[11]

Massive siltation has sharply reduced the useful life span of the Ambuklao Dam on the Agno River, which was built for hydroelectric power generation in the 1950s with US Export-Import Bank financing. At the time of its construction, Ambuklao was the second-highest earth and rock fill dam in the world, and it created the largest man-made lake in the Philippines (Zablan, 1961, p. 2). In its cost-benefit analysis, Ambuklao was projected to operate for 75 years, but siltation cut this in half.[12] Similarly, the World Bank reports that the Magat reservoir in Cagayan, intended to supply water to the largest irrigation system in the country, has had its probable life span cut by siltation from 100 years at the project appraisal in the 1970s to as little as 25 years.[13]

Floods have also imposed large social costs. In the typhoon belt from northern Luzon to southern Samar, flooding has increased greatly as a result of watershed degradation, according to a 1982 FAO study.[14] In the Cagayan Valley, for example, entire villages have 'washed into the rivers during some typhoons, a catastrophe people in the valley had never witnessed before the loggers came to the mountains' (Porter and Ganapin, 1988, p. 25). In Zambales province in central Luzon, rainy-season floods regularly wash out highways and bridges, while during the dry season, owing to the loss of the forest sponge, droughts have curtailed vegetable gardening and fishing (*ibid.*). In Mindanao, south of the typhoon belt, denuded forests have also led to catastrophic floods. Floods in Northern Mindanao in 1981, for example, killed 283 people, injured 14,000, and left tens of thousands homeless (Tadem, Reyes and Magno, 1984, p. 4).

In addition to these severe local externalities, tropical deforestation contributes to worldwide climatic change by altering the global carbon cycle. Tropical forests contain about 20 per cent of the world's terrestrial carbon, roughly half in the living forest and half in the soil. Much of this is released as carbon dioxide when the forest is destroyed (Guppy, 1984, p. 931). The accumulation of carbon dioxide and other gases in the atmosphere traps more heat near the earth's surface, and a number of scientists predict that the resulting global 'greenhouse effect' will cause temperatures to rise in coming decades, triggering far-reaching disruptions in weather patterns and world agriculture. Potential consequences in the Philippines include changes in rainfall patterns and the submergence of low-lying coastal areas, including parts of metropolitan Manila, by rising sea levels caused by the melting of the polar ice caps. The Philippines bears only a minor share of responsibility for the global greenhouse effect, however, since the primary cause of rising atmospheric carbon dioxide levels has been fossil fuel combustion in the industrialized countries.[15] Like most Third World countries, the Philippines is likely to be mainly on the receiving end of the greenhouse effect, its share of the adverse impacts outweighing its contribution to the problem.

Loss of Biological Diversity

Although tropical rainforests cover a only small fraction of the earth's surface, they are home to roughly half of the world's plant and animal species. Rainforests in general support extraordinarily diverse plant and animal populations, and those of Southeast Asia exceed all others in this respect. Dr. T. C. Whitmore, a leading authority on this subject, concludes: 'The tropical rain forests of the Far East include the most complex and species-rich ecosystems which have ever existed on this planet'.[16] For example, the slopes of a single volcano in Luzon's Laguna and Batangas provinces, Mt. Makiling, contain as many woody plant species as the entire continental United States (Caufield, 1985b, p. 60). Many rainforest species remain unknown to scientists. About half a million species have been identified, but Raven (1987, p. 11) estimates that 'there are at least 3 million, and perhaps ten times that many, yet to be discovered'.

Tropical deforestation currently results in the extinction of an estimated 10,000 plant and animal species each year (Scott, 1989, p. 34). Caufield (1985a, p. 59) reports that, 'Fewer than one per cent of tropical-forest species have been examined for their possible use to mankind – that is, screened for chemical compounds'.

Although the economic value of rainforest species is unknown, and indeed unknowable given uncertainty as to future human needs, a few examples will give an indication of the stakes. In searching for a rice plant gene for resistance to grassy-stunt virus, scientists at the International Rice Research Institute screened thousands of varieties. They found only one such gene, in two seeds of a wild rice variety which had been collected in central India. When scientists returned to the source area, they were unable to find any more. As a result, Caufield (1985a, p. 59) reports, 'every modern rice plant has a gene derived from one of those two original seeds'. In addition to agriculture, biological resources have important medical uses. One-quarter of all pharmaceuticals originate from plants and animals of tropical forests (World Bank, 1989c, p. 67). The US National Cancer Institute has identified three thousand plants with anti-cancer properties, 70 per cent of which are rainforest species (Caufield, 1985a, p. 60).

Since the potential benefits extend to all of humankind, the preservation of biological diversity is a textbook example of a public good.[17] The loss of species through deforestation hence arises from the combined effect of three disjunctures between individual and social rationality: (1) the myopia, or excessively high discount rates, of individuals; (2) the externality problem that the costs of species losses are social while the benefits of forest destruction are private; and (3) the 'free rider' problem that *even if* costs exceeded benefits for the individual, a 'rational' maximizer of self-interest would continue to cut the forest to minimize his personal loss, on the assumption that others would cut if he did not.[18]

Various proposals have been put forward to conserve the genetic resources of tropical rainforests. These range from 'living gene banks' in the form of parks and reserves to the collection and preservation of samples in botanical gardens, seed banks, and tissue culture centers (Raven, 1987, p. 16). In practice, such efforts have been quite limited, and even if they were much better developed, they would provide only an imperfect substitute for natural environments for at least two reasons. First, centralized conservation means putting one's eggs in a few baskets, with the attendant risks discussed in the case of rice germ plasm in Chapter 3. Second, for both scientific and aesthetic purposes (including tourism), natural environments are more than the sum of their component species.

In sum, the social costs of Philippine deforestation include the loss of future forestry income, the degradation of watersheds, climatic disruptions, and the reduction of biological diversity. While the benefits of deforestation have accrued to a small number of people, notably the captains of the logging industry, the costs have been distributed widely. Some of the costs affect people outside the Philippines, but the heaviest ones have been imposed on present and future generations of Filipinos.

PUBLIC RESOURCES AND PRIVATE INTERESTS

Most of the Philippines' forests are in the public domain, and over the years successive governments have promulgated forestry rules and regulations which aim, at least in theory, to safeguard the public interest. The inefficacy of these attempts reflects not only a lack of resources for enforcement, but also the distribution of wealth and power in Philippine society.

The allocation of logging licenses in the Philippines has long been a vehicle for political patronage. During martial law, there were reportedly 'two ways to obtain a timber concession: either by knowing the President, or knowing someone in the Wood Industries Development Board' (Hurst, 1990, p. 187). Lucrative concessions were 'gobbled up by cronies of Marcos' (Porter and Ganapin, 1988, p. 27). Defence Minister Juan Ponce Enrile controlled logging companies with leases totalling hundreds of thousands of hectares. Another close Marcos associate, Herminio Disini, obtained nearly 200,000 ha in timber concessions in northern Luzon, including tribal lands of the Tinggian cultural minority.[19]

Foreign firms have long been involved in Philippine timber extraction. The rapid exploitation of the country's forests began early in the twentieth century, as US firms entered in partnership with logging companies formed by the landowning elite.[20] Major transnationals in the Philippine timber industry in the 1970s and 1980s included Georgia-Pacific, Boise-Cascade, International Paper, Weyerhaeuser, and Mitsubishi.[21]

Forest management provisions in the logging licenses – such as selective cutting and reforestation requirements – are often ignored by licensees. Much unlicensed logging also occurs, often with *de facto* official protection. For example, in an area of northern Luzon in which logging is nominally banned, trucks loaded with logs reportedly pay 'tolls' as they pass military checkpoints in leaving the forest (Mackenzie, 1988, p. 43). On the Agusan River in northeastern Mindanao, Tadem, Reyes and Magno (1984, p. 156) found numerous unauthorized military checkpoints involved in extortion, sarcastically called by loggers the 'fourteen stations of the cross'. A retired forestry official remarked, 'There is reason to believe that illegal logging will not prosper if there is no backing from some law enforcers and the military' (Reyes, 1984, p. 49).

Some loggers deploy their own private armies. The main logging baron in Palawan, for example, 'routinely operates outside the nominal boundaries of the Timber Concession Agreements granted by the central government', but objections are muted by the fact that he 'maintains considerable numbers of private security guards and has an intemperate reputation' (Clad and Vitug, 1988, p. 50). Similar circumstances are expressed in the rhetorical question of a Mindanao official: 'What would you do as a forestry officer manning an isolated road block if a dozen armed men pushed the barrels of their rifles down your nose and politely requested you to let their log-laden trucks through?'[22] The total volume of illegal logging in the Philippines is unknown, but the World Bank (1989c, p. 11) states that its addition to the licensed timber cut might double the total volume of annual extraction.

Some logging also takes a quasi-legal form. For example, logging firms owned by friends of President Marcos were allowed to cut timber on lands legally leased to others, under the pretext of clearing the forest for Ministry of Agrarian Reform resettlement projects (Porter and Ganapin, 1988, p. 27).

When the Philippine government imposed a quota on log exports in the late 1970s, in an attempt to slow deforestation and encourage domestic wood processing industries, the law was flaunted by smugglers. Comparisons of trade data reveal massive under-reporting of log exports: in 1980, for example, Japan reported 1.1 billion cubic meters of hardwood log imports from the Philippines, while Philippine government data on exports to Japan recorded less than half that amount.[23] Ernesto Maceda, who became Minister of Natural Resources after the February 1986 revolution, estimated that between 1974 and 1980, US $960 million worth of timber was smuggled out of the country by friends and associates of President Marcos (Crewdson, 1986, p. 21).

The level of government license fees – in effect, the rent paid by private loggers for the appropriation of public resources – similarly reveals the weakness of public *vis-à-vis* private interests. The pattern was established in the early years of US colonial rule, when logging concessions were dispensed on 'ruinously favorable terms'.[24] Including export tax receipts as well as license fees, total Philippine government revenue from the forestry sector from 1979 to 1982 amounted to $170 million, only 11.4 per cent of the $1.5 billion potential rent.[25] Repetto (1988, p. 15) notes that annual government revenues 'have not covered even the administrative and infrastructure costs incurred for timber harvesting'.

The Bureau of Forestry Development (BFD), the government agency charged with the implementation of forest policies, was dubbed the 'Bureau of Forest Destruction' by critics because of 'its readiness to protect loggers for a price' (Porter and Ganapin, 1988, p. 28). The Assistant Director of the BFD frankly assessed the agency's reputation in 1982: 'For the past many years, government foresters have time and again been accused of catering mostly to the whims and fancies of moneyed politicians and cunning timber and other forest product exploiters'.[26]

With the advent of the Aquino government, the BFD has sought to improve its image by aiming to 'democratize the disposition of public lands' (Alvarez, 1987, p. 2). This is easier said than done, however. The dominant logger in Palawan, for example, reportedly maintained his control of 168,000 ha of logging concessions simply by switching political allegiance after February 1986.[27]

International actors have played key roles in Philippine forestry. Foreign demand has provided the main impetus for the logging industry; foreign firms have directly engaged in logging; and international agencies have influenced government policy. As early as 1962, a World Bank report described the country's forestry policies as 'irresponsible' and 'suicidal':

> Earnings from forestry and forest products have skyrocketed since World War II, though at a cost which is beginning to resemble a bargain sale of the Filipino birthright. The combined effects of *kaingin* farming and "legal" slaughter of the forest include widespread erosion and a reported deterioration in climatic conditions.   (World Bank, 1962, pp. 16, 18)

This warning went unheeded not only by the Philippine government but by the Bank itself.

A decade later, at the height of the country's forestry export boom, the World Bank's primary concern was 'efficiency', writ small:

> The extensive forest resources of the Philippines appear to offer good prospects for increasing export earnings during the 1970s, but they are not

managed well. Output of trees under license falls short of the allowable cut level. . . . Policies which encourage more efficient use of the forests and low-cost production in order to compete with other log exporters to Japan should be established.   (World Bank, 1973, Vol. I, p. 20)

The World Bank offered more than words of encouragement for continued forest exploitation.[28] As part of its Smallholder [*sic*] Tree Farming and Forestry Project, for example, the Bank funded a tree plantation on ancestral lands of the Tinggian minority to supply a pulp mill of Cellophil, a corporation established by Marcos associate Herminio Disini.[29] The same firm received $113.5 million in loans from European commercial banks, repayment of which was guaranteed by the government's Development Bank of the Philippines (Kramer, 1978, p. 18).

UPLAND AGRICULTURE: BLAMING THE VICTIM

Once opened up by the loggers, many forest areas have been cleared for agricultural use. The usual technique is slash-and-burn cultivation, known as *kaingin* in the Philippines, an imprecise term often used to encompass the 'harmonic', ecologically sustainable techniques of traditional forest dwellers as well as the 'disharmonic', ecologically non-sustainable, techniques of migrants from the lowlands.[30]

In recent decades the upland population appears to have grown at roughly the same rate as the country's population as a whole.[31] Some regions, such as Southern and Central Mindanao, witnessed considerable migration into upland areas. In other regions, such as the Visayas, the upland population grew more slowly than the national average, implying net out-migration (Cruz *et al.*, 1986).

The allocation of agricultural land-use rights in upland areas, like the allocation of logging rights, has been shaped by the distribution of power. In the Philippines, as elsewhere, the new property rights established in the land frontier bear the indelible imprint of the colonists' social order. As elsewhere, too, the newcomers have often disregarded the traditional rights of the tribal 'cultural minorities' who have inhabited the uplands for many generations.[32]

The disregard of traditional rights can be traced as far back as Magellan's annexation of the Philippines on behalf of the Spanish royal family in 1521: 'The legal effect of Magellan's gesture was to convert all of the indigenous forest occupants of the still unexplored archipelago into squatters'.[33] This usurpation continued under US colonial rule, notwithstanding a 1909 US Supreme Court decision recognizing 'native titles'.[34]

Although they occupy what is nominally public land, many upland settlers pay rent to private 'landlords'. Little documentation of the origins, extent, and nature of these *de facto* tenancy relationships is available. Porter and Ganapin (1988, p. 29) report that 'an unknown number' of upland cultivators 'are part of a well-organized occupation of forest land being carried out by wealthier individuals hoping to lay claim to the land by paying taxes on it'. These 'taxes' are paid to local officials in an attempt to purchase their support. Cornista (1985, pp. 2–3) reports that these 'non-cultivating claimants' are 'generally absentees', and that they act as 'virtual landowners', usually extracting share rents from their tenants.

In some instances, local judicial systems have been mobilized in support of these claims. For example, Borlagdan (1990, p. 273) mentions a case in Cebu in which an absentee claimant filed a legal complaint against a settler who had not surrendered a share of his harvests:

> Because the landlord had no legal title to the land, he filed a complaint for breach of contract over the sharing agreement, a personal contract between the tenant and the claimant. The case was dismissed after the tenant apologized to the claimant and swore to resume compliance with the sharing agreement.

In those areas of settlement in which legal titles are issued, Lopez (1987, p. 235) remarks that 'landed elites, with their strong political connections, wealth, and access to legal expertise, can more readily obtain titles than settlers or cultural minorities', and adds that 'even settlers enjoy a comparative advantage over indigenous groups'.

Official Philippine government policy towards agricultural settlement in public-domain forest areas traditionally has been one of repression. The Bureau of Forestry Development (BFD) 'long sought to eradicate *kaingin*-making and forest occupancy, declaring them illegal and in fact prosecuting those that have been caught' (Aguilar, 1982, p. 2). Local populations, who bear many of the heaviest social costs of deforestation, were seen as part of the problem, rather than as part of the solution.

In the mid-1970s, the Philippine government moved towards 'social forestry' policies, which accept the reality of upland settlement and seek to channel settler activities in what the government defines as socially desirable directions. The revised Forestry Code, promulgated as Presidential Decree No. 705 in 1975, stated:

> *Kaingineros*, squatters, cultural minorities and other occupants who entered into forest lands before the effectivity of this Code, without

permits or authority, shall not be prosecuted: *provided*, that they do not increase their clearings; *provided, further*, that they undertake within two (2) months from notice thereof, the activities *which will be imposed upon them by the Bureau* in accordance with a management plan calculated to conserve and protect forest resources.[35]   (Final emphasis added)

The top-down approach of the new government policy is evident in the language of the decree.

The social forestry policies included two long-term land tenure instruments: the Certificate of Stewardship Contract issued to individuals, and the Community Forest Lease issued to associations of individuals who will use the land communally. Both extend for 25 years and are renewable thereafter, with provisions for transfer to the next-of-kin. The programs encountered resistance, however, from three sources: first, the cultivators themselves, many of whom 'believe that it is simply a means of getting them to plant trees and that BFD will reclaim the land once the trees have been grown'; second, the elite non-cultivating claimants, who view the programs as a threat to their efforts to appropriate the land; and third, local officials, who 'tend to side with the claimants because they get revenues from the taxes paid on the land'.[36] As of 1986, the BFD had issued stewardship certificates covering only 162,000 ha, and community forest leases covering only 16,000 ha, to a total of 65,000 households (Alvarez, 1987, p. 5). The vast majority of upland cultivators thus continued to lack secure tenure.[37]

Loggers and government officials often identify the *kaingineros* as the principal culprits in Philippine deforestation. A 1980 government study, for example, attributed 55 per cent of annual forest cover losses to *kaingineros*, 40 per cent to legal logging and forest fires, and less than 5 per cent to illegal logging (McCue, 1982). Officials of a lumber company with a 95,000-ha forest concession in Mindanao similarly complain of 'the unstoppable entry and destruction caused by hordes of settlers and forest residents'.[38]

Although upland farmers often do contribute to deforestation, it is misleading to cast them as the main villains. Since clearing for cultivation typically follows the logging of the land, and in turn grazing often follows cultivation, one cannot neatly assign percentage shares of responsibility for deforestation to the different parties. Moreover, what distinguishes upland farmers from other agents of deforestation – loggers, government officials, absentee landlords, and international firms and institutions – is that the upland farmers themselves are among the principal *victims* of the deforestation process. Not coincidentally, they are also the poorest.

Some observers consider population pressure to be 'the underlying factor' behind Philippine deforestation.[39] This analysis in effect blames the victims twice, first for what they do, and then for why they do it. As Frederick Engels observed more than a century ago, 'the pressure of population is not upon the means of subsistence but upon the means of *employment*'.[40] The land hunger which drives impoverished cultivators to clear the forests is an outcome of the land ownership concentration documented in preceding chapters, and of the absence of sufficient non-agricultural employment opportunities.[41]

On a visit to Bataan province in January 1989, I spoke with some cultivators who had occupied and cleared forest land belonging to a nearby paper mill. After slashing and burning the vegetation on the steep hillsides, they had planted bananas, papayas, and cassava. A recent typhoon had destroyed the flowers which would have produced their first fruit crop. For the past year they had subsisted almost entirely on boiled cassava root, the only food they could offer to a visitor. The cultivators had previously been working as agricultural laborers in Bataan, having migrated from the Visayas some fifteen years earlier. Their last employer had been a landlord and trader, one of the richest men in the province, who had paid them poorly and often not on time. Although they were now suffering extreme deprivation in the hills, they assured me that they were in fact better off than they had been as laborers. 'Population pressure' in the Philippine uplands can be understood only within this political and economic context.

In an impassioned 1988 pastoral letter, the Catholic Bishops Conference of the Philippines protested the despoliation of the country's environment. 'Our forests are almost gone, our rivers are almost empty', the bishops wrote. 'During the monsoon rains, flash-floods destroy everything in their path'. Blaming 'the relentless drive of our plunder economy', the bishops posed the crucial question: 'Who has benefited most, and who has borne the real costs?'[42]

This question is important not only for a diagnosis of the problem, but also for its implications as to the political impetus for change. The clash between private and public interests in Philippine forestry is at the same time a clash between rich and poor. Those who bear the heaviest costs of deforestation have the greatest motivation to change the country's forestry policies. First and foremost, this means the rural poor.

For example, in 1987 a non-governmental organization successfully blocked logging on ancestral lands of the Mangyan cultural minority in Mindoro.[43] In the battle over the fate of the country's largest remaining virgin forest on the island of Palawan, the national environmental organization Haribon is attempting to forge links with diverse local residents, including former workers for the island's dominant logging firm.[44] Local communities often need national and even international support to thwart powerful logging interests, but their active engagement is likely to be the most basic precondition for the emergence of an alternative forestry policy.

CONCLUSIONS

Philippine forestry in the Marcos era provides a case study in the political economy of environmental degradation.[45] A natural inheritance has been squandered, as future income opportunities are sacrificed for short-term gains. At the same time, the social costs of soil erosion, floods, droughts, and lost of biological diversity have been imposed on current and future generations.

The neoclassical economist diagnoses these symptoms as a case of 'market failure': the pursuit of individual self-interest does not generate a socially desirable outcome, due to myopia and externalities. The political economist, however, recognizes a further source of the malady: the distribution of power. The ability to seize natural resources for personal benefit and to impose social costs on others is not distributed without limit to everyone, as freely as the air we breathe. Nor is it apportioned in equal measure to rich and poor alike. It is not mere coincidence that the primary beneficiaries of Philippine forestry in the Marcos era were presidential cronies and local political bosses, nor that its primary losers were poor Filipinos in general, and cultural minorities in particular. Given the distribution of wealth and power in the Philippines, the despoliation of the country's forests was virtually inevitable.

British forester Nicholas Guppy (1984, p. 944) likens tropical deforestation to a four-layered cake. The topmost layer is population growth and land hunger. Beneath it lie the social conditions under which non-forested land is not available to those who need it. Beneath this layer lies the local and national power structure, or what Guppy terms 'political motivations and unwillingness to face realities'. And beneath this is the foundation layer of the deforestation cake: the ready availability of financial backing from external sources which sustains the political *status quo*. Deforestation in the Philippines is a case in point.

The neoclassical prescriptions for market failure are straightforward. Whenever feasible, resources should be privatized and rights to them made secure, so that individuals have an incentive to plan with longer-term time horizons and are compelled to internalize externalities. When, as is often the case, this is not feasible, the government should step in to regulate resource use. Both prescriptions presume the existence of a non-partisan, efficiency-maximizing state, the role of which is either to allocate and enforce property rights or to regulate individual behavior.

The political economist recognizes that such states have never existed, and probably never will. The actions of states, whether in creating the preconditions for markets or in redressing market failures, are invariably shaped by the prevailing distribution of power. In a setting of marked political and economic inequalities, one can expect state policies with respect to the natural environment to favor the interests of the rich and powerful over those of the poor and powerless. If environmental degradation benefits the former at the expense of the latter, it will continue until such time as it is blocked by the mobilization of countervailing power. Herein lies the vital link between environmentalism and democracy.

NOTES

1. Roque (1987, p. 308). Similarly, Quisumbing (1987b, p. 1) reports that about 130 holders of logging licenses controlled 33 per cent of the country's forest area in the mid-1980s.
2. The politically contingent nature of these rights was vividly demonstrated after the February 1986 revolution, when 150 of the 157 major concession licenses were reportedly revoked within three months (Hurst, 1990, p. 189).
3. A nationwide forest resources inventory conducted from 1979 to 1988 by the Philippine government with German assistance reached similar conclusions. Total forest area as of 1988 was estimated at 6.5 million ha, with average annual loss of 210,000 ha/year from 1969 to 1988 (Philippine-German Forest Resources Inventory Project, 1988, p. 20).
4. Japan remained the single largest market despite the fact that its share in the total value of Philippine forestry exports fell from roughly 60 per cent in the 1960s to 30 per cent in the early 1980s (United Nations, *Foreign Trade Statistics of Asia and the Far East*, various issues). Japan mainly imported logs and lumber, imposing tariffs to product its domestic wood processing industry. As Philippine forest resources dwindled, veneer and plywood (for which the US, EEC, and Hong Kong are major markets) claimed an increasing share of total Philippine exports, and this contributed to the diminishing Japanese share. See also Takeuchi (1974) and Nectoux and Kuroda (1989).
5. Professor Hans Steinlin, Albert Ludwig University, Freiburg, West Germany, quoted by Caufield (1985b, p. 155). See also Ledec (1985, p. 196) and Nectoux and Kuroda (1989, pp. 105–6).
6. The World Bank (1989c, p. 20) reports that extracted wood is 55 per cent of total volume reduction, and that a further 30–50 per cent is lost in processing, so that total end recovery is one-fifth to one-third of the growing stock reduction. This is compared to recovery rates of 85 per cent each in logging and processing in some industrialized countries.

7. Boychuck (1987, p. 20), citing research conducted by the Manila-based Appropriate Technology Center for Rural Development. See also USAID (1980, p. 19); Porter and Ganapin (1988, p. 29); and World Bank (1989c, pp. 24–6).

8. The magnitude of the decline reported in Table 8.1 may be exaggerated owing to a rise in illegal exports of logs and lumber and export underinvoicing, but there is no dispute as to the direction of the trend. Exports of other wood products (mainly veneer and plywood) peaked in the late 1970s (FAO, *Yearbook of Forest Products*, various issues).

9. The extent to which past prices would have supported sustainable-yield forestry exports is an open question. The United Nations Industrial Development Organization (1983, pp. 338, 349–53) identifies the Philippines as a country with very strong 'revealed comparative advantage' in wood products, indicated by a low ratio of domestic consumption to gross output. However, this calculation ignores the social costs of past forestry practices.

10. Myers (1988) reports that 'there appears to be a timber famine in the making' in the Philippines. The President of the Philippine Wood Products Association predicted in 1986 that the country would have to import logs from Malaysia in the early 1990s (cited by Hurst, 1990, p. 170).

11. USAID (1985, pp. 21–2). For a review of soil erosion estimation problems, see W. David (1984, pp. 18–25). David's estimates for the Magat reservoir watershed in northern Luzon indicate that soil loss rates range from 3 mt/ha/year from primary forests with small patches of clearings to 250 mt/ha/year from overgrazed areas.

12. Caufield (1985b, p. 24) states that Ambuklao's operational life span was reduced to 30 years. USAID (1979, p. 70) states that siltation reduced the useful life of the dam from 60 years to 32 years.

13. World Bank (1989c, p. 27). See also Myers (1988, p. 208).

14. FAO and UNDP, 'Watershed Problems and Status of Watershed Management, Country Brief, Philippines', FAO:RAS/81/053, June 1982, p. 10, cited by Porter and Ganapin (1988, p. 24).

15. The World Resources Institute (1990, p. 15) estimates, for example, that the United States accounted for 17.6 per cent of the world's net greenhouse gas emissions in 1987, while the Philippines accounted for 0.7 per cent. On a per capita basis, US emissions were more than six times higher than those of the Philippines (calculated from World Resources Institute, 1991, pp. 254–5, 348–9). Moreover, these estimates have been criticized for *understating* the share of the industrialized countries and *overstating* that of the developing countries (see Agarwal and Narain, 1990). See also Kellogg and Schware (1982, p. 1080) and references therein.

16. Whitmore (1984, p. 288). Whitmore notes (p. 6), however, that forests of comparable richness may yet be discovered in Latin America.

17. See, for example, Tietenberg (1988, pp. 49–53).

18. The latter problem is often described as the 'tragedy of the commons', but as Bromley and Cernea (1989) point out, it is more accurately termed the tragedy of *open access*, since collective action can, and often does, result in socially rational use of common property resources.

19. For details, see Aguilar (1982, pp. 154–6); Anti-Slavery Society (1983, pp. 74–90); Hurst (1990, pp. 194–6); Nectoux and Kuroda (1989, pp. 84–5); and Porter and Ganapin (1988, p. 27).

20. See Porter and Ganapin (1988, p. 25) and Roth (1983).

21. For details, see Tadem, Reyes and Magno (1984, pp. 104–45) and Anti-Slavery Society (1983, Ch. 4).

22. Quoted by Hurst (1990, p. 189).

23. Power and Tumaneng (1983, p. 8). See also Nectoux and Kuroda (1989, pp. 71–73).

24. Moore (1910, p. 80), cited by Roth (1983, p. 46).

25. Boado (1988, p. 184). 'Granted that the government's capture might have been higher by another 5 per cent owing to unaccounted domestic sales and realty taxes', Boado (p. 185) concludes, 'the profit margin of the timber operators would still remain high'. The World Bank (1989c, pp. 146–7) cites similar figures from an earlier draft of Boado's paper. See also Power and Tumaneng (1983) and Gillis (1988).

26. J. B. Alvarez, Jr., 'Forests and Rural Communities', paper presented at the Integrated Natural Resources Symposium, Manila, July 1982, quoted by Porter and Ganapin (1988, p. 28).

27. For details, see Clad and Vitug (1988).

28. In 1987, the World Bank, like the BFD, vowed to reform. 'If the World Bank has been part of the problem in the past', Bank president Barber Conable proclaimed in a speech on the environment, 'it can and will be a strong force in finding solutions in the future' (quoted by Rich, 1989, p. 73). This declaration came in the wake of vigorous campaigning by environmental organizations, including well-publicized demonstrations at the World Bank's Washington headquarters. 'They're scaling the walls at the Bank!' a senior consultant told me. 'On the outside, not on the inside like we used to do'.

29. Anti-Slavery Society (1983, p. 79); Bello *et al.* (1982, pp. 89–90). When entering the Tinggian lands, Cellophil personnel were 'accompanied and guarded by elements of Marcos's special Presidential Guard Battalion' (Anti-Slavery Society, 1983, p. 77).

30. Olofson (1981, p. 3), cited by Lopez (1987, p. 230). Shifting cultivators are referred to in official documents as '*kaingineros*', which Tadem, Reyes and Magno (1984) consider a disparaging term for tribal Filipinos and settlers. For a discussion of differences between the agricultural practices of traditional swidden cultivators and those of the migrant settlers, see also Fujisaka and Sajise (1986) and Hurst (1990, pp. 184–5).

31. Cruz *et al.* (1986, pp. 39–49) estimate that 'upland population' grew from an estimated 8.2 million in 1960 to 14.4 million in 1980, maintaining a fairly constant share of 30 per cent in the country's total population.

The Bureau of Forestry Development estimated upland population in the early 1980s at 7.5 million (Capistrano and Fujisaka, 1984, p. 2).

32. For a review of the government policies with respect to cultural minorities in the Marcos years, see Anti-Slavery Society (1983).

33. Owen Lynch, Jr., quoted by Poffenberger (1990, p. 12).

34. See Lynch (1984, p. 187) and Lynch and Talbot (1988, p. 686).

35. P. D. 705, Section 53, quoted in Anti-Slavery Society (1983, p. 67).

36. Porter and Ganapin (1988, p. 29). For example, attempts to award stewardship certificates under the World Bank-assisted Central Visayas Regional Project foundered, among other reasons, on the opposition from *de facto* landlords who 'fear loss of revenue generated by illegal land claims' (Reid, Barnes and Blackwelder, 1988, p. 31).

37. Moreover, in some cases certificate holders are reported to 'lease out portions of the land grants to other farmers with minuscule farms or to the landless' (Cornista, 1985, p. 6).

38. Natonton and Abraham (1984, p. 121). For contrasting views of a lumber company's activities, compare this account to that of Tadem, Reyes and Magno (1984, pp. 138–45).

39. See, for example, Ooi (1987). In a cross-sectional analysis of Philippine provinces, however, Kummer (1992) finds no significant correlation between population growth and the loss of forest cover from 1970 to 1980.

40. Letter to F. A. Lange, 29 March 1865, quoted by Baran (1957, p. 242). Emphasis in original.

41. The Philippines is not unique in this respect. See, for example, Guppy (1984, pp. 939–44) on Brazil and Indonesia.

42. Quoted by Clad (1988a) and by Lynch and Talbot (1988, p. 680).

43. This and other examples are of grassroots environmental movements in the Philippines are discussed by Lynch and Talbot (1988, pp. 702–9).

44. See Broad and Cavanagh (1989). For examples from other countries, see Durning (1990).

45. A parallel story could be related for the country's mining sector. See McAndrew (1983) and Briones (1987).

9 Foreign Borrowing

INTRODUCTION

Foreign borrowing was a key element in Philippine development strategy in the Marcos era. The primary rationale advanced by the government and the external creditors was 'development': borrowed money would speed the growth of the Philippine economy, improving the well-being of present and future generations of Filipinos. If this was the goal, the strategy must be judged a historic failure.

The most evident legacy of this borrowing was the $28 billion external debt bequeathed by the Marcos regime to the new government of Mrs. Corazon Aquino in 1986. Payments on this inherited debt in the late 1980s absorbed some $3.5 billion per year, or about ten per cent of the country's gross national product.[1] The legacy of the debt runs deeper, however, for the uses to which the borrowed funds were put have had profound consequences for the Philippine economy.

This chapter traces the growth of Philippine external indebtedness in the Marcos era. It begins with an exposition of the net transfer cycle, a simple yet often ignored feature of any debt-for-development strategy. It then reviews the country's balance-of-payments from 1962 to 1986, to set forth the context within which the external debt was accumulated. Finally, it documents the growth of the debt and its changing composition by type of borrower, type of lender, and maturity length. Chapter 10 investigates the mechanisms and magnitude of capital flight, which involved large flows of foreign exchange in the opposite direction. Chapter 11 then analyzes the impact of foreign borrowing on country's political economy, and concludes with some implications for future debt management strategy.[2]

THE NET TRANSFER CYCLE

Debt service does not pose a serious burden as long as enough new money can be borrowed to pay for it. The Philippines' mounting debt service obligations were met in precisely this fashion until 1983. It is in the nature of debt, however, that new money sufficient to service past loans cannot be borrowed forever. The reason, of course, is that loans must be repaid with

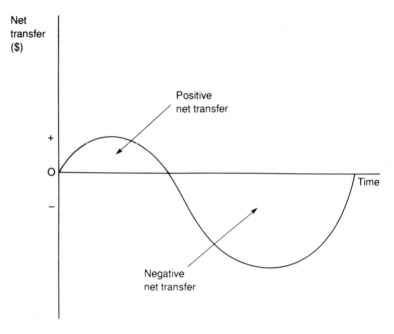

Figure 9.1:   The Net Transfer Cycle

interest. Ever larger sums must be borrowed to repay prior debts, until the creditors eventually are unable or unwilling to lend enough new money to meet debt service requirements. At that point, the *net transfer* – new money minus interest and principal repayment on past loans – turns negative.

This inexorable course of events is depicted in Figure 9.1. Starting with no debt and zero net transfer, the borrowing country initially receives a positive net transfer: the credit inflow comes first, the debt service outflow follows. As debt service rises over time, more and more new money is needed to maintain the positive net transfer. Sooner or later, assuming that the loans are repaid with interest, the country reaches the critical breaking point at which debt service payments surpass the inflow of new money. The stage of negative net transfers begins.[3]

The total amount of the negative net transfer is represented by the area above the curve and below the horizontal axis. It is, of course, much larger than the earlier positive net transfer (the area below the curve and above the axis). The difference between the two is total interest payments.

The net transfer cycle depicted in Figure 9.1 is not merely a theoretical possibility: it is a logical necessity. Creditors cannot increase lending indefinitely. The only question is timing, which depends on the interest rate and on the willingness of creditors to supply new money. The question is not *if* the breaking point will come, but *when*. For the Philippines, it arrived in 1983.

Consider the circumstances under which a country, once it reaches the stage of negative net transfers, could be deemed 'better off' than it would have been had it never borrowed at all.

If the borrowed money were invested productively, generating a rate of return greater than the interest rate, then the country would be better off in the aggregate sense that national income, net of external transfers, would be higher than it would have been without the loans. This rate of return must, of course, be calculated in hard currency. If inadequate foreign exchange earnings force devaluation of the local currency, the required rate of return is pushed correspondingly higher.

What if, in practice, part of the borrowed money is not invested, but rather is spent on consumption items such as imports of food or arms? What if part of it leaks out of the country as capital flight? What if part of that capital invested domestically fails to yield the necessary rate of return? In all these cases, the necessary condition for the country to be judged 'better off' becomes still more stringent: the rate of return on the remaining capital must be high enough to cover not only its own repayment with interest (in foreign exchange), but also interest and principal repayment for that portion of borrowed money which was consumed, lost in capital flight, or invested at inadequate rates of return. Only then could a debt-for-development strategy succeed in raising aggregate income net of external transfers during the stage of negative net transfers.

In practice, these stringent conditions are seldom fulfilled. The share of loans invested productively and the rate of return on that investment are typically insufficient to provide a net income gain once the inevitable negative net transfer occurs. Instead, net income during the era of negative net transfers is *lower than it would have been if no money had ever been borrowed.*[4]

External borrowing for unproductive (or insufficiently productive) purposes becomes addictive. At first, small doses of foreign funds may offer temporary relief from various economic woes. But in the end, the woes remain unsolved, sending the borrower back for more of the financial narcotic in ever larger doses. Over time, dependence on the lender grows.

The term 'cold turkey' refers to the intensely painful withdrawal symptoms suffered by a narcotics addict when deprived of the drug. It is also used by economists to describe sharply recessionary anti-inflation strategies.[5] This economic analogy is even more apposite in the case of a heavily indebted country facing the inevitability of a negative net transfer, and desperate for new money to ease the pain of debt service.

Why, then, do countries embark upon the perilous road of large-scale external debt? There are two reasons: myopia and social heterogeneity.

Individuals tend to be myopic, or short-sighted: they value the present more than the future. Standing at time zero in Figure 9.1, they see the alluring mountain of the positive net transfer but lose sight of the deep valley of the negative net transfer which lies beyond it.

One may hope that governments will resist this short-sightedness and pursue a longer-term vision of the public interest. Alas, this often proves not to be the case: governments succumb to a myopia of their own.

Social heterogeneity helps to explain governmental myopia. A country comprises many individuals, groups, and classes, who have diverse and often contradictory interests. In general, the costs of the negative net transfer are not distributed across this population in proportion to the benefits of the positive net transfer. The distribution of benefits and costs is shaped, among other things, by the exercise of political power, as individuals, groups, and classes seek to appropriate the benefits for themselves and to impose the costs on others. While debt is a doubtful route to long-term gains in aggregate income, it can lead to handsome income gains for particular individuals or groups.

THE BALANCE OF PAYMENTS, 1962–86

The build-up of the Philippine external debt began well before the oil price increases of the 1970s. It can be traced to the foreign exchange decontrol and trade liberalization announced by President Macapagal in 1962, after which lending by international financial institutions, Western governments, and private commercial banks grew steadily. An increasing supply of new loans ensured that the country had the means to service prior loans.

A balance-of-payments crisis in 1970 foreshadowed the inevitable turning point at which debt service payments surpass the inflow of new money, and the net transfer turns negative. This premonition was temporarily exorcised, however, by means of fresh lending unlocked by an IMF adjustment program. External borrowing then accelerated greatly in the 1970s, as the Philippines pursued a development strategy of 'debt-led growth'. For a time, the country – or more accurately, some of its citizens – was able to live 'beyond its means', thanks to a positive net transfer of external resources.

The day of reckoning arrived in October 1983. Private international lending, already in short supply following the Mexican near-default of August 1982, virtually dried up after the August 1983 assassination of Benigno Aquino, precipitating the worst balance-of-payments crisis in the Philippines' postwar history. The net transfer turned negative.

This history is reflected in the Philippine balance of payments from 1962 to 1986, as summarized in Table 9.1. Before reviewing the chronology, it may be useful to discuss briefly the categories in which international financial transactions are grouped for the purposes of the table.

Reading the Balance of Payments

The *current account*, consisting of payments for goods and services and unrequited transfers, is here subdivided into four components:

— *Exports* and *imports* refer to merchandise trade; when their sum was negative, as in every year shown except for 1963 and 1973, the Philippines experienced a trade deficit. Export and import value estimates are based on Philippine government data, which do not necessarily agree with data of trading partners (a problem discussed in Chapter 10).

— *Investment income* refers to interest on international loans and profits on foreign direct investment. The loans and investments are themselves recorded in the capital account, but their returns are classified as payments for the 'services' this capital renders and hence recorded in the current account – an accounting practice which effectively prohibits countries from placing controls on interest payments and profit repatriation under the IMF Articles of Agreement.[6] Investment income is reported here in net form, subtracting outflows from the smaller inflows generated by Philippine investment abroad. In the Philippines, as in many third world countries, net investment income is consistently negative; hence, as Payer (1974, p. 8) remarks, this item could more accurately be termed 'investment payments'.[7]

— *Other* current account transactions is a residual category which includes freight and insurance services, travel, earnings of non-resident Filipino workers overseas, and unrequited transfers (including remittances from Filipinos who are classified as residents of other countries).

The *capital account* consists of loans and investments which will give rise to future 'service' payments. These are reported net of amortization payments and recorded capital outflows. The capital account is subdivided into the following categories:

TABLE 9.1 The Philippine Balance of Payments, 1962–1986 (US $ million)

Year	1962	1963	1964	1965	1966	1967	1968	1969	1970	1971	1972	1973	1974
Current Account	30	182	85	137	161	-25	-250	-253	-48	-2	7	474	-207
Exports	556	727	742	769	828	821	858	855	1064	1136	1136	1871	2695
Imports	-587	-618	-780	-808	-853	-1062	-1150	-1132	-1090	-1186	-1261	-1596	-3145
Investment Income	-17	-17	-26	-31	-37	-76	-97	-78	-130	-101	-126	-113	-54
Other	78	90	149	207	223	292	139	102	108	148	257	312	297
Capital Account	-28	0	-18	4	-117	72	375	299	242	242	283	212	867
Direct Investment	-3	-4	-4	-10	-15	-9	-3	6	-29	-4	-22	64	-40
Long-term Loans:	9	-53	56	119	-3	18	225	152	159	-5	137	68	267
Official	6	-27	18	127	-5	-6	40	36	54	13	104	73	72
Private	3	-26	38	-8	2	24	185	116	105	-18	33	-5	195
Short-term Loans	-34	57	-70	-105	-99	63	153	141	112	251	168	80	640
Official	NA	NA	NA	NA	NA	106	-33	62	4	42	-60	-129	132
Deposit Money Banks	-7	28	39	12	-82	-55	8	12	32	117	173	134	277
Other Private	-27	29	-109	-118	-17	12	178	67	76	91	55	75	231
Reserves and Related Items	-21	-23	-16	-67	12	25	74	81	-46	-97	-184	-668	-591
Net Errors and Omissions	19	-159	-51	-73	-56	-72	-199	-127	-148	-142	-106	-19	-70

TABLE 9.1 *(Continued)*

Year	1975	1976	1977	1978	1979	1980	1981	1982	1983	1984	1985	1986
Current Account	-924	-1102	-755	-1093	-1496	-1901	-2089	-3198	-2753	-1257	-26	991
Exports	2263	2520	3151	3419	4600	5791	5711	5019	5008	5396	4632	4836
Imports	-3459	-3634	-3916	-4725	-6141	-7727	-7957	-7664	-7492	-6074	-5118	-5045
Investment Income	-126	-253	-333	-406	-565	-832	-1042	-1826	-1176	-2104	-2002	-1950
Other	398	265	343	618	610	867	1199	1273	1506	1526	2460	3150
Capital Account	1094	1194	513	1855	1627	2739	2244	2868	1056	1424	-755	215
Direct Investment	124	142	215	100	21	-103	176	17	111	6	20	140
Long-term Loans:	393	938	661	886	1151	1030	1332	1553	1349	291	3096	1652
Official	255	599	391	630	987	536	836	1305	965	400	1677	1798
Private	138	398	270	257	164	493	496	248	384	-109	1419	-147
Short-term Loans	577	54	-363	869	455	1812	736	1298	-404	1126	-3871	-1577
Official	297	64	-530	19	422	781	248	699	617	821	-1222	-5
Deposit Money Banks	177	89	335	930	628	712	478	505	-376	-240	-940	-759
Other Private	102	-98	-167	-79	-596	319	11	95	-646	545	-1709	-813
Reserves and Related Items	16	57	30	-876	-376	-960	349	703	2044	-263	122	-1111
Net Errors and Omissions	-186	-148	210	115	245	122	-503	-373	-347	97	659	-94

SOURCES   International Monetary Fund, *Balance of Payments Statistics Yearbook*, various issues (in cases of conflict, data from more recent issues are used) and *International Financial Statistics* (SDR/$ exchange rate).

NOTE
'Direct investment' includes portfolio investment. 'Reserves and related items' includes counterpart items.

— *Direct investment* refers to the acquisition by foreigners of productive land or physical capital, or of securities issued by Philippine firms (distinguished in recent volumes of the *Balance of Payments Yearbooks* as 'portfolio investment'). In theory, this includes reinvested profits, which are entered as a debit on the investment income line of the current account and again as a credit on this line. In the Philippines, net flows of direct investment have been small relative to loans.

— *Long-term loans* are loans with maturities of more than one year. These are subdivided into *official* and *private* loans depending on whether the borrower is the government or a private firm.

— *Short-term loans* are loans with maturities of less than one year. *Official* short-term loans include net drawings by the Central Bank. *Deposit money banks* refer to foreign exchange assets and liabilities of commercial banks. *Other private* short-term loans include trade credits and other non-bank assets and liabilities.

The *reserves and related items* line refers to changes in the country's official foreign exchange reserves, including 'counterpart items' such as monetization of gold and valuation changes in reserves. These represent 'accommodating' foreign exchange movements undertaken by Philippine monetary authorities so as to effect a balance between the current and capital accounts. In the absence of statistical discrepancies, the sum of the current account, the capital account, and changes in reserves and related items would be zero. Net reductions in reserves are recorded with a positive sign (in effect, foreign exchange is being provided to the economy by the change in reserves); net additions to reserves are recorded with a negative sign.

Net errors and omissions arise from data imperfections as a result of which the above categories do not, in fact, sum to zero. Unrecorded capital flows are believed to be a major source of these discrepancies, and hence errors and omissions are often incorporated in measures of capital flight.

In 1970 and 1983, the Philippines experienced balance-of-payments crises. Shortages of foreign exchange forced the government to turn to the IMF and undertake longer-term 'adjustments' ostensibly designed to remedy the problems which led to the crises. These crises serve as convenient points for demarcating the 1962–86 period into the three segments discussed below.

The Aftermath of Decontrol, 1962–70

The year 1962 saw the abrupt abandonment of foreign exchange controls by the newly elected government of President Diosdado Macapagal. These controls, which had been imposed in the wake of a balance-of-payments crisis in 1949, restricted the access of private firms to foreign credits, and required that any foreign payments be approved by the Central Bank. Their effect was to curtail imports of consumption goods in particular, setting the stage for import substitution. As Power and Sicat (1971, pp. 33–4) remarked: 'What began as an emergency tactic in balance of payments policy became the principal policy instrument for promoting industrialization over the decade of the 1950s'.

The abandonment of controls is sometimes attributed to the influence of the United States and the International Monetary Fund[8], but domestic politics appear to have played the decisive role. A foreign exchange crisis in 1958 had been resolved through the imposition of a foreign exchange tax, in defiance of US and IMF pressures for decontrol and devaluation, with the help of short-term commercial borrowing rather than IMF drawings. Corruption and political favoritism in the rationing of foreign exchange and import licenses, however, fueled growing anti-control pressure, resulting in the passage in 1959 of legislation requiring a gradual decontrol. In the event, decontrol came quite precipitously upon Macapagal's assumption of the Presidency.[9] Alburo and Canlas (1986, p. 9) conclude that 'it is doubtful that the IMF had earlier been consulted or participated in [the decontrol] policy analysis and decision'. Decontrol and the *de facto* devaluation of almost 100 per cent (from 2.0 to 3.9 pesos per US dollar) which accompanied the freeing of the foreign exchange market, however, quickly won backing from the US government and the IMF in the form of a $300 million stabilization loan package commitment.[10]

Despite the devaluation and imposition of higher tariffs which accompanied decontrol, imports climbed rapidly in the following years. By 1969 the dollar value of imports had risen to nearly twice the 1962 level, while the value of exports had grown by little more than 50 per cent. The resulting trade deficits were financed in large part by foreign borrowing, the magnitude of which is documented below.[11]

The growing trade deficit and repayment obligations for the loans which financed it set the stage for the balance-of-payments crisis which culminated in further devaluation of the peso in February 1970. Massive spending in Marcos's 1969 re-election campaign, financed by further external borrowing and an increase in the domestic money supply, provided 'simply the spark that ignited the crisis'.[12] The ILO mission (1974, p. 280) observed that a sharp rise in debt service payments (amortisation and interest) 'was a major factor in the balance-of-payments crisis of 1970'; indeed, the event was described by at least one observer (Wellons, 1977, p. 161) as a 'debt crisis' well before that phrase acquired its current popularity. The 1970 crisis thus underscored the likelihood of an eventual balance-of-payments crisis whenever external borrowing is used for purposes which do not generate sufficient foreign exchange for their ultimate repayment with interest. It was a lesson soon forgotten.

Debt-driven Growth, 1970–83

The balance-of-payments crisis of 1970 and the associated adjustment measures inaugurated what several analysts have characterized as 'the period of debt-driven growth'.[13] This time the Philippine government turned to the IMF; as Payer (1974, p. 71) writes, it 'had virtually no alternative to the acceptance of the IMF programme other than repudiation of its debts, and it did not have the social backing or political courage to face the consequences of a cut-off of aid and trading credits which that course would involve'. A $27.5 million IMF stand-by credit was arranged in February.

Three important developments occurred in connection with the 1970 crisis: (1) the floating of the peso and devaluation, the centerpieces of a stabilization package 'dictated by the IMF'[14]; (2) the adoption of policies to promote 'non-traditional' exports; and (3) the formation of a consortium of aid donors chaired by the World Bank.

The day after the stand-by agreement took effect, the Philippine government announced that henceforth the value of the peso would be allowed to float.[15] The devaluation was swift and sharp. The peso/dollar rate fell from 3.9 before the float to 6.4 by the end of the year. The extent of the devaluation surprised the IMF, which had predicted that a rate of 5.0 to 5.2 pesos/dollar would emerge (Broad, 1988, p. 35).

The inflationary consequences of the devaluation were severe: the consumer price index for low-income families in Manila, for example, jumped from 116.4 in 1970 (with 1966 = 100) to 155.5 in 1971 and to 296.6 in 1974 (NEDA, 1976, Table 14.4, p. 470). 'Floating rate' entered the Filipino vocabulary as a synonym for inflation (Payer, 1974, p. 72). A number of private firms were unable to service their external debts at the new exchange rate, and many of their obligations passed to the government's Development Bank of the Philippines, which had liberally dispensed loan guarantees in the months preceding the 1969 election.[16]

Philippine inflation eroded the impact of the devaluation on real (as opposed to nominal) exchange rates. After a 34 per cent drop in 1970, the peso actually appreciated in real terms in the 1970s, and by the end of the decade the real peso/dollar rate had returned to its pre-float level (see Table 11.1). The Philippine trade deficit meanwhile grew from $26 million in 1970 to $2.2 billion in 1981 (see Table 9.1). The co-existence of an appreciating real effective exchange rate with this growing trade imbalance was made possible by a concomitant influx of foreign borrowing.

Export promotion was a second important policy response to the 1970 crisis. The Export Incentive Act of 1970 provided for tariff exemptions on imported capital equipment and tax credits for domestic capital equipment.[17] A November 1972 Presidential Decree provided for the creation of the country's first export-processing zone in Bataan (Alburo and Shepherd, 1985, p. 61).

The Consultative Group for the Philippines, an international consortium of official development assistance donors chaired by the World Bank, met for the first time in April 1971.[18] The formation of the consultative group was important for two reasons. First, it served to mobilize substantially larger official financial flows. As the World Bank (1976, p. 467) observed, 'the importance of foreign aid increased dramatically' after the formation of the consultative group, with the total committed in 1971–74 exceeding that in the previous twenty years. The Philippines was designated a 'country of concentration' by the World Bank itself, and received lending from the Bank 'somewhat higher than average for countries of similar size and income'.[19] Second, the consultative group increased the leverage and influence of the World Bank, providing a vehicle for its 'attempts to rally other donors around its recommendations' (Bello *et al.*, 1982, p. 137, quoting a 1981 US Treasury Department report).

The 1974 ILO mission was optimistic about Philippine balance-of-payments prospects in the wake of the floating of the peso. Notwithstanding the faster inflation since the devaluation, the mission observed (p. 127), 'the prices of many goods and services, and especially money wage rates, have risen by much less than the devaluation', and 'consequently, much of the competitive gain still remains'. In other words, lower real wages would help to put the Philippine economy on a sounder international footing. The report noted that 'the balance of payments has gone into surplus and foreign exchange reserves have reached their highest levels since the Second World War'. A substantial trade surplus was achieved in 1973. However, this was primarily attributable to the world-wide commodity boom of that year which brought about a 50 per cent jump in Philippine export prices (Wellons, 1977, p. 174), and the experience has yet to be repeated.

The World Bank (1976, pp. 469–72) was similarly sanguine about the post-1970 growth of the Philippine external debt, remarking that 'it would be unfortunate for the Philippines to curb its potential for rapid development unnecessarily' by failing to borrow on commercial markets in the years ahead. Hence the Bank called for 'sustained and vigorous efforts . . . to ensure that the volume of funds available is sufficient for the needs of the Philippines'. Anticipating a rise in the shares of official and medium and long-term debt, the Bank predicted: 'The present careful control over external borrowings will undoubtedly continue, and, provided that the composition of inflows is along the lines already indicated, the projected increase in external ebt and debt service, though large, is not expected to present serious difficulties'.

These optimistic prognoses can be contrasted with Cheryl Payer's (1974, pp. 72, 74) remarkably prescient conclusion that the Philippines was already facing 'crippling debt obligations', and that the reliance of the Marcos government on fresh loans to service external debt 'will only create more and larger obligations in the future'. Similarly, commenting on the influx of new lending which followed the imposition of martial law in 1972, the editors of *Pick's Currency Yearbook* noted wryly, 'Despite the excellent chance of these debts possibly never being repaid, certain banks or bankers considered dictator Marcos an excellent credit risk' (Steve and Cowitt, 1976, p. 466).

It would be misleading, therefore, to date the origins of the Philippine debt problem from the oil price shock of 1973–74. The oil price boom did, however, contribute to an acceleration in the build-up of external debt: the Philippine demand for foreign exchange to pay for more expensive oil imports rose, and more importantly, the supply of external finance increased as international banks sought to 'recycle' the surpluses of the oil exporters. The direct, demand-side impact of the higher oil prices was limited by the fact that crude oil and petroleum products constituted only 12 per cent of the value of Philippine imports in 1973, rising to 21 per cent in 1974.[20] Moreover, the Philippines had some success in substituting away from oil imports: the quantum index of crude petroleum imports fell from 100 in 1973 to 92 in 1974, rose gradually to 108 in 1978, and thereafter declined to 71 in 1985. And the growing demand for Philippine labor in the Middle East partially offset the current account impact of the higher oil prices.[21]

More serious impacts on the Philippine demand for external finance arose from the deterioration in Philippine terms of trade, in which the oil price shock played an indirect role by contributing to the recession in the industrialized countries.[22] At the same time, Philippine efforts to develop non-oil energy sources led to increased imports of capital goods, the prices of which rose sharply in the mid-1970s, contributing almost as much as oil itself to the deterioration of the trade balance (Remolona, Mangahas and Pante, 1985, pp. 12–13).

The infusion of 'petrodollars' into world financial markets caused a dramatic shift in the supply of foreign lending, evidenced not only by the growth in the volume of debt but also by a marked shift in its composition, with a growing proportion of the loans originating from private commercial banks. These banks found themselves with a large volume of cash to lend, at a time when investment demand was slack in the industrialized countries themselves; their response was to increase dramatically their lending to Third World countries. The Philippine debt accumulation in the 1970s hence was part of this larger picture, with its counterparts in many other Asian, Latin American and African countries.

The relative importance of demand-side and supply-side factors in the post-1973 debt accumulation in the Third World is open to debate.[23] But two items of evidence suggest that the increased supply of foreign loans played the dominant role. First, the debt build-up was not limited to oil-importing nations like the Philippines, whose demand for foreign exchange was directly and indirectly increased by the oil price rises. Oil-exporting nations, including Mexico, Venezuela, Indonesia, and Nigeria also saw a rapid accumulation of debt.[24] Second, real interest rates were low and even negative in the 1970s, implying that at the international level supply shifts dominated.

In the Philippine case, the combination of increased lending from official sources and increased lending from private commercial banks led to massive capital account surpluses in the 1970s.

Following the second round of oil price increases in 1979–80, the Philippine external position grew still more precarious. Fresh borrowing now had to cover the rising burden of debt service on old money. At the same time, tight monetary policies in the industrialized countries pushed up real interest rates and plunged the world into the worst recession since the 1930s. Moreover, as commercial banks grew worried about their Third World loans, they shifted their new lending to shorter maturities. The stage was set for a new and deeper crisis.

The Long Crisis, 1983–86

On 17 October 1983, the Philippine government was forced by the depletion of its foreign exchange reserves to declare a 90-day moratorium on the amortization of its external debt, marking the onset of the worst balance-of-payments crisis in postwar Philippine history. The economic and political impacts of the ensuing 'adjustment' measures were so severe that the period up to the overthrow of the Marcos government in February 1986 can be characterized as one long, protracted crisis.

The accumulation of external debt, analogous in many ways to a 'Ponzi scheme' in which ever-increasing quantities of new money are borrowed to service past borrowing of dubious productive value, made a crisis inevitable.[25] The growing proportion of short-term debt, the 'interest rate shock' of the early 1980s, the sharp deterioration of the country's terms of trade, and the Mexican quasi-default of August 1982 brought the Philippine debt bubble close to the bursting point. According to Philippine Prime Minister and Finance Secretary Cesar Virata, 'our credit lines were already being cut towards the end of 1982' and by early 1983 foreign banks had withdrawn $709 million in credit facilities (Peagam, 1984, p. 53).

The final rupture was precipitated by the assassination of Benigno Aquino as he stepped from a plane at Manila airport on 21 August 1983. This event 'triggered a torrent of closures of commercial credit lines to the country' (Montes, 1987, p. 18). In addition, political unrest in the wake of the murder is said to have accelerated capital flight, which 'significantly contributed to the dwindling of international reserves' (Remolona and Lamberte, 1986, p. 113).[26]

The government's debt moratorium was accompanied by further devaluation of the peso (to P14/$, after having been devalued from P9 to P11 in June), and by an announcement that it was negotiating a new agreement with the IMF. Negotiations with the IMF and with commercial banks collapsed, however, when it was revealed in November that the Central Bank had been systematically overstating its foreign exchange reserves, to the tune of $600 to $800 million, by double-counting dollars cycled through overseas branches of the government-owned Philippine National Bank.[27] This deception, later described by Virata as a 'window-dressing effort' (Peagam, 1984, p. 54), led to the resignation of the Central Bank governor, and provoked further disenchantment in international financial circles. As a result, no new money was forthcoming, and the debt moratorium had to be repeatedly extended. A $608 million stand-by agreement with the IMF was finally concluded in December 1984, and a rescheduling agreement with the country's 483 foreign bank creditors followed in May 1985.[28]

In 'prior action commitments' preceding the signing of the IMF accord, the Philippine government implemented a number of 'classic IMF adjustment measures', including the devaluation and floating of the peso (which fell to P20/$ by the end of 1984), tight monetary policies, interest rate increases as high as 40 per cent, reduction of the government budget deficit, and the lifting of price controls (Montes, 1987, pp. 23–24; Lamberte *et al.*, 1985, pp. xvi–xx). These measures had a severe contractionary impact: GDP declined and real wages plummeted.

In terms of fulfillment of the targets set forth in the IMF agreement, including balance-of-payments targets, the 'adjustment' program was a great success. The current account deficit was virtually eliminated in 1985, and a substantial current account surplus was achieved in 1986. The adjustment did not, however, provide a secure basis for a longer-term recovery. As Montes

(1987, pp. 46–48) observes, exports declined in 1985 and 1986 (and would have declined in 1984, too, but for a boom in commodity prices), leaving the adjustment to be achieved primarily through precipitous declines in imports, particularly of capital goods and industrial inputs.[29]

THE EXTERNAL DEBT: MAGNITUDE AND COMPOSITION

Between 1962 and 1986 the external debt of the Philippines grew from $355 million to $28.3 billion. By the end of the Marcos years, the Philippines was the ninth most indebted nation in Asia, Africa, and Latin America in absolute terms. In terms of the ratio of external debt to gross domestic product, the Philippines ranked second among the top ten Third World debtor countries.[30]

This section reviews the available data on growth of the Philippine external debt and its composition in terms of type of borrower (public or private sector), type of lender (official or commercial), and maturity (long, medium, or short term).

Definitional Problems

The Philippine Central Bank's statistical system established in 1971 to monitor the country's external debt is 'one of the best in Asia and the Far East', according to the World Bank (1984, p. 43). Even so, substantial discrepancies exist among Philippine external debt estimates reported by different sources. One reason for these discrepancies is that many estimates rely on incomplete data on the volume of debt. This justifies a general presumption in favor of larger rather than smaller estimates; as I. David (1984, pp. 4–5) observes, 'in matters of debtor reporting, errors of omission are more likely than double counting'.[31]

Different definitions of external debt also contribute to apparent discrepancies. One distinction is between loan *commitments* and loan *disbursements*. In the case of official development assistance project loans, for example, funds committed at the start of the project are typically disbursed over a number of years as construction or other project activities proceed. More generally, the opening of a credit line represents a commitment, while drawings on that credit line represent disbursements. The data presented here pertain to actual disbursements.[32]

A second distinction is between gross and net external liabilities of the Central Bank and commercial banks. The Central Bank has both external liabilities and international reserves; similarly Philippine commercial banks have cross-border deposits which constitute external liabilities, but at the same time they hold external assets including deposits in foreign banks. Net external liabilities of the banking system are gross external liabilities minus gross external assets. In keeping with the general practice, the Philippine external debt is here defined to include gross external liabilities of the banking system.[33] The augmentation of the banking system's international reserves is thus one possible use of foreign borrowing. One rationale for including gross rather than net external liabilities of the Central Bank in the measure of the external debt is 'the assumption that Central Bank assets should be available to cover imports' (World Bank, 1984, p. 8).[34]

A final definitional problem concerns the distinction between public sector and private sector debt. This distinction is blurred in the Philippines, as in many countries, by two common practices. The first is external borrowing by government agencies for on-lending to the private sector. The government-owned Philippine National Bank, for example, provided 'the chief conduit for private external debt' in the early 1970s (Wellons, 1977, p. 163). Similarly, under the Consolidated Foreign Borrowing Program (CFBP) established in 1978, the Central Bank of the Philippines borrows (primarily from foreign commercial banks) in its own name and on-lends the proceeds to private and public sector borrowers by way of Philippine banks. By the end of 1982 total CFBP on-lending stood at $2.0 billion, more than half of which represented refinancing of prior foreign obligations (IMF, 1984, p. 65; World Bank, 1984, p. 39). In theory, foreign funds on-lent to the private sector are recorded by official record-keepers as private external debt, together with direct borrowing by the private sector. In practice, classifications vary.

A second practice which blurs the public-private debt distinction is the Philippine government's issuance of guarantees for repayment of most private debt. 'The creditors, in general, considered the Philippines to be a very high risk country', former Finance Minister Cesar Virata testified before a Congressional hearing in 1987, 'and they would not like to lend to the private sector without government guarantee'.[35] Considerable amounts of publicly guaranteed private obligations were assumed in the end by the public sector, as private borrowers defaulted, but the classification of such debt prior to default differs among data sources (see Wellons, 1977, pp. 164, 186).

Total External Debt Outstanding by Borrowing Sector

Table 9.2 summarizes data on the Philippine external debt from several sources. These provide the basis for the constructed time series reported in Table 9.3.

TABLE 9.2 *Alternative Estimates of Total Philippine External Debt Outstanding,*
1961–1986 [1] *(US $ million)*

Year	Central Bank [2]	IMF	Alfiler	World Bank	Jurado	Wellons & NEDA [3]
1961					355	278
1962					358	271
1963					376	252
1964						304
1965						481
1966						516
1967						680
1968						737
1969						840
1970	2297	2297		1613		956
1971	2393	2368		1777		1009
1972	2732	2663		1962		1171
1973	2886	2846		2029		1225
1974	3755	3538	3900	2465		1519
1975	4939	4392	5200	3053		2234
1976	6768	6345	7200	4471		3323
1977	8069	8035	8600	8221		3889
1978	10694	10608	11200	10817		5281
1979	13352	13192	13900	13307		6528
1980	17252	17122	18100	17390		8522
1981	20893	20291	21800	20750		11304
1982	24677	23797	25000	24299		13887
1983	24816	24972	26200	24124		14482
1984	25418		25900	24358		
1985	26252			26190		
1986	28256			28853		

NOTES

1. End-of-year estimates.
2. Unpublished data provided by the Central Bank of the Philippines, Department of Economic Research (International) and Financial Plan Data Center.
3. 'Public sector' debt only; see text for discussion.

SOURCES IMF (1984, Table 12, p. 72); Alfiler (1986, Table 1, p. 23); World Bank (1989b, Vol. II, p. 310; Vol. III, p. 180); Jurado (1966, Table 4, p. 373); Wellons (1977, Table 1 (1), p. 162); NEDA (1976, Table 11.8, pp. 398–9; 1986, Table 15.12, pp. 606–7).

TABLE 9.3   *External debt of the Philippines by borrowing sector, 1961–1986: A constructed time series*[1] *(US $ billion)*

| Year | Total Outstanding | Borrowing Sector | | Real Total (1986 $)[2] |
		Public	Private	
1961	0.36	0.17	0.19	1.14
1962	0.36	0.19	0.17	1.14
1963	0.38	0.23	0.15	1.21
1964	0.48	0.28	0.20	1.52
1965	0.80	0.46	0.34	2.48
1966	0.91	0.50	0.41	2.73
1967	1.28	0.68	0.60	3.84
1968	1.49	0.76	0.73	4.36
1969	1.83	0.90	0.93	5.15
1970	2.30	1.10	1.20	6.25
1971	2.39	0.92	1.47	6.28
1972	2.73	1.11	1.62	6.87
1973	2.89	1.15	1.74	6.43
1974	3.76	1.57	2.19	7.04
1975	4.94	2.33	2.61	8.47
1976	6.77	3.52	3.25	11.09
1977	8.07	4.03	4.04	12.46
1978	10.69	5.69	5.00	15.31
1979	13.35	7.65	5.70	16.99
1980	17.25	10.25	7.00	19.24
1981	20.89	12.80	8.09	21.35
1982	24.68	15.43	9.25	24.72
1983	24.82	16.73	8.09	24.55
1984	25.42	17.55	7.87	24.56
1985	26.25	19.12	7.13	25.49
1986	28.26	21.83	6.43	28.26

NOTES
1. End-of-year estimates of external debt outstanding, including gross banking system liabilities.
2. US wholesale price index (from IMF, 1987, pp. 698–9) used as proxy for inflation rate.

SOURCES   1961–63: Jurado (1966, p. 373). 1964–69: Wellons (1977, p. 162); original estimates scaled up to adjust for incompleteness. 1970–86: Unpublished data provided by Central Bank of the Philippines, Department of Economic Research (International) and Financial Plan Data Center. For details, see text.

After the Philippine debt moratorium was declared in October 1983, the Philippine government revealed that the country's total indebtedness as of October 17 was $24.6 billion, a sharp jump from the previously accepted figure of $18 billion.[36] The discrepancy arose primarily from the exclusion of monetary sector debt and revolving (as opposed to fixed short-term) credits from prior estimates issued by the Central Bank. These turned out to be much higher than had been previously known. The Central Bank subsequently extended the more comprehensive debt estimates to earlier years.

The Central Bank's Financial Plan Data Center has compiled the official data on external debt from 1983 onwards. The Central Bank's Department of Economic Research (International) has prepared comparable estimates for the years 1970 through 1982. The annual totals reported in Table 9.2 include the monetary sector (that is, gross external liabilities of the Central Bank and commercial banks) as well as the nonmonetary sector.

The Central Bank estimates for the nonmonetary sector are broken down into public and private sector debt, and into short versus medium and long-term debt. The estimates for the monetary sector for 1983–86 are classified into liabilities of the Central Bank, government commercial banks, and private commercial banks, again permitting a public/private breakdown. Commercial bank liabilities for 1970–82 are not subdivided into government and private banks; the public and private sector debt estimates reported in Table 9.3 for these years are based on the assumption that government banks accounted for 20 per cent of total commercial bank liabilities in those years.

The IMF (1984) and Alfiler (1986) present estimates which accord fairly closely with the Central Bank data. The OECD (1985, 1987) presents estimates for the years 1983–86 which also are reasonably consistent with those presented above.[37]

The World Bank, in the 1988–89 edition of its *World Debt Tables*, also presents revised figures on external debt extending back to 1970. Past editions of the *World Debt Tables*, which were often used for international comparisons, woefully understated the Philippine external debt. The 1984–85 edition, for example, reported total Philippine external debt in 1983 to have been $13.7 billion.[38] The Bank's revised figures redress this problem from 1977 onwards, but the estimates for 1970–1976 remain well below those reported by the Central Bank, Alfiler, and the IMF, apparently owing to continued under-reporting.

Debt estimates for the 1960s must be drawn from other sources. Jurado (1966) presents data on Philippine foreign loans from 1906 to 1963; only his 1961–63 figures are reported here. His estimates, the source of which was the Central Bank's Department of Economic Research, appear to be quite comprehensive. Data on both public and private sector debt are reported, and from notes to the table it appears that monetary sector debt is included.

Wellons (1977) presents figures on Philippine external debt for the years 1960–73. These correspond to the estimates of external debt classified by institutional source reported in various issues of the *Philippine Statistical Yearbook* published by the government's National Economic and Development Authority (NEDA). The Central Bank is stated to be the source of these data. Wellons reports, on the basis of a 1975 interview, that the data for the 1960s are 'incomplete'. The data refer only to 'public sector' debt, although as Wellons notes, the categories of public and private debt overlap since (1) the government-owned Philippine National Bank was the 'chief conduit for private external debt'; and (2) the government's Development Bank of the Philippines 'guaranteed substantial private foreign debt'. The extent to which these are included in the Wellons/NEDA series is 'unclear', but Wellons suggests that the inclusion of some publicly guaranteed private debt may help to account for the 'astonishing' discrepancy between these figures and (lower) estimates reported at the time by the World Bank.[39]

The time series on total, public, and private external debt reported in Table 9.3 is constructed on the basis of these data. For the years 1970–86, the time series uses the Central Bank data. Estimates for 1961–63 are taken directly from Jurado. For the intervening years, 1964–69, estimates are derived from the data presented by Wellons and NEDA. Owing to their incompleteness, these are scaled up to make them comparable to the earlier and later data.[40] The estimates in Table 9.3 for the years 1964–69 should therefore be regarded as rougher approximations than those for other years.

The total external debt at the end of 1961 stood at $355 million, of which slightly more than half represented private external debt. A review of the country's external debt up to the early 1960s concluded that most loans had been 'channeled to economically productive enterprises', and that the volume of foreign loans had been 'relatively light' (Jurado, 1966, p. 378). The foreign debt was equivalent to approximately 5 per cent of GNP, valued at the pre-devaluation exchange rate of 2 pesos per dollar, or 10 per cent when valued at the post-devaluation rate of 3.9 (calculated from GNP data in NEDA, 1976, p. 114).

By 1970, the debt had increased more than six-fold, to $2.30 billion, equivalent (at the new post-devaluation exchange rate of 6.4 pesos per dollar) to 36 per cent of the country's GNP. Private sector debt registered the strongest increase in the 1960s, a period marked by the relaxation of government control over private foreign transactions, as noted above. The rapid growth of debt in the late 1960s, the service requirements of which played a key role in the 1970 balance-of-payments crisis, led to the implementation of the control system administered by the Central Bank (IMF, 1984, p. 73). The tasks of debt monitoring and management were entrusted to the Central Bank's Management of External Debt and Investment Accounts Department (MEDIAD), which must approve all public and private non-monetary sector borrowing (World Bank, 1984, pp. 37–42).

In the period 1970–74 the external debt 'grew moderately', in the words of the IMF (1984, p. 73), 'reflecting the improved balance of payments position and the close monitoring of approvals'. Although the growth can be termed 'moderate' relative to that in preceding and subsequent years, the external debt, already large enough to precipitate a crisis in 1970, continued to rise. Rapid world price inflation in 1973 and 1974 eroded the real value of the external debt outstanding in those years. Nevertheless new borrowing left total real debt at the end of 1974 above what it had been at the end of 1970. Outstanding external debt now stood at 26 per cent of GNP.[41]

The external debt build-up again accelerated in the mid-1970s, rising from \$3.8 billion in 1974 to \$17.3 billion in 1980, and to \$24.8 billion in 1983. New borrowing far outpaced the erosion of the real value of the accumulated debt by world price inflation, and by 1980 the real debt was three times its level in the early 1970s, and sixteen times higher than in the early 1960s. When the Philippine debt crisis broke in 1983, the external debt had swollen to 114 per cent of GNP.[42] The World Bank (1984, p. 12) nevertheless characterizes the growth rate of real Philippine debt during the 1970s as 'quite modest', suggesting that modesty, like beauty, lies in the eye of the beholder.[43]

In contrast to the debt build-up which preceded the 1970 crisis, the debt accumulation of the 1970s and early 1980s was marked by a generally rising share of the public sector in total debt. Indeed, the 'leading role' of the public sector is understated by the figures in Table 9.3 insofar as private debt was publicly guaranteed. After 1983, the 'socialization' of private debt is evident in the decline of outstanding private external debt and the concomitant rise in outstanding public external debt.

The World Bank (1984, p. 24) interprets the declining share of private debt in the late 1970s and early 1980s as an indication of weakening private demand for foreign funds, which 'perhaps reflected the combined effect of domestic recession, increased government use of foreign funds, take-over of private concerns by public enterprises, and the private sector's response to hardening of loan terms'. In this context, the Bank continues, it would be useful 'to further investigate if the private sector really responded to the changed economic and financial conditions and whether the public sector failed to do so'. The rapid expansion of external debt after 1978, according to the Bank (1984, p. 6) 'suggests that the Philippine authorities were not sufficiently responsive to the sharp rise in real interest rates in international markets'.

This analysis is flawed in three respects. First, it rests on the questionable premise that Philippine government borrowing was based on cost-benefit comparisons of expected internal rates of return with real interest rates, rather than an increasingly desperate effort to service past debt by means of new money and thereby forestall the inevitable crisis. Second, the inability of the private borrowers to service their debt, much of which was then assumed by the public sector, is transmuted into evidence of greater private sector responsiveness to market conditions, in a rather heroic effort to find virtue in private enterprise. And finally, the analysis conveniently omits mention of the active encouragement provided by international financial institutions, not least among them the World Bank itself, to the government's strategy of debt-driven growth.

The year 1983 marked the breaking point of the debt cycle in the Philippines, in which the net transfer turned negative. The net flow (that is, new lending minus amortization payments) shrank to $140 million, and this was far exceeded by an outflow of $2.0 billion in interest payments (see Table 9.4).[44] The net transfer remained negative in subsequent years; even in 1986, with the influx of new credits following the February revolution, interest payments exceeded the net flow of lending.

Distribution of External Debt by Creditor

The distribution of the Philippine public external debt among creditors is reported in Table 9.5. Most private sector loans were received from private creditors, although the Philippine government channelled concessional funds from bilateral and multilateral donors and long-term export credits to private entrepreneurs 'from time to time' (World Bank, 1984, p. 21). The available data indicating the breakdown by creditor refer only to public external debt.

Perhaps the most notable feature of the data is the fairly consistent percentage distribution of the rapidly growing debt among different types of creditors. Thus the private creditors' share of total public external debt was 44 per cent in 1963 and 48 per cent in 1983, with an intervening peak of 58 per

TABLE 9.4 *Net Flow and Net Transfer, 1962–1986 (US $ million)*

Year	Change in external debt outstanding[1]	Interest payments[2]	Net Transfer
1962	0	10	−10
1963	20	9	11
1964	100	25	75
1965	320	33	287
1966	110	29	81
1967	370	36	334
1968	210	33	177
1969	340	38	302
1970	470	116	354
1971	90	91	−1
1972	340	115	225
1973	160	119	41
1974	870	146	724
1975	1180	223	957
1976	1830	246	1584
1977	1300	236	1064
1978	2620	439	2181
1979	2660	625	2035
1980	3900	975	2925
1981	3640	1378	2262
1982	3790	1993	1797
1983	140	1988	−1848
1984	600	2328	−1728
1985	830	2219	−1389
1986	2010	2048	−38
Total	27900	15499	12401

NOTES
1. Including gross external liabilities of the banking system.
2. Investment income debits other than earnings on direct investment.

SOURCES   Change in external debt outstanding from Table 9.3; interest payments from IMF, *Balance of Payments Statistics Yearbook*, various issues.

TABLE 9.5 *Public External Debt by Creditor, 1963–1983*
(percentage distribution)

Year	Official Creditors					Private Creditors	
	World Bank	IMF	US	Japan	Others	Commercial banks	Suppliers' credits
1963	13.9	21.2	20.3	0	0	34.9	9.7
1964	14.8	15.4	16.6	0	11.8	34.6	6.6
1965	12.9	14.0	14.6	0	3.1	49.5	5.8
1966	13.6	17.5	11.5	0	2.7	49.1	5.5
1967	12.4	17.4	8.7	0	2.0	53.5	6.0
1968	12.9	23.3	8.8	0	2.9	43.2	8.9
1969	13.6	20.8	8.8	0	1.6	45.8	9.2
1970	13.4	24.2	8.9	0	1.7	45.2	6.5
1971	14.8	25.6	9.7	0	1.7	36.4	11.7
1972	13.6	28.7	10.0	0.2	4.7	27.3	15.5
1973	13.6	30.5	11.4	1.8	5.5	20.0	17.2
1974	11.4	23.6	10.3	5.3	5.6	28.5	15.0
1975	11.6	21.0	10.8	8.0	7.7	36.1	4.8
1976	10.0	18.4	9.0	6.8	17.0	34.3	4.5
1977	10.7	18.3	9.3	6.6	20.7	25.9	8.5
1978	10.2	17.3	9.0	8.3	20.4	25.5	9.3
1979	10.4	16.7	9.2	5.8	18.9	29.0	9.0
1980	10.2	17.4	8.0	5.6	18.8	33.3	6.6
1981	11.0	17.8	6.5	6.1	18.4	35.5	4.7
1982	11.4	14.1	4.8	5.4	12.5	49.6	2.3
1983	14.4	12.3	5.1	5.6	14.5	45.6	2.6

SOURCES   NEDA (1974, pp. 280–1; 1976, pp. 398–9; 1986, pp. 606–7).

cent in 1967 and low of 34 per cent in 1977. The World Bank accounted for 10 to 15 per cent of total public external debt throughout the period. The growth of the Philippine debt hence cannot be attributed to lending by one or a few groups of creditors: it was a broadly-based process. The creditor structure of the debt did, however, show some variation over time. For example, in the 1970s lending from Japan and other official creditors (including European governments and the Asian Development Bank) came to play an important role, whereas in the 1960s official lending came almost entirely from the US, the World Bank and the IMF.

The change in the composition of official creditors was accompanied by a parallel shift towards greater Japanese and European involvement in

TABLE 9.6 *Term Structure of External Debt, 1965–1986*
(percentage distribution)

| Year | Non-monetary Sector | | Monetary Sector [3] |
	Medium and long-term[1]	Short-term [2]	
1965–69 (average)[4]	47	53	
1970	65	13	21
1971	64	13	23
1972	61	11	28
1973	60	10	30
1974	55	9	36
1975	53	9	38
1976	60	11	30
1977	65	12	23
1978	58	12	31
1979	53	14	33
1980	50	15	36
1981	47	18	35
1982	45	18	37
1983	50	16	33
1984	51	17	32
1985	52	14	34
1986	55	10	35

NOTES
1. Debt with maturities of one year or more.
2. Debt with maturities less than one year.
3. Gross external liabilities of the banking system (Central Bank and commercial banks).
4. Public debt only.

SOURCES 1965–69: Wellons (1977, p. 163). 1970–87: unpublished data provided by Central Bank of the Philippines, Department of Economic Research (International) and Financial Plan Data Center.

commercial bank lending. The early 1970s saw the formation of separate syndicates of Japanese, US, and European banks which established revolving Eurocurrency credit lines (Wellons, 1977, p. 167). In 1983, outstanding public external debt to non-US commercial banks surpassed that to US banks for the first time.[45]

Term Structure of External Debt

The distribution of total external debt by maturity type is reported in Table 9.6. Non-monetary sector debt (public and private) is broken down into two categories: (a) medium- and long-term (MLT) debt, with maturities of one year or more, and (b) short-term debt, with maturities of less than one year. Medium-term debt (with 1–5 year maturities) comprised a small fraction of the former, at least towards the end of the period. In 1982, for example, medium-term debt represented only 1.4 per cent of all medium- and long-term debt, while 51.6 per cent carried maturities of 5–12 years, and 47.0 per cent carried maturities over 12 years (World Bank, 1984, p. 72). Short-term non-monetary sector debt includes revolving credits, some of which are trade-related; a relatively small amount of fixed-term debt, primarily bridging finance for development projects that will subsequently be financed with MLT loans; and trade financing, usually carrying maturities of 30–60 days following the shipment of goods to the Philippines, in the form of documents against acceptance (D/As) provided by foreign banks, and open accounts (O/As) provided by foreign suppliers.[46]

Monetary sector debt – the gross external liabilities of the Central Bank and commercial banks – is reported separately in the table. This is not broken down by term structure owing to the inadequacy of available data, but most of it is probably short-term.[47]

The rapid growth of short-term debt in the late 1960s played an important role in precipitating the 1970 balance-of-payments crisis. Among the responses to the crisis (others of which were discussed above) was a restructuring of this debt: 'In early 1970, faced with a large volume of maturing debt during the year, the authorities negotiated longer maturities for a sizable proportion of outstanding debt and obtained new medium-term credits to replace maturing short-term loans' (IMF, 1984, p. 76).

In the late 1970s, however, the share of short-term debt again began to rise, even as the total volume of debt grew rapidly. The share of short-term non-monetary debt and gross monetary sector liabilities rose from 35 per cent in 1977 to 55 per cent in 1982. In absolute terms, such debt grew during this period from $3 billion to $14 billion.

As the volume of short-term debt mounted, its composition shifted. The share owed to banks and other financial institutions (as opposed to suppliers' credits) registered a 'phenomenal rise' from 45 per cent in 1979 to 77 per cent in 1982 (World Bank, 1984, p. 13). Two developments played key roles in this shift: credits from major oil suppliers dried up, forcing importers to turn to financial intermediaries; and short-term credit was increasingly used not only to finance trade, but also 'to replace maturing longer term debts' and 'to continually finance their working capital needs' by some producers in both the public and private sector (World Bank, 1984, pp. 13–14). Public sector enterprises – such as the Philippine National Oil Company, Philippine Airlines, the National Power Corporation, the Development Bank of the Philippines, the National Sugar Trading Corporation, the National Food Authority, and the National Steel Corporation – accounted for about two-thirds of the increase in short-term debt in the early 1980s (IMF, 1984, p. 76). Discussing this period, the World Bank (1984, p. 12) remarks, 'In general, the financial markets interpret a sudden accretion of short-term debt as a sign of reduced creditworthiness'. This initiates a vicious circle:

> At this stage, a debtor is often faced with restrictions on the type of credits available, with creditors showing a preference for short-term rather than medium-term commitments. Thus, a country with an increasing share of short-term borrowings in its debt portfolio faces a serious dilemma: lenders' perceptions of its creditworthiness erode as the weight of short-term borrowings increases; on the other hand, in order to service the debt and thereby maintain creditworthiness, the borrowing country's dependence on short-term rollovers continues to grow. (World Bank, 1984, pp. 12–13.)

This was the predicament of the Philippine economy as it approached the crisis of 1983.

By the end of 1986, restructuring had reduced the share of short-term debt in total external liabilities. In this respect, the pattern following the 1970 crisis was repeated. In other respects, however, the aftermaths of the two crises were profoundly different. In the early 1970s, the reduction in short-term debt had been achieved in a context of growing availability of external finance, although the exercise of restraint by Philippine authorities (notably in the Central Bank), anxious not to repeat the 1970 experience, acted for a time as a check on new borrowing in general, and on short-term borrowing in particular. In the mid-1980s, by contrast, the Philippines faced much tighter supplies of external finance, both from official sources and, most drastically, from private lenders. A resumption of the 'Ponzi scheme' in this changed international financial environment seems quite unlikely. Rather than an infusion of new external finance, the country now faces the prospect of protracted negative net transfers.

NOTES

1. In 1988, for example, interest payments totalled $2.1 billion and principal repayments totalled $1.5 billion (World Bank, 1990a, p. 310).
2. These chapters draw heavily on Boyce (1990).
3. The precise shape of the net transfer curve depends, of course, upon loan timing and interest rates. For a depiction of the net transfer cycle assuming 'World Bank-type terms' of 7 per cent interest, 25-year maturity, and a 5-year grace period, see Frank (1972, p. 31).
4. For expositions of the net transfer cycle, see also Griffin (1978, Ch. 3), Reisen and von Trotsenburg (1988), and Payer (1991).
5. See, for example, Dornbusch and Fischer (1990, p. 536).
6. The IMF Articles of Agreement prohibit restrictions on payments on the current account, but allow controls on the capital account. Evans (1968, p. 34, cited by Payer, 1974, p. 8) remarks that this 'may indicate why the drafters of the Fund Agreement specifically included interest and net income as payments for current transactions'.
7. Following the Philippines government's declaration of a debt repayment moratorium, interest payments fell into arrears in 1983 and 1984. These payments were nevertheless recorded in the balance of payments as if they had been made, with corresponding short-term capital inflows (a form of 'exceptional financing'); the reverse occurred in 1985, when repayment of arrears is recorded as a short-term capital outflow and not reported on the investment income line.
8. For example, Bello *et al.* (1982, p. 131) state: 'Pressured by US investors seeking freer repatriation of their profits and US exporters frustrated by protectionist obstacles, the US government forced President Diosdado Macapagal to abolish import and exchange controls'. Montes (1987, p. 3) refers to the dismantling of controls as part of an 'IMF adjustment program' imposed in connection with 'the 1962 crisis'.
9. For an account of these events, see Payer (1974, pp. 59–66).
10. The stabilization package included a $40 million stand-by agreement with the IMF, credits from the USAID and the US Export-Import Bank, a loan (against gold) from the US Federal Reserve, and stand-by financing and refinancing from private banks (Alburo and Canlas, 1986, p. 6; Broad, 1983, p. 85; Broad, 1988, p. 33).
11. The growth of the Philippine external debt is not fully captured by the data in Table 9.1, partly because the balance of payments data are net of recorded capital outflows. In addition, differences between debt and balance-of-payments reporting procedures, involving the adjustment for

late reporting by borrowers, valuation adjustments for exchange rate movements, and the classification of short-term capital movements, give rise to discrepancies (World Bank, 1984, p. 44).

12. Power and Sicat (1971, p. 50). See also Payer (1974, pp. 70–1); Bello *et al.* (1982, p. 136); and Montes (1987, p. 3).

13. Montes (1987, p. 6). Ranis (1984, p.6) has also referred to the Philippines' 'debt-driven growth of the 70s'.

14. Broad (1988, p. 34), quoting Benito Legarda, Jr., who was Assistant Director of the Central Bank's Department of Economic Research at the time.

15. Alburo and Canlas (1986, p. 9). A Central Bank circular stated: 'The free market rate shall not be administratively fixed but shall be determined through transactions in the foreign exchange market on a day-to-day basis. The authorities shall not intervene in the market except to the extent necessary to compensate for excessive fluctuations but shall not operate against the trend in the market'. (Quoted in ILO, 1974, p. 128.) In practice, a fairly stable dollar exchange rate was maintained in the 1970s (see Table 11.1) – an accomplishment made possible by massive foreign exchange inflows on the capital account, as discussed below. As a result, the exchange rate regime during this period has been variously described as 'fixed' and 'on a managed float' (Canlas, 1985, pp. 3, 4); as a policy of 'limited flexibility in contrast to a policy of full flexibility' (Panganiban, 1983, p. 10); as a 'flexible' policy which 'was not used effectively to adjust to the imbalances in the country's external accounts' (Remolona, Mangahas and Pante, 1985, p. 10); by the IMF in 1980 as a 'policy of keeping the exchange rate of the peso closely in line with the dollar' (quoted by Thompson and Slayton, 1985, p. 72); and as a 'dirty float' policy, 'wherein, although the peso was technically free to float, the Central Bank intervened in foreign exchange markets to maintain the peso's value against the dollar' (Broad, 1988, p. 94). The float became 'cleaner' in the early 1980s, a change which Broad attributes to World Bank pressure.

16. Interview with Benito Legarda, Jr., Central Bank representative at the Embassy of the Republic of the Philippines, Washington, D.C., 11 May 1988. Legarda suggests that the DBP's demand for foreign exchange to service these debts 'drove the market' after the float, causing the devaluation to be more substantial than it otherwise would have been.

17. See Ofreneo (1985, pp. 171–2); Alburo and Shepherd (1985, pp. 60–3); and Dohner and Intal (1989, pp. 443–5, 455).

18. Wellons (1977, p. 187, n. 27); Ofreneo (1985, p. 173). In addition to the Bank, its members included bilateral donor countries (among them the United States and Japan), the IMF, the UNDP, the ADB, and the OECD. The first aid coordination group had been organized by the Bank for India in 1958; by May 1971 the Bank was chairman of fifteen such groups (World Bank, 1971, p. 42).

19. Gould (1976, pp. 2, 17), cited by Bello *et al.* (1982, p. 24).

20.   Calculated from data in World Bank (1986, Vol. III, Tables 3.8 and 3.10, pp. 26, 28).

21.   Personal income remittances from overseas contract workers, included in the 'other' line of the current account in Table 9.1, rose from US$103 million in 1975 to a peak of $944 million in 1983, with workers in the Middle East accounting for roughly half of the total in the 1980s (Tabora, 1986, Table 3, p. 24). The Philippine import bill for crude oil and petroleum products in 1983 stood at $1,752 million (World Bank, 1986, Vol. III, Table 3.10, p. 28).

22.   Power (1983, p. 9) reports that with 1971–73 = 100, the terms-of-trade index (that is, the ratio of export prices to import prices) for the Philippines in 1982 was 52. See also Chapter 6, above.

23.   For discussion, see Taylor (1985), Darity (1986), Darity and Horn (1988), and Devlin (1989).

24.   Oil wealth made such countries appear to be good credit risks; in the words of the Mexican official who managed that country's external debt in the late 1970s, 'Mexico was really sexy then. We were contracting on terms as fine as Sweden's'. (Quoted by Moffett and Truell, 1988.) Oil was not essential to rouse the animal spirits of foreign bankers, however. Regarding the Philippines, the president of Bancom Development Corporation observed in 1976: '[I]n banking, like anything else, there are fads. There will be fads for a particular country. This means all of a sudden the credit of a particular country becomes hot in the market, a situation wherein everybody tries to push financing to that country. I think the Philippines is very much in this position now'. (Quoted in Thompson and Slayton, 1985, p. 77.) One indicator of lender perceptions of risk is the interest rate spread above LIBOR charged on public and publicly-guaranteed loans. The average spread for the Philippines from 1979 through 1982 was 0.9, while for Mexico it was 0.6; in 1983, however, it fell to 0.7 in the Philippines, while it rose to 1.9 in Mexico (Folkerts-Landau, 1985). Alternative measures, based upon the ratio of interest payments to total external debt, show the Philippines to have paid a substantially *lower* risk premium than Mexico throughout the 1978–83 period (Dooley, 1986, p. 9).

25.   Charles Ponzi, the 'Boston swindler', was an early twentieth century entrepreneur who offered high interest rates in a fraudulent investment scheme (based on ostensible profits to be made in exchange rate arbitrage using international postal reply coupons) which depended upon new depositors' money to pay dividends to earlier investors. Payer (1985, p. 17; 1991, Chapter 3) draws the analogy with international commercial bank lending in the 1970s.

26.   This widely accepted version of the timing of capital flight has been disputed; for example, Weiner (1987) states that capital flight out of the Philippines peaked 'in the months before, and not after, the murder of Benigno Aquino'. Statistical evidence reviewed in Chapter 10 suggests that capital flight in fact peaked in 1981.

27. For details of the reserve overstatement scandal, see Peagam (1984); Henry (1989); and Dohner and Intal (1989, p. 533). The latter authors report that 'the overstatement had run as high as $1.1 billion, or 50 per cent of stated international reserves'.

28. The negotiations are described by Montes (1987, pp. 19–24); Remolona and Lamberte (1986, p. 23); and Dohner and Intal (1989, pp. 542–4).

29. In addition, the balance of payments record a notable increase in net 'other' payments, the reasons for which are unclear. Noting the further deterioration in the ratios of the country's debt burden to GDP and exports, the World Bank (1986, Vol. II, p. 6) warned that rescheduling alone 'is not a sustainable strategy for the medium term'.

30. The debt/GDP ratio for the Philippines was 0.88. Among the top ten debtors, this was surpassed only by Egypt, with a ratio of 1.05, and was equal to that of Venezuela. The average ratio for the other seven countries was 0.54. Based on 1985 data from OECD (1987, Table 2) and World Bank (1987, Table 3).

31. This is reflected in the fact that total world lending of banks to non-banks reported by creditors exceeds that ascribed to individual borrowers; in 1983 $98 billion (of a total of $679 billion) remained unaccounted for in the IMF's international financial statistics (David, 1984, p. 5).

32. Similarly, in the case of the monetary sector (the Central Banks and commercial banks), credit lines may be drawn down gradually; indeed, sometimes they are never drawn at all (as, for example, in the case of the country's first stand-by credits from the IMF in the 1960s; see Alburo and Canlas, 1986, p. 6).

33. Annual data on changes in official reserves and commercial banking system external assets for the period under review are provided in Table 10.2; debt flows net of these can thus be readily calculated.

34. A further definitional point relates to the treatment of the assets and liabilities of offshore banking units (OBUs), whose establishment in the Philippines was permitted by a 1976 Presidential Decree. Twenty-eight foreign banks had set up OBUs in the Philippines as of 1984; they borrow and lend in foreign currencies 'outside the regulatory framework of banks operating in the Philippines' (IMF, 1984, pp. 69–70). Contrary to standard practice in many countries, the Philippine statistical authorities treat OBUs as overseas banks. Thus OBU lending to Philippine residents is included in the country's external debt statistics, while OBU external liabilities are not. As of June 1986, Philippine debt to OBUs stood at $2.5 billion, while the OBUs owed $3.7 billion to other foreign entities. The net effect was to understate the Philippine external debt (compared with that which would result from the conventional treatment of OBUs) by $1.2 billion. The debt statistics reported here were provided by Philippine authorities, and hence follow their practice in this regard.

35. Official minutes of the testimony of Cesar Virata before the Philippine House of Representatives Subcommittee on Monetary, Credit and Financial Matters, 26 August 1987, p. IV–1. The World Bank (1984, p. 20)

reports that 34 per cent of private medium and long-term debt was publicly guaranteed in 1975, and that this share fell to 20 per cent in 1980 and rose to 29 per cent in 1982. These appear to be underestimates.

36. Rafferty (1983, p. 101); Peagam (1984, p. 57); IBON (1984, p. 32).

37. The OECD (1985) reports estimated Philippine indebtedness at the end of 1983 to be $28.4 billion (including $5.3 billion in 'other liabilities', representing cross-border deposits of entities other than banks in Philippine banks); and $29.0 billion (including $5.2 billion in other liabilities) at the end of 1984. The OECD (1987) estimates for 1985 and 1986 (presented in a different format, which may not be entirely comparable with those of the 1985 report) are $28.6 billion and $27.2 billion, respectively. Earlier data published by the OECD were much less complete; see David and Lee (1986) for a comparison of the old and new OECD series.

38. The Bank's figure comprised $10.4 billion public or publicly guaranteed debt and $3.3 billion private debt. Power (1983, p. 8) notes that the *World Debt Table* figures do not fully capture non-guaranteed private debt; in this instance they also appear to understate public debt.

39. Wellons (1977, pp. 163–4, 186).

40. The ratio of the Wellons/NEDA estimate to Jurado's estimate for 1963 is 0.67; the ratio of the Wellons/NEDA estimates to the Central Bank estimates for 1970–73 is 0.425. Accordingly, the Wellons/NEDA figures for the intervening years were scaled up on the assumption that they represent a proportion of total external debt which declined linearly between these points (that is, 0.635 in 1964, 0.60 in 1965, . . ., 0.46 in 1969). The resulting estimates are partitioned into public and private debt in a similar fashion, interpolating the trend in their relative shares from the observation that the public share of total debt declined from 0.61 in 1963 to 0.48 in 1970. These trends are consistent with other evidence: NEDA (1976, pp. 400–1), in an alternative debt series (which includes private debt but is apparently less comprehensive with respect to public debt than the series cited here), indicates that the public share of total external debt declined in the late 1960s. The World Bank (1976, p. 472) similarly reports that the share of the public sector in total medium and long-term debt declined from 48 per cent in 1964 to 29 per cent in 1969. Both sources indicate that the public share then rose in the early 1970s.

41. The apparent decline in the debt/GNP ratio in the early 1970s is quite sensitive to the exchange rate. Real Philippine GNP rose between 1970 and 1974 by 29 per cent; the implicit Philippine GNP deflator (1970=100) was 192.1 (calculated from NEDA, 1976, pp. 115, 119). At the same time the real value of the external debt rose by only 13 per cent (using the US wholesale price index, which rose by 45 per cent, as the debt deflator). Despite the differences in inflation rates, the peso/dollar exchange rate rose by only 10 per cent, from 6.435 to 7.065 (see Table 11.1); more rapid depreciation of the peso would have resulted in a higher debt/GNP ratio in 1974, by lowering the dollar value of GNP.

42. Converting the 304,876 million peso GNP (NEDA, 1986, p. 163) at the end-of-year exchange rate of 14 pesos/dollar; if the 1984 exchange rate of 19.76 pesos/dollars is used on the grounds that the peso remained overvalued at the end of 1983, the debt/GNP ratio rises to 161 per cent.

43. As evidence, the World Bank (1984, p. 68) cites data indicating that real outstanding medium and long-term debt grew at 'only' 5.0 to 9.7 per cent per annum from 1970–79, depending upon the price index used. Short-term debt grew even faster, as discussed below.

44. The 'net transfer' estimates reported in Table 9.4 are inexact insofar as changes in the dollar value of external debt outstanding arose not from new money inflows but from exchange rate effects (notably changes in the yen/dollar rate). These effects were substantial in 1985 and 1986 (see Table 10.2), and as a result Table 9.4 understates the net transfer in those years. Alternative data for the 1980s presented by the World Bank (1990, p. 310) indicate that the negative net transfer from the Philippines commenced two years earlier, in 1981.

45. As of 1985, the four commercial banks with the greatest exposure in the Philippines were US-based: Citibank ($1.8 billion), Manufacturers Hanover Trust Co. ($489 million), Bank of America ($487 million), and Chase Manhattan Bank ($427 million). They were followed by the Bank of Tokyo ($404 million), Barclays Bank ($386 million), Bank of Montreal ($362 million), Banque Nationale de Paris ($284 million), Credit Lyonnais ($267 million), Morgan Guaranty Trust Co. ($252 million), and the Fuji Bank ($251 million). Data reported in *The Manila Chronicle*, November 4, 1986, p. 5; see Lind (1984) for further details.

46. The latter method has been used primarily for oil imports and by subsidiaries of transnational corporations (IMF, 1984, pp. 67, 76).

47. Unpublished Central Bank data indicate that 64 per cent of monetary sector liabilities were short-term in 1983. For the next two years the corresponding figures were 63 per cent and 56 per cent; in 1986 it fell to 26 per cent, presumably as a result of rescheduling. Maturity breakdowns of monetary sector liabilities for earlier years are not available, but the Central Bank data indicate that commercial bank liabilities, a higher proportion of which are short-term, constituted a larger fraction of total monetary sector liabilities from 1972 to 1982 than they did thereafter.

10   Capital Flight

INTRODUCTION

A substantial fraction of Philippine external borrowing was 'recycled' out of the country via capital flight, or what Filipinos often refer to as 'dollar salting'. The best-publicized instances involve the assets of ex-President Marcos, his family, and his close associates.[1] But Philippine capital flight was not restricted to members of the ruling family and their friends. The first Finance Minister of the Aquino government, the late Jaime Ongpin, told a group of bankers in 1986 that 'every successful businessman, lawyer, accountant, doctor, and dentist I know has some form of cash or assets which he began to squirrel abroad after Marcos declared martial law in 1972 and, in the process, frightened every Filipino who had anything to lose' (Shaplen, 1986, p. 61).

The Philippines was not unusual in this respect. Many Asian, Latin American, and African countries experienced large-scale capital flight in the 1970s and 1980s even as they accumulated large external debts. Morgan Guaranty Trust Company (1986) estimates that capital flight from eighteen major Third World countries totalled $198 billion from 1976 to 1985. During the same period the total external indebtedness of these countries rose by $451 billion.[2]

Several estimates of the ratio of cumulative capital flight to external debt for major Latin American and Asian debtor countries are reported in Table 10.1. As a fraction of external debt, Philippine capital flight appears to have exceeded that of Brazil, Korea, and Indonesia, but to have remained less than that of Argentina, Venezuela, Malaysia, and possibly Mexico.

A noteworthy feature of the estimates in Table 10.1, and virtually all commonly-cited estimates of capital flight, is that the reported cumulative totals are simply the summation of *nominal* annual flows, with no adjustment for inflation or interest earnings on externally held assets. That is, a dollar that left the Philippines or Mexico in, say, 1975, is valued the same as a dollar that left in 1986. Such cumulative totals substantially understate the real value of flight capital, imparting a downward bias to the ratios reported in the table. This bias and others are corrected in measures of Philippine capital flight derived in this chapter.

TABLE 10.1 *Ratio of Capital Flight to External Debt, Selected Countries*

Country	Ratio of capital flight to external debt[1]			External debt outstanding end 1986[2] (US$ billion)
	Morgan Guaranty (1976–85)	Dooley (to 1983)	Khan & Ul Haque (1974–82)	
Argentina	0.62	0.61	0.72	55.2
Brazil	0.12	0.08	0.04	115.4
Mexico	0.71	0.44	0.34	109.6
Venezuela	1.15	0.77	0.49	42.5
Indonesia	0.19	NA	NA	42.2
Korea	0.30	0.27	0.22	54.4
Malaysia	0.63	NA	NA	22.9
Philippines	0.39	0.30	0.36	27.2

NA = not available

NOTES

1. Ratios differ due to differences in time periods covered and in measures employed; see original sources for details. All are likely to be underestimates in that they omit interest earnings on flight capital.
2. OECD estimates.

SOURCES   Morgan Guaranty Trust Company (1986, p. 13); Dooley (1986, p. 17); Khan and Ul Haque (1987, p. 4); OECD (1987, Table 1).

The chapter is organized as follows. First, the concept of capital flight is discussed. Next, some mechanisms by which capital fled the Philippines are enumerated. Annual measures of capital flight are then presented. These indicate that the cumulative flight from 1962 to 1986 totalled $13.5 billion in 1986 dollars. With imputed interest earnings, the stock of Philippine flight capital amounted to $19.9 billion, equivalent to 70 per cent of the country's external debt outstanding. The causes of this capital flight are explored in Chapter 11.

THE CONCEPT OF 'CAPITAL FLIGHT'

Capital is mobile, albeit not perfectly so. Worldwide cumulated gross external liabilities from 1977 to 1983 amounted to $2621 billion.[3] What portion of these liabilities should be considered 'capital flight' is a matter of debate.

Capital flight is here defined as the movement of private capital from one jurisdiction to another *in order to reduce the actual or potential level of social control over that capital.* Within a country, capital can flee a particular province or region to escape legal or other social constraints. International capital flight, the object of this study, refers to such movements of capital from one sovereign nation to another.

This definition is close to that advanced by several contributors to the recent literature on the subject. Dooley (1986, p. 15), for example, defines capital flight as those capital outflows which are 'motivated by the desire of residents to obtain financial assets and earnings on those assets which remain outside the control of the domestic authorities'. Similarly, Deppler and Williamson (1987, p. 41) write that the 'problem with capital flight is that resources escape those who seek to exercise some degree of control over how the funds may be used'.

This concept of capital flight rests on the proposition that private control over capital is seldom absolute. Rather, it is circumscribed by a range of social controls. Some of these social controls are codified in existing laws. Examples include taxation, exchange controls which restrict the free exit of capital from the country, and regulations on the uses of capital. Social controls also include societal norms and expectations which, though not formalized in law, constrain individual control over capital, and extra-legal exactions by governmental or non-governmental authorities. Moreover, there is always a *potential* for further social controls to be extended should economic or political circumstances change. This risk itself constitutes a further dimension of social control over private capital.

The phenomenon of capital flight thus arises from the fact that control over capital is contested.[4] In the real world, absolute private control, unfettered by social control, is the exception rather than the rule. The degree and nature of social control differs among nations, and it is this differential which triggers capital flight.[5]

Capital flight is sometimes contrasted to 'normal' capital outflows motivated by higher expected returns or portfolio diversification (see Cumby and Levich, 1987, pp, 30–1). But while capital flight may be a response to abnormal circumstances, it is not an abnormal activity. As Lessard and Williamson (1987, p. 201) remark, capital flight is 'the result of individual agents reacting in the way that is posited as rational by economic theory and accepted as normal in industrial countries'.

Whether capital flight is regarded as socially beneficial or harmful depends, of course, on one's notion of social welfare. Judgments are likely to vary from case to case according to the specific circumstances. One may, for example, laud the flight of capital from Nazi Germany, but deplore the export of capital by a dictator in anticipation of his future retirement.

In theory, efforts by private owners of capital to reduce social control over their assets can be distinguished from efforts to increase the rate of return on those assets.[6] Indeed, as Walter (1987, p. 105) observes, one cost of the confidentiality obtained through capital flight may be a lower expected rate of return. In practice, the two motives are often conflated, thus making it difficult to distinguish capital flight from the broader concept of 'resident capital outflow', which comprises all private, non-banking system capital exports. Moreover, the flight and non-flight motives for capital outflows may be mutually reinforcing. For example, capital flight contributes to pressure on the exchange rate, which in turn may spark efforts to increase the rate of return on assets via dollarization. This would add to pressure on the peso-dollar rate, and if this in turn increases the probability of greater social controls on private capital, further capital flight could result.

The export of capital from the Philippines occurred for the most part in violation of Philippine law. The boundary between legal and illegal transfers is fuzzy, however, since a number of 'laws' were made and modified by secret presidential decrees.[7] As a US congressional staffer told journalists, 'Marcos could have exempted his friends from any one of the regulations, and you'd never be able to tell' (Carey and Ellison, 1985).

In such a setting, the problem of distinguishing capital flight from other capital movements is simplified: virtually all resident capital outflows can be classified as capital flight by virtue of their illegality. The diminution of social control over capital may not have been the sole motivation for capital flight, but it was one intended effect.

MECHANISMS OF CAPITAL FLIGHT

The process of capital flight involves two necessary steps: the acquisition of hard currency, and the exit of capital from the country. These can be accomplished by a number of mechanisms, including cash transfers, false invoicing, 'kickbacks' and inter-bank transfers.

Cash Transfers

The physical transfer of cash or other monetary instruments payable to the bearer (such as traveller's checks or cashier's checks) is one mechanism of capital flight. In the case of the Philippines, the main currency trans-ferred was reportedly US dollars, which were exchanged for pesos on the black market by tourists, visiting businessmen, US military personnel, and Philippine residents working abroad.[8] At least until the early 1980s, dollars were reportedly also sold on the 'Binondo' black market by the government-owned Philippine National Bank. 'The primary motivation behind such action', according to Thompson and Slayton (1985, p. 72), 'was to hurt black market traders and to facilitate their "financial cooperation" with certain highly-placed government officials'.

Having acquired dollars in the Philippines, the physical transfer can be achieved in three principal ways: (1) via personal smuggling; (2) via the use of hired couriers who charge a fee – Carey and Ellison (1985) report a figure of five per cent – for guiding the money past customs officials; and (3) via the mails.[9] Newspaper reports indicated that following the Aquino assassination in 1983 as much as $3 million per day was leaving the Philippines through the Manila airport (Carey and Ellison, 1985).

A variant on the cash transfer mechanism was the wire transmission services provided by the black marketeers based in Manila's Binondo district, collectively known as the 'Binondo Central Bank'. The Binondo bankers acquired dollars on the black market and smuggled them to Hong Kong for deposit in major banks. An individual could provide pesos to a Binondo intermediary, who instructed a Hong Kong bank to wire dollars to the customer's overseas account. The customer could then confirm that the deposit was made by contacting his or her overseas bank.[10]

False Invoicing of Exports and Imports

Manipulation of trade invoices provides another important mechanism of capital flight. Exporters of goods from the Philippines are required by law to surrender their foreign currency earnings to the government for conversion into pesos. To circumvent this requirement and accumulate foreign currency abroad, the exporter can understate the true price or quantity of the goods in question on the invoice. The difference between the invoice value and the actual value is then deposited abroad. In the case of imports, the same objective can be achieved through overinvoicing: the importer takes an invoice with an inflated value to the Central Bank to obtain the necessary foreign exchange, which is then transferred to the supplier, who in turn deposits the difference in accordance with the importer's instructions.

False invoicing is widely believed to have been a major avenue for Philippine capital flight. Cowitt (1985, p. 675) reports that 'underinvoicing of exports and overinvoicing of imports represented a major part of the trade [in the foreign currency black market], while banknote smuggling accounted for less than 10%'. For example, a 1984 US State Department cable on the coconut monopoly cited a shipment of coconut oil valued 8 cents per pound below the world market price, and noted that at 1983 export levels 'each one cent of undervaluation in the price of coconut oil would mean over 21 million dollars which could be deposited abroad'.[11]

Kickbacks

The provision of kickbacks on import contracts, referred to in polite company as 'commissions', is similar in effect to import overinvoicing. In this case, the foreign supplier pays an individual a portion of its proceeds from the sale of goods or services to the Philippines. The exchange occurs abroad, but the ultimate source of the hard currency is the payment for the imports in question. Perhaps the most famous example of this in the Philippines is the $80 million paid to Herminio Disini by Westinghouse Corporation 'for assistance in obtaining the contract and for implementation services' in the sale of a nuclear power plant to the Philippine government. A lawyer who worked on the contract for the supply of the power plant told *The New York Times*:

> There was nothing illegal about this contract. But if you look at the terms closely, you will see that the price of the equipment being sold to the Philippines was inflated, as a way to cover the cost of the fees to Disini.

In a memo to President Marcos, the Secretary of Industry of the Philippines described the transaction as 'one reactor for the price of two'.[12]

Another documented example is the purchase of telecommunications equipment, financed by the US government's Foreign Military Sales program, from shell companies which in turn obtained 'sham marketing contracts' with the actual producers 'in order to kick back between 35% and 50% of their proceeds' (Pasztor, 1987).[13] Similarly, prioritization of Japanese aid projects reportedly hinged on 'the willingness of the Japanese companies implementing the projects either to pad costs or reduce profit margins, with the difference being remitted to the agents of the top Philippine government officials'.[14]

Inter-bank Transfers

The role of inter-bank transfers in capital flight is among the most controversial aspects of the phenomenon, particularly in countries such as the Philippines which have capital controls aimed at limiting outflows of foreign exchange. Local banks, or local affiliates of foreign banks, have the ability both to provide foreign exchange and to transfer it to designated recipients abroad; the only problem is that this is often illegal.

Walter (1987, p. 115) asserts that 'banks of international standing tend to avoid direct involvement in the capital flight process itself'. More precisely, they seek to preserve what in the US political lexicon is termed 'deniability':

> They generally have multiple domestic and foreign relationships with governments, public – and private-sector entities, individuals and multinational firms, and exposure, especially of illegal capital flight activities, is likely to lead to business losses greater than prospective gains.

Subject to this constraint, however, the banks are by no means averse to flight capital:

> [A]ll such institutions will actively solicit fiduciary and other business from individuals and institutions engaged in capital flight once the assets are safely offshore. They will also assiduously cultivate the various clients involved. In that sense they may help to reduce information and transaction costs.

While the first-tier banks 'will tend to stay well clear of illegal acts', Walter notes that 'among the foreign-based financial institutions there are plenty of second-tier players and shady operators who have far fewer long-term stakes in the game, and are more than willing to turn a fast profit at the edge of the law or ethical behavior'.[15]

One variant of the inter-bank transfer mechanism is the 'hidden deposit' placed by a Philippine resident in the local branch of a domestic or international bank with overseas branches:

> He or she deposits $115 in the Philippine branch and makes a private agreement with the bank never to withdraw that money. The bank then provides the depositor with a $100 loan from an overseas branch of the bank.

The bank profits by the difference between the amount deposited and the amount 'loaned', and through 'tax advantages it gains by having an outstanding loan in its overseas branch' (Carey and Ellison, 1985).

THE MEASUREMENT OF CAPITAL FLIGHT

The measurement of capital flight requires statistical detective work, for as Lessard and Williamson (1987, p. 205) remark, the individuals involved 'are unlikely to make a point of informing the compilers of balance-of-payments statistics of their actions'.

The capital flight estimates reported below differ from previous estimates in several respects: they span a longer period of time; they are based on more complete estimates of the country's external debt outstanding; they include adjustments for changes in debt outstanding arising from fluctuations in the yen/dollar exchange rate; they incorporate the net effect of misinvoicing of exports and imports; and they calculate the cumulative stock of flight capital in real terms and with imputed interest earnings.

Most of the recent literature on capital flight employs one of two measurement techniques, here termed the residual and 'hot money' measures.

The Residual Measure

The most widely used measure begins with annual changes in the country's total external debt outstanding, including gross banking system liabilities. Various non-flight uses of this external finance are then deducted, and the residual is taken as a measure of capital flight. In most cases, this measure is calculated as changes in gross foreign debt minus the net direct investment outflow, the current account deficit, and increases in official reserves.[16] The relevant data for the Philippines are reported in Table 10.2.

One problem with residual measures of capital flight is that the dollar value of external debt outstanding is affected by exchange rate variations among the currencies in which the debt is denominated. In the case of the Philippines, where a substantial fraction of the debt is owed in Japanese yen, the dollar value of the external debt rises as the yen appreciates against the dollar, and declines as it depreciates. Such variations contribute to the year-to-year changes in external debt outstanding reported in Table 9.3.

Precise data on the currency composition of the Philippine external debt are not available, but National Economic Development Authority (NEDA) data permit the calculation of the share of debt to Japanese private and official creditors.[17] Multiplying this percentage by total external debt yields an estimate of the dollar value of yen-denominated debt at the end of each year. The yen/dollar adjustment factor reported in Table 10.2 is the change in the dollar value of the previous year's yen-denominated debt when revalued

TABLE 10.2 *Change in External Debt and Non-flight Uses of Foreign Exchange, 1962–1986 (US $ million)*

Year	Change in external debt outstanding[1]	Yen/dollar adjustment[2]	Current account deficit			Net direct investment	Increase in official reserves	Increase in commercial banks' external assets
			Total	Non-investment income	Net investment income			
1962	0	0	-30	-47	17	3	21	-19
1963	20	0	-182	-199	17	4	23	17
1964	100	0	-85	-111	26	4	16	-7
1965	320	0	-137	-168	31	10	67	37
1966	110	0	-161	-198	37	15	-12	45
1967	370	0	25	-51	76	9	-25	4
1968	210	0	250	153	97	3	-74	24
1969	340	0	253	175	78	-6	-81	-26
1970	470	0	48	-82	130	29	46	-9
1971	90	27	2	-99	101	4	97	25
1972	340	5	-7	-132	126	22	184	168
1973	160	22	-474	-588	113	-64	668	320
1974	870	-29	207	153	54	40	591	329
1975	1180	-10	924	798	126	-124	-16	117

Foreign exchange outflows[3]

TABLE 10.2 (Continued)

| Year | Change in external debt outstanding[1] | Yen/dollar adjustment[2] | Current account deficit | | | Net direct investment | Increase in official reserves | Increase in commercial banks' external assets |
			Total	Non-investment income	Net investment income			
1976	1830	27	1102	849	253	-142	-57	-405
1977	1300	146	755	422	333	-215	-30	-77
1978	2620	185	1093	687	406	-100	876	394
1979	2660	-300	1496	932	565	-21	376	403
1980	3900	357	1901	1069	832	103	960	816
1981	3640	-164	2089	1047	1042	-176	-349	-29
1982	3790	-176	3198	1372	1826	-17	-703	207
1983	140	38	2753	977	1776	-111	-2044	-710
1984	600	-325	1257	-848	2104	-6	263	122
1985	830	1155	26	-1975	2002	-20	-123	-68
1986	2010	1298	-991	-2941	1950	-140	1111	39

Foreign exchange outflows[3]

TABLE 10.2 *(Continued)*

Years	Change in external debt outstanding[1]	Yen/dollar adjustment[2]	Current account deficit Total	Non-investment income	Net investment income	Foreign exchange outflows[3] Net direct investment	Increase in official reserves	Increase in commercial banks' external assets
			Cumulative totals					
1962–69	1470	0	−67	−446	379	42	−65	75
1970–75	3110	15	700	49	651	−94	1569	950
1976–80	12310	415	6346	3958	2388	−375	2125	1131
1981–86	11010	1826	8332	−2367	10699	−469	−1845	−439
1962–86	27900	2255	15311	1194	14117	−896	1784	1717

NOTES

1. Including gross external liabilities of the banking system.
2. Adjustment for appreciation (+) or depreciation (−) of yen-denominated debt.
3. Outflows positive, inflows negative (opposite of balance of payments sign convention).

SOURCES   Change in external debt outstanding from Table 9.3. Yen/dollar adjustment based upon percentage share of Japanese in total liabilities from NEDA (1976, pp. 400–1; 1986, pp. 607–7) and unpublished Central Bank data, and exchange rates reported in IFS (1987, pp. 424–5). Current account deficit, net direct investment, and change in reserves from Table 9.1; commercial banks' external assets from IMF, *International Financial Statistics, 1987*, pp. 558–9, line 7a.d.

at the end-of-year exchange rate. The adjustment was zero in the 1960s, when the yen share of total debt was relatively low and the yen/dollar rate relatively stable, and largest in 1985 and 1986, when the yen appreciated strongly.

The residual measure of capital flight reported in Table 10.3 incorporates this yen/dollar adjustment. The arithmetic by which this measure is derived can be traced in Table 10.2. The total increase in external debt outstanding in this period was $27.9 billion; of this, $2.3 billion was attributable to the rise in the dollar value of yen-denominated debt, for an adjusted inflow of $25.6 billion. In addition, direct investment contributed a net inflow of $0.9 billion. The adjusted 'gross capital inflow' was thus $26.5 billion. Of this amount, $1.2 billion covered the cumulative deficit on the non-investment income portion of the current account. A further $14.1 billion covered net investment income payments, primarily interest payments on the external debt itself. Net additions to the country's official reserves amounted to $1.8 billion. The remainder – $9.4 billion – is the residual estimate of capital flight.[18]

A more restrictive variant of the residual measure excludes the external assets accumulated by the country's commercial banks.[19] Philippine commercial banks accumulated $1.7 billion in external assets over the 1962–86 period; deducting these the total capital flight estimate would be $7.7 billion. There is no convincing reason, however, to assume that banks cannot engage in capital flight, and hence following the usual practice their external assets are included in the residual measure developed here.[20]

These residual measures are incomplete in that they exclude capital flight through false trade invoicing and the interest earnings of flight capital. Adjustments for these are considered below.

The 'Hot Money' Measure

The second measure of capital flight is relatively narrow: the sum of net errors and omissions plus certain private, non-bank short-term capital movements as recorded in the balance of payments. The aim is to capture only highly liquid 'speculative' capital outflows; errors and omissions are included 'because of the widespread belief that [they] largely reflect unrecorded short-term capital flows'.[21]

This measure is excessively restrictive since, as Deppler and Williamson (1987, p. 43) observe, long-term assets such as equities and real estate 'may be relatively close substitutes' for short-term assets. Even if the aim is to focus only on the 'hot' component of flight capital, which moves most quickly in response to changing economic and political conditions, the measure

TABLE 10.3   *Capital Flight: Residual and Hot Money Measures*
(without adjustments, US $ million)

| Year | Residual measures[1] | | Hot money[2] |
	Inclusive	Non-bank	
1962	6	25	8
1963	175	158	130
1964	165	172	160
1965	380	343	191
1966	268	223	73
1967	361	357	60
1968	31	7	129
1969	174	200	117
1970	347	356	158
1971	−41	−66	99
1972	136	−32	104
1973	10	−310	25
1974	62	−267	120
1975	406	289	220
1976	900	1305	460
1977	645	722	127
1978	566	172	227
1979	1108	705	643
1980	579	−237	267
1981	2240	2269	1205
1982	1487	1280	734
1983	−495	215	248
1984	−589	−711	−197
1985	−208	−140	−248
1986	732	693	506
Cumulative Totals			
1962–69	1560	1485	868
1970–75	920	−30	727
1976–80	3798	2667	1724
1981–86	3167	3606	2248
1962–86	9446	7729	5567

NOTES
1. Residual measures calculated from data in Table 10.2: 'Inclusive' = Increase in
external debt outstanding minus yen/dollar adjustment minus current account
deficit minus net direct investment outflow minus increase in official reserves.
'Non-bank' = Inclusive measure minus increase in commercial banks' external
assets.
2. Hot money = Sum of 'other short-term capital of other sectors: other assets' (or
equivalent entries in earlier years) plus 'net errors and omissions', as reported in
IMF, *Balance of Payments Statistics Yearbooks*.

may be too narrow. As Cumby and Levich (1987, p. 35) remark: 'In today's international financial markets there is very little loss of liquidity associated with acquiring long-term bonds (especially US government bonds, corporate bonds traded on US markets, or Eurobonds) or equities'. The hot money measure can thus be regarded as an estimate of the lower bound on total capital flight.

The application of this measure to the Philippines yields the hot money estimate reported in the final column of Table 10.3.[22] Net outflows (here bearing a positive sign) were recorded every year except 1984 and 1985, with a peak of $1.2 billion in 1981. The cumulative (nominal) outflow by this measure, with no adjustment for inflation or interest earnings on externally held assets, was $5.6 billion, of which $4.0 billion fled from 1976 to 1986. Notwithstanding the narrowness of this measure, the volume of capital flight it captures is thus quite substantial.

Misinvoicing Adjustment

A problem with both of the usual capital flight measures is that they fail to incorporate the effects of false trade invoicing. The underinvoicing of exports and overinvoicing of imports are widely believed to be important vehicles for capital flight. Such practices would inflate the trade and current account deficits, leading to underestimation of capital flight by the residual and hot money measures.

At the same time, however, 'technical smuggling' via *under*invoicing of imports, and 'pure smuggling' in which legal import channels are bypassed completely, are also reported to have been widespread in the Philippines. The motive in this case is the evasion of tariff and other import barriers. Smuggling has the opposite effect: understatement of the trade and current account deficits, and overstatement of capital flight, as funds which appear to have fled the country are in fact used to finance unrecorded imports.

The net impact of trade misinvoicing on estimated capital flight is the sum of these two contradictory effects. Its direction and magnitude cannot be judged on *a priori* grounds, but the net effect can be estimated by means of trading partner data comparisons.

Table 10.4 presents annual estimates of the net impact of misinvoicing for the period under review. These are based on comparisons of trade flows as recorded by the Philippines and its industrial country trading partners, as reported in the IMF's *Direction of Trade Yearbooks*. In 1986, for example, the Philippines reported exports to the United States as having a total value of $1.71 billion, while the US reported imports from the Philippines with a total value of $2.15 billion. Adjusting for freight and insurance costs (using

TABLE 10.4 *Trade Invoicing Discrepancies, 1962–1986 (US $ million)*

Year	Export discrepancy [1]	Import discrepancy [2]	Capital flight misinvoicing adjustment [3]
1962	81	51	30
1963	−3	209	−212
1964	37	161	−124
1965	29	183	−155
1966	72	184	−111
1967	144	223	−79
1968	178	305	−127
1969	305	312	−7
1970	129	319	−190
1971	112	286	−174
1972	101	248	−147
1973	−46	298	−344
1974	63	−32	96
1975	458	203	255
1976	133	253	−121
1977	250	266	−16
1978	438	659	−221
1979	593	640	−47
1980	949	623	326
1981	1071	593	477
1982	1181	541	640
1983	870	1194	−324
1984	1395	803	592
1985	1516	886	630
1986	1223	923	300
Total	11277	10332	945

NOTES
1. Export discrepancy = Trading partners' imports from the Philippines – (recorded Philippine exports × cif/fob factor).
2. Import discrepancy = (Trading partners' exports to the Philippines × cif/fob factor) – recorded Philippine imports.
3. Misinvoicing adjustment = export discrepancy – import discrepancy.

SOURCES IMF, *Direction of Trade Yearbooks*; cif/fob factors from IMF, *International Financial Statistics 1987*, pp. 126–7.
[For method of calculation, see text].

the Philippine fob/cif ratio reported annually in the IMF's *International Financial Statistics*), the comparison indicates that Philippine exports to the US were underinvoiced by $320 million in that year. Total discrepancies for industrial country trading partners are scaled upwards (by their ratios to total Philippine exports and imports in a given year) to generate the global estimates reported in the table.[23]

On the export side, the data reveal a consistent pattern of underinvoicing. In all but two of the 25 years, the value of imports from the Philippines recorded by its trading partners exceeded the value of exports (adjusted for shipping costs) recorded by the Philippines. In the period as a whole, the average discrepancy was equivalent to 13 per cent of the recorded value of exports; in the 1980s it rose to 24 percent, or nearly $1.2 billion per year.[24]

On the import side, the data reveal consistent under- rather than over-invoicing. This indicates that capital flight through import overinvoicing was exceeded in magnitude by smuggling through underinvoicing or non-reporting of imports. The average net discrepancy was equivalent to 15 per cent of the recorded value of imports; in the 1980s it fell to 11 per cent.[25]

In the 1960s, the misinvoicing adjustment to capital flight estimates is downward: the impact of smuggling swamped not only import overinvoicing but export underinvoicing as well. In the 1970s, the picture is mixed, with export underinvoicing exceeding the net import underinvoicing in two years and almost equalling it in two others. In the 1980s, the capital flight effect generally overwhelmed the smuggling effect, necessitating upward adjustments of our previous capital flight estimates. The misinvoicing adjustment consequently has a noticeable impact on the time trend of capital flight. Its net effect on total estimated nominal capital flight in 1962–86 is an additional $945 million.

It should be emphasized that this fairly modest total does not imply that trade invoice manipulation has been a relatively unimportant mechanism of capital flight. On the contrary, in the period as a whole, export underinvoicing alone amounted to $11 billion. The misinvoicing adjustment captures the *net* effect of (1) capital flight via false trade invoicing and (2) the use of unrecorded capital outflows to finance the undeclared portion of Philippine imports.[26] It is quite possible that cash and wire transfers were major mechanisms for undeclared import finance, while export underinvoicing and import overinvoicing were significant vehicles of capital flight.

Inflation and Interest Adjustments

Table 10.5 presents two alternative summary estimates of capital flight from the Philippines. Measure A is the residual measure reported in Table

TABLE 10.5 *Summary Estimates of Philippine Capital Flight, 1962–1986 (US $ million)*

Year	Annual flow				Cumulative stock (with interest adjustment)[2]	
	Nominal (current $)		Real (1986 $)[1]			
	A	B	A	B	A	B
1962	36	38	115	121	37	39
1963	–37	–82	–116	–260	1	–43
1964	41	36	130	115	42	–8
1965	226	36	700	113	274	29
1966	157	–38	471	–115	448	–9
1967	282	–19	846	–56	756	–29
1968	–96	2	–280	6	698	–28
1969	167	110	470	309	917	84
1970	157	–32	425	–88	1138	56
1971	–215	–75	–565	–197	967	–18
1972	–12	–43	–29	–109	995	–63
1973	–334	–319	–744	–710	719	–398
1974	158	216	295	404	939	–205
1975	661	474	1133	814	1674	272
1976	779	339	1277	556	2556	633
1977	628	111	970	171	3336	780
1978	345	6	494	8	3934	842
1979	1061	596	1351	759	5444	1553
1980	905	593	1010	661	7035	2361
1981	2717	1682	2777	1719	10934	4494
1982	2127	1374	2130	1376	14347	6423
1983	–820	–76	–810	–75	14728	6898
1984	3	395	3	381	16141	7971
1985	422	382	409	371	17787	8965
1986	1032	806	1032	806	19912	10329
Total	10391	6512	13492	7080	19912	10329

Key: A = Residual measure plus misinvoicing adjustment.
B = Hot money measure plus misinvoicing adjustment.

NOTES
1. Converted to 1986 dollars using US wholesale price index as reported in IMF (1987, pp. 698–9).
2. End-of-year cumulative totals, including interest calculated on mid-year cumulated stock (using short-term US Treasury bill rate as reported in IMF, 1987, pp. 698–9).

10.3 plus the misinvoicing adjustment reported in Table 10.4. Measure B is the 'hot money' measure reported in Table 10.3 plus the misinvoicing adjustment. Measure A is the more comprehensive of the two. Measure B is reported as a minimal alternative estimate. In nominal terms, total capital flight from the Philippines from 1962 to 1986 amounted to $10.4 billion by the former measure, and $6.5 billion by the latter.

The magnitude of capital flight (relative, for example, to the country's $28.3 billion external debt outstanding at the end of 1986) can be better appreciated by imputing interest earnings to derive the cumulative stock of flight capital, or alternatively by converting the annual flows into real terms. Both adjustments are reported in Table 10.5. The interest adjustment is made using the short-term US Treasury bill rate;[27] the inflation adjustment is made using the US wholesale price index. Capital flight by measure A in the 1962–86 period, calculated with the inflation adjustment, totalled $13.5 billion in 1986 dollars, equivalent to almost half of the Philippines' external debt outstanding. This is a conservative estimate in that it assumes that externally held assets earned zero real interest. With the interest adjustment the total stock of flight capital amounted to $19.9 billion, equivalent to 70 per cent of the external debt outstanding.

CONCLUSIONS

Capital flight from the Philippines, like the country's external debt problem, did not commence in the mid-1970s. In the eight years preceding the 1970 foreign exchange crisis, capital flight (by measure A) amounted to $776 million, equivalent to $2.3 billion in 1986 dollars. The outflow of flight capital in real terms appears to have peaked in 1975–76 and again in 1981–82 (see Figure 11.1). At the end of 1986 the cumulative stock of flight capital was equivalent to a sizeable fraction of the country's external debt. A key difference, of course, is that the external debt was largely public, while the external assets were strictly private.

The apparent net inflow of flight capital in 1983 and the relatively small outflow in 1984 are at variance with the conventional wisdom that massive capital flight followed the August 1983 Aquino assassination. One possible explanation is that with the collapse of foreign lending to the Philippines, an important source of financing for capital flight dried up; another is that speculative capital was drawn back to the country by the very high-interest 'Jobo bills' issued by the Central Bank in 1984.

If anything, the capital flight estimates reported here may err on the conservative side. None of the measures captures capital flight which occurred through 'commissions' or kickbacks paid abroad on import contracts. Unlike false invoicing, these cannot be detected by trading partner data comparisons since the kickbacks enter into the purchase price reported by both parties. If capital flight by this mechanism was substantial, the estimates reported here may be too low. Similarly, the practice of export 'reinvoicing', whereby Philippine exporters 'sell' goods at a low price to a foreign-based company which in turn resells them at a higher price to the final buyer, escapes detection.[28] Moreover, insofar as dollars supplied to the black market are unrecorded in the Philippine balance of payments, their re-export also escapes detection.[29] In each of these cases, the current account deficit is in effect overstated, and capital flight is correspondingly understated.

One measure of the cost of capital flight to the Philippine economy would be the productive investment which could have been financed within the country with the same resources. The extent to which individual flight capitalists would have undertaken such investments, had capital flight been blocked as an alternative with all else unchanged, is an open question. It is quite possible that much of the money instead would have been channeled into unproductive, speculative investment or the consumption of imported goods. It is difficult to imagine, however, that capital flight could in fact have been eliminated while leaving the rest of the country's political economy unchanged. Hence there are as many answers to the question of what would have happened in a counterfactual setting as there are different conceivable settings. No doubt many Filipinos would have preferred other uses of the missing billions.

NOTES

1. Estimates of the amount of capital exported by Marcos and his associates vary widely. According to Kessler (1986, p. 41), 'Marcos's own fortune is estimated at anywhere between $2 billion and $20 billion'. Press reports in July 1988 indicated that Marcos had offered to repatriate $5 billion to the Philippines in return for the right to return to the country and be exempt from criminal prosecution ('Marcos Bids $5 Billion to Return to Philippines', *Los Angeles Times*, 26 July 1988). On the search for Marcos's hidden wealth, see WGBH Educational Foundation (1987) and Mydans (1990).

2. The countries included were Argentina, Bolivia, Brazil, Chile, Colombia, Ecuador, India, Indonesia, Malaysia, Mexico, Nigeria, Peru, Philippines, South Africa, South Korea, Thailand, Uruguay, and Venezuela. For other estimates, see Dooley *et al.* (1986), Dooley (1986),

Cumby and Levich (1987), Khan and ul Haque (1987), and Pastor (1990).

3. IMF (1987b, Table 3, p. 13). At the same time, the reported increase in cumulated external assets was $2324 billion. In other words, nearly $300 billion of recorded inflows (liabilities) were unmatched by recorded outflows (assets).

4. This phenomenon of 'contested endowments' is akin to 'contested exchange' (on which see Bowles and Gintis, 1988).

5. In recent years international competition for funds among 'haven' countries has contributed to further loosening of taxation on nonresident investment income; see Lessard and Williamson (1987, pp. 240–1).

6. Consider the difference between a shift from local currency into domestically-held dollars in anticipation of a devaluation and the export of capital out of the country. Dollarization could protect the asset owner's rate of return, without the loss of social control involved in capital flight. This was the Philippine government's rationale for permitting commercial and foreign banks to set up Foreign Currency Deposit Units under Central Bank Circular Nos. 343 and 547. The difficulties inherent in such a distinction were demonstrated in Mexico when dollar-indexed financial instruments ('Mex-dollars') were declared inconvertible at the free market rate when that country's debt crisis broke in August 1982 (Zedillo, 1987, p. 182).

7. Presidential decrees in the early 1970s and again in 1983 made it illegal to export large amounts of cash or to hold foreign exchange accounts without Central Bank approval. For details regarding currency transferability restrictions, see Cowitt (1985, pp. 669–70) and various issues of the IMF's *Annual Report on Exchange Arrangements and Exchange Restrictions*. The legal situation was different in the mid-1960s, when Philippine residents lived 'under a nearly liberal currency control system' (Pick, 1968, p. 417).

8. Exports of pesos are less common, although there is a market for Philippine currency in Hong Kong.

9. Carey and Ellison (1985) report a case in which Deak & Company's San Francisco office received $11 million sent from the Philippines in envelopes marked 'documents'; the company was convicted of banking law violations by US federal court for failing to report the transaction.

10. This process is described by Carey and Ellison (1985). From early 1984 to February 1986, the Binondo Central Bank reportedly functioned with quasi-official control over its exchange rates (Dohner and Intal, 1989, pp. 525–7).

11. 'The Philippine Coconut Monopoly', Cable No. 05607 from US Embassy, Manila, to Secretary of State, Washington, D.C., March 1984, p. 14.

12. The *Times* reported that 95 per cent of Disini's fees were then transferred to Marcos (Butterfield, 1986). Criminal investigations of the payments by the US Justice Department were dropped without bringing charges

(Pasztor, 1987). Further details on the financial negotiations leading to the reactor sale are reported by Bello, Hayes and Zarsky (1979, pp. 9–10) and Dumaine (1986).

13. Former Philippine armed forces commander General Fabian Ver was reported to be 'a principal subject' of grand jury investigations into this case. See also Ellinson and Carey (1985).

14. Dohner and Intal (1989, p. 471). See also Smith (1986).

15. Among such 'second-tier' institutions was the Australia-based Nugan Hand Bank, whose Manila representative was General LeRoy Manor, the former commander of US military bases in the Philippines, who negotiated their renewal with the Philippine government in 1979. Nugan Hand's known clients included Elizabeth Marcos (sister of the President) and her husband Ludwig Rocka, who deposited $3.5 million with the bank according to records found after its collapse in 1980. See Kwitny (1987, pp. 34–37, 186–93). Affidavits filed with the Philippine Presidential Commission on Good Government indicate that President Marcos himself deposited $51.8 million in Hong Kong between 1981 and 1985 via inter-bank transfers by the Security Bank & Trust Company; and documents found in Malacanang Palace indicate that Marcos funds were also transferred abroad via the Traders Royal Bank (Malone, 1987, pp. 29, 31).

16. See, for example, Diaz-Alejandro (1984, pp. 362–3), Sachs (1984, p. 397), the Bank for International Settlements (1984, p. 101), Erbe (1985), and the World Bank (1985c, p. 64). In keeping with the usual practice in the literature, direct investment outflows from the Philippines are treated here as non-flight capital. The definition of capital flight proposed above does not, however, necessarily exclude direct investment outflows. In the present instance, the quantities involved are so small that their treatment makes little difference.

17. NEDA (1974, pp. 280–1; 1976, pp. 398–9; 1986, pp. 606–7). This share averaged approximately 10 per cent in the period as a whole, and rose over time. Unpublished data furnished by the Central Bank indicate that 25.7 per cent of foreign exchange liabilities, excluding liabilities to multilateral agencies, were to Japan at end of 1985; this is equivalent to 20 per cent of total liabilities.

18. This estimate is reasonably consistent with those reported for the Philippines by other sources; for a review, see Boyce and Zarsky (1988, Appendix B).

19. This is the measure used by the Morgan Guaranty Trust Company of New York (1986) in its widely reported capital flight estimates. The Morgan Guaranty estimates for the Philippines are $7 billion in the period 1976–82 and a further $2 billion in 1983–85; these are somewhat higher than the corresponding estimates of $6.2 billion and – $0.6 billion reported in Table 10.3. The reason for the discrepancy is not clear, but it may be due to different debt estimates used by Morgan Guaranty and/or to a slightly different definition of banking system external assets.

Cumby and Levich (1987, pp. 60–1) and Lessard and Williamson (1987, p. 206) report an estimate of $3.7 billion by this method for the years 1976–84 (versus $5.7 billion reported here); their lower figure arises from an error (amounting to $639 million) in their recording of banking system foreign assets for the year 1983, and to their lower debt estimates.

20.   Cumby and Levich (1987, pp. 32–33) question whether there is sound 'justification for treating the banking system differently from other firms and individuals'. Cuddington (1986, p. 4, n. 2) offers the rationale that 'the central bank directly or indirectly controls a large fraction of commercial banks' foreign assets in many developing countries'. In the Philippines, government financial institutions (such as the PNB and DBP) and 'political banks' enjoying a 'special relationship with the group in government' accounted for more than half of the total assets of the commercial banking system in 1982 (De Dios *et al.*, 1984, p. 38). As Patrick and Moreno (1985, p. 363) observe, the political power of major financial groups implies that 'they do not have to take as given the rules of the economic game as determined by government'. The degree of social control over the external assets of the commercial banking system is hence open to doubt. In the Philippine case, the more inclusive measure of capital flight thus seems preferable to the non-bank measure.

21.   Cuddington (1986, pp. 2–3). Indeed, 'Net errors and omissions' are reported as a subheading under 'Short-Term Capital' in the 'analytic presentation' for the Philippines in some issues of the IMF *Balance of Payments Yearbook*; see, for example, Vol. 28 (1977), p. 489. The IMF (1977, p. 51) states that this practice is followed when 'there is evidence to suggest that the variations reflect mostly unrecorded short-term movements of capital'. Dornbusch (1985, pp. 227–9) employs a similar definition of capital flight.

22.   This measure includes, in addition to net errors and omissions, those short-term, non-bank private capital movements recorded as 'other assets' or 'other liabilities' in the balance of payments. Entries under the heading 'other loans received' (which correspond to entries under the heading 'trade credits' in earlier volumes) are excluded, since these primarily refer to trade financing. The same technique is used by Cumby and Levich (1987, pp. 60–1) in their calculation of the Cuddington measure for the Philippines for the years 1976–84.

23.   This methodology relies on the assumption that the trade data reported by the industrial countries are reasonably accurate. Gulati (1987, p. 70), who employs the same technique, reports that trade data comparisons among the industrial countries indicate that this assumption is 'for the most part realistic'.

24.   Exports to the Philippines top three trading partners – the United States, Japan, and West Germany – were underinvoiced by averages of 7%, 20%, and 71%, respectively. The extraordinarily high figure for West Germany may be partly attributable to misidentification of the final

export destination as the Netherlands; trade data comparisons reveal consistent 'overinvoicing' of Philippine exports to the latter.

25. Imports by the Philippines from the US, Japan, and West Germany were underreported by averages of 12%, 25%, and 4%, respectively in the period as a whole.

26. A notion of the scale of the latter can be derived from Alano's (1984, pp. 185–7) estimate that in the period 1965–78 smuggled imports represented 29 per cent of the value of exports to the Philippines as recorded by its trading partners.

27. The actual interest rate earned by flight capital is an open question; de Vries (1987, p. 188) considered the current Treasury bill rate of 6% to be a 'low' proxy for the rate of return on overseas assets, while a European banker stated that most foreign depositors in Swiss banks received *negative* interest, 'implying that they were willing to pay a substantial premium for security' (Lessard and Williamson, eds, 1987, p. 83). Nor is it necessarily the case that all capital sent abroad was saved; some may well have been used to finance consumption overseas. The interest imputation in Table 10.5 thus should be regarded as a measure of the opportunity cost of capital flight, rather than of actual accumulated external assets.

28. Carey and Ellison (1985) report that some exporters established front companies in Hong Kong for this purpose.

29. A further avenue for non-detectable capital flight may be transactions between Philippine residents working abroad who wish to obtain pesos at the black market rate, and those in the Philippines who wish to acquire dollars for transfer abroad. Rather than smuggling dollars to their families in the Philippines via a 'network of couriers' (as reported by Cowitt, 1985, p. 671), overseas workers could sell dollars abroad for pesos at home, eliminating the costs and risks of currency smuggling in both directions. I have found no reference to such transactions in the literature, but it is unlikely that the opportunities for intermediation escaped the notice of the Binondo bankers.

11 Debt for Development?

When Philippine policy makers embraced the debt-for-development strategy, its attraction lay in the positive net transfer. Perhaps they realized that the stage of negative net transfers would eventually dawn. Perhaps some even anticipated the bitter, morning-after sensation of debt regret. But the lure of the positive net transfer proved irresistible.

How sweet was the kiss of debt? Did the inflows of borrowed capital allow the people of the Philippines to live, for a time, 'beyond their means', reaping short-term benefits at the price of long-term indebtedness? What impact did external borrowing have on savings, investment, and growth? Were debt-creating capital inflows a cause of capital flight, or was it mere coincidence that the two occurred in the same time period? How did external borrowing affect the character and role of the Philippine state?

This chapter explores these questions.

DEBT AND THE CURRENT ACCOUNT

The usual view of the external debt of Third World countries is that borrowing on the capital account is a result of current account deficits, particularly trade deficits. Transactions in goods and services lead, and capital movements follow.

In discussing the Philippine experience in the 1960s, for example, Baldwin (1975, p. 14) states that imports were 'stimulated by the government's easy credit policies and expanded development-oriented expenditure programs', and that the resulting balance-of-payments problems 'were held off for a few years by extensive foreign borrowing from official and private sources'.

Similarly, referring to the experience of the late 1970s and early 1980s, the World Bank (1984, pp. i, ii) states that 'adverse exogenous developments . . . combined with expansionary demand policies, led to an increase in the country's current account deficit and a rapid accumulation of external debt'. In particular, declining terms of trade and rising interest payments 'were mainly responsible for the increase in the current account deficit (and *consequent* debt accumulation) in recent years' (emphasis added). In the same vein, Power (1983, p. 12) models external financing as an 'accommodation' to current account deficits resulting from the gap between external shocks and other adjustments.

Yet it is evident that without capital account surpluses, the current account deficits which they financed could not have endured for long. Indeed, an explicit objective of some lending – for example, official export credits and much bilateral aid – was the promotion of exports from the creditor countries.

The relationship between current account deficits and capital account surpluses can hence be given interpretations in which causality does not run in a unilinear fashion from the former to the latter.

Remolona, Mangahas and Pante (1985, p. 1), for example, state: 'The worsening of the current account was due in part to a severe deterioration in the country's terms of trade and in part to a policy response that relied heavily on foreign borrowing to the neglect of other adjustment measures'. They observe (p. 11) that 'easy external financing led to the postponement of required adjustments in the exchange rates' (or, it might be added, of other, non-exchange rate measures to redress the imbalance).

Montes (1987, p. 4) states that the 'foreign exchange bonanza' of the 1970s resulted in the appreciation of the real effective exchange rate by 18 per cent between 1970 and 1982. He remarks: 'This was a period of increasing overvaluation of the peso, which was made possible, ironically, by the consistent support of the IMF and the World Bank to the country's economic management'.

Indeed, one can venture the stronger statement that overvaluation was *caused* by large-scale foreign borrowing.[1] All else equal, an increase in the supply of foreign exchange results in a decline in its price, that is, it causes appreciation of the local currency. This makes imports more competitive in the domestic market, and makes exports less competitive in the world market. Both effects contribute to a widening of the trade deficit.[2]

An examination of trends in the real effective exchange rate of the Philippine peso (that is, the nominal exchange rates adjusted for inter-country differences in inflation and weighted among countries by trade share) reveals significant real devaluations in the years 1970 and 1980 (see Table 11.1). The overall extent of real devaluation from 1962 to 1986 was far less, however, than that of the nominal exchange rate. Moreover, between 1970 and 1980 the real effective exchange rate actually appreciated, notwithstanding widening current account deficits.

In the 1970s the country's official foreign exchange reserves grew, even as the current account deficit widened.[3] In other words, during much of the period of debt-driven growth the supply of external finance grew faster than

TABLE 11.1 *Exchange Rates of the Philippine Peso, 1962–1986*

Year	Pesos per US dollar [1]		Dollar/ peso index (official rate)	Real exchange rate [2]	Real effective exchange rate [3]
	Official rate	Black market rate			
1962	3.92	3.97	100.0	100.0	100.0
1963	3.91	3.92	100.3	107.1	104.5
1964	3.91	3.91	100.3	115.0	110.7
1965	3.91	4.00	100.3	116.7	110.3
1966	3.90	3.97	100.5	119.0	111.7
1967	3.93	4.20	99.7	121.4	113.6
1968	3.93	5.00	99.7	118.9	110.4
1969	3.93	6.00	99.7	114.3	105.8
1970	6.44	7.10	60.9	75.9	69.9
1971	6.44	6.88	60.9	88.4	76.3
1972	6.78	7.35	57.8	87.9	74.2
1973	6.73	6.85	58.2	97.2	77.7
1974	7.06	7.45	55.5	112.0	88.2
1975	7.50	8.50	52.3	103.2	81.6
1976	7.43	8.10	52.8	107.5	82.6
1977	7.37	7.57	53.2	111.8	80.6
1978	7.38	8.10	53.1	111.4	76.5
1979	7.42	7.90	52.8	117.0	86.1
1980	7.60	7.85	51.6	119.0	86.1
1981	8.20	8.70	47.8	113.0	85.8
1982	9.17	9.85	42.7	104.9	82.4
1983	14.00	21.00	28.0	73.3	58.2
1984	19.76	20.00	19.8	74.9	62.3
1985	19.03	20.30	20.6	92.4	70.7
1986	20.53	21.00	19.1	84.7	60.2

NOTES

1. End-of-year rates.
2. Official dollar/peso rate divided by ratio of US consumer price index to Philippine consumer price index (increase indicates appreciation).
3. Average of real exchange rates against the US dollar, Japanese yen, and Deutsche mark, weighted by average trade shares in the period (increase indicates appreciation).

SOURCES IMF, *International Financial Statistics Yearbook 1987*, lines ae and 64. Black market rates from *Pick's Currency Yearbook 1968* (p. 419), *1975–76* (p. 469), *1985 World Currency Yearbook* (p. 675), and *1988–89 World Currency Yearbook* (p. 516).

demand for it. The relative importance of supply and demand in the post-1973 burst of international lending to Third World countries was considered briefly in Chapter 9.[4] In Philippine case, Ranis (1984, pp. 6–7) refers to an 'unholy alliance between foreign banks eager to lend and public and private Filipinos eager to borrow – without much regard to the allocative efficiency of the projects'. He concludes: 'While the Government has generally responded rather well to the OPEC impact via higher oil prices, that is, in terms of its energy policies, the OPEC impact via petro-dollars seeking an outlet in the "good investment climate" of the Philippines has thus had much more serious consequences'.

Hence a case can be made that in the Philippines the capital-account tail wagged the current-account dog.[5] The apportionment of responsibility for capital flows between the Philippine borrowers and the foreign lenders is a matter which need not be judged here; suffice it to say that the transactions occurred between mutually consenting adults. Undoubtedly, 'the willingness, and in some cases, the eagerness of commercial banks to lend to dubious projects . . . is one of the root causes of the debt crisis' (Alburo *et al.*, 1986, pp. 46–7). At the same time, 'the public sector could have exercised more restraint in incurring such debt'.[6] Why borrowers, both public and private, did not exercise more restraint will be more apparent when we examine the relationship between external debt and capital flight.

The extent to which debt financed excessive spending on imports is an open question. Much of the borrowing financed interest payments on previous loans and capital flight, as documented in Chapter 10. The Philippines ran merchandise trade deficits throughout the 1962–86 period (the sole exceptions being the years 1963 and 1973; see Table 9.1). However, when other non-investment income current account transactions (such as labor remittances) are included, the picture is more mixed, with surpluses in the mid-1960s, early 1970s and mid-1980s (see Table 10.2). The cumulative merchandise trade deficit from 1962 to 1986 was $17.8 billion, but the cumulative non-investment income current account deficit was only $1.2 billion. Both figures are well below the $27.9 billion debt accumulation in the period. Substantial non-investment income current account deficits were run only from 1975 to 1983, and even then these deficits amounted to only one-third of the debt inflow.

It is impossible to say what items would or would not have been imported in the absence of foreign borrowing. Given the balance of political power and the distribution of effective demand in the country, it is quite conceivable that, in the absence of external finance, some necessities would have been foregone while luxury imports continued. The important role of well-to-do consumers in the demand for imports is evident from a comparison of the growth in numbers of buses and private automobiles in the country. Between 1962 and 1985, the number of registered private passenger cars rose from 55,693 to 332,473, an increase of 500 per cent. At the same time the number of buses *declined* from 14,055 to 11,641, a 17 per cent drop.[7] The World Bank (1976, pp. 80–3) observed that the 'large growth in private passenger vehicles' exacerbated Manila's chronic traffic congestion, and cited a survey which found that while private cars accounted for two-thirds of vehicular traffic and buses for less than five per cent, buses carried almost as many passengers. Morrell (1979, p. 6) estimated the cost of the allocation of resources for cars instead of buses in the 1970s at $3.25 billion.

To a limited extent, then, one can say that the Philippine external debt was used to finance imports. Yet an analogy between the Philippines and a spendthrift individual, who buys now and pays later, would be misleading for at least four reasons. First, borrowing caused spending rather than vice versa, as imports were artificially stimulated by the income and exchange rate effects of the loan influx. Second, the non-investment income current account deficit accounted for only a small fraction of the debt – less than five per cent of the cumulative total from 1962 to 1986. Third, a country differs from an individual in that it comprises many people, some of whom benefitted considerably from the spending of the borrowed money, and others of whom did not. Owners of private automobiles, for example, benefitted more than bus passengers. Finally, those who borrowed are not those from whom repayment is demanded – a point to which we return below.

DEBT, SAVINGS, INVESTMENT, AND GROWTH

A primary rationale of the debt-for-development strategy is the belief that external capital can and will be used to finance investment and growth. 'Sure, we're up to our eyeballs in debt', a Finance Ministry official admitted in 1980, 'but to "take off" you have to spend'.[8]

The impact of foreign capital on growth in Third World countries has long been a matter of debate. The simplest view is that foreign capital (or more precisely, that fraction of foreign capital which finances investment rather than consumption) is entirely additional to domestic savings, and that its impact on growth can be calculated simply by dividing its volume by the incremental capital output ratio (ICOR), which measures the efficiency with which capital is used to generate additional output. Even allowing for the possibility of diminishing returns to capital (rising ICORs), the impact on growth is necessarily positive.

TABLE 11.2   *Savings, Investment, and Growth, 1971–1983*

Year	Foreign saving (% of GNP)	Domestic saving (% of GNP)	Investment (% of GNP)	Incremental capital output ratio	Real GNP growth rate (%)
1971	1.9	19.2	21.1	3.46	5.8
1972	1.8	19.0	20.8	3.46	4.9
1973	–3.3	24.9	21.6	1.87	9.6
1974	2.8	24.0	26.8	3.55	6.3
1975	7.1	24.1	31.2	3.56	5.9
1976	7.4	23.5	30.9	3.54	6.1
1977	4.3	25.2	29.5	3.35	6.9
1978	6.0	23.5	29.5	4.31	6.2
1979	5.3	25.9	31.2	3.87	7.5
1980	5.9	24.8	30.7	5.22	4.4
1981	6.0	24.7	30.7	6.72	3.7
1982	8.2	20.7	28.9	8.24	2.8
1983	7.4	19.5	26.9	22.55	1.4

SOURCES   Remolona, Mangahas and Pante (1985, Table 2.6, p. 33).

This simple view was widely held by development economists in the 1950s and 1960s (see, for example, Chenery and Strout, 1966). Griffin and Enos (1970) challenged this conventional wisdom, suggesting that the positive impact of foreign savings on growth could be partially or even fully offset by two phenomena: a decline in domestic savings, for which foreign savings act as a substitute; and a decline in the efficiency of capital owing to specific attributes of foreign capital. These include a bias towards the purchase of capital-intensive technology, long gestation periods for infrastructure investments, the hindering of local entrepreneurship, and the strengthening of internal political forces which resist needed institutional reforms. The resulting inefficiencies may also affect domestically financed investment, particularly if much of it is tied up in counterpart funding for foreign-assisted projects.

The subsequent debate has been conducted primarily by means of international cross-country comparisons.[9] Yet the impact of foreign capital inflows can be expected to vary from country to country, depending on their specific economic and political circumstances. Time-series analyses may help to illuminate the relationships within particular countries.

An examination of data on foreign capital inflows, domestic savings, investment, and output growth in the Philippines from 1971 to 1983 suggests

TABLE 11.3 *Foreign Savings Correlations*

| Variable | Simple correlation coefficient (Pearson's r) | Simple regression | |
		Constant	Coefficient (t-ratio in parentheses)
Domestic savings	0.09	23.0	0.07 (0.3)
Investment	0.83	23.0	1.07 (4.7)
Incremental capital output ratio	0.66	2.7	0.35 (2.8)
Real GNP growth rate	–0.65	7.5	–0.36 (–2.7)

NOTES
Number of observations = 12 (1971–82). Variables as reported in Table 11.2.

that while foreign capital did not depress domestic savings, it had a negative short-run impact on both investment efficiency and the rate of growth of output. The relevant data are presented in Table 11.2.[10] Correlations between foreign savings and domestic savings, investment, the incremental capital output ratio (ICOR), and the GNP growth rate are reported in Table 11.3.[11]

The results indicate that a one per cent increase in foreign savings (as a percentage of GNP) was associated with a slight increase in domestic savings (not significantly different from zero), such that investment rose by slightly more than one percentage point. The incremental capital output ratio also rose with foreign savings, however, indicating that the efficiency with which capital was utilized was inversely related to the influx of foreign savings. This may help to explain the strong negative correlation between foreign savings and output growth: a one percentage point increase in foreign savings was associated with a 0.36 per cent *decrease* in the GNP growth rate. Such correlations cannot conclusively establish cause and effect, but they are consistent with the Griffin-Enos hypothesis that foreign capital inflows lower the efficiency of investment.

The World Bank (1984, p. 35), remarking on the rising ICOR's of the late 1970s and early 1980s, expressed concern that 'the investment pattern was not especially geared to expanding the DSC [debt servicing capacity]'. The Bank stated that this 'was partly a result of the large weight of public sector infrastructure projects in total investment with relatively long gestation periods', but noted that 'the relatively high ICOR has also been interpreted to reflect investment inefficiency in the economy'.

Other analysts have been more blunt. Remolona and Lamberte (1986, p. 117), for example, interpret the rising ICOR as a result of 'wasteful investment'. Oshima (1983, p. 42) cites 'rampant misallocation of funds borrowed abroad' as a cause of the country's disappointing economic performance. And Ranis (1987, p. 117) writes of the 'many parastatals which have come to rest in government hands as a consequence of the inflow of foreign capital, its misallocation, and the exercise of government guarantees'.

The effect of foreign borrowing on the direction of technological change bears special mention. Foreign borrowing can be expected to cause a capital-intensive bias in the direction of technological change for three reasons. First, by causing overvaluation of the domestic currency (that is, making foreign exchange cheaper than it otherwise would have been), the capital inflow shifts relative prices in favor of imported capital goods and against labor. Second, foreign borrowing is often tied to purchases of imported capital goods. In the case of official bilateral lending ('tied aid'), these imports are often bought at a premium above the world market price.[12] Third, capital-goods imports provide opportunities for capital flight through kickbacks and overinvoicing. Insofar as debt drives capital flight (a possibility examined below), the bias toward capital-intensive technology is thereby exacerbated.

This bias adversely affects both efficiency and employment. Tied purchases, kickbacks, and import overinvoicing inflate the prices of capital goods, raising the ICOR. Moreover, the 'true' ICOR, corrected for exchange-rate overvaluation, would be even higher insofar as the peso cost of investment is undervalued. The relatively slow employment growth documented in Chapter 2 can be traced, at least in part, to this capital-intensive bias in the direction of technological change.[13]

In discussing the potential contribution of foreign capital to investment in the Philippines, the International Labour Office mission (ILO, 1974, p. 279) observed that 'the qualitative significance of foreign capital . . . in affecting the orientation of the total effort, both foreign and domestic, may be quite substantial'. This prediction appears to have withstood the test of time, albeit in retrospect with an unintended irony.

THE REVOLVING DOOR: DEBT AND CAPITAL FLIGHT

In addition to financing the current account deficit (much of which was attributable to interest payments on previous borrowings) and investment, a substantial fraction of foreign borrowing appears to have financed capital flight from the Philippines.

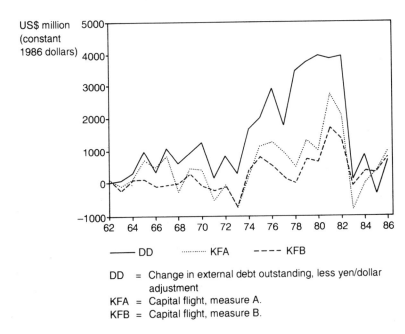

DD = Change in external debt outstanding, less yen/dollar
      adjustment
KFA = Capital flight, measure A.
KFB = Capital flight, measure B.

Sources: See Tables 10.5 and 11.5

Figure 11.1:   External Debt Inflows and Capital Flight, 1962 – 1986

The relationship between the timing of debt-creating external capital inflows and of capital flight is depicted in Figure 11.1. The solid line represents the annual change in the outstanding Philippine external debt (adjusted for yen/dollar exchange rate effects), and the broken lines represent alternative measures of capital flight derived in the preceding chapter. All are expressed in constant 1986 dollars to eliminate the effect of inflation. It is apparent from the figure that the two phenomena are positively correlated.[14]

Linkages Between Debt and Capital Flight: A Classification

In a textbook world in which 'capital is capital', money would move across borders in response to international differences in rates of return and risk. Favorable conditions in any given country would attract foreign and domestic investment alike; unfavorable conditions would repel foreign investment and trigger resident capital outflows. The result would be a negative correlation between debt-creating inflows and resident outflows: capital flight would be lowest in those years in which foreign borrowing was greatest, and vice versa.

In the Philippines and other real-world settings the opposite occurs: capital flight is larger in years of greater lending. How is this to be explained? Answers to this question can be grouped into five categories.

Indirect Linkages

The explanation favored by bankers, at least in their public statements, is that debt disbursements and capital flight bear no direct causal relation to each other. Rather, both are results of a common set of exogenous factors, notably poor economic management by the debtor government. The Morgan Guaranty Trust Company (1986, p. 15) declares, for example, that the simultaneous occurrence of debt accumulation and capital flight in Third World countries 'was no coincidence' since 'the policies and track records that engendered capital flight also generated demands for foreign credit'.

This line of reasoning seems plausible as an explanation for a positive cross-sectional correlation between external borrowing and cumulative capital flight, both measured over an appropriately long interval. Over a decade or two, irresponsibly-governed country A may witness more public-sector demand for external credit, and more private-sector propensity for capital flight, than prudently-governed country B. It is far less convincing, however, as an explanation for a positive time-series correlation between annual debt disbursements and capital outflows in a given country, since the time frame for the relevant 'policies and track records' is clearly longer than a single year.

Moreover, while this line of reasoning may help to explain the *demand* for external borrowing, it leaves open the question of why foreign creditors were willing to *supply* large sums of money to governments whose own residents were voting no confidence by shifting their capital abroad. As Pastor (1990, p. 7) remarks, 'If the "investment climate" in a country is negative enough to push out local capital, why would savvy international bankers extend their own capital in the form of loans?' Either the creditors were not so savvy, or they faced risks and returns systematically different from those perceived by residents.

Direct Causal Linkages

The latter possibility lies at the heart of explanations which posit direct causal linkages between debt and capital flight. Direct linkages can be classified into four groups on the basis of (1) whether the direction of causality runs from debt to capital flight, or vice versa, and (2) whether one simply provided the *motive* for the other, or whether it provided the *means* as well.

Indirect:	Exogenous variables:	Debt disbursements Capital flight	

Direct:		Causal mechanism:	
		Motive only	Motive & capital
Direction of linkage:	Debt to capital flight (*DD* → *KF*)	Debt-driven capital flight	Debt-fueled capital flight
	Capital flight to debt (*KF* → *DD*)	Flight-driven external borrowing	Flight-fueled external borrowing

Figure 11.2:　Linkages between Debt Disbursements and Capital Flight

Figure 11.2 summarizes these linkages. Explanations in which the causality runs from debt to capital flight can be divided into those in which external borrowing motivates residents to shift their own capital abroad (for example, by generating expectations of exchange rate devaluation or fiscal crisis), and those in which the borrowed funds are themselves transferred abroad. I shall term these 'debt-driven' and 'debt-fueled' capital flight, respectively. Similarly, explanations in which the causality runs from capital flight to debt can be divided into 'flight-driven external borrowing', in which the export of capital generates an economy-wide demand for replacement funds, and 'flight-fueled external borrowing', in which residents who exported capital then 'borrow' their own money back.

In each of these direct linkages, capital flows in both directions as if through a revolving door. Pursuing this analogy, we can think of *debt-driven* capital flight as a case in which Mr. Dollar arrives through the revolving door, and Mr. Peso upon seeing him anticipates trouble and decides to leave. In *debt-fueled* capital flight, by contrast, Mr. Dollar enters, attends to a few formalities discussed below, and then slips out again. In *flight-driven* external borrowing, Mr. Peso leaves and Mr. Dollar is invited to take his place. And in *flight-fueled* external borrowing, Mr. Peso steps out and then comes back dressed as Mr. Dollar. Let us examine each scenario more closely.

Debt-driven Capital Flight
Debt-driven' capital flight refers to capital which flees a country in response to economic circumstances attributable to the external debt itself.

Consider the impact of external borrowing on the exchange rate. In the short run, the capital inflow increases the supply of foreign exchange, applying upward pressure to the local currency. If, however, this debt is incurred for purposes which are unlikely to generate adequate foreign exchange for repayment, then in the long-run an opposite pressure will result: when the net transfer (new borrowing minus amortization and interest payments on past loans) turns negative, increased demand for foreign currency (compared to the no-borrowing counterfactual) will depress the value of the local currency. The rational response for any asset holder who can do so at reasonable cost is to dollarize when the local currency is artificially inflated in the expectation of its eventual decline.[15] Since this dollarization further increases demand for foreign exchange, the pressure for devaluation gets an additional boost from self-fulfilling expectations.

Similarly, external borrowing temporarily eases the pressure on government to tax residents either overtly or through the 'inflation tax'. Further down the road, however, domestic asset holders may expect exceptionally onerous taxes in the wake of an eventual debt crisis. 'Taxes' can here be considered as a broad range of regulations which reduce the value of domestic financial assets (Dooley, 1987, p. 79). The desire to avoid such taxes in the future provides a further motivational link between debt inflows and capital flight. External funds may also preempt favorable investment opportunities, or drive down the domestic rate of return, 'crowding out' domestic capital and pushing it overseas.[16]

Note, however, that debt-driven capital flight need not be hasty, particularly if the major impetus comes from anticipation of future consequences of the debt accumulation. The net transfer seldom alternates sign in successive years. Rather, a number of years of positive net transfers typically precedes a number of years of negative ones. In the Philippines, for example, the net transfer was positive from 1963 through 1970, briefly dipped below zero in 1971 in the wake of a balance-of-payments crisis, and then remained positive until crisis struck again in 1983. In such a setting one would expect debt-driven capital flight only when the warning signs of the negative net transfer appear in the form of diminishing official reserves, increasing reliance on short-term finance, and so on. Lacking perfect foresight, some residents may even wait too long, and export whatever capital they can only after the crisis has broken. In other words, the timing of debt-driven capital flight would not be expected to generate a terribly strong positive year-to-year correlation between net debt disbursements and capital flight.

In addition to economic impacts, it is worthwhile to consider possible 'extra-economic' impacts of external borrowing. These too could spur capital flight. Imagine, for example, that external borrowing increases the leverage of an avaricious tyrant and his greedy cronies, who control the borrower government. Imagine, further, that they employ this leverage to wrest control of assets and markets from their rivals in the national economy, using a combination of legal, quasi-legal and illegal methods. The resulting increase in 'expropriation risk' may well propel further capital flight. These hypothetical circumstances, not dissimilar to those faced by Filipino capitalists under the Marcos regime, might strengthen the phenomenon of debt-driven capital flight. But again the relevant time frame would extend well beyond a single year. A strong year-to-year correlation implies that other, tighter linkages were at work.

Debt-fueled Capital Flight
In 'debt-fueled' capital flight, the inflow of external resources provides the resources as well as a possible motive for capital flight. The same individual borrows external resources and then transfers part or all of his assets abroad. Debt directly fuels capital flight. In some cases the fuel is fungible, as in Pastor's (1990, p. 7) example in which 'an investor could draw a publicly-guaranteed external loan cheaply and ship his/her own resources abroad to acquire foreign assets'. In other cases the capital never enters the country: the money is borrowed and immediately deposited in a foreign bank, possibly the same one making the loan, so that 'the entire cycle is completed with a few bookkeeping entries in New York' (Henry, 1986, p. 20).

To differentiate between debt-driven and debt-fueled capital flight, it is useful to contrast two scenarios. In the first, the government borrows dollars (or any other hard currency) and then sells them to its own residents. Some of the buyers then legally or illegally transfer these dollars abroad. In this case, external borrowing merely furnishes foreign exchange; it does not provide the *resources* transferred abroad since residents must purchase the dollars with resources acquired in some other way. In the second scenario, the government again borrows dollars but on-lends these funds to private borrowers through a national development bank. The borrowers then transfer part or all of this capital abroad. In this case, unlike the first, external borrowing provides the resources – the fuel – for capital flight.

Debt-fueled capital flight typically involves a process of 'layering' between the external creditor and the private resident in whose name external assets are acquired. On the creditor's books, the debt is owed by the government or by a corporate entity, typically with a government guarantee of repayment in case of default. The external assets, by contrast, are in the names of individuals: government officials who siphoned part of the proceeds of the loan, or private residents who borrowed in the name of a firm. The holder of the external asset thus is not identical to the holder of the external liability. Yet in practice the same individual is engaged in both transactions.

This legal discrepancy is by no means coincidental. Public guarantees posed a 'moral hazard' for creditors and borrowers alike. Insured against the risk of default, neither party had an incentive to minimize it. Creditors might have been more reluctant to finance capital flight if repayment were the sole responsibility of the individual flight capitalist. With the debt in the name of the government, or secured by government guarantee, the creditors could draw comfort from their faith that 'countries do not go bankrupt'.

For the flight capitalist, the evasion of responsibility for eventual re-payment of the external loan was often a key element in the transaction's rationale. It is not likely that the capitalist could turn a profit by borrowing money from a bank and then redepositing it there or in another bank, for banks derive their own profit from the opposite spread between interest rates. It is conceivable that some borrowers were astute enough to identify lucrative overseas investment opportunities which permitted retention of a profit spread after repayment, but it is doubtful that all flight capitalists possessed such acumen. In many cases, the principal motive for debt-fueled capital flight was the opportunity to exploit the legal dichotomy between the holder of the liability and the holder of the asset. Whenever there are opportunities for the acquisition of private assets by means of public debts, 'rational' profit maximizers can be expected to seize them.[17]

Debt-fueled capital flight could generate a rather strong year-to-year correlation between net debt inflows and capital flight. Unlike debt-driven capital flight, the causal relation is not mediated by changing perceptions of the economic and political environment. Nor are the lags between borrowing and flight likely to extend over a period of several years. Rather the loan is obtained for the intended purpose of capital flight, and the borrower may well be anxious to consummate the circuit expeditiously, while the window of opportunity is open. Mr. Dollar's round trip through the revolving door is likely to be quick.

Flight-driven External Borrowing

We now turn to causal linkages running in the opposite direction, from capital flight to external borrowing. Here too we can distinguish between the case in which the link is solely motivational ('flight-driven' external borrowing) and that in which flight capital directly provides the resources which re-enter the country ('flight-fueled' external borrowing). Let us start with the former.

The demand-side of flight-driven external borrowing is straightforward: the drain of domestic resources through capital flight generates demand for replacement funds on the part of the government and private sectors.

Why are external creditors willing to meet this demand, when local residents are not? The answer is likely to be found in different risks and returns facing resident and non-resident capital, rather than in different perceptions of the same risks and returns. An inflation tax, for example, will erode the returns to holders of fixed-interest domestic-currency liabilities, whereas non-residents who hold claims denominated in foreign currency are unaffected.[18] Systematic differences in the risk-adjusted financial returns to domestic and external capital could also arise from disparities in taxation, interest-rate ceilings, and risk-pooling capabilities (Lessard and Williamson, 1987, pp. 215–18).

In addition, foreign creditors may enjoy a 'comparative advantage' in risk mitigation thanks to the 'direct or indirect sanctions' they can bring to bear upon the borrower (Lessard, 1986, p. 16). If so, they may believe that 'domestic assets held by residents are effectively subordinated to sovereign external obligations in the case of a fiscal crisis' (Lessard, 1987, p. 99). In the Philippine case, the creditors received official encouragement for this belief: Presidential Decree No. 1177, issued by Marcos in 1977, provided for automatic appropriation of government monies for external debt service, bypassing the usual requirement for Congressional appropriation of government expenditures.[19]

Such differences can be expected to lead to 'offshore financial intermediation', by which foreign creditors provide fresh loans as domestic capital is exported, in effect transforming resident capital into non-resident capital. This in turn can intensify debt-driven capital flight, since 'the substitution of foreign funds backed by international leverage for resident savings may increase the likelihood of crises and the relative exposure of (the remaining) resident holdings of domestic assets' (Lessard, 1987, p. 98). A vicious circle is set in motion, in which debt and capital flight feed upon each other.

Flight-fueled External Borrowing
In flight-fueled external borrowing, Mr. Peso flees and then re-enters the country in the guise of Mr. Dollar. The flight capitalist seeks to arbitrage the yield and risk differentials between resident and external capital, by

engaging in a series of transactions sometimes known as 'round-tripping' or 'back-to-back loans'. Resident capital is dollarized and deposited in an overseas bank, and the depositor then takes a 'loan' from the same bank (for which the deposit may serve as collateral).

As in the case of offshore financial intermediation, government guarantees provide a crucial part of the rationale for back-to-back loans. As Khan and Ul Haque (1985, p. 625) remark:

> To the extent that the investor believed that foreign debt implicitly carried a government guarantee, he was assured that, if the domestic firm or enterprise went bankrupt or was expropriated, the foreign lender's claim would be assumed by the government. Savings held abroad would obviously not be at risk, so that the investor was protected if he relied as much as possible on foreign borrowing. Given this scenario, the domestic investor was behaving in a completely rational fashion.

In many cases, of course, the government guarantees have been explicit.

A further motive for flight-fueled external borrowing is the concealment of the sources of funds from present or prospective government authorities. This was the main objective of the pioneer of back-to-back loans, US organized crime financier Meyer Lansky, who developed the technique in the 1930s as a means to launder funds in Switzerland.[20] In this respect back-to-back loans have a motivational dimension beyond more general offshore financial intermediation: The laundry service not only bleaches out systematic yield differentials, but also removes the stain of the money's origins.[21]

Which of the flight-to-borrowing linkages would be more likely to result in a strong positive correlation in the year-to-year variations of capital flight and external borrowing? In the case of flight-*driven* external borrowing, where the link is only motivational, there may be a longer lag between the outflow and inflow of capital than in the case of flight-*fueled* borrowing, where the same individual first exports and then imports the capital. Hence it seems reasonable to hypothesize that flight-*fueled* external borrowing would generate a stronger year-to-year correlation.

Linkages Between Debt and Capital Flight: Some Implications

The distinctions drawn above have been often blurred in the recent literature on Third World debt and capital flight. The debt-to-flight linkage has been described, for example, as a 'liquidity effect', in which 'the availability of foreign exchange enables capital flight to take place' (Lessard, 1987, p. 99). This formulation could encompass both debt-*fueled* and debt-*driven* capital flight.[22] Yet the two have quite different implications.

The 'fuel' linkages – debt-fueled capital flight and flight-fueled external borrowing – imply that international creditors bear a particularly heavy responsibility for the debt crisis. Knowingly or unknowingly, they colluded in transactions whereby public debts were transformed into private assets, and vice versa, transactions which come perilously close to what is commonly understood as fraud. The 'drive' linkages place the creditors in a relatively favorable light: they may have lent unwisely, but they did not act unethically.

Members of the banking community would prefer to be viewed as slightly soft-headed providers of 'easy money' than as operators of a toll booth at the revolving door:

It is . . . a gross distortion to claim, as some have done, that the "private banking" departments of some lending banks were deliberately seeking the money that their loan departments were putting out; rather, the point is that easy money contributed to lax policies, especially exchange overvaluation, which provided the incentive for private capital outflows.[23]

The distinction here is precisely that between debt-fueled and debt-driven capital flight.[24]

In the Philippines, however, debt-fueled capital flight was very much in evidence. Guarantees and on-lending by government institutions were the major avenues for external borrowing by the Philippine private sector. Two months after the onset of the Philippine debt crisis, Prime Minister Cesar Virata explained to an interviewer:

We were quite liberal in guaranteeing loans, so that investors could go on with their projects on the basis of commercial loans. We found out later that their motives were not as pure as we would have liked. In other words, *some of the companies really wanted to make money out of purchases of equipment rather than by operating it*. This has been one of the major faults of our system. (Virata, 1984, p. 274; *emphasis added*)

With 'commissions' on the purchases safely deposited abroad, private investors could rest secure in the knowledge that when repayment of the loans came due (or the net transfer to their companies turned negative), the Philippine government would be left with the debt.

Many of the government guarantees were what Rosendo Bondoc, the former president of the Philippine Export and Foreign Loan Guarantee Corporation, termed 'behest guarantees', issued at the express instructions of President or Mrs. Marcos. Asked whether he considered rescinding a guarantee on one loan which he knew had been diverted to capital flight, Bondoc explained: 'In the light of the instructions being given, it was either follow or . . . You know it was an autocratic rule'.[25]

Similarly, much of the foreign borrowing on-lent to the private sector by the Development Bank of the Philippines (DBP) and the Philippine National Bank was in the form of 'behest loans', also issued on the instructions of the Marcoses. In an extraordinary 1983 memorandum to President Marcos and Prime Minister Virata, Acting DBP Chairman Jose Tengco, Jr. listed that institution's exposure to 'behest accounts' amounting to 28.2 billion pesos (equivalent to $2.54 billion at the average 1983 official exchange rate). Nearly a quarter of this exposure (6.6 billion pesos) was in the form of guarantees; the remainder was DBP loans, much of which represented on-lending of external borrowings.[26]

A DBP governor later recounted the following example of debt-fueled capital flight to a journalist:

> Persons seeking the loan would just come around here and say that we need 100–200 million dollars for this project which looks viable. It's not viable but Marcos says it is viable. When he says that then it better be viable. For instance, we were recently sent an account for 65 million dollars that we are supposed to pay. Now, apparently this money was supposed to have put up a steel mill, a factory. . . So we asked to see where the factory is, and to this day, after several months, nobody has found it. In short, this factory does not exist.[27]

This represents the most extreme case, in which an entire loan apparently vanished into thin air.

In other cases, a portion of the borrowed funds was invested, but the underlying motive for the loan was the diversion of the remainder into capital flight. 'Kickbacks are apparently the name of the game in the expansion of the sugar industry here', the *Far Eastern Economic Review* reported in 1976:

> Whether or not the new [sugar mill] centrals make any money may be of little consequence to the owners. The investors who are favoured generally have to put up only about P2.5 million (US $333,330) for centrals costing

$65 million. The remainder is loan money from or guaranteed by the Government-owned Philippine National Bank.   (Wideman, 1976)

The requirement that loans be approved by the Central Bank did not provide effective oversight:

> Say there is an application for a loan to set up a new sugar mill. What is the right price for a sugar mill? It is hard to say. Likewise, it was hard for MEDIAD [the Central Bank's Management of External Debt and Investment Accounts Department] to evaluate the soundness of the particular project. So, for example, a mill was built in a very rainy region which produces only poor quality, watery cane. Or mills were installed close to existing mills, creating excess milling capacity and raising unit costs. We know why these things were done. The profit was not in the mill. *The profit was in the procurement of the mill equipment.*[28]

According to a senior Japanese government official, kickbacks averaged 12 per cent of contract prices, or $7.8 million on a $65 million sugar mill.[29]

The extent to which creditors knowingly lent money to fuel capital flight is an open question. The case of the largest single loan to the Philippines – the $900 million in direct loans and loan guarantees provided by the US Export-Import Bank for the Bataan nuclear plant – may be instructive in this regard. When asked in 1978 why the Bank had financed the plant despite the fact that its cost was roughly double that of a comparable reactor being built in South Korea, also by Westinghouse with Export-Import Bank backing, the Bank's general counsel replied with a rhetorical question: 'The Ex-Im Bank is going to say the price is wrong when the two big boys have agreed to it?' William J. Casey, the chairman of the Export-Import Bank (later the director of the Central Intelligence Agency), clarified where the buck stops:

> You couldn't tell Westinghouse what to charge. If they charge too much, the Philippines has to pay it. It's their government; they have to protect themselves from getting fleeced.[30]

Many creditors apparently shared Mr. Casey's view that what happened to the money they lent was not their problem. The international debt crisis of the 1980s may have altered that perception.

The statistical analysis reported below strongly supports the hypothesis that direct linkages existed between external borrowing and capital flight in the Philippines.

A Model of Philippine Capital Flight

There are plausible *a priori* grounds to expect the positive correlation between capital flight and debt-creating capital inflows depicted in Figure 11.1: External borrowing can both drive and fuel capital flight, and capital flight can drive and fuel external borrowing. Since the causality may run in either or both directions, the relationship between the two must be modelled to permit simultaneity.

The Model
A complete model of the relationship between capital flight and debt disbursements must incorporate other variables. Other possible determinants of capital flight include:

1. The level of the country's official foreign exchange reserves: Higher reserves, as an indicator of a lower likelihood of a balance-of-payments crisis, are expected to lead to less capital flight.[31]
2. The rate of growth of gross domestic product: Higher growth, and the associated opportunities for investment, could be expected to result in less capital flight.
3. The difference between international and domestic real interest rates: A larger real interest rate gap would be expected to induce more capital flight.
4. The government budget surplus or deficit: As a signal of the likelihood of a fiscal crisis, a higher surplus (or lower deficit) would be expected to result in less capital flight.

Each of these variables could also affect the level of debt disbursements. Higher foreign exchange reserves, interest rate differences, and budget surpluses could be expected to lead to lower demand for external capital and to greater supply; the direction of the net effects, if any, would hence depend on the relative importance of supply and demand in determining the amount of external borrowing. The net effect of GDP growth is also uncertain. Higher growth would presumably boost private investment demand (and perhaps supply), but public sector demand for external credit could be counter-cyclical.[32]

In addition, the Mexican near-default of August 1982 had a drastic effect on the supply of external credit from commercial banks in subsequent years. In the Philippine case, this was followed by the assassination of Senator Benigno Aquino in August 1983. As new lending dried up and the net transfer (new lending minus debt service payments) turned negative, the

TABLE 11.4 *Predicted Effects of Independent Variables in Debt-Capital Flight Regressions*

Independent variable	Dependent variable		
	KF	*DD*	
		Demand	Supply
KF		+	+
DD	+		
RES	–	–	+
GDPR	–	?	+
INT	+	–	+
BS	–	–	+
MEXD	+	+	–

country was plunged into its worst balance-of-payments crisis in the its postwar history.

A general model incorporating these variables is:

$$KF = f(DD, RES, GDPGR, INT, BS, MEXD) \quad (1A)$$
$$DD = f(KF, RES, GDPGR, INT, BS, MEXD) \quad (1B)$$

where *KF* = annual capital flight (in 1986 dollars); *DD* = net debt disbursements (in 1986 dollars); *RES* = the level of the country's official foreign exchange reserves (in 1986 dollars); *GDPGR* = the percentage growth rate of gross domestic product; *INT* = the real US Treasury bill rate minus the real time deposit rate in the Philippines (in both cases, the real interest rate is calculated as the nominal rate minus the relevant consumer price index inflation rate); *BS* = the government budget surplus as a percentage of gross domestic product; and *MEXD* = a dummy variable to allow for the impact of the Mexican debt crisis, taking the value 0 prior to 1983 and 1 thereafter. The predicted effects of each of these variables are summarized in Table 11.4.

A fairly general initial dynamic specification of this model is:

$$KF = a_0 + a_1 KF_{-1} + b_0 DD + b_1 DD_{-1} + cRES_{-1} + dGDPGR_{-1} + e_0 INT + e_1 INT_{-1} + f_0 BS + f_1 BS_{-1} + gMEXD + v_t \quad (2A)$$

$$DD = a'_0 + a'_1 DD_{-1} + b'_0 KF + b'_1 KF_{-1} + c'RES_{-1} + d'GDPGR_{-1} + e'_0 INT + e'_1 INT_{-1} + f'BS_{-1} + g'MEXD + v'_t \quad (2B)$$

TABLE 11.5 *Independent Variables for Analysis of Determinants of Philippine Capital Flight*

Year	DD	RES	GDPGR	INT	BS
1962	0.00	237.21	4.820	0.106	0.31
1963	64.45	345.82	7.100	5.292	−0.58
1964	315.54	389.35	3.214	6.345	0.14
1965	993.82	583.52	5.228	0.394	−1.29
1966	330.75	868.25	4.571	0.574	−0.59
1967	1109.10	896.36	5.366	1.104	−0.81
1968	614.01	763.35	5.268	−2.954	−0.82
1969	957.44	551.83	5.126	−3.877	−2.82
1970	1277.02	1208.93	5.021	9.013	0.14
1971	164.88	1798.20	5.104	14.611	−0.37
1972	842.57	1382.35	4.843	2.176	−1.96
1973	308.11	2307.85	9.307	10.548	−1.17
1974	1683.96	2815.16	5.020	21.814	0.45
1975	2040.80	2385.06	6.433	−5.806	−1.19
1976	2954.13	2688.47	7.985	−1.448	−1.74
1977	1781.29	2354.21	6.217	−1.226	−1.82
1978	3488.51	2697.05	5.381	−2.920	−1.22
1979	3766.92	3083.92	6.302	6.215	−0.16
1980	3950.63	3518.46	5.233	3.595	−1.28
1981	3887.89	2630.37	3.915	2.070	−3.98
1982	3972.52	1713.92	2.953	−0.649	−4.23
1983	101.11	855.72	1.014	0.069	−1.94
1984	894.22	856.14	−6.122	33.365	−1.84
1985	−315.20	1030.15	−4.183	5.058	−1.83
1986	712.00	2459.00	0.999	−9.460	−4.48

Key:

DD = net debt disbursements (1986 $ million) with an adjustment for yen/dollar exchange rate effects as reported in Table 10.2.

RES = level of official foreign exchange reserves. Source: Unpublished Central Bank of the Philippines data provided to the author, converted to 1986 dollars using US wholesale price index from IMF (1987, pp. 698–9).

GDPGR = percentage growth rate of real gross domestic product. Source: Calculated from IMF (1987, pp. 562–3, lines 99b and 99aip).

INT = real U.S. Treasury bill rate minus real time deposit rate in the Philippines. Sources: U.S. Treasury bill rate, U.S. and Philippines consumer price indexes from IMF (1987 , pp. 560–1, 698–9). Time deposit rate in the Philippines from unpublished Central Bank of the Philippines data provided to the author.

BS = government budget surplus as percentage of gross domestic product. Source: Calculated from IMF (1987, pp. 562–3).

Owing to possible simultaneity, only lagged values of *RES* and *GDPGR* are included in the equations, and for the same reason only the lagged value of *BS* appears in equation (2B). Simultaneity between *KF* and *DD* is addressed below by the use of instrumental variables.

Both of the capital flight measures derived in Chapter 10 are used in the following analysis: *KFA* = the broad measure A, and *KFB* = the narrow measure B (see Table 10.5). Although measure B is less comprehensive, it has the advantage that it is calculated independently of the external debt.[33] The other variables used in the analysis are presented in Table 11.5.

Estimation of the Determinants of Capital Flight
Ordinary least-squares estimation of equation (2A), using each of our two measures of capital flight as the dependent variable, gave the following results (absolute values of t-ratios in parentheses):

$$KFA = -15 - 0.12KFA_{-1} + 0.54DD + 0.07DD_{-1} - 0.25RES_{-1}$$
$$ (0.4) \qquad (2.7) \qquad (0.3) \qquad (0.6)$$
$$ -35.8GDPGR_{-1} - 6.7INT + 14.4INT_{-1} - 228BS$$
$$ (0.3) \qquad\qquad (0.4) \qquad (0.6) \qquad\quad (1.6)$$
$$ + 22.5BS_{-1} - 433MEXD \qquad\qquad\qquad (3A)$$
$$ (0.1) \qquad\quad (0.6)$$

$\bar{R}^2 = 0.59$; DW = 2.19; n = 24.
LM test of residual serial correlation: $\chi^2(1) = 1.32$.

$$KFB = -708 - 0.13KFB_{-1} + 0.39DD + 0.11DD_{-1} - 0.31RES_{-1}$$
$$ (0.4) \qquad\quad (3.1) \qquad (0.9) \qquad\quad (1.3)$$
$$ + 62.9GDPGR_{-1} + 2.8INT + 27.3INT_{-1} - 243BS$$
$$ (1.0) \qquad\qquad (0.3) \qquad (1.8) \qquad\quad (2.5)$$
$$ + 617BS_{-1} + 590MEXD \qquad\qquad\qquad (3B)$$
$$ (0.7) \qquad\quad (1.2)$$

$\bar{R}^2 = 0.63$; DW = 2.31; n = 24.
LM test of residual serial correlation: $\chi^2(1) = 2.87$.

On elimination of the less significant variables, we obtain the following:

$$KFA = -303 + 0.62DD - 0.30RES_{-1} + 21.0INT_{-1} - 218BS \quad (4A)$$
$$ (4.5) \qquad (1.6) \qquad\quad (1.7) \qquad\quad (2.8)$$

$\bar{R}^2 = 0.69$; DW = 2.20; n = 24.
LM test of residual serial correlation: $\chi^2(1) = 0.29$.

$$KFB = -412 + 0.25DD + 16.3INT_{-1} - 176BS \tag{4B}$$
$$\qquad\quad (5.3) \qquad (2.2) \qquad\quad (3.6)$$
$$\bar{R}^2 = 0.70; \text{DW} = 2.05; \text{n} = 24.$$
LM test of residual serial correlation: $\chi^2(1) = 0.04.$

The models performed well on various diagnostic tests.[34] To check for simultaneity bias, an instrumental variables estimator (DD^*) was tested. Using the lagged variables and the Mexican crisis dummy variable as instruments, a similar result was obtained:

$$KFA = -218 + 0.87DD^* - 0.57RES_{-1} + 31.9INT_{-1} + 167BS \tag{5A}$$
$$\qquad\quad (2.9) \qquad (1.6) \qquad\quad (1.7) \qquad\quad (1.7)$$
$$\bar{R}^2 = 0.56; \text{DW} = 1.67; \text{n} = 24.$$
LM test of residual serial correlation: $\chi^2(1) = 0.76.$

$$KFB = -360 + 0.22DD^* + 15.2INT_{-1} - 170BS \tag{5B}$$
$$\qquad\quad (3.3) \qquad\quad (1.7) \qquad\quad (2.7)$$
$$\bar{R}^2 = 0.54; \text{DW} = 1.75; \text{n} = 24.$$
LM test of residual serial correlation: $\chi^2(1) = 0.45.$

To summarize, the results indicate that debt disbursements were a highly significant determinant of Philippine capital flight in the 1962–86 period: Greater borrowing led to greater capital flight, implying the existence of what are here termed 'debt-fueled' and 'debt-driven' capital flight. In addition, the real interest rate differential, government budget surplus or deficit, and, in the case of the broad capital flight measure, the level of official reserves, had moderately significant effects with the expected signs.

Estimation of the Determinants of Net Debt Disbursements
What of the reverse linkages, from capital flight to debt? Estimation of equation (2B), using each of our measures of capital flight, yields the following results:

$$DD = 529 - 0.03DD_{-1} + 0.57KFA + 0.14KFA_{-1} + 0.94RES_{-1}$$
$$\qquad\quad (0.1) \qquad\quad (2.4) \qquad (0.4) \qquad\quad (3.2)$$
$$-118GDPGR_{-1} + 24.9INT - 46.3INT_{-1} + 32.3BS_{-1}$$
$$\quad (1.1) \qquad\qquad (1.3) \qquad\quad (2.2) \qquad\quad (0.2)$$
$$-1190MEXD \tag{6A}$$
$$\quad\; (1.5)$$
$$\bar{R}^2 = 0.81; \text{DW} = 2.47; \text{n} = 24.$$
LM test of residual serial correlation: $\chi^2(1) = 6.06.$

$$DD = 960 - 0.02\,DD_{-1} + 0.81\,KFB + 0.08\,KFB_{-1} + 0.96\,RES_{-1}$$
$$ (0.1) \qquad (2.2) \qquad (0.2) \qquad (3.4)$$
$$-166\,GDPGR_{-1} + 18.6\,INT - 56.4\,INT_{-1} - 10.6\,BS_{-1}$$
$$ (1.7) \qquad\qquad (1.0) \qquad (2.8) \qquad (0.1)$$
$$-1885\,MEXD \qquad\qquad\qquad\qquad\qquad\qquad\qquad (6B)$$
$$ (2.6)$$

$\bar{R}^2 = 0.81$; DW = 2.40; n = 24.

LM test of residual serial correlation: $\chi^2(1) = 5.52$.

Using instrumental variables estimators (*KFA** and *KFB**), again based on the lagged variables and *MEXD*, and eliminating variables the estimated coefficients of which are not significantly different from zero, the serial correlation is eliminated and the equations collapse to:[35]

$$DD = 108 + 0.84\,KFA^* + 0.71\,RES_{-1} - 34.6\,INT_{-1} - 361\,MEXD \quad (7A)$$
$$ (2.6) \qquad (3.4) \qquad\quad (2.2) \qquad\quad (1.0)$$

$\bar{R}^2 = 0.79$; DW = 2.23; n = 24.

LM test of residual serial correlation: $\chi^2(1) = 0.49$.

$$DD = 557 + 1.74\,KFB^* + 0.50\,RES_{-1} - 41.5\,INT_{-1} - 1011\,MEXD \quad (7B)$$
$$ (2.4) \qquad (1.7) \qquad\quad (2.6) \qquad\quad (2.3)$$

$\bar{R}^2 = 0.78$; DW = 2.21; n = 24.

LM test of residual serial correlation: $\chi^2(1) = 0.48$.

These results indicate that debt disbursements were significantly and positively affected by capital flight. Taken with the results reported in equations (5A) and (5B), this supports the hypothesis that the causal linkages between debt and capital flight did in fact run in both directions. In addition, debt disbursements were positively related to the (lagged) level of official reserves, suggesting that, at least in this respect, supply-side factors drove the credit market, since higher reserves were presumably associated with a greater willingness to lend but with a lesser need to borrow. Similarly, the negative impact of the Mexican debt crisis on subsequent disbursements is clearly a supply-side phenomenon. The negative sign on the lagged interest rate differential suggests, however, that demand-side considerations also influenced the level of external borrowing.

In sum, statistical analysis of the relationship between net debt disbursements and capital flight in the Philippines in the 1962–86 period indicates that the two were strongly linked. Larger debt disbursements led to more capital flight, and more capital flight led to larger debt disbursements.

While neither capital flight nor debt disbursements can be completely explained in terms of each other, this vicious circle appears to have been an important feature of the financial interactions between the Philippines and the world economy which culminated in the country's debt crisis. The Philippines was probably not unique in this respect.[36]

Nominal legal restrictions apparently did little to stem Philippine capital flight. The country's experience thus is consistent with the general conclusion that capital controls are 'nigh impossible to administer against the clever and the guileful' (Kindleberger, 1987, p. 58). In South Korea, however, where illegal overseas transfer of $1 million or more was punishable with a maximum sentence of death, capital controls 'are believed to have been a credible deterrent to private investors who might otherwise have used public subsidies to build personal fortunes abroad' (Amsden, 1989, pp. 17–18). Moreover, an analysis of capital flight from Latin America found that 'capital availability' (defined as the ratio of net long-term capital flows to GDP) significantly increased capital flight only in countries without capital controls; in countries with controls there was no significant correlation.[37] Our findings for the Philippines suggest that controls are not an either-or proposition, but rather extend along a continuum in terms of their efficacy. The Philippines apparently was situated near the low end of this scale.

The finding that debt disbursements and capital flight are most strongly correlated with each other's values *in the same year* suggests that they not only *drove* each other by providing motives, but also *fueled* each other by providing capital for the reverse flow. In other words, external resources did not simply 'crowd out' or scare off domestic capital, nor did capital flight simply create a vacuum into which external capital was pulled; rather, the same capital flowed in both directions through the revolving door.

THE AGGRANDIZEMENT OF THE STATE

External finance does not flow to countries as a whole, but to specific institutions and individuals within countries. In the Philippines, much foreign borrowing was channelled to the state. Seventy-seven per cent of the country's $28.3 billion external debt outstanding at the end of 1986 was public sector debt (see Table 9.3). Even this understates the state role in foreign borrowing, since much private debt was on-lent by public sector financial institutions or was publicly guaranteed, and even direct, non-guaranteed private borrowings required Central Bank approval. Control over the allocation of billions of dollars in borrowed money provided the financial basis for the aggrandizement of the Philippine state.[38]

'The most durable support of the Marcos regime', according to political scientist William Overholt, 'came from its own senior military officers and from the United States government'. In light of the political predilections of these supporters, it is rather surprising to find that regime described by the same author as 'socialist in the strict sense of radically increasing the state's ownership of the means of production' (Overholt, 1987, pp. 100–1). Similarly, Kwitny (1984, p. 307), wrote that 'socialism is certainly not the name that the US embassy gives to it; but socialism is a fairly apt term for what Marcos has done to Philippine industry'. The US embassy did have a different name for it: 'creeping state capitalism'.[39]

External financial backing, in the form of lending from official institutions and private banks, unquestionably played a crucial role in this process. During his first administration (1965–69), President Marcos relied on external and internal borrowing to expand the direct role of the government in the economy, notably through rural infrastructure investments. In so doing, he built 'an extensive patronage machine of a scale unmatched in postwar years', laying the basis for an unprecedented centralization of political authority (Doronila, 1985, pp. 111–14).

When Marcos declared martial law in 1972, the World Bank and IMF 'looked forward to funding another of the series of Pacific Basin economic miracles' (Overholt, 1987, p. 92). At the end of the decade, the World Bank (1979b, pp. 5, 14) applauded 'the Government's remarkable success in raising the level of public investment', and claimed that while the efficiency of private investment had been damaged by import substitution policies, 'public investment projects have generally been well selected'. Foreign-assisted projects accounted for 75 per cent of the public investment program, a ratio which the Bank conceded was 'probably undesirably high' because it limited 'the Government's room for maneuver' (pp. ii, 17). Nevertheless the Bank called for an increase in official development assistance from the Consultative Group to 'at least $1 billion' in the following year (p. iv). At the same time the Bank actively encouraged lending by commercial banks. Overholt (p. 99) reports: 'The authority of the World Bank greatly weakened Marcos's critics inside private banks and greatly strengthened advocates of increased lending'.

During the Marcos era, government involvement in both agriculture and industry grew substantially. As Overholt (p. 108) remarks, the regime 'not only seized the commanding heights of the economy but also a good many of the minor foothills'. In some cases the takeovers were hostile, as in the establishment of the predatory coconut and sugar monopolies.

In others they were friendly, as the liabilities of private firms whose assets had been stripped to finance capital flight were handed over to the state.

A panel of Filipino economists described the situation in 1984:

> The most damaging economic consequence of political monopoly is the potential abuse of the state machinery and its functions to dispense economic privileges and positions to certain private entities. . . . Hence it might be a mistake to view the expansion of the government's role in recent years as an instance of "creeping socialism", or to regard the essence of the economic debate as being about the virtues of public intervention versus private enterprise. On the contrary, it could well be a conflict between different groups in society, being distinguished only in that one group has obtained exclusive access to the government.   (De Dios *et al.*, 1984, pp. 61–2)

In such a setting, the economists observed, it would be natural to expect the expanded government role to be attended by inefficiency, for 'what might appear from the public viewpoint as government waste and inefficiency might in reality be gain and profit for private interests' (De Dios *et al.*, 1984, p. 62). This reality conforms to the ideal versions of neither socialism nor capitalism.

Administrative power in the Philippines was exercised by a coalition of two groups known in the country as 'cronies' and 'technocrats'. The economists explained, 'Most major economic decisions were formulated and approved by a rather small circle of people – consisting of so-called technocrats as well as political and business allies – gathered around a powerful chief executive' (De Dios *et al.*, p. 59). Notwithstanding conflicts among them, the technocrats and cronies shared a common belief in the virtues of the authoritarian state.

Is there an irony in the support extended by foreign official and private lenders to this state apparatus? Not if one superimposes upon the traditional dichotomy between capitalism and socialism another equally overarching one: that between technocracy, in which power is concentrated at the 'top' in the hands of self-proclaimed leaders and experts, and democracy, in which power resides in the hands of the citizenry. The Philippines from 1962 to 1986, and particularly after the declaration of martial law, pursued a technocratic development strategy, in which the aggrandizement of state power was legitimated by an ideology of disinterested expertise. That in reality private interests enriched themselves behind this official veneer is, sadly, not an experience unique to the Philippines.

POLICY ALTERNATIVES IN THE ERA OF NEGATIVE
NET TRANSFERS

The Philippines entered the era of negative net transfers in 1983, when debt
service payments surpassed the inflow of new money. As of this writing,
it appears likely that the country will remain in this stage of the net
transfer cycle for many years to come. Four policy options for this era are
considered below: (1) dutiful debt service; (2) debt buy-backs; (3) selective
disengagement; and (4) outright default.

Dutiful Debt Service

The policy option most popular among debtor governments (if not their
citizens) in the 1980s was dutiful debt service. To be sure, most governments
failed to meet the repayment schedules set forth in the original loan documents. They negotiated with their creditors to reschedule debt payments, and
some who failed to make scheduled payments on time slipped into the vast
intermediate terrain between zero and total default. By and large, however,
the debtor country governments have accepted the obligation to eventually
repay their debts with interest, and they have demonstrated their willingness
to extract remarkably large negative net transfers from their populations in
order to do so.

The Philippines was not an exception, notwithstanding the historic rupture
between the government which accumulated the debt and that from which
repayment is now demanded. In her September 1986 address to a joint ses-
sion of the United States Congress, President Corazon Aquino described the
foreign debt as a form of 'slavery' and denounced 'the previous government
that stole this debt', but she pledged to repay it 'if only for honor'.

Dutiful debt service is clearly desirable from the standpoint of the
creditors, but its attractions from the debtors' standpoint are less evident. As
inducements creditors have deployed the carrot of new money and the stick
of threatened reprisals.

The carrot is proffered in a recent World Bank country report on the Philippines, for example, which holds forth the 'restoration of creditworthiness'
as a critical goal for the country's future.[40] Dutiful behavior will surely be
rewarded: one day the country can re-enter the enchanted world of positive
net transfers. This prospect does not seem imminent, however. Private
creditors are seeking to reduce their Third World exposure, not to increase
it, and official creditors have limited funds and other competing priorities.
Moreover, borrowers may be less enamored of the lure of 'creditworthiness'
in light of their recent experience of its consequences.

Hence the importance of the stick. A month after the February revolution, Central Bank Governor 'Jobo' Fernandez (1986, p. 1) warned in the *Central Bank Review* of the risk of 'economic retaliation against the country' should it take unilateral actions in defiance of its creditors. Trade credit lines could be withheld 'paralyzing foreign trade', and foreign assistance could be terminated. In July 1986 Citibank President John Reed visited Manila to deliver the same message. If the Philippines were to repudiate its debts, he warned in an address to the American Chamber of Commerce and the Rotary Club of Manila, 'it would produce immense suffering and difficulty for the people' (Andrei, 1986, p. 76).

The credibility of these threats is, however, open to serious doubt. Brazil defied its commercial creditors for 18 months, beginning with the unilateral suspension of debt service announced in February 1987. Its defiance provoked much posturing by the banks, but little genuine retaliation.[41] The holders of paper assets proved to be paper tigers. Similarly, the well-publicized but less drastic debt service ceiling imposed by Peruvian President Alan Garcia did not bring grievous penalties; the Garcia government's heterodox economic program ultimately failed *despite* the debt policy, not because of it.[42] More quietly, Bolivia halted most debt service payments in 1984, and three years later won the very favorable debt buy-back deal described below.

The credibility of creditor threats was carefully dissected by London *Financial Times'* correspondent Anatole Kaletsky in his slim book *The Costs of Default*, published in 1985. Kaletsky's central conclusion is that debtor countries have relatively little to fear from their private creditors. A more serious concern is the reaction of the governments of creditor countries to alternative debtor government policies.[43] Kaletsky argues persuasively that creditor country governments are unlikely to impose punitive sanctions against debtor governments which adopt a policy of 'conciliatory default'.

Indeed, there are important interests within creditor countries who stand to gain from the reduction or elimination of the negative net transfer from debtor countries. These include the management, shareholders, and workers of firms which have seen their export markets wither as indebted countries slash imports to meet debt service obligations; farmers whose export markets have met the same fate; and producers of goods for domestic markets who face stiff competition from countries obliged to run large trade surpluses to service their debts. To date, Third World debt policy in creditor countries, notably the United States, has favored financial interests over industrial and farm interests, but the political equilibrium on this issue is not necessarily stable.[44]

Debt Buy-backs

The widely held belief that much Third World debt will never be repaid, however long it lingers in the purgatory of rescheduling, drives a wedge between the face value of the debt and its real value. The emergence of a secondary market in which Third World debt is traded at a discount provides a market-based assessment of the latter. In recent years a variety of debt-management mechanisms have been fashioned to trade on the difference between the two.

Debt-equity swaps are one such mechanism, but they have a number of drawbacks from the debtor country's standpoint. Something real must be exchanged for the debt, such as ownership rights in domestic enterprises. This transfer often generates fears of some loss of national economic sovereignty. This loss may not be more onerous than that arising from indebtedness, but it is more visible and hence politically suspect. In addition, the country sacrifices part of the resources and foreign exchange which would have entered as direct foreign investment anyway in the absence of the swaps. And if domestic currency is printed to finance swaps on a large scale, it can fuel inflation.

Direct debt buy-backs on the secondary market avoid these shortcomings. If debt is trading at 36 cents on the dollar, for example – as was Philippine debt in March 1989 – then a dollar devoted to repurchase of debt would clearly reduce future obligations more than a dollar devoted to debt service (which is equivalent to repurchasing debt at face value). The creditor banks have attempted to block such buy-backs for obvious 'moral-hazard' reasons: if countries can buy their own debt at a discount, they have an incentive to withhold debt service so as to drive down its value. Hence the clauses in rescheduling agreements prohibiting debt repurchases and requiring *pro rata* sharing of any debt payments among all the creditor banks.

This curious arrangement – whereby one party is excluded from participating in an otherwise open market – invites creative responses. One possibility is for debtor countries to buy each other's debt on the secondary market and then swap it.[45] But even direct buy-backs are possible, as the Bolivian government demonstrated in 1987–88 when it repurchased roughly half of its commercial bank debt at an average price of 11 cents on the dollar. Sixty of the country's 130 creditor banks accepted the terms of the buy-back, including the Bank of America, which chaired Bolivia's bank advisory committee.[46]

The banks sought to depict the Bolivian buy-back as a one-time-only special deal, but in retrospect it looks more like a precedent. In 1989, reports

The Economist of London, Third World countries quietly repurchased some $30 billion of their foreign debt in secondary markets.[47]

From the debtor's standpoint, a buy-back clearly is a better use of scarce resources than paying interest, but its advantages are less clear if the alternative use of resources is investment or consumption. Moreover, the buy-back may result in an increase in the secondary market valuation of the remaining debt, partially or wholly offsetting the reduction in the market value of debt outstanding. For these reasons, Bulow and Rogoff (1988) conclude that debtor countries should agree to buy-backs only when they receive new loans to cover part of the cost or gain other substantial concessions from their creditors.

Selective Disengagement

A third option is selective disengagement: a decision to honor some debts, but to repudiate others. The primary political and legal basis for selectivity lies in the uses to which the loans in question were put.

As documented above, upper-class Filipinos accumulated large-scale private external assets in the same decades in which the country accumulated its public external debt. Econometric as well as anecdotal evidence indicates that the two phenomena in many cases were causally linked through a financial revolving door. As Diaz-Alejandro (1984, p. 379) observed in Latin America, 'this situation reduces the political legitimacy of efforts to service the external debt'. It also raises the possibility of legal challenges to continued debt service.

Debtor country governments and their citizens might well ask why they should bear the cost of repayment of debts not of their making, from which they derived no benefit. Rather than continue to service the entire debt, debtor countries might instruct the creditors to seek repayment from the owners of the private external assets which are the real counterpart of a substantial component of the public external debt.

The compulsory mobilization of foreign private assets for debt service has been proposed by Felix (1985), who argues that creditor banks and governments might collaborate in this unorthodox endeavor so as to collateralize otherwise uncollectible debts. Pastor (1990) notes the practical problems of implementing such a plan: the identification of assets, the banks' reluctance to damage relations with private clients, and the political resistance from holders of foreign assets. In addition, unless such a plan were implemented on a world-wide scale, it could be evaded by shifting assets to safe-haven countries.

Debtor nations could, however, capitalize on the debt-flight connection in another way. Rather than seeking to recapture the flown capital, either by luring it home (which, as Pastor notes, amounts to ceding veto power over national economic policy to wealthy elites) or by impounding it abroad, governments could tell their creditors: Resources permitting, we will scrupulously repay all loans or portions thereof which were used for *bona fide* investment or consumption in our country. However, until such time as you furnish proof of such use, we shall assume no obligation to repay.

Such a move could claim a legal basis in the 'doctrine of odious debt', which holds that for sovereign debt:

> An interest which a creditor possesses in a debt must, in order to constitute an acquired right protected by international law, be an interest in funds utilized for the needs and interests of the State. Any debts contracted for other purposes is a debt intrinsically 'hostile to the interests of the territory'.   (O'Connell, 1967, p. 459)

The landmark application of this doctrine occurred nearly a century ago, in 1898, when the United States seized control of the Philippines and Cuba in the Spanish-American War. At issue was the Cuban external debt accumulated under Spanish rule. At the Paris peace conference, the US authorities contended that this debt had not been incurred for the benefit of the Cuban people, that it had been contracted without their consent, that the creditors must have appreciated that the purpose of the loans was to finance 'the continuous effort to put down a people struggling for freedom from the Spanish rule', and that 'the creditors, from the beginning, took the chances of the investment'.[48]

The legal circumstances under which the doctrine of odious debt can be applied are far from unambiguous. In particular, there is considerable room for different interpretations as to whether and to what extent its application requires proof that the creditor was aware of the ultimate use of the loan proceeds.[49] 'On this topic politics assume dominance over legal analysis', O'Connell (1967, p. 460) concludes, 'and for this reason the only exact test of whether or not a debt is odious is the extent to which it is unbeneficial to the population of the territory it burdens'.

The debts foisted upon the Philippine government via debt-fueled capital flight and flight-fueled external borrowing were unquestionably 'unbeneficial to the population'. The same argument could be advanced regarding some debts incurred for other purposes, for example, the construction of the Bataan nuclear power plant. Hence there is considerable scope for legal and political challenges to the legitimacy of a significant fraction of the country's external debt.

Outright Default

A final option is outright default. In its most naked form, this means informing creditors that debts will not be repaid. The attraction of such a policy is that it would immediately halt the hemorrhage of national income and foreign exchange in the negative net transfer. The drawback is the possibility of retaliation, not so much from private commercial creditors as from their governments.

Kaletsky (1985, p. 45) points out the important differences between such naked repudiation and more conciliatory forms of default, in which the country ceases or curtails debt payments without announcing that it never intends to repay:

> A conciliatory default would be like a slow leak in the banks' balance sheets; it could be patched up with profit retentions and reserve additions for long enough to keep the banking system afloat. A repudiation, by contrast, would be like an explosion below decks: it would blow a hole right through the center of the banks' capital structure.

In terms of minimizing the likelihood of retaliation, the former has much to recommend it.

Here too there is room for selectivity. Although the net transfer has turned negative in the aggregate, some individual (official) creditors continue to provide new money in excess of the interest and amortization payments they receive. In other respects as well, the retaliatory capabilities of some official creditors exceed those of private commercial banks. Hence a country may choose to default upon only the private subset of its total external debt.

There is ample historical precedent for one or another variant of the default option. 'For at least five hundred years', Kaletsky remarks, 'governments and nations have regularly defaulted on their foreign debts'.[50] Yet it has not been exercised in the current international debt crisis. A number of reasons for this have been advanced. MacEwan (1990, pp. 113–15) cites the availability of rescheduling alternatives, the benefits which ruling elites derive from the imposition of austerity measures on the working classes (while themselves evading the consequences by holding foreign assets), and the integration of these elites as 'junior partners' in the international economic power structure.

Magee and Brock (1986, p. 190) argue that ruling elites accede to creditor demands in order to safeguard their own external assets, and that this helps to explain the banks' collaboration in capital flight:

> The strategy of all banks is not to lend to projects that have the highest expected return, but to individuals or groups with the greatest likelihood of repaying. This practice encourages redistributive loans to "flight capitalists" rather than to LDC [less developed country] capital development: collateral outside of the LDC is safer than capital inside it.

Magee and Brock (p. 186) maintain that even though private external assets cannot be seized by the banks in the event of a public sector default, they can be 'tied up legally so that their owners cannot use them'. The validity of this claim is rather doubtful, however.[51]

More plausibly, Sachs (1988, p. 710), like Kaletsky, emphasizes 'fear of a foreign policy rupture with the United States'. This again brings politics – within the debtor and creditor countries and between them – to center stage. The Reagan administration's debt policy, Sachs remarks, was built around the single goal of preventing write-downs which 'might threaten the survival of the current management of even one or two of the most heavily exposed banks'. Other conceptions of the US national interest are readily conceivable, however, as evidenced by the earlier example of President Franklin D. Roosevelt who in 1943 not only accepted a Bolivian default, but also apologized to the President of Bolivia for 'some Americans [who] sold to the Bolivian government through supersalesmanship the idea that it needed a loan'.[52]

Who Should Forgive Whom?

The case for a tougher debt strategy, including selective repudiation of debts in which 'the creditor was negligent or was not acting in good faith when the loan was granted', was considered in the 'Yellow Paper' prepared by a team of leading Filipino economists immediately after the February revolution (Alburo *et al.*, 1986, pp. 46–9). Concerning the possibility of reprisals, such as a cut-off of trade credits, in response to such a strategy, they noted that 'public opinion, both local and global, may be the critical determinant', and may provide 'the best deterrent against lethal retaliation'.

The analysis of the Philippine external debt presented above suggests that a compelling case for disengagement could be put before the court of world opinion.

In a lawsuit filed against ex-president Marcos in US District Court in California, the Aquino government's Presidential Commission on Good Government characterized the former government under Marcos as a 'RICO [Racketeer Influenced and Corrupt Organizations] enterprise' as defined in the US criminal code.[53] If this is a tenable characterization of the Marcos regime, then it is reasonable to ask whether the repayment of loans contracted or guaranteed by that regime should now be the responsibility of the Filipino people.

It is not a question of debt 'forgiveness', but of the legitimacy of the debt itself. Indeed, those Filipinos who saw their real incomes decline in the years of debt-driven growth and their aftermath may well ask who should forgive whom.

Selective disengagement is, by its very nature, a flexible debt-management strategy which does not exclude dutiful debt service in some cases, debt buy-backs in others, or outright default as a last resort. An advantage of selective disengagement over other options is that it focuses political and public attention on the uses to which loans were put, and thereby fosters a broader awareness of the pitfalls of a debt-for-development strategy. If this awareness enables the country to resist the temptations of a positive net transfer at some future date when the present crisis has passed, then the debt tragedy will have had at least one redeeming feature.

CONCLUSIONS

The Philippines, like many Asian, African, and Latin American countries, accumulated a massive external debt in recent decades. Until 1983 the country received positive net transfers: Inflows of new money exceeded amortization and interest payments on past debt. Since then, however, the net transfer has turned negative, forcing the country to live 'below its means' in order to service the accumulated debt.

The extent to which the majority of Filipinos benefitted from the country's foreign borrowing is open to serious question. During the era of positive net transfers, the borrowing helped to finance a persistent current account deficit, but interest payments on the debt itself were an important component of the deficit, and luxury imports absorbed part of the remainder. The borrowing financed some investment, but much of it was so inefficient that the short-run impact on output growth appears to have been negative. Foreign borrowing also financed large-scale capital flight, and by 1986 the cumulative stock of externally held assets was equivalent to 70 per cent of the country's outstanding external debt. The borrowing also helped to sustain the political regime which presided over this state of affairs.

Although national income per capita rose during the stage of positive net transfers, the real incomes of millions of Filipinos declined, as documented elsewhere in this book. At the same time, the real incomes of many wealthy Filipinos rose. Much of this increased wealth flowed abroad, either to escape the political and economic climate engendered by the Marcos regime or, in the case of crony capital, to ensure a pleasant retirement should the climate change.

While the benefits of the positive net transfer proved illusory for many Filipinos, the costs of the negative net transfer have been all too apparent. In the first three years of the Aquino administration, the net transfer from the Philippines – that is, payments of debt service in excess of new lending – amounted to $4.7 billion. By 1988 the net transfer had risen to $2 billion, equivalent to six per cent of the country's gross national product (World Bank, 1990, p. 310). This required what are euphemistically termed 'adjustments': domestic consumption and investment had to be curtailed to free resources for debt service. The payments were not sufficient to make a dent in the total principal owed; on the contrary, external debt outstanding crept upwards to $29.4 billion by the end of 1988.

The negative net transfer can be expected to continue indefinitely, unless temporary relief arrives in the form of a massive infusion of new lending (implying in turn still larger debt service obligations in the future) or a more permanent solution is achieved by means of an alternative debt management strategy.

NOTES

1. Edwards (1987) notes that large capital inflows in response to capital-account liberalization can trigger real appreciation, adversely affecting profitability in the tradeable goods sector. Capital-account liberalization is neither necessary nor sufficient for this result.

2. In reality, of course, all else was not equal. Import expenditures (as well as capital flight and debt service) reduced the supply of foreign exchange. Commenting on the relatively modest exchange rate appreciation between 1970 and 1983, Dohner and Intal (1989, p. 449) state that 'the Philippines avoided the significant currency overvaluation that characterized many of the LDC borrowers'. They argue that heavy spending on capital goods imports prevented sharper appreciation of the currency. If the demand for foreign exchange were taken as given, however, there can be no doubt that foreign borrowing caused significant

overvaluation *relative to a counterfactual situation of no borrowing.* That such demand cannot be taken as given is precisely the point of the argument presented here.

3.   See Table 9.1, recalling the balance-of-payments convention that a negative sign indicates additions to reserves.

4.   See p. 256–7, above.

5.   Wallich (1984) uses this phrase in a discussion of the United States balance of payments. A number of writers have put forward variants of this capital account-led view of the US trade deficit in the 1980s. One variant is the 'safe-haven' model developed by Dooley and Isard (1986, 1987), in which capital flows from developing countries in response to variations in relative after-'tax' rates of return. Branson (1985, p. 50) notes that the safe-haven explanation for the rise in the US dollar is based on a shift in the supply of funds to the US, and adduces from the rise in real interest rates in the 1980s that 'the dominant effect must have come from the demand side'. In the case of the Third World debt in the 1970s, by contrast, the behavior of real interest rates supports the view that the supply side dominated. See also Marris (1985, pp. 28–29), and Hooper and Mann (1987, pp. 9–11). The potential (if not inevitable) leading role of capital movements was quite clearly recognized in an earlier era, when US economists argued against European repayment of postwar capital inflows from the US on the grounds that, as 'the balance of trade and service transactions adjusted to accommodate the change in investment items' (Lary, 1946, p. 678), domestic production and full employment would be undermined; for discussion, see Payer (1991, Ch. 4). For an analysis of the role of capital account movements in the behavior of current accounts in Latin America, see Pastor (1989).

6.   Remolona, Mangahas and Pante (1985, p. 24). The duality was nicely captured by Finance Minister Cesar Virata (1984, pp. 272–3), who asserted that 'the problem of external indebtedness has arisen largely from the desires and plans of the developing countries to move ahead' by boosting investment, but then conceded: 'It is probably true that things got out of hand in a number of instances because of the relative ease of obtaining finance from the commercial market.'

7.   Jeepneys, which seat 15–20 passengers, accounted for a rising share of public transportation; their number grew from 22,556 in 1962 to 57,961 in 1985 (NEDA, 1976, p. 298; 1986, p. 508).

8.   Quoted in Broad (1988, p. 197). 'To paraphrase top Philippine technocrats', Broad adds, 'the dollar amount of the debt was irrelevant, for the loans were being channeled into productive export-oriented industrialization'.

9.   The results have been mixed. See, for example, Papanek (1972), Weisskopf (1972), Chenery and Carter (1973), Bornschier, Chase-Dunn and Rubinson (1978), Mosley (1980), and, for a survey, Riddell (1987, Ch.10).

10. The ICOR data in Table 11.2, taken from Remolona, Mangahas and Pante (1985), differ in magnitude from those implicit in the final column of Table 2.6 in this book. The two sets of estimates are fairly consistent, however, in their year-to-year variations.

11. The crisis year 1983 is omitted from these correlations because of the exceptionally high ICOR in that year.

12. In effect, the premium is traded against the concessional component of the credit. 'Interlocking factor markets' (Bardhan, 1984, Chapter 12) thus are not confined to agriculture.

13. Examples have been presented above in the cases of agricultural mechanization in rice (Chapter 5) and sugarcane (Chapter 7). For a discussion of the employment effects of exchange-rate overvaluation, see Oshima, de Borja and Paz (1986, pp. 168–9).

14. The correlation between debt inflows and capital flight by 'measure A' (from Table 10.5) is 0.77, when both variables are expressed in constant 1986 dollars to eliminate the effects of inflation. The correlation between debt inflows and capital flight by 'measure B' is 0.69.

15. Conesa (1987, p. 55) advances this explanation for his finding of a positive association between capital flight and debt disbursements in Argentina and Mexico: 'The excessive supply of credit to a country without an adequate and efficiently implemented growth strategy only overvalues national currency and acts as a provider of counterpart funds for local citizens who then deposit their money abroad'. Duwendag (1987, p. 25) advances this and other debt-driven mechanisms to explain a positive correlation between foreign borrowing and capital flight.

16. For a model incorporating this possibility, see Diwan (1989).

17. The phenomenon of 'wealthy businessmen, bankrupt businesses' was not unique to the Philippines; see Maxfield (1989, pp. 76–78) on Latin America.

18. In some cases, residents are permitted to hold dollar-denominated assets domestically. The protection against inflation afforded by dollar-indexed instruments is often incomplete, however, as demonstrated for example in Mexico in 1982 (see Zedillo, 1987, p. 182). Moreover, other risks such as internal debt repudiation are not mitigated by mere dollarization.

19. This decree remained in force under the Aquino government. Describing this provision as 'one of the onerous impositions on the Philippine government in exchange for loan availments', Senators Jovito Salonga and Alberto Romulo filed an act in August 1988 which sought to amend the decree, so as to subject appropriations for the servicing of debts and guarantees incurred under the Marcos regime to annual Congressional approval (Senate Bill No. 702, 5 August 1988).

20. Lansky's clients also reaped a fringe benefit: interest payments on the 'loans' were tax-deductible (Naylor, 1987, pp. 21–2).

21. In practice, financial laundry services can be costly. For discussion, see Walter (1987, pp. 105–9, 119–20). One European banker estimates that much of the $600 billion deposited by foreigners in Swiss banks receives

negative interest returns, implying that depositors 'were willing to pay a substantial premium for security' (Lessard and Williamson, eds, 1987, p. 83).

22.   Similar ambiguity surrounds the use of the verb 'finance', as, for example, in the statement that 'large external debt increases have been used to finance the private accumulation of foreign assets' (Gulati, 1988, p. 168). In domestic contexts the verb 'finance' means providing resources, usually on credit, as when an individual obtains a mortgage to finance the purchase of a house. The above passage therefore may appear to refer to debt-fueled capital flight. In this instance, however, the author means something else: 'Central banks have been borrowing abroad and *selling* foreign currency to domestic residents who simply purchase external assets with the obtained foreign exchange' (Gulati, 1988, p. 169; emphasis added). This scenario may represent debt-driven capital flight (if motivated by economic and political circumstances attributable to the debt itself), but it is not debt-fueled by our definition since domestic resources are exchanged for the hard currency.

23.   Pedro-Pablo Kuczynski, Co-Chairman of First Boston International, in Lessard and Williamson, eds (1987, p. 192).

24.   Note that debt-fueled capital flight is not necessarily redeposited in the same bank which lent the money. Moreover, it is conceivable that officers in a bank's lending division could operate in ignorance of the deposit-taking activities of the same bank's 'international private banking' division. Thus, in reply to the allegation that his bank facilitated capital flight through the provision of 'private banking' services to residents of major debtor countries, a senior research officer of Morgan Guaranty Trust Company 'protested his ignorance of the actions of other parts of the bank and averred that Morgan would compete in whatever banking field it was legal to do so' (Lessard and Williamson, eds, 1987, pp. 198–9).

25.   Official minutes of the testimony of Rosendo Bondoc before the House of Representatives Subcommittee on Monetary, Credit and Financial Matters, 2 October 1987, pp. VII–1, VIII–4, and IX–1.

26.   J. R. Tengco, Jr., 'Memorandum for His Excellency, President Ferdinand E. Marcos, Thru Prime Minister Cesar E. A. Virata, Subject: Action Program for the Rehabilitation of DBP', 25 November 1983. For discussion of behest loans and guarantees, see also Reyes and Reyes-Cantos (1989); Dohner and Intal (1989, pp. 427–9, 499–501); and Haggard (1990, pp. 234–40).

27.   Jose Mari Velez, quoted in WGBH Educational Foundation (1987).

28.   Interview with a senior Central Bank official, May 1988, anonymity requested.

29.   Quoted by Wideman (1976). McCoy (1984, pp. 27–8) similarly reported that 'the Japanese contractors pay a minimum 10 per cent kickback on their machinery'. In some cases, the Central Bank may have deliberately looked the other way. McCoy (1984, p. 31) reports that a Governor of the

Central Bank resigned 'when it was discovered that his office had been accepting "commissions" from borrowers for approving their loans'.

30. Quoted by Crittenden (1978). The Philippine nuclear plant was the largest deal the Export-Import Bank had backed anywhere in the world; Casey personally approved it after a visit to Manila, despite a US Embassy report to Washington cautioning that the price was inflated and that there were reports of payoffs (Butterfield, 1986).

31. See, for example, Conesa (1987). Note that this expectation is unambiguous only for private owners of capital. In the hypothetical case in which public officials engage in capital flight by diverting resources from government coffers, higher reserves might permit *more* capital flight.

32. Some analysts (e.g., Cuddington, 1987, p. 90) have used a real effective exchange rate variable as an additional determinant of capital flight, taking upward movements to indicate an 'expectation that the domestic currency is soon to be devalued'. This entails the assumption that there exists an equilibrium exchange rate which persists through time. There is no tenable basis for such an assumption. Upward movements in the real effective exchange rate could occur owing to upward shifts in the equilibrium rate itself. For this reason, the level of official reserves would seem to be a more appropriate indicator of expected devaluation.

33. Measure A, derived by the residual method, has the potential drawback that any measurement errors in the debt variable would be passed on to the capital flight variable, potentially giving rise to a spurious correlation. The results obtained using measure B can thus be regarded as a check on those obtained using the broader measure.

34. Lagrange multiplier tests for second – and third-order residual serial correlation, Ramsey's RESET test for functional form mis-specification, and LM tests for normality and heteroscedasticity (see Pesaran and Pesaran, 1987) were also performed.

35. Third-order autoregressive error models, estimated by the Cochrane-Orcutt method, gave similar results with the difference that the estimated coefficient on $GDPGR_1$ remained moderately significant (and negative).

36. Conesa (1987) and Cuddington (1987) report a positive correlation between debt disbursements and capital flight in Mexico, Argentina, and Uruguay.

37. Pastor (1990, pp. 11–12). The countries with controls were Brazil, Chile, Colombia, and Peru; those without controls were Argentina, Mexico, Uruguay, and Venezuela.

38. The link between foreign borrowing and the growth of the state sector was a characteristic feature of the 'indebted industrialization' policies pursued by a number of Third World countries in this period; see Frieden (1981).

39. This is the title of a 1983 embassy cable dealing with the Development Bank of the Philippines, the Philippine National Bank, the National Development Company, and their client companies. 'Creeping State Capitalism in the Philippines', Airgram from the US embassy to the

Department of State, 83 Manila A–008, April 6, 1983 (declassified). The author is grateful to the National Security Archive (1775 Massachusetts Avenue, Washington, DC 20036) for providing this document.

40. World Bank (1989a, p. iii). The World Bank (1984, p. 47) emphasized this prospect from the outset of the Philippine debt crisis: 'One of the main objectives of the Government's adjustment efforts will have to be to improve the country's creditworthiness'.

41. Short-term credit lines (trade credits and inter-bank deposits) slipped from $15 billion at the outset of the moratorium to $13.5 billion near the end. In addition, interest rate spreads on these credits may have risen somewhat above their pre-moratorium level. These costs pale when compared to the benefit of $6 billion per year in suspended interest payments alone.

42. Griffith-Jones (1988, p. 360) observes: 'The Peruvian experience has shown that after two years of unilateral action no legal response has come from the creditor banks to confiscate assets or other drastic measures; the only "cost" of the unilateral action, as regards creditor banks, has been their curtailment of short-term credit lines'.

43. The terms 'creditor country' and 'debtor country' here refer to the bilateral relationship between a borrower government and its private and official external creditors. The United States, for example, is a 'creditor country' *vis-à-vis* the Philippines despite being the world's largest debtor country.

44. For a view from General Motors Corporation, see Whitman (1987). Berg (1988) presents an empirical analysis indicating that 11 per cent of the US trade deficit in 1985 was attributable to debt-related austerity measures in five major Third World countries, including the Philippines, and that these caused a 0.5 per cent decrease in US GNP. For a discussion of the so-called Bradley Plan, a debt initiative sponsored by a US Senator representing a heavily industrial state, see Dornbusch (1986).

45. In May 1990 Brazil and Bolivia agreed that Bolivia would buy Brazilian debt with $300 million face value on the secondary market (at 25.5 to 27.5 cents on the dollar) to exchange for Bolivian debt held by Brazil (Truell, 1990).

46. For details, see Whitelaw (1987), Truell (1988), Sachs (1988), and 'Bolivia Buys Back $334 Million of Debt', *The Wall Street Journal*, 11 August 1988.

47. 'Brady's Bazaar', *The Economist*, 12 May 1990, p. 77. For example, Costa Rica reached an agreement in 1989 to repurchase more than 60 per cent of its $1.8 billion commercial bank debt at 16 cents on the dollar; see Saborio (1990) and Blustein (1989).

48. Quoted in O'Connell (1967, pp. 459–60) and Hoeflich (1982, pp. 53–55).

49. O'Connell (1967, p. 459) states that this is a 'dangerous' doctrine, which if not limited 'tends to be expanded as States seek a pretext for avoiding obligations which otherwise would be imposed upon them', and notes

that one legal authority suggests that to justify its invocation a successor state 'should be required to prove, first, that the debt was contrary to the interests of the population of all or part of the absorbed territory and, secondly, that the creditors were aware of this. Once these two things have been proved . . . the onus is upon the creditors to show that the funds have in fact been utilized for the benefit of the territory'. Citing the same authority, however, Frankenberg and Knieper (1984, p. 434) argue that the burden of proof should fall upon the creditor: '[T]he creditor (or supplier) would first have to show evidence that the credit (or supply) was used or was supposed to be used in the debtor country's national (developmental) interest.'

50. Kaletsky (1985, p. 1). For reviews of historical default experiences, see Fishlow (1985), Eichengreen and Portes (1986), and Felix (1987).
51. As an example the authors cite the freezing of Iranian assets by the United States in 1979. But this exceptional action applied only to Iranian *government* assets, not to the private assets of Iranian nationals (for details, see Gwertzman, 1979).
52. Cited by Kaletsky (1985, p. 90), quoting an account which appeared in *The New York Times* on 8 May 1943.
53. *The Republic of the Philippines v. Ferdinand E. Marcos et al.*, Case No. CIV 86–3859, filed before the United States District Court, Central District of California, 16 June, 1986, p. 13.

12 Conclusions

If the central aim of economic development is the reduction of poverty, then the Philippine development strategy in the Marcos era was an abysmal failure. Poverty deepened despite a modest increase in average national income, demonstrating that immiserizing growth is not merely a theoretical possibility.

Even by the narrower objective of economic growth, the Philippine strategy could not claim great success. Growth was slow compared to that in other East and Southeast Asian countries, and by the mid-1980s it was grinding to a halt. The low purchasing power of the poor depressed the market for rice, choking off growth in the country's most important crop. Deteriorating terms of trade and the predations of the Marcos regime crippled export agriculture. The nation's once-plentiful forest resources were nearing depletion. And the country had entered the stage of negative net transfers to its international creditors, forcing the Filipino people to live 'below their means' for the indefinite future.

These adverse developments did not unfold in an isolated backwater of the world economy, deprived of the modernizing influences of technocratic expertise and foreign capital. Quite the contrary. The three central elements of the government's development strategy – the 'green revolution' in rice agriculture, continued growth in agricultural and forestry exports, and massive external borrowing – received strong support, both intellectual and financial, from international officialdom. The private sector was equally enthusiastic; as Dohner and Intal (1989, p. 373) remark, 'the Philippine desk became a path for rapid advancement within the international divisions of many commercial banks'. The failure of the Philippine development strategy thus was also a failure of the international development establishment.

The Philippines experienced immiserizing growth not only in the descriptive sense that growth and impoverishment proceeded at the same time, but also in the causal sense that the two processes were closely intertwined. The income gains from the green revolution, agricultural and forestry exports, and foreign borrowing accrued disproportionately to the wealthiest strata of the population. As income inequalities widened, the balance of power shifted correspondingly, setting the stage for further economic polarization and absolute impoverishment.

The new rice technology increased output, but failed to bring a substantial reduction in poverty. Higher rice yields saved land for export crops and saved foreign exchange for non-rice imports, but neither saving was mobilized to benefit the poor. Within the rice sector income became concentrated in the hands of new producer and commercial elites, who extracted surplus from those who actually tilled the soil. Initial employment gains for rice laborers were soon reversed by the introduction of labor-saving machinery and herbicides, which were privately profitable but socially of questionable net benefit.

Export agriculture and forestry, the traditional economic mainstays of the ruling elite, failed to provide an engine for economic growth. Export prices suffered from pervasive 'imperfections' in world markets, including protection for industrialized-country farmers, oligopsonistic market structures, and competition from synthetic substitutes whose prices omit the external costs of pollution. Output gains were offset by declining terms of trade. Meanwhile the relations of production and exchange within export agriculture systematically concentrated income in a few hands. The coconut and sugar monopsonies stand as classic examples of the use of political power to expand market power. In the forestry sector, political power was similarly deployed to appropriate public resources for private gain, squandering a valuable natural inheritance and imposing high social costs on current and future generations.

Foreign borrowing financed too little genuinely productive investment and too much capital flight. A financial revolving door spun billions of dollars in public external debts and private external assets. Capital flight eroded the quality as well as the quantity of domestic investment, since the investment was often merely a pretext for obtaining foreign loans with the aim of diverting a percentage to safe havens abroad. The most striking monument to this wasteful charade is the Bataan nuclear power plant, built at a cost of more than $2 billion, which never generated a kilowatt of electricity. Because borrowings were not invested to yield a rate of return at least equal to the interest rate in hard currency, the Philippines today has a lower income, net of debt service payments and new money inflows, than if the country had never borrowed a cent. Ironically, but not surprisingly, the resulting austerity measures have fallen most heavily on those who benefitted least from past borrowing.

The failure of the Philippine development strategy starkly illuminates two core misconceptions common not only to the technocrats of the Marcos era, but to much of contemporary social science. The first concerns the market, the second the state.

The starting point for orthodox economic theory is a world of complete and perfect markets underpinned by secure property rights. Given individual preferences, technology, and the initial distribution of endowments, voluntary market exchanges yield an 'efficient' outcome in the specific sense that no one can be made better off without making someone else worse off. This is the celebrated fable of the invisible hand.

A complementary political theory lurks in the background, although it is seldom explicitly stated. Its starting point is an impartial and omnipotent state. This idealized state remains curiously untouched by the individual self-interest which animates the market; instead it exists only to promote the public interest. The state's appropriate functions are limited but absolutely crucial. It guarantees the sanctity of property rights and contractual exchange. It redresses market failures through the provision of public goods and the internalization of externalities. It remedies market imperfections by preventing the exercise of market power and correcting for individual myopia. The invisible hand of the market wears the visible glove of the state.

Imagine how the Philippine development strategy might have fared in this imaginary world. The new rice technology would have reduced income inequalities among both consumers and producers. Farm laborers would have benefitted from higher employment, or higher wages, or both. Efficiently managed export agriculture and forestry would have brought the blessings of comparative advantage in international trade. External borrowing would have augmented domestic savings, bringing higher rates of productive investment and more rapid growth. The net result would have been sustained growth of national income, in which most if not all Filipinos would have shared.

Whatever its charm in the rarified atmosphere of pure theory, the orthodox hand-and-glove fable is woefully unsatisfactory as a guide to economic reality. Real-world markets are seldom perfect or complete, and the property rights which underpin them are never absolutely secure. Real-world states are neither impartial nor omnipotent. Instead, market failures arising from public goods and externalities abound. Market imperfections are the rule, not the exception. Property rights are contested. And the state is an arena in which divergent private interests battle for advantage.

If we follow the logic of self-interest to its conclusion, we can predict that whenever individuals, groups, or classes have the power to benefit themselves at the expense of others, they will do so. Whenever profitable, they will seize other people's properties, appropriate public resources, inflict external costs on others, and reap above-normal profit through the exercise of market power. 'Rational' actors will pursue these socially injurious but privately profitable activities just as energetically as the socially beneficial ones of the invisible hand fable, equating their net private benefits at the margin.

The state does not stand apart from the resulting clash of private interests, impartially dispensing efficiency or justice. Contests among individuals, groups, and classes extend to attempts to control the government and to influence its policies. Hence there can be no guarantee that the state will promote the public interest; this is a comforting possibility, but by no means a foregone certainty. Instead, government interventions may deliberately benefit one party at the expense of all others.

The national and international technocrats who framed the Philippine development strategy assumed that the fable of the invisible hand and the visible glove provides a workable model of the market and the state. Their strategy foundered in the end on the political and economic realities of a profoundly inequitable social order. The technocrats were not unaware of the extreme income disparities in the Philippines, nor could they fail to perceive the absence of meaningful democracy. They refused, however, to face the implications of economic inequity and political authoritarianism.

A Filipino businessman explained the technocratic *modus operandi* to the US ambassador in 1980. He termed Finance Minister Cesar Virata 'number one among the technocrats', while characterizing sugar czar Roberto Benedicto as a 'purely political' appointee:

> He described the President [Marcos] as the hub of a wheel whose spokes go out to such diverse personalities as Virata and Benedicto, whom the President uses for very different purposes. The spokes never touch except through the President. If the Benedicto and Virata spokes did touch, Virata would resign.[1]

Although the technocrats could erect tenuous personal shields against the unsavory realities of the country's political economy, no such insulation guarded the virtue of their development strategy.[2]

Free from the restraints of a more equitable distribution of wealth and power, the Philippine ruling elite single-mindedly followed the maxim of the orthodox economist: they pursued their self-interest.[3] In this quest they benefitted greatly from the support of external powers, notably the United States government, whose foreign policy elevated 'anti-communism' and hospitality to US military bases above all else. In pursuing their self-interest, the Philippine rulers and their foreign patrons not only failed to promote the public interest of the Filipino people, they trampled upon it.

The history of the Philippines demonstrates that interactions between wealth and power can set in motion a cumulative process of economic and political polarization. In the absence of countervailing forces, political economy would be a dismal science indeed. Initial disparities would inexorably widen as the rich and powerful used their power to become richer, more powerful, and richer still, until finally the poor would be reduced to bare subsistence.

History also demonstrates, however, that wealth is not the only source of power. The vicious circle is not closed. The Philippine 'people's power' revolution of February 1986, which drove Marcos to his involuntary retirement, bore testament to the fact that popular mobilization can and sometimes does counter the power of accumulated wealth.

Yet the events of February 1986 did not alter several fundamental features of the Philippine political economy. The promise of a thorough land reform, which had enhanced Corazon Aquino's electoral appeal, receded like a mirage after she came to power. Rather than challenging the legitimacy of those external debts from which the Filipino people had derived no benefit, the new government chose the path of dutiful debt service, pursuing the chimera of a 'restoration of creditworthiness'. When the dust settled, the downfall of Marcos appeared to have brought little more than 'a shake in the kaleidoscope of oligarchic power'.[4]

The analysis of this book suggests that, far from being subject to a 'great trade-off', the goals of equity and efficiency are complementary in the Philippines. Only a more equitable distribution of wealth and power can prevent individuals from advancing their self-interest at the expense of the public interest. A comparison between the Philippines and its East Asian neighbors may be instructive in this regard: China, Japan, Korea, and Taiwan are not models of perfect egalitarianism, but after World War Two each had a redistributive land reform which broke the power of the landed oligarchy. In the Philippines this historic task has yet to be completed.

Our analysis also suggests that the current controversy over the relative merits of the market and the state is somewhat misplaced. In a highly inegalitarian society, neither the market nor the state can be expected to advance greatly the well-being of the poor, whereas in a less inimical setting both could play positive roles. The need to establish a more egalitarian social order implies a broader role for the state, however, than that envisaged in orthodox economic theory. The challenge is to create a state which is able to redistribute wealth and power, yet willing to do so only in the interests of the poor. In the Marcos-era Philippines, as in many times and places, the first condition held but not the second.

NOTES

1. Embassy of the United States of America, Manila, Philippines, 'Confidential Memorandum of Conversation. Participants: Washington Sycip [of] Sycip, Gorres and Velayo (SGV); Ambassador Richard W. Murphy; Edson W. Kempe, EC/COM Counselor. Time & Place: January 10, 1980, Ambassador Murphy's Office. Subject: Prospects for the Philippine Economy – An Overview', p. 4. This document was released to the author under the United States Freedom of Information Act.
2. On the relationships among Marcos, his cronies, and the technocrats, see also Stauffer (1979, pp. 189–91); Bello *et al.* (1982, Ch. 7); and Haggard (1990, pp. 216–19).
3. Mangahas (1986, p. 6) remarks: 'Explaining the many errors of economic management in the Marcos era is relatively simple once one assumes that the real objectives were perpetuation of power and accumulation of incredible wealth'. For a lucid discussion of the economic effects of political authoritarianism, see also De Dios *et al.* (1984, pp. 59–66).
4. Anderson (1988, p. 28). For an account of political developments in the first four years of the Aquino government, see Goodno (1991).

Bibliography of Works Cited

ABADILLA, D. C. (1987) 'The Coconut Jigsaw Puzzle', *Malaya*, 6 July, pp. 4–5.

ABDULLAH, A. A. (1980) 'Landlord and Rich Peasant under the Permanent Settlement', *Calcutta Historical Journal*, Vol. 4, No. 2, pp. 1–27 and Vol. 5, No. 1, pp. 89–154.

ADAMS, F. G. and BEHRMAN, J. R. (1982) *Commodity Exports and Economic Development: The Commodity Problem and Policy in Developing Countries*. Lexington: D. C. Heath.

AGARWAL, A. and NARAIN, S. (1990) *Global Warming in an Unequal World*. New Delhi: Centre for Science and Environment.

AGRICULTURAL POLICY and STRATEGY TEAM (1986) *Agenda for Action for the Philippine Rural Sector*. Manila: Univeristy of the Philippines at Los Banos Agricultural Policy Research Program and Philippine Institute for Development Studies, October. [The 'Green Paper'.]

AGUILAR, F., Jr. (1981) *Landlessness and Hired Labor in Philippine Rice Farms*. Swansea, U. K.: University College of Swansea, Centre for Development Studies, Monograph Series No. 14, September.

AGUILAR, F. V., Jr. (1982) *Social Forestry for Upland Development: Lessons from Four Case Studies*. Quezon City: Institute of Philippine Culture.

AGUILAR, F. V., Jr. (1984) *The Making of Cane Sugar: Poverty, Crisis and Change in Negros Occidental*. Bacolod: La Salle Social Research Center, Monograph Series No. 2.

AHLUWALIA, M. S. and CHENERY, H. (1974) 'The Economic Framework', in H. Chenery *et al.* (1974) *Redistribution with Growth*. Oxford: Oxford University Press, pp. 38–51.

ALANO, B. P., Jr. (1984) 'Import Smuggling in the Philippines: An Economic Analysis', *Journal of Philippine Development*, Vol. 11, No. 2, pp. 157–90.

ALBURO, F., *et al.* (1986) *Economic Recovery and Long-Run Growth: Agenda for Reforms*. Volume I: Main Report (the 'Yellow Paper'). Manila: Philippine Institute for Development Studies, 1 May.

ALBURO, F. and CANLAS, D. (1986) 'Balance of Payments, Output, and the IMF', Paper presented at the Conference on Development Alternatives and Prospects, Manila, 5–6 December.

ALBURO, F. and SHEPHERD, G. (1985) 'Trade Liberalization Experience in the Philippines, 1960–1984', Philippine Institute for Development Studies Working Paper No. 86–01, December.

ALFILER, F. R. (1986) 'An Analysis of the Onset of the Philippine Debt Crisis', *Central Bank Review*, Vol. 38, Nos. 1 & 2, pp. 22–4.

ALFONSO, F. B. (1983) 'Assisting Farmer Controlled Development of Communal Irrigation Systems', in D. C. Korten and F. B. Alfonso, eds., *Bureaucracy and the Poor: Closing the Gap*. West Hartford, Conn.: Kumarian Press, pp. 44–52.

ALIX, J. C. (1979) 'The Impact of the Masangana 99 Program on Small Farmer Production and Income in the Philippines', Paper presented to the FAO Workshop on Price and Income Support and Their Impact on the Small Farmers, Bangkok, 22–7 January.

ALVAREZ, J. B., Jr. (1987) 'DNR [Department of Natural Resources] Tenure Program in the Public Domain', Paper presented at the Workshop on the Accelerated Agrarian Reform Program, University of the Philippines, Diliman, 11–12 March.

AMSDEN, A. H. (1989) *Asia's Next Giant: South Korea and Late Industrialization*. New York: Oxford University Press.

ANDERSON, B. (1988) 'Cacique Democracy and the Philippines: Origins and Dreams', *New Left Review*, No. 169, May/June, pp. 3–31.

ANDERSON, J. N. (1987) 'Lands at Risk, People at Risk: Perspectives on Tropical Forest Transformations in the Philippines', in P. D. Little and M. M. Horowitz, eds., *Lands at Risk in the Third World: Local-level Perspectives*. Boulder: Westview, pp. 249–67.

ANDREI, M. T. (1986) 'Awaiting the Renaissance', *Asiabanking*, September, pp. 75–80.

ANTI-SLAVERY SOCIETY (1983) *The Philippines: Authoritarian Government, Multinationals and Ancestral Lands*. London: Anti-Slavery Society, Indigenous Peoples and Development Series, Report No. 1.

AQUINO, R. M., CASTILLO, R. A. DEL, and PAYUAN, E. V. (1987) 'Mounting a National Social Forestry Program: Lessons Learned from the Philippine Experience', Honolulu: East-West Center Environment and Policy Institute, Working Paper No. 87–9, May.

ASIAN DEVELOPMENT BANK (ADB) (1987) *A Review of Forestry and Forest Industries in the Asia Pacific Region*. Manila: ADB, Agriculture Department.

ADB (1988) *Key Indicators of Developing Member Countries of ADB*. Vol. 19. Manila: ADB, Economics Office, July.

BAGADION, B. U. (1988) 'The Evolution of the Policy Context: An Historical Overview', in Korten and Siy, eds., pp. 1–19.

BALAGOT, Q. M. and LIBRERO, A. R. (1975) 'Analysis of Agricultural Wage Rates in the Philippines', Bureau of Agricultural Economics Working Paper No. 10, December.

BALDWIN, R. E. (1975) *Foreign Trade Regimes and Economic Development: The Philippines*. New York: Columbia University Press for the National Bureau of Economic Research.

BALE, M. (1983) 'Philippines: Agricultural Trade Policies, Resource Flows and the Competitiveness of Agriculture', Washington: World Bank, CPD Discussion Paper No. 1983–19, December.

BALE, M. D. (1985) 'Agricultural Trade and Food Policy: The experience of five developing countries', Washington: World Bank Staff Working Paper No. 724.

BANK FOR INTERNATIONAL SETTLEMENTS (1984) *Fifty-Fourth Annual Report*. Basle: BIS, 18 June.

BANZON, J. A. and VELASCO, J. R. (1982) *Coconut Production and Utilization*. Manila: Philippine Coconut Research and Development Foundation.

BANZON-BAUTISTA, C. (1989) 'The Saudi Connection: Agrarian Change in a Pampangan Village, 1977–1984', in Hart, Turton, and White, eds., pp. 144–58.

BARAN, P. (1957) *The Political Economy of Growth*. New York: Monthly Review.

BARDHAN, P. K. (1984) *Land, Labor, and Rural Poverty: Essays in Development Economics*. New York: Columbia University Press.

BARDHAN, P. K. (1987) 'Poverty and "Trickle-Down" in Rural India: A Quantitative Analysis', in Mellor and Desai, eds., pp. 76–94.

BARKER, R. (1978) 'Barriers to Efficient Capital Investment in Agriculture', in T. W. Schultz, ed., *Distortions in Agricultural Incentives*. Bloomington: Indiana University Press, pp. 140–60.

BARKER, R. and CORDOVA, V. G. (1978) 'Labor Utilization in Rice Production', in International Rice Research Institute, pp. 113–36.

BARKER, R., COWARD, E. W., Jr., LEVINE, G. and SMALL, L. (1984) 'Irrigation Development in Asia: Past Trends and Future Directions', Ithaca: Cornell University, Center for International Studies, Cornell Studies in Irrigation No. 1, March.

BARKER, R., HERDT, R. W., and ROSE, B. (1985) *The Rice Economy of Asia*. Washington, D. C.: Resources for the Future; Manila: International Rice Research Institute.

BARTLETT, R. (1989) *Economics and Power: An Inquiry into Human Relations and Markets*. Cambridge: Cambridge University Press.

BASU, K. (1984) *The Less Developed Economy: A Critique of Contemporary Theory*. Oxford: Basil Blackwell.

BAUTISTA, G. M., THIESENHUSEN, W. C., and KING, D. J. (1983) 'Farm Households on Rice and Sugar Lands: Margen's Village Economy in Transition', in Ledesma, Makil, and Miralao, eds., pp. 73–92

BAUTISTA, R. M. (1987) 'Production Incentives in Philippine Agriculture: Effects of Trade and Exchange Rate Policies', Washington: International Food Policy Research Institute, Research Report No. 59, May.

BAUTISTA, R. M., POWER, J. H., *et al.* (1979) *Industrial Promotion Policies in the Philippines*. Makati: Philippine Institute for Development Studies.

BECKFORD, G. L. (1972) *Persistent Poverty: Underdevelopment in Plantation Economies of the Third World*. Oxford: Oxford University Press.

BELLO, W. *et al.* (1982) *Development Debacle: The World Bank in the Philippines*. San Francisco: Institute for Food and Development Policy.

BELLO, W., HAYES, P., and ZARSKY, L. (1979) '500 Mile Island:

The Philippine Nuclear Reactor Deal', *Pacific Research*, Vol. 10, No. 1, pp. 1–29.

BERG, G. C. (1988) 'The Effects of the External Debts of Mexico, Brazil, Argentina, Venezuela, and the Philippines on the United States', *Applied Economics*, Vol. 20, pp. 939–56.

BERRY, R. A. (1978) 'Income and Consumption Distribution Trends in the Philippines, 1950–1970', *Review of Income and Wealth*, Vol. 24, No. 3, pp. 313–31.

BERRY, R. A. and CLINE, W. R. (1979) *Agrarian Structure and Productivity in Developing Countries*. Baltimore: Johns Hopkins University Press.

BHAGWATI, J. N. (1958) 'Immiserizing Growth: A Geometrical Note', *Review of Economic Studies*, Vol. 25, No. 3, pp. 201–5.

BIGSTEN, A. (1988) 'Poverty, Inequality and Development', in N. Gemell, ed., *Surveys in Development Economics*. Oxford: Basil Blackwell, pp. 135–71.

BLUSTEIN, P. (1989) 'Costa Rica, Banks Said to Agree on Debt Plan,' *The Washington Post*, 27 October, p. G3.

BOADO, E. L. (1988) 'Incentive Policies and Forest Use in the Philippines', in R. Repetto and M. Gillis, eds., *Public Policies and the Misuse of Forest Resources*. Cambridge: Cambridge University Press, pp. 165–203.

BONNER, R. (1987) *Waltzing with a Dictator: The Marcoses and the Making of American Policy*. New York: Times Books.

BORLAGDAN, S. B. (1990) 'Social Forestry in Upland Cebu', in M. Poffenberger, ed., *Keepers of the Forest: Land Management Alternatives in Southeast Asia*. West Hartford: Kumarian Press, pp. 266–76.

BORLAUG, N. (1990) 'Setting the Grass Roots on Fire', *Newsletter from the International Center for Economic Growth* (Panama City), Vol. 4, No. 1, July, pp. 5–6.

BORNSCHIER, V., CHASE-DUNN, C., and RUBINSON, R. (1978) 'Cross-national Evidence of the Effects of Foreign Investment and Aid on Economic Growth and Inequality: A Survey of Findings and a Reanalysis', *American Journal of Sociology*, Vol. 84, No. 3, pp. 651–83.

BOSERUP, E. (1965) *The Conditions of Agricultural Growth: The Economics of Agrarian Change under Population Pressure*. London: George Allen & Unwin.

BOUIS, H. E. (1982) *Rice Policy in the Philippines*. Unpublished Ph.D. dissertation, Stanford University, Food Research Institute.

BOUIS, H. E. (1983) 'Seasonal Rice Price Variation in the Philippines: Measuring the Effects of Government Intervention', *Food Research Institute Studies*, Vol. 19, No. 1, pp. 81–92.

BOUIS, H. E. (1989) 'Measuring the Rate of Technological Change for Rice Production in the Philippines: Implications for Agricultural Policy under Economic Recovery', Washington: International Food Policy Research Intitute, mimeo.

BOWLES, S. (1985) 'The Production Process in a Competitive Economy', *American Economic Review*, Vol. 75, No. 1, pp. 16–36.

BOWLES, S. and EDWARDS, R. (1985) *Understanding Capitalism: Competition, Command, and Change in the US Economy*. New York: Harper & Row.

BOWLES, S. and GINTIS, H. (1988) 'Contested Exchange: Political Economy and Modern Economic Theory', *American Economic Review*, Vol. 78, No. 2, pp. 145–50.

BOWRING, P. (1981) 'The Poverty Puzzle', *Far Eastern Economic Review*, 27 March, pp. 125–31.

BOWRING, P. and SACERDOTI, G. (1983) 'Time for a Real Debate', *Far Eastern Economic Review*, June 9, pp. 54–66.

BOYCE, J. K. (1986) 'Kinked Exponential Models for Growth Rate Estimation', *Oxford Bulletin of Economics and Statistics*, Vol. 48, No. 4, pp. 385–91.

BOYCE, J. K. (1987) *Agrarian Impasse in Bengal: Institutional Constraints to Technological Change*. Oxford: Oxford University Press.

BOYCE, J. K. (1988) 'Technological and Institutional Alternatives in Asian Rice Irrigation', *Economic and Political Weekly* (Bombay), Vol. 23, No. 13, March, pp. A6-A22.

BOYCE, J. K. (1990) *The Political Economy of External Indebtedness: A Case Study of the Philippines*. Makati: Philippine Institute for Development Studies, Monograph Series No. 12.

BOYCE, J. K. (1991) 'Agricultural Development under State Planning: A Comment,' mimeo, to be published in T. J. Byres and D. Taylor, eds., *The State and Development Planning in India*. Oxford: Oxford University Press [forthcoming].

BOYCE, J. K. and ZARSKY, L. (1988) 'Capital Flight from the Philippines, 1962–1986', *Journal of Philippine Development*, Vol. 15, No. 2, pp. 191–222.

BOYCHUCK, R. (1987) 'Exodus of the Hungry: The Environmental Consequences of Rural Poverty in the Philippines', mimeo, London, September.

BRADFIELD, R. (1970) 'Increasing Food Production in the Tropics by Multiple Cropping', in D. G. Aldrich, Jr., ed., *Research for the World Food Crisis*. Washington: American Association for the Advancement of Science, Publication No. 92, pp. 229–42.

BRANSON, W. H. (1985) 'Causes of Appreciation and Volatility of the Dollar', in *The US Dollar -Recent Developments, Outlook, and Policy Options*, Symposium sponsored by the Federal Reserve Bank of Kansas City, pp. 33–52.

BRAVO, M. R., CORNISTA, L. B., and RAMOS, E. A. (1986) 'The Agrarian Situation in the Sugarlands', Paper presented at the Policy Workshop on Agrarian Reform, PCARRD Headquarters, Los Banos, December 4–6.

BRIONES, N. D. (1987) 'Mining Pollution: The Case of the Baguio Mining District, the Philippines', *Environmental Management*, Vol. 11, No. 3, pp. 335–44.

BROAD, R. (1980) '"Our Children Are Being Kidnapped!"' *Bulletin of Concerned Asian Scholars*, Vol. 12, No. 3, pp. 2–9.

BROAD, R. (1983) 'Beyond Philippine Policy Making: The Role of the World Bank and the International Monetary Fund'. Ph.D. dissertation, Woodrow Wilson School of Public and International Affairs, Princeton University, June.

BROAD, R. (1988) *Unequal Alliance, 1979–1986: The World Bank, the International Monetary Fund, and the Philippines*. Quezon City: Ateneo de Manila University Press; Berkeley: University of California Press.

BROAD, R. and CAVANAGH, J. (1989) 'Marcos's Ghost', *Amicus Journal* (Washington, D. C.: Natural Resources Defense Council), Vol. 11, No. 4, Fall, pp. 18–29.

BROMLEY, D. W. and CERNEA, M. M. (1989) 'The Management of Common Property Resources', Washington, D. C.: World Bank Discussion Paper No. 57.

BULOW, J. and ROGOFF, K. (1988) 'The Buyback Boondoggle', *Brookings Papers on Economic Activity* 2:1988, pp. 675–704.

BURBACH, R. and FLYNN, P. (1980) *Agribusiness in the Americas*. New York: Monthly Review Press.

BUTTERFIELD, F. (1986) 'Filipinos Say Marcos Was Given Millions for '76 Nuclear Contract', *The New York Times*, March 7.

BUTWELL, R. (1966) 'The Philippines: Changing of the Guard', *Asian Survey*, Vol. 6, No. 1.

CALDWELL, J. (1982) *Theory of Fertility Decline*. London: Academic Press.

CANLAS, D. B. (1985) 'The Balance of Payments Crisis and the Economy', *PIDS Development Research News*, Vol. 3, No. 2, March-April, pp. 1–5.

CANLAS, D. B. and ALBURO, F. A. (1989) 'Trade, Protectionism, and Vertical Integration in Agro-Industrial Processing: The Philippine Coconut Oil Industry', in J. T. L. Hoe and S. Sharma, eds., *Trade, Protectionism, and Industrial Adjustment in Vegetable Oils: Asian Responses to North America*. Singapore: Institute of Southeast Asian Studies, pp. 75–94.

CAPISTRANO, A. D. and FUJISAKA, S. (1984) 'Tenure, Technology, and Productivity of Agroforestry Schemes', Philippine Institute for Development Studies Working Paper No. 84–06.

CAREY, P. and ELLISON, K. (1985) 'How Smugglers Drain the Philippines', *San Jose Mercury News*, 27 October.

CASTILLO, G. T. (1975) *All in a Grain of Rice*. College, Laguna: Southeast Asian Regional Center for Graduate Study and Research in Agriculture.

CAUFIELD, C. (1985a) 'A Reporter at Large: The Rain Forests', *The New Yorker*, 14 January, pp. 41–101.

CAUFIELD, C. (1985b) *In the Rainforest*. New York: Knopf.

CENTRAL BANK OF THE PHILIPPINES (1973) *Statistical Appendix to the 25th Annual Report*. Manila.

CENTRAL BANK OF THE PHILIPPINES (1980) *Thirty-Second Statistical Bulletin, 1980: Statistical Appendix to Annual Report 1980*. Manila.

CERNOHOUS, Z. (1966) 'The Marketing of Agricultural Products in the Philippines', *Philippine Economic Journal*, Vol. 5, No. 1, pp. 64–94.

CHANDLER, R. F., Jr. (1975) 'Case History of IRRI's Research Management

During the Period 1960 to 1972', Taiwan: Asian Vegetable Research and Development Center.

CHANDLER, R. F., Jr. (1979) *Rice in the Tropics*. Boulder, Colorado: Westview.

CHAPMAN, W. (1987) 'Still Without Land: For Filipino. peasants, Aquino. brings no. change', *The Progressive*, Vol. 51, No. 6, June, pp. 26–8.

CHENERY, H. B. and Carter, N. G. (1973), 'Foreign Assistance and Development Performance, 1960–1970', *American Economic Review*, Vol. 63, No. 2, pp. 459–68.

CHENERY, H. B. and STROUT, A. M. (1966) 'Foreign Assistance and Economic Development', *American Economic Review*, September.

CLAD, J. (1988a) 'The Fragile Forests: Church Pastoral Letter Protests Against Despoliation', *Far Eastern Economic Review*, 25 February, p. 19.

CLAD, J. (1988b) 'Philippines: Poor Get Poorer', *Far Eastern Economic Review*, 18 August, p. 34.

CLAD, J. and VITUG, M. D. (1988) 'The Politics of Plunder: Palawan's Forests Appear Doomed in a Power Struggle', *Far Eastern Economic Review*, 24 November, pp. 48–52.

CLARETE, R. L. and ROUMASSET, J. A. (1983) 'An Analysis of the Economic Policies Affecting the Philippine Coconut Industry', Philippine Institute for Development Studies Working Paper 83–08.

COCHRANE, W. W. (1958) *Farm Prices: Myth and Reality.* Westport, Connecticut: Greenwood Press.

COLLINS, J. (1987) 'Philippine Land Reform: Cory's Broken Promise', *The Nation*, November 14, pp. 549–52.

COMMODITY RESEARCH BUREAU (1982) *1982 Commodity Year Book.* New York: Commodity Research Bureau.

COMMODITY RESEARCH BUREAU (1988) *1988 CRB Commodity Year Book.* New York: Commodity Research Bureau.

COMMONER, B. (1990) *Making Peace with the Planet.* New York: Pantheon.

CONESA, E. R. (1987) 'The Flight of Capital from Latin America', Washington: Inter-American Development Bank, mimeo.

CONSTANTINO, R. (1975) *A History of the Philippines: From Spanish Colonization to the Second World War.* New York: Monthly Review.

COOTE, B. (1987) *The Hunger Crop: Poverty and the Sugar Industry.* Oxford: OXFAM.

CORDOVA, V. G. (1979) 'New Rice Technology and Its Effect on Labor Use and Shares in Rice Production in Laguna, Philippines: 1966–1978'. Paper presented at the First International Conference of the Canadian Council for Southeast Asian Studies at the University of British Columbia, Vancouver, November. IRRI Agricultural Economics Department Paper 80–02.

CORDOVA, V. G., MANDAC, A. M., and GASCON, F. (1980) 'Some Conclusions on the Energy Costs of Rice Production in Central Luzon'. Paper presented at the PAEDA 26th Annual Convention, Munos, Nueva Ecija, June.

CORDOVA, V. G., OTSUKA, K., and GASCON, F. (1988) 'Technological Change and Labor Use in Rice Farming'. Paper prepared for the 4th Meeting of the Federation of Crop Science Society of the Philippines, Davao City, April.

CORNISTA, L. B. (1981) *Social Dynamics of Coconut Farming: The Case of Two Philippine Villages*. Unpublished Ph.D. dissertation, University of Wisconsin at Madison, November.

CORNISTA, L. B. (1985) 'Land Tenure System in the Philippine Uplands: Its Implications to Agroforestry'. Los Banos: UPLB, Agrarian Reform Institute, Seminar Papers Series No. 1, July.

CORNISTA, L. B. and ESCUETA, E. F. (1983) 'The Structure of the Coconut Farming Industry'. Los Banos: UPLB, Agrarian Reform Institute, Occasional Paper No. 10, August.

CORNISTA, L. B. and PAHM, E. A. (1987) 'Directions of Agrarian Reform in the Coconut Sector'. Los Banos: UPLB, Institute of Agrarian Studies, Occasional Paper No. 17, April.

COURTENAY, P. P. (1980) *Plantation Agriculture*. Revised edn., Boulder, Colorado: Westview.

COWARD, E. W., Jr. (1979) 'Principles of Social Organization in an Indigenous Irrigation System', *Human Organization*, Vol. 38, No. 1, pp. 28–36.

COWITT, P. P. (1985) *1985 World Currency Yearbook*. Brooklyn, N. Y.: International Currency Analysis, Inc.

CRISOSTOMO, C. and BARKER, R. (1972) 'Growth Rates of Philippine Agriculture: 1948–1969', *Philippine Economic Journal*, Vol. 11, No. 1, pp. 88–148.

CREWDSON, J. (1986) 'Marcos Graft Staggering: Investigators Trace Billions in Holdings', *The Chicago Tribune*, 23 March, pp. 1, 20–1.

CRISOSTOMO, C. *et al.* (1971) 'The New Rice Technology and Labor Absorption in Philippine Agriculture', *Malayan Economic Review*, Vol. 16, No. 2, pp. 117–58.

CRITTENDEN, A. (1978) 'Behind the Philippine Loan', *The New York Times*, February 12.

CRUZ, M. C. J., ZOSA-FERANIL, I. and GOCE, C. L. (1986) 'Population Pressure and Migration: Implications for Upland Development in the Philippines', Los Banos: UPLB, Center for Policy and Development Studies, Working Paper No. 86–06, August.

CUDDINGTON, J. T. (1986) *Capital Flight: Estimates, Issues, and Explanations*. Princeton: Princeton University, Department of Economics, Princeton Studies in International Finance No. 58, December.

CUDDINGTON, J. T. (1987) 'Macroeconomic Determinants of Capital Flight: An Econometric Investigation', in Lessard and Williamson, eds., pp. 85–100.

CUMBY, R. and LEVICH, R. (1987) 'On the Definition and Magnitude of Recent Capital Flight', in Lessard and Williamson, eds., pp. 27–67.

CUNNINGTON, T. J. (1988) Review of 'Hot Money and the Politics of Debt',

Bankers Magazine, Jan.–Feb., pp. 74–7.

DALRYMPLE, D. G. (1971) *Survey of Multiple Cropping in Less Developed Nations*. Washington: US Department of Agriculture, Foreign Economic Development Service, Report No. 12, October.

DALTON, K. (1978) 'The Undernourished Philippines', *Far Eastern Economic Review*, 1 September, pp. 35–6.

DARITY, W., Jr. (1986) 'Did Commercial Banks Push Loans on the LDC's?' in M. P. Claudon, ed., *World Debt Crisis: International Lending on Trial*. Cambridge, Mass.: Ballinger, pp. 199–225.

DARITY, W., Jr. and HORN, B. L. (1988) *The Loan Pushers: The Role of Commercial Banks in the International Debt Crisis*. Cambridge, Mass.: Ballinger.

DAVID, C. C. (1979) 'Structure and Performance of Rural Financial Markets in the Philippines', Columbus, Ohio: Ohio State University, Department of Agricultural Economics and Rural Sociology, Occasional Paper No. 589, May.

DAVID, C. C. (1983) 'Economic Policies and Philippine Agriculture', Manila: Philippine Institute for Development Studies Working Paper 83–02.

DAVID, C. C. (1985) 'Why the Philippines Imported Rice in Recent Years', Los Banos: IRRI Agricultural Economics Department Paper No. 85–11, October.

DAVID, C. C. and BALISACAN, A. M. (1981) 'An Analysis of Fertilizer Policies in the Philippines', *Journal of Philippine Development*, Vol. 8, Nos. 1 & 2, pp. 21–37.

DAVID, C. C., BARKER, R. and PALACPAC, A. (1984) 'The Nature of Productivity Growth in Philippine Agriculture, 1948–1982', Los Banos: IRRI Agricultural Economics Paper No. 84–22. Subsequently published in *Productivity Measurement and Analysis: Asian Agriculture*. Tokyo: Asian Productivity Organization, 1987, pp. 409–38, 741–60.

DAVID, C. C. and OTSUKA, K. (1987) 'Differential Impact of Technical Change Between Favorable and Unfavorable Areas', Paper presented at the First Workshop on Differential Impact of Modern Rice Technology on Favorable and Unfavorable Production Environments, International Rice Research Institute, Los Banos, 23–5 March.

DAVID, I. P. (1984) 'Estimates of the Total External Debt of the Developing Member Countries of ADB: 1981–1983', Manila: Asian Development Bank Economics Office, Statistical Report Series No. 1, September.

DAVID, I. P. (1989) 'The State of Agricultural Statistics in Southeast Asia', Manila: Asian Development Bank Economics Office, Statistical Report Series No. 12, March.

DAVID, I. P. and LEE, J. (1986) 'External Debt Situation in Asian Developing Countries', Manila: Asian Development Bank Economics Office, Statistical Report Series No. 6, March.

DAVID, I. P., NENETTE, A., MENDOZA, C. and BESA, D. C. (1990) 'Evaluation of Philippine Corn Statistics', *Journal of Philippine Development*, Vol. 17, No. 1, pp. 33–66.

DAVID, R. (1982) 'Bananas and Underdevelopment: The Philippine Experience', *Alternatives*, Vol. 7, Spring, pp. 451–65.

DAVID, R. *et al.* (1983) 'Transnational Corporations and the Philippine Banana Export Industry', in *Political Economy of Philippine Commodities*, Quezon City: University of the Philippines, Third World Studies Center, pp. 1–133.

DAVID, V. (1977) *The Barriers in the Development of the Philippine Coconut Industry*. Unpublished M. B. A. dissertation, Ateneo de Manila University.

DAVID, W. P. (1984) 'Environmental Effects of Watershed Modifications', Manila: Philippine Institute for Development Studies Working Paper 84–07.

DE DIOS, E. S., *et al.* (1984) *An Analysis of the Philippine Economic Crisis: A Workshop Report*. Quezon City: University of the Philippines Press.

DE LOS REYES, R. P. (1985) 'Managing through Persuasion: Experiences in a Philippine Community Irrigation System', *Philippine Sociological Review*, Vol. 33, Nos. 3–4, pp. 5–18.

DE LOS REYES, R. P. and JOPILLO, S. M. G. (1988) 'The Impact of Participation: An Evaluation of the NIA's Communal Irrigation Program', in Korten and Siy, eds., pp. 90–115.

DEPPLER, M. and WILLIAMSON, M. (1987) 'Capital Flight: Concepts, Measurement, and Issues,' *IMF Staff Studies for the World Economic Outlook*, August, pp. 39–58.

DEVLIN, R. (1989) *Debt and Crisis in Latin America: The Supply Side of the Story*. Princeton: Princeton University Press.

DE VRIES, R. (1986) 'LDC Debt: Debt Relief or Market Solutions?' *World Financial Markets* (Morgan Guaranty Trust Company of New York), September, pp. 1–11.

DE VRIES, R. (1987) 'Panel on Policy Issues', in Lessard and Williamson, eds., pp. 187–91.

DIAZ-ALEJANDRO, C. F. (1984) 'Latin American Debt: I Don't Think We Are in Kansas Anymore', *Brookings Papers on Economic Activity* 2:1984, pp. 335–89.

DIWAN, I. (1989) 'Foreign Debt, Crowding Out and Capital Flight', *Journal of International Money and Finance*, Vol. 8, pp. 121–36.

DOHNER, R. S. and Intal, P., Jr. (1989) 'The Marcos Legacy: Economic Policy and Foreign Debt in the Philippines', in J. D. Sachs and S. M. Collins, eds., *Developing Country Debt and Economic Performance. Volume 3: Country Studies -Indonesia, Korea, Philippines, Turkey*. Chicago: University of Chicago Press, pp. 371–614.

DOOLEY, M. P. (1986) 'Country-Specific Risk Premiums, Capital Flight and Net Investment Income Payments in Selected Developing Countries', International Monetary Fund Research Department Memorandum DM/86/17, March 11.

DOOLEY, M. P. (1987) 'Comment', in Lessard and Williamson, eds., pp. 79–81.

DOOLEY, M. P., HELKIE, W., TRYON, R. and UNDERWOOD, J. (1986) 'An Analysis of External Debt Positions of Eight Developing Countries Through 1990', *Journal of Development Economics*, Vol. 21, No. 3,

pp. 283–318.

DOOLEY, M. P. and ISARD, P. (1986) 'Tax Avoidance and Exchange Rate Determination', International Monetary Fund, Research Department Memorandum DM/86/1, 2 January.

DOOLEY, M. P. and ISARD, P. (1987) 'Country Preferences, Currency Values and Policy Issues', *Journal of Policy Modeling*, Vol. 9, No. 1, pp. 65–81.

DORNBUSCH, R. (1985) 'External Debt, Budget Deficits, and Disequilibrium Exchange Rates', in Smith and Cuddington, eds., pp. 213–35.

DORNBUSCH, R. (1986) 'The Bradley Plan: A Way Out of the Latin Debt Mess', *The Washington Post*, 27 August, p. A19.

DORNBUSCH, R. and FISCHER, S. (1990) *Macroeconomics*. Fifth edn., New York: McGraw-Hill.

DORONILA, A. (1985) 'The Transformation of Patron-Client Relations and its Political Consequences in Postwar Philippines', *Journal of Southeast Asian Studies*, Vol. 16, No. 1, pp. 99–116.

DORONILA, A. (1987) 'The Decline of the Sugar Industry', *The Manila Chronicle*, 29 December, pp. 1, 6.

DOWLING, J. M. (1984) 'Income Distribution and Poverty in Selected Asian Countries', *Asian Development Bank Economic Staff Paper* No. 22, November.

DUFF, B. (1986) 'Changes in Small-farm Rice Threshing Technology in Thailand and the Philippines', International Rice Research Institute, Research Paper Series No. 120, November.

DUMAINE, B. (1986) 'The $2.2 Billion Nuclear Fiasco', *Fortune*, September 1, pp. 39–46.

DURNING, A. (1990) 'Environmentalism South', *Amicus Journal* (Washington, D. C.: Natural Resources Defense Council), Vol. 12, No. 3, Summer, pp. 12–18.

DUWENDAG, D. (1987) *Capital Flight from Developing Countries: Estimates and Determinants for 25 Major Borrowers*. Tilburg, Netherlands: Société Universitaire Européenne de Recherches Financières.

ECHAUZ, R. (1978) *Sketches of the Island of Negros*. Athens, Ohio: Ohio University Center for International Studies, Southeast Asia Program.

EDQUIST, C. (1985) *Capitalism, Socialism and Technology: A Comparative Study of Cuba and Jamaica*. London: Zed Books.

EDWARDS, S. (1987) 'Sequencing Economic Liberalization in Developing Countries', *Finance and Development*, Vol. 24, No. 1, pp. 26–9.

EICHENGREEN, B. and PORTES, R. (1986) 'Debt and Default in the 1930s: Causes and Consequences', *European Economic Review*, Vol. 30, pp. 599–640.

EISNER, R. (1988) 'Extended Accounts for National Income and Product', *Journal of Economic Literature*, Vol. 26, No. 4, pp. 1611–84.

ELLISON, K. and CAREY, P. (1985) 'Military Aid and Manila: Pentagon probes US contractors for links to top Philippine officials', *San Jose Mercury News*, June 28.

ERBE, S. (1985) 'The Flight of Capital from Developing Countries',

Intereconomics, Vol. 20, November/December, pp. 268–75.

ESGUERRA, E. (1981) 'The Redistributive Potential of the Masagana 99 Credit Subsidy', University of the Philippines School of Economics, Masters thesis, August.

ESPIRITU, C. E. (1987) 'Monopoly Still Controls Local Coconut Industry', *Business Star* (Manila), 4 August, pp. 1, 2.

EVANS, J. G. (1968) 'Current and Capital Transactions: How the Fund Defines Them', *Finance and Development*, Vol. 5, No. 3, September, pp. 30–5.

EVENSON, R. E. and FLORES, P. M. (1978) 'Social Returns to Rice Research', in *Economic Consequences of the New Rice Technology*, Los Banos: International Rice Research Institute, pp. 243–65.

EVENSON, R. E., WAGGONER, P., and BLOOM, P. (1980) 'Investing in Technology for Philippine Agriculture', Report for the USAID Asia Bureau/University of Minnesota Asian Agricultural Research Review (mimeo).

FALCON, W. P. (1970) 'The Green Revolution: Generations of Problems', *American Journal of Agricultural Economics*, Vol. 52, No. 5, pp. 698–709.

FARMERS ASSISTANCE BOARD (1982) *Profits from Poison: A Look into the Socio-economics and Politics of Pesticides.* Manila: Farmers Assistance Board, Inc.

FEDER, E. (1983) *Perverse Development.* Quezon City: Foundation for Nationalist Studies.

FEGAN, B. (1972a) 'Between the Lord and the Law: Tenants' Dilemma', in Lynch, ed., pp. 113–27.

FEGAN, B. (1972b) 'Jobs and Farms: The Lessee's Alternatives and Peasantization', in Lynch, ed., pp. 134–41.

FEGAN, B. (1979) 'Folk-Capitalism: Economic Strategies of Peasants in a Philippine Wet-Rice Village.' Unpublished Ph.D. dissertation, Yale University, Department of Anthropology.

FEGAN, B. (1982a) 'The Social History of a Central Luzon Barrio', in McCoy and de Jesus, eds., pp. 91–129.

FEGAN, B. (1982b) 'Land Reform and Technical Change in Central Luzon: The Rice Industry Under Martial Law', Diliman, Quezon City: University of the Philippines, Third World Studies Center, Philippine Commodity Paper Series No. 4, September.

FEGAN, B. (1989a) 'The Philippines: Agrarian Stagnation Under a Decaying Regime', in Hart, Turton, and White, eds., pp. 125–43.

FEGAN, B. (1989b) 'Accumulation on the Basis of an Unprofitable Crop', in Hart, Turton, and White, eds., pp. 159–78.

FELIX, D. (1985) 'How to Resolve Latin America's Debt Crisis', *Challenge*, Vol. 28, No. 5, pp. 44–51.

FELIX, D. (1987) 'Alternative Outcomes of the Latin American Debt Crisis: Lessons from the Past', *Latin American Research Review*, Vol. 22, No. 2, pp. 3–46.

FERNANDEZ, J. (1986) 'Honoring an International Commitment', *Central Bank Review*, Vol. 38, No. 3, p. 1.

FIELDS, G. (1980) *Poverty, Inequality, and Development.* Cambridge: Cambridge University Press.

FISHLOW, A. (1985) 'Lessons from the Past: Capital Markets during the 19th Century and the Interwar Period', *International Organization*, Vol. 39, No. 3, pp. 383–439.

FLORENTINO, R. F., NARCISO, Z. V., and VALERIO, T. E. (1986) *1986 Situation Analysis of Children in the Philippines: Food and Nutrition.* Manila: National Science and Technology Authority, Food and Nutrition Research Institute, Monograph Series No. 2, July.

FLORESCA, R. F. (1980) 'Are We Exporting Rice at a Loss?' *Philippine Farmers' Journal*, September, pp. 24–5.

FLORO, S. L. (1986) 'Credit Relations and Market Interlinkage in Philippine Agriculture', Unpublished Ph.D. dissertation, Food Research Institute, Stanford University, September.

FOLKERTS-LANDAU, D. (1985) 'The Changing Role of International Bank Lending in Development Finance', *IMF Staff Papers*, Vol. 32, June.

FOOD AND AGRICULTURE ORGANIZATION OF THE UNITED NATIONS (FAO) (1972) *Processed Tropical Fruit: Trends and outlook for production and trade of canned pineapple and processed exotic fruit.* Rome: FAO Commodity Bulletin Series No. 51.

FAO (1975) 'Problems of Rice Trade Liberalization and Pricing Policy', in *FAO Rice Report 1974/75*. Rome: FAO, pp. 14–21.

FAO (1976a) 'Recent Trends in the Canned Pineapple Market', *Monthly Bulletin of Agricultural Economics and Statistics*, Vol. 25, May, pp. 23–30.

FAO (1976b) *Development and Forest Resources in Asia and the Far East: Trends and Perspectives 1961–1991.* Rome: FAO Forest Economics and Statistics Unit.

FAO (1977) *1975 Yearbook of Forest Products.* Rome: FAO.

FAO (1982) *FAO Commodity Review and Outlook, 1981–1982.* Rome: FAO Economic and Social Development Series No. 22.

FAO (1985) *Rice: Selected Aspects of Production, Trade and Price Policies.* Rome: FAO Economic and Social Development Paper No. 54.

FAO (1986) *The World Banana Economy, 1970–1984: Structure, Performance and Prospects.* Rome: FAO Commodities and Trade Division, Economic and Social Development Paper No. 57.

FAO (1987a) *FAO Trade Yearbook 1986* (Vol. 40). Rome: FAO.

FAO (1987b) *FAO Production Yearbook 1986.* (Vol. 40). Rome: FAO.

FOOD AND NUTRITION RESEARCH INSTITUTE (FNRI) (1984) *Second Nationwide Nutrition Survey, Philippines, 1982.* Manila: National Science and Technology Authority.

FOODWATCH RESEARCH TEAM (1988) 'Ang Sistema ng Pagsasapamilihan ng Palay: Panimulang Resulta ng Ilang Case Study sa Luson' ['The System of Marketing Palay: Initial Result of Case Studies in Luzon'], Quezon City: Philippine Peasant Institute, August.

FRANCISCO, L. (1987) 'The Philippine-American War', in D. B. Schirmer and S. R. Shalom, eds., *The Philippines Reader: A History of Colonialism,*

Neocolonialism, Dictatorship, and Resistance. Boston: South End Press, pp. 8–19.

FRANK, C. R., Jr. (1972) 'Debt and Terms of Aid', in C. R. Frank *et al.*, *Assisting Developing Countries: Problems of Debts, Burden-Sharing, Jobs, and Trade.* New York: Praeger, pp. 3–68.

FRANKENBERG,, G. and KNIEPER, R. (1984) 'Legal Problems of the Overindebtedness of Developing Countries: The Current Relevance of the Doctrine of Odious Debts', *International Journal of the Sociology of Law*, Vol. 12, pp. 415–38.

FRIEDEN, J. (1981) 'Third World Indebted Industrialization: International Finance and State Capitalism in Mexico, Brazil, Algeria, and South Korea', *International Organization*, Vol. 35, No. 3, pp. 407–32.

FRIEND, T. (1963) 'The Philippine Sugar Industry and the Politics of Independence, 1929–1935', *Journal of Asian Studies*, Vol. 22, pp. 179–92.

FRIESEN, D. and STOLTZFUS, G. (1978) 'Castle and Cooke in Mindanao', Diliman: University of the Philippines, Third World Studies Discussion Paper No. 8, January.

FUJISAKA, S. and SAJISE, P. (1986) 'Change and "Development" in the Uplands: A Synthesis of Lessons, Unresolved Issues, and Implications', in S. Fujisaka, P. E. Sajise and R. A. del Castillo, eds., *Man, Agriculture and the Tropical Forest: Change and Development in the Philippine Uplands.* Bangkok: Winrock International Institute for Agricultural Development, pp. 337–60.

GALANG, J. (1987) 'Wealth Rooted Deep in a Sugar Empire', *Far Eastern Economic Review*, 26 March, p. 73.

GALANG, J. (1988) 'Landlocked in Manila', *Far Eastern Economic Review*, 6 October, p. 64.

GALANG, J. (1988b) 'The Coconut Crisis', *Far Eastern Economic Review*, 24 November, pp. 72–3.

GATES, J. M. (1983) 'War-Related Deaths in the Philippines, 1898–1902', *Pacific Historical Review*, Vol. 53, pp. 367–78.

GEERTZ, C. (1963) *Agricultural Involution: The Processes of Ecological Change in Java.* Berkeley: University of California Press.

GEORGHIOU, G. P. (1986) 'The Magnitude of the Resistance Problem', in National Academy of Sciences, *Pesticide Resistance: Strategies and Tactics for Management.* Report of the Committee on Strategies for the Management of Pesticide Resistant Pest Populations, Board on Agriculture, National Research Council. Washington, D. C.: National Academy Press, pp. 14–43.

GILLIS, M. (1988) 'The Logging Industry in Tropical Asia', in J. S. Denslow and C. Padoch, eds., *People of the Tropical Rain Forest.* Berkeley: University of California Press, pp.177–84.

GOLAY, F. H. (1961) *The Philippines: Public Policy and National Economic Development.* Ithaca: Cornell University Press.

GOLDENMAN, G. and RENGAM, S. (1987) *Problem Pesticides, Pesticide Problems: A Citizens' Action Guide to the International Code of Conduct on the Distribution and Use of Pesticides.* Penang: International Organization of Consumers Unions and Pesticide Action Network.

GOLDMAN, H. W. and RANADE, C. G. (1977) 'Analysis of Income Effect of Food Consumption in Rural and Urban Philippines', *Journal of Agricultural Economics and Development*, Vol. 7, pp. 150–65.

GONZAGA, V. L. (1983) *Mechanization and Labor Employment: A Study of the Sugarcane Workers' Responses to Technological Change in Sugar Farming in Negros*. Bacolod: La Salle Bacolod Monograph Series No. 1.

GONZAGA, V. L. (1986) *Crisis in Sugarlandia: The Planters' Differential Perceptions and Responses and their Impact on Sugarcane Workers' Households*. Bacolod: La Salle Social Research Center.

GOODNO, J. B. (1991) *The Philippines: Land of Broken Promises*. London: Zed Books.

GOPINATH, C. (1976) 'Problems and Concepts in Irrigation Use', in *Role of Irrigation in the Development of India's Agriculture*, Bombay: Indian Society of Agricultural Economics, Seminar Series No. 13.

GOULD, M. (1976) 'Philippines: Country Program Paper', World Bank Office Memorandum, 26 March.

GRACE, B. (1978) 'Food and Small Farm Strategies in the Philippines: Cooperatives and Credit', *American Universities Field Staff Reports*, No. 40.

GRIFFIN, K. B. (1974) *The Political Economy of Agrarian Change: An Essay on the Green Revolution*. London: Macmillan.

GRIFFIN, K. B. (1978) *International Inequality and National Poverty*. London: Macmillan.

GRIFFIN, K. B. (1978b) 'Comments on "Labor Utilization in Rice Production"', in International Rice Research Institute, pp. 137–43.

GRIFFIN, K. B. and ENOS, J. L. (1970) 'Foreign Assistance: Objectives and Consequences', *Economic Development and Cultural Change*, Vol. 18, No. 3, pp. 313–27.

GRIFFIN, K. B. and GHOSE, A. K. (1979) 'Growth and Impoverishment in Rural Areas of Asia', *World Development*, Vol. 7, No. 4/5, pp. 361–83.

GRIFFITH-JONES, S. (1988) 'Conclusions and Policy Recommendations', in S. Griffith-Jones, ed., *Managing World Debt*. New York: St. Martin's.

GROSSHOLTZ, J. (1964) *Politics in the Philippines*. Boston: Little, Brown.

GUERRERO, S. H. (1985) 'A Review of Welfare Issues in the Coconut Industry', Philippine Institute for Development Studies Working Paper 85–01.

GUIEB, E. R. III (1990) 'The Rice Mafia', *Midweek*, Vol. 5, No. 24, 9 May, pp. 3–7.

GULATI, S. K. (1987) 'A Note on Trade Misinvoicing', in Lessard and Williamson, eds., pp. 68–78.

GULATI, S. (1988) 'Capital Flight: Causes, Consequences and Cures', *Journal of International Affairs*, Vol. 42, No. 1, pp. 165–85.

GUPPY, N. (1984) 'Tropical Deforestation: A Global View', *Foreign Affairs*, Vol. 62, No. 4, pp. 928–65.

GWERTZMAN, B. (1979) 'Carter Freezes Billions in Iranian Assets as Khomeini Regime Tries to Withdraw Them', *The New York Times*, 15

November.

HABITO, C. (1987a) 'Policy Issues in the Coconut Industry: A Survey', in UPLB Agricultural Policy Working Group, *Policy Issues on the Philippine Rice Economy and Agricultural Trade*. College, Laguna: UPLB, Center for Policy and Development Studies, pp. 193–224.

HABITO, C. (1987b) 'Should Scale Economies Stand in the Way of Philippine Agrarian Reform?' Paper presented to the Philippine Economic Society, 29 May.

HAGGARD, S. (1990) 'The Political Economy of the Philippine Debt Crisis', in J. M. Nelson, ed., *Economic Crisis and Policy Choice: The Politics of Adjustment in the Third World*. Princeton: Princeton University Press, pp. 215–55.

HAINSWORTH, G. B. (1979) 'Economic Growth and Poverty in Southeast Asia: Malaysia, Indonesia and the Philippines', *Pacific Affairs*, Vol. 52, No. 1, pp. 5–41.

HARRIS, S. (1987) 'Current Issues in the World Sugar Economy', *Food Policy*, Vol. 12, No. 2, pp. 127–45.

HART, G., TURTON, A., and WHITE, B., eds., (1989) *Agrarian Transformations: Local Processes and the State in Southeast Asia*. Berkeley: University of California Press.

HARTMANN, B. (1987) *Reproductive Rights and Wrongs: The Global Politics of Population Control and Contraceptive Choice*. New York: Harper & Row.

HAWES, G. (1987) *The Philippine State and the Marcos Regime: The Politics of Export*. Ithaca: Cornell University Press.

HAWES, G. (1990) 'Theories of Peasant Revolution: A Critique and Contribution from the Philippines', *World Politics*, Vol. 42, No. 2, pp. 261–98.

HAYAMI, Y. (1971) 'Elements of Induced Innovation: A Historical Perspective for the Green Revolution', *Explorations in Economic History*, Vol. 8, No. 4, pp. 445–72.

HAYAMI, Y. (1987) 'Kasupong in Central Luzon: "Indianization" of the Philippine Rice Bowl?' Los Banos: International Rice Research Institute, Department of Agricultural Economics Paper No. 87–22.

HAYAMI, Y., ADRIANO, L. S. and QUISUMBING, M. A. (1987) *Agribusiness and Agrarian Reform: A View from the Banana and Pineapple Plantations*. Los Banos: UPLB Center for Policy and Development Studies, November.

HAYAMI, Y., AKINO, M., SHINTANI, M. and YAMADA, S. (1975) *A Century of Agricultural Growth in Japan: Its Relevance to Asian Development*. Minneapolis: University of Minnesota Press and Tokyo: University of Tokyo Press.

HAYAMI, Y., DAVID, C. C., FLORES, P. and KIKUCHI, M. (1976) 'Agricultural Growth Against a Land Resource Constraint: The Philippine Experience', *Australian Journal of Agricultural Economics*, Vol. 20, No. 3, pp. 144–59.

HAYAMI, Y. and KIKUCHI, M. (1978) 'Investment Inducements to Public Infrastructure: Irrigation in the Philippines', *Review of Economics and*

Statistics, Vol. 60, No. 1, pp. 70–7.

HAYAMI, Y. and KIKUCHI, M. (1982) *Asian Village Economy at the Cross-roads: An Economic Approach to Institutional Change.* Tokyo: University of Tokyo Press, and Baltimore: Johns Hopkins University Press.

HAYAMI, Y. and RUTTAN, V. W. (1985) *Agricultural Development: An International Perspective.* Revised edn., Baltimore: Johns Hopkins University Press.

HAYAMI, Y., QUISUMBING, M. A. and ADRIANO, L. S. (1987) *In Search of a Land Reform Design for the Philippines.* Los Banos: UPLB Agricultural Policy Research Program, Monograph Series No. 1, June.

HAYAMI, Y., QUISUMBING, M. A. and ADRIANO, L. S. (1990) *Toward an Alternative Land Reform Paradigm: A Philippine Perspective.* Quezon City: Ateneo de Manila University Press.

HENIG, R. M. (1979) 'Human Disease Linked to Dioxin: Congress Calls for 2,4,5-T Ban After Dramatic Herbicide Hearings,' *BioScience*, Vol. 29, No. 8, pp. 453–4.

HENRY, J. (1986) 'Where the Money Went: Third World Debt Hoax', *The New Republic*, April 14, pp. 20–3.

HENRY, J. (1989) 'The New Philippines: Revolution, Recovery and Reality', *International Development Review* (New York), Vol. 2, No. 1, pp. 64–85.

HERDT, R. W. (1983) 'Studies in Water Management Economics at IRRI', in *Report of a Planning Workshop on Irrigation Water Management.* Los Banos: IRRI, pp. 115–38.

HERDT, R. W. (1987) 'A Retrospective View of Technological and Other Changes in Philippine Rice Farming, 1965–1982', *Economic Development and Cultural Change*, Vol. 35, No. 2, pp. 329–50.

HERDT, R. W. and CAPULE, C. (1983) *Adoption, Spread, and Production Impact of Modern Rice Varieties in Asia.* Los Banos: IRRI.

HERDT, R. W. and MANDAC, A. M. (1981) 'Modern Technology and Economic Efficiency of Philippine Rice Farmers', *Economic Development and Cultural Change*, Vol. 29, No. 2, pp. 375–99.

HICKS, G. L. (1967) *The Philippine Coconut Industry: Growth and Change, 1900–1965.* Washington, D. C.: National Planning Association, Center for Development Planning, Field Work Report No. 17, June.

HICKS, G. L. and McNICOLL, G. (1971) *Trade and Growth in the Philippines: An Open Dual Economy.* Ithaca: Cornell University Press.

HILL, H. and JAYASURIYA, S. (1985) 'The Philippines: Growth, Debt and Crisis; Economic Performance During the Marcos Era'. Canberra: Australian National University, Development Studies Centre, Working Paper No. 85/3.

HOEFLICH, M. E. (1982) 'Through a Glass Darkly: Reflections Upon the History of the International Law of Public Debt in Connection with State Succession', *University of Illinois Law Review*, Vol. 1982, No. 1, pp. 39–70.

HOOLEY, R. and RUTTAN, V. W. (1969) 'The Philippines', in R. T. Shand, ed., *Agricultural Development in Asia.* Canberra: Australian National University Press, pp. 215–50.

HOOPER, P. and MANN, C. L. (1987) 'The US External Deficit: Its Causes and Persistence', Board of Governors of the Federal Reserve System, International Finance Discussion Paper No. 316, November.

HOPPER, W. D. (1968) 'Investment in Agriculture: The Essentials for Payoff', in *Strategy for the Conquest of Hunger: Proceedings of a Symposium Convened by The Rockefeller Foundation, April 1 and 2, 1968, at the Rockefeller University.* New York: Rockefeller Foundation, pp. 102–13.

HSIEH, S. C. and RUTTAN, V. W. (1967) 'Environmental, Technological, and Institutional Factors in the Growth of Rice Production: Philippines, Thailand, and Taiwan', *Food Research Institute Studies*, Vol. 7, No. 3, pp. 307–41.

HUKE, R. E. (1963) *Shadows on the Land: An Economic Geography of the Philippines.* Manila: Bookmark, Inc.

HUKE, R. E. and DUNCAN, J. (1969) 'Spatial Aspects of HYV Diffusion', in Department of Agricultural Economics, School of Agriculture and International Rice Research Institute, *Seminar on Economics of Rice Production in the Philippines.*

HURST, P. (1990) *Rainforest Politics: Ecological Destruction in South-East Asia.* London: Zed Books.

HUSAIN, S. S. (1985) 'Where Does CGIAR Go from Here?' Interview in *The Bank's World* (Washington, D. C.: The World Bank), Vol. 4, No. 12.

IBON DATABANK PHILS., Inc. (1984) *What Crisis? Highlights on the Philippine Economy 1983.* Manila: IBON.

ILLO, J. F. I. (1985) 'Wives at Work: Patterns of Labor Force Participation in Two Rice-farming Villages in the Philippines', in International Rice Research Institute, *Women in Rice Farming.* Aldershot: Gower, pp. 71–89.

INTERNATIONAL LABOUR OFFICE (1974) *Sharing in Development: A Programme of Employment, Equity and Growth for the Philippines.* Geneva: ILO.

INTERNATIONAL MONETARY FUND (IMF) (1977) *Balance of Payments Manual.* Fourth Edition. Washington: IMF.

IMF (1984) *Philippines: Recent Economic Developments.* June 8.

IMF (1987) *International Financial Statistics Yearbook 1987.* Washington: IMF.

IMF (1987b) *Report on the World Current Account Discrepancy.* Final Report of the Working Party on the Statistical Discrepancy in World Current Account Balances, September.

IMF (1989) *International Financial Statistics Yearbook 1988.* Washington: IMF.

INTERNATIONAL RICE RESEARCH INSTITUTE (IRRI) (1978) *Economic Consequences of the New Rice Technology.* Los Banos: IRRI.

IRRI (1979) *Annual Report for 1978.* Los Banos: IRRI.

IRRI (1986) *World Rice Statistics 1985.* Manila: IRRI.

IRRI (1989) *Annual Report for 1988.* Los Banos: IRRI.

ISHIBASHI, N., Kondo, E. and Ito, S. (1983) 'Effects of Application of Certain Herbicides on Soil Nematodes and Aquatic Invertebrates in Rice Paddy Fields in Japan,' *Crop Protection*, Vol. 2, No. 3, pp. 289–304.

ISHIKAWA, S. (1967) *Economic Development in Asian Perspective.* Tokyo: Kinokuniya.

ISHIKAWA, S. (1970) *Agricultural Development Strategies in Asia: Case Studies of the Philippines and Thailand.* Manila: Asian Development Bank.

JAGAN, L. (1987) 'Philippines: Land to the Hungry', *International Labour Reports*, No. 23, September-October.

JAMES, W. E. (1978) 'Agricultural Growth Against a Land Resource Constraint: The Philippine Experience: Comment', *Australian Journal of Agricultural Economics*, Vol. 22, No. 3.

JAPAN COMMITTEE FOR THE NEGROS CAMPAIGN (1987) 'The Prospects for Economic Self-Reliance and International Cooperation on Negros Island, the Philippines', Report to the Toyota Foundation, Tokyo (mimeo).

JAYASURIYA, S. K. and SHAND, R. T. (1986) 'Technical Change and Labor Absorption in Asian Agriculture: Some Emerging Trends', *World Development*, Vol. 14, No. 3, pp. 415–28.

JESENA, A. C. (1969) 'The Sacadas of Sugarland', in D. Shoesmith, ed., *The Politics of Sugar: Studies of the Sugar Industry in the Philippines.* Victoria: Asian Bureau Australia.

JOSE, F. S. (1959) 'The Philippine Agrarian Problem', *Comment*, Vol. 9, pp. 85–143.

JOSLING, T. (1984) 'Agricultural Prices and Export Earnings: The Experience of Developing Countries in the 1970s', Rome: FAO Economic and Social Development Paper No. 43.

JOSON, J. J. (1989) 'The Plight of Palay Producers', *Midweek*, Vol. 4, No. 31, 2 August, pp. 14–16.

JURADO, G. M. (1966) 'Philippine Foreign Loans: 1906–1963', *Philippine Economic Journal*, Vol. 5, No. 2, pp. 362–79.

KALETSKY, A. (1985) *The Costs of Default.* New York: Priority Press.

KAMM, H. (1981) 'Poor Filipinos Lose Farms, Then Lives', *The New York Times*, January 29, p. A3.

KELLOGG, W. W. and SCHWARE, R. (1982) 'Society, Science and Climate Change', *Foreign Affairs*, Vol. 60, No. 5, pp. 1076–110.

KELLY, W. (1982) 'Irrigation Management in Japan: A Critical Review of Japanese Social Science Research', Ithaca: Cornell University East Asia Papers No. 30.

KERKVLIET, B. J. (1974) 'Land Reform in the Philippines Since the Marcos Coup', *Pacific Affairs*, Vol. 47, pp. 286–304.

KERKVLIET, B. J. (1977) *The Huk Rebellion: A Study of Peasant Revolt in the Philippines.* Berkeley: University of California Press.

KERKVLIET, B. J. T. (1990) *Everyday Politics in the Philippines: Class and Status Relations in a Central Luzon Village.* Berkeley: University of California Press.

KESSLER, R. J. (1986) 'Marcos and the Americans', *Foreign Policy*, No. 63, pp. 40–57.

KHAN, A. R. (1977) 'Growth and Inequality in the Rural Philippines', in *Poverty and Landlessness in Rural Asia*, Geneva: International Labor

Organization.

KHAN, M. S. and UL HAQUE, N. (1985) 'Foreign Borrowing and Capital Flight: A Formal Analysis', *IMF Staff Papers*, Vol. 32, No. 4, pp. 606–28.

KHAN, M. S. and UL HAQUE, N. (1987) 'Capital Flight from Developing Countries', *Finance and Development*, Vol. 24, March, pp. 2–5.

KIKUCHI, M. (1983) 'Recent Changes in a Laguna Rice Village: A New Generation of Changes?' in Ledesma, Makil and Miralao, eds., pp. 59–72.

KIKUCHI, M., DOZINA, G., Jr., and HAYAMI, H. (1978) 'Economics of Community Work Programs: A Communal Irrigation Project in the Philippines', *Economic Development and Cultural Change*, Vol. 26, No. 2, pp. 211–25.

KIKUCHI, M. and HAYAMI, Y. (1978a) 'Agricultural Growth against a Land Resource Constraint: A Comparative History of Japan, Taiwan, Korea, and the Philippines', *Journal of Economic History*, Vol. 38, No. 4, pp. 839–64.

KIKUCHI, M. and HAYAMI, Y. (1978b) 'New Rice Technology and National Irrigation Development Policy', in *Economic Consequences of the New Rice Technology*, Los Banos: International Rice Research Institute, pp. 315–32.

KIKUCHI, M. and HAYAMI, Y. (1980) 'Inducements to Institutional Innovations in an Agrarian Community', *Economic Development and Cultural Change*, Vol. 29, No. 1, pp. 21–36.

KIKUCHI, M. and HAYAMI, Y. (1983) 'New Rice Technology, Intrarural Migration, and Institutional Innovation in the Philippines', International Rice Research Institute, Research Paper Series No. 86, January.

KIKUCHI, M., HUYSMAN, A., and RES, L. (1983) 'New Rice Technology and Labor Absorption: Comparative Histories of Two Philippine Rice Villages', IRRI Research Paper Series No. 90, April.

KINDLEBERGER, C. P. (1987) *International Capital Movements*. Cambridge: Cambridge University Press.

KORTEN, F. F. and SIY, R. Y., Jr. (1988) *Transforming a Bureaucracy: The Experience of the Philippine National Irrigation Administration*. West Hartford, Connecticut: Kumarian Press.

KRAMER, B. (1978) 'Ties to the Top: In the Philippines, It's Whom You Know That Can Really Count', *Wall Street Journal*, 12 January, pp. 1, 18.

KRINKS, P. (1983a) 'Rectifying Inequality or Favouring the Few? Image and Reality in Philippine Development', in D. A. M. Lea and D. P. Chaudhuri, eds., *Rural Development and the State*, London: Methuen, pp. 100–26.

KRINKS, P. (1983b) 'Rural Transformation under Peripheral Capitalism: The Philippine Banana Export Industry', *Philippine Sociological Review*, Vol. 31, Nos. 1–2, pp. 101–14.

KRUEGER, A. O. (1990) 'The Political Economy of Controls: American Sugar', in M. Scott and D. Lal, eds., *Public Policy and Economic Development*. Oxford: Clarendon, pp. 170–216.

KUCZYNSKI, P. P. (1987) Remarks in the Panel on Policy Issues, in Lessard and Williamson, eds., pp. 191–3.

KUMMER, D. M. (1992) *Deforestation in the Post-War Philippines*. Chicago: University of Chicago Press.

KUZNETS, S. (1955) 'Economic Growth and Income Inequality', *American Economic Review*, Vol. 49, pp. 1–28.

KUZNETS, S. (1963) 'Quantitative Aspects of the Economic Growth of Nations', *Economic Development and Cultural Change*, Vol. 11, No. 2, Part II, pp. 1–80.

KWITNY, J. (1984) *Endless Enemies: The Making of an Unfriendly World.* New York: Congdon & Weed.

KWITNY, J. (1987) *The Crimes of Patriots: A True Tale of Dope, Dirty Money, and the CIA.* New York: Norton.

LAARMAN, J. G. (1988) 'Export of Tropical Hardwoods in the Twentieth Century', in J. F. Richards and R. P. Tucker, eds., *World Deforestation in the Twentieth Century.* Durham: Duke University Press, pp. 147–63.

LACSON, M. V. (1981) 'Mechanization is the Only Way to Profitability', *Sugarland* (Bacolod), Vol. 18, No. 2, pp. 5–10.

LAL, D. (1986) 'Stolper-Samuelson-Rybczynski in the Pacific: Real Wages and Real Exchange Rates in the Philippines, 1956–1978', *Journal of Development Economics*, Vol. 21, pp. 181–204.

LAMBERTE, M. B. *et al.* (1985) *A Review and Appraisal of the Government Response to the 1983–84 Balance-of Payments Crisis.* Manila: PIDS Monograph Series No. 8, October.

LANDE, C. H. and HOOLEY, R. (1986) 'Aquino. Takes Charge', *Foreign Affairs*, Vol. 64, pp.1087–107.

LANDE, C. H., ed. (1987) *Rebuilding a Nation: Philippine Challenges and American Policy.* Washington: Washington Institute Press.

LAPPE, F. M. and COLLINS, J. (1979) *Food First: Beyond the Myth of Scarcity.* Revised edn., New York: Ballantine.

LAPPE, F. M. and McCALLIE, E. (1978) 'Banana Hunger', *Food Monitor*, March/April, pp. 11–13.

LARKIN, J. A. (1982) 'Philippine History Reconsidered: A Socioeconomic Perspective', *American Historical Review*, Vol. 87, No. 3, pp. 595–623.

LARY, H. B. (1946) 'The Domestic Effects of Foreign Investment', *American Economic Review Papers and Proceedings*, Vol. 36, No. 2, pp. 672–86.

LEDEC, G. (1985) 'The Political Economy of Tropical Deforestation', in H. J. Leonard, ed., *Divesting Nature's Capital: The Political Economy of Environmental Abuse in the Third World.* New York: Holmes & Meier, pp. 179–226.

LEDESMA, A. J. (1982) *Landless Workers and Rice Farmers: Peasant Subclasses under Agrarian Reform in Two Philippine Villages.* Los Banos: International Rice Research Institute.

LEDESMA, A. J., MAKIL, P. Q., and MIRALAO, V. A., eds., (1983) *Second View from the Paddy: More Empirical Studies on Philippine Rice Farming and Tenancy.* Manila: Institute of Philippine Culture, Ateneo de Manila University.

LEE, A. H., YU, P. Y., METCALF, R. L. and HSU, E. L. (1976) 'The Environmental Fate of Three Dichlorophenyl Nitrophenyl Herbicides in a Rice Paddy Model Ecosystem,' *Journal of Environmental Quality*, Vol. 5, No. 4,

pp. 482–6.

LEE, G. M. and KNUTSON, R. D. (1987) 'US Sugar Policy: Costs, Benefits, Consequences', Paper presented at Western Economic Association, July.

LEGARDA, B. (1962) 'Foreign Exchange Decontrol and the Redirection of Income Flows', *Philippine Economic Journal*, Vol. 1, No. 1, pp. 18–27.

LESSARD, D. R. (1986) 'Country Risk and the Structure of International Financial Intermediation', Paper presented at the Federal Reserve Bank of St. Louis Conference on Financial Risk, November 14–15.

LESSARD, D. R. (1987) 'Comment' [on Cuddington's 'Macroeconomic Determinants of Capital Flight'], in Lessard and Williamson, eds., pp. 97–100.

LESSARD, D. R. and WILLIAMSON, J. (1987) 'The Problem and Policy Responses', in Lessard and Williamson, eds., pp. 201–54.

LESSARD, D. R. and WILLIAMSON, J., eds., (1987) *Capital Flight and Third World Debt*. Washington, D. C.: Institute for International Economics.

LEWIS, H. T. (1971) *Ilocano. Rice Farmers: A Comparative Study of Two Philippine Barrios*. Honolulu: University of Hawaii Press.

LIM, J. (1986) 'Review of Literature on Rural Finance: A Sub-Reading', Manila: Presidential Committee on Agricultural Credit, Technical Board for Agricultural Credit.

LIND, J. E. (1984) 'Philippine Debt to Foreign Banks', San Francisco: Northern California Interfaith Committee for Corporate Responsibility, November.

LIPTON, M. and LONGHURST, R. (1989) *New Seeds and Poor People*. Baltimore: Johns Hopkins University Press.

LITTLE, I. M. D. (1976) Review of 'Economic Growth and Social Equity in Developing Countries', *Journal of Development Economics*, Vol. 3, No. 1, pp. 99–106.

LOEVINSON, M. E. (1987) 'Insecticide Use and Increased Mortality in Rural Luzon, Philippines', *The Lancet*, No. 8546, 13 June, pp.1359–62.

LOPEZ, M. E. (1987a) 'Has the "Coconut Monopoly" Really Been Cracked?', Center for Research and Communication Staff Memo No. 22, November, pp. 2–5.

LOPEZ, M. E. (1987b) 'The Politics of Lands at Risk in a Philippine Frontier', in P. D. Little and M. M. Horowitz, eds., *Lands at Risk in the Third World: Local-Level Perspectives*. Boulder: Westview, pp. 230–48.

LUKES, S. (1974) *Power: A Radical View*. London: Macmillan.

LUZON SECRETARIAT OF SOCIAL ACTION (LUSSA) (1982) *Countryside Report: Focusing on Five Major Industries: Rice, Coconut, Sugar, Fishing and Abaca*. Manila: LUSSA.

LYNCH, F., ed. (1972) *View from the Paddy: Empirical Studies of Philippine Rice Farming and Tenancy*. Special issue of *Philippine Sociological Review*, Vol. 20, Nos. 1 & 2.

LYNCH, F. (1976) 'Some Empirically-based Conclusions about the Masagana 99 Rice Production Program in Camarines Sur'. Paper presented at the Population Center Foundation's Secondary Analysis Training Course, 7 May.

Reprinted in *A Tribute to Frank Lynch S. J.*, Special issue of Philippine Social Science Information (Quezon City: Philippine Social Science Council), October-December 1978, pp. 2–3, 24.

LYNCH, O., Jr. (1984) 'Withered Roots and Landgrabbers: A Survey of Research on Upland Tenure and Displacement', in C. P. Castro, ed., *Uplands and Uplanders: In Search of New Perspectives*. Quezon City: Bureau of Forest Development, Upland Development Program, pp. 167–230.

LYNCH, O., Jr., and TALBOT, K. (1988) 'Legal Responses to the Philippine Deforestation Crisis', *New York University Journal of International Law and Politics*, Vol. 20, No. 3, pp. 679–713.

MACEWAN, A. (1990) *Debt and Disorder: International Economic Instability and US Imperial Decline*. New York: Monthly Review.

MACKENZIE, D. (1988) 'Uphill Battle to Save Filipino. Trees', *New Scientist*, 30 June, pp. 42–3.

MAGEE, S. P. and BROCK, W. A. (1986) 'Third World Debt and International Capital Market Failure as a Consequence of Redistributive Political Risk Sharing', in M. P. Claudon, ed., *World Debt Crisis: International Lending on Trial*. Cambridge, Mass.: Ballinger, pp. 173–98.

MAITRA, T. and LAHIRI, R. K. (1975) 'Land Utilisation and Crop Yield Estimation', in V. M. Dandekar and P. Venkataramaiah, eds., *Data Base of the Indian Economy, Volume II: Role of Sample Surveys*. Calcutta: Statistical Publishing Society, pp. 153–68.

MAKIL, L. P. R. and FERMIN, P. N. (1978) 'Landless Rural Workers in the Philippines: A Documentary Survey', Final report submitted to the Rural Workers Office of the Department of Labor by the Institute of Philippine Culture, Ateneo de Manila University, January.

MALONE, W. S. (1987) 'Ferdinand E. Marcos: A Trail of Corruption', Investigative report for the Public Broadcasting System/WGBH.

MALTHUS, T. R. (1817) *An Essay on the Principle of Population*. 5th edn., London: John Murray.

MANGAHAS, M. (1975) 'The Political Economy of Rice in the New Society', *Food Research Institute Studies*, vol. 14, No. 3, pp. 295–309.

MANGAHAS, M. (1981) 'Workers' Welfare and Income Distribution: Recent Economic Trends', *Philippine Labor Review*, Vol. 6, No. 3, pp. 53–68.

MANGAHAS, M. (1982) 'What Happened to the Poor on the Way to the Next Development Plan?' *Philippine Economic Journal*, Vol. 21, Nos. 3 & 4, pp. 126–46.

MANGAHAS, M. (1984) 'Perception Indicators of Economic Well-Being: The Philippines in Relation to Other Countries', *ESCAP Seminar on Social and Related Statistics*. Seoul: Republic of Korea, Economic Planning Board, National Bureau of Statistics, pp. 387–437.

MANGAHAS, M. (1985a) 'Growth, Equity and Public Policy in the Rural Sector: A Philippine Case Study with Subnational Data'. Draft report submitted to the Food and Agriculture Organization of the United Nations, November.

MANGAHAS, M. (1985b) 'Rural Poverty and Operation Land Transfer in the Philippines,' in R. Islam, ed., *Strategies for Alleviating Poverty in*

Rural Asia.. Bangkok: ILO/ARTEP and Dhaka: Bangladesh Institute of Development Studies, pp. 201–41.

MANGAHAS, M. (1986) 'The Political Economy of Land Reform and Land Redistribution in the Philippines,' Quezon City: Social Weather Stations, Inc. Mimeo, November.

MANGAHAS, M. (1987) 'Dimensions of Poverty,' Quezon City: Social Weather Stations, Inc. Mimeo.

MANGAHAS, M. and BARROS, B. (1980) 'The Distribution of Income and Wealth: A Survey of Philippine Research', in Philippine Institute for Development Studies (PIDS), *Survey of Philippine Development Research I.* Manila: PIDS, pp. 51–132.

MANGAHAS, M. and LIBRERO, A. R. (1973) 'The High-Yielding Varieties of Rice in the Philippines: A Perspective', Diliman: University of the Philippines School of Economics, Institute of Economic Development and Research Discussion Paper No. 73–11.

MANGAHAS, M., QUIZON, J. L., and LIM, A. (1977) 'A Critique of the NCSO 1975 Family Income and Expenditure Survey', Quezon City: University of the Philippines School of Economics/PREFP Papers, Vol. IV. –3.B, September.

MANGAHAS, M., RECTO, A. and RUTTAN, V. W. (1966) 'Market Relationships for Rice and Corn in the Philippines', *Philippine Economic Journal*, Vol. 5, No. 1.

MANLOGON, M. and LACABA, J. F. (1989) 'Carlos Dominguez: Of Rice and Prices', *Midweek*, Vol. 4, No. 22, 10 May, pp. 13–15, 44.

MARRIS, S. (1985) *Deficits and the Dollar: The World Economy at Risk.* Washington, D. C.: Institute for International Economics.

MARX, K. (1967) *Capital.* New York: International Publishers.

MAXFIELD, S. (1989) 'National Business, Debt-Led Growth, and Political Transition in Latin America', in B. Stallings and R. Kaufman, eds., *Debt and Democracy in Latin America.* Boulder: Westview, pp. 75–90.

McANDREW, J. P. (1983) *The Impact of Corporate Mining on Local Philippine Communities.* Davao City: Alternate Resource Center.

McCOY, A. W. (1982) 'A Queen Dies Slowly: The Rise and Decline of Iloilo City', in McCoy and de Jesus, eds., pp. 297–358.

McCOY, A. W. (1983) '"In Extreme Unction": The Philippine Sugar Industry', in *Political Economy of Philippine Commodities*, Quezon City: University of the Philippines, Third World Studies Program, pp. 135–79.

McCOY, A. W. (1984) *Priests on Trial.* New York: Penguin.

McCOY, A. W. (1985) 'Rural Philippines: Technological Change in the Sugar Industry', in R. J. May and F. Nemenzo, eds., *The Philippines After Marcos.* London & Sydney: Croom Helm.

McCOY, A. (1988) 'Oligarchy: Filipino. Families and the Politics of Survival', Paper presented at the Annual Meeting of the Association for Asian Studies, San Francisco, 26 March.

McCOY, A. W. and DE JESUS, E. C., eds., (1982) *Philippine Social History: Global Trade and Local Transformations.* Quezon City: Ateneo de Manila

University Press; Sydney: George Allen & Unwin; Honolulu: University of Hawaii Press.

McCUE, A. (1982) 'Philippines Facing Ecological Disaster As Villagers, Loggers Denude Hillsides', *The Wall Street Journal*, 27 April.

McEWAN, F. L. and STEPHENSON, G. R. (1979) *The Use and Significance of Pesticides in the Environment*. New York: John Wiley & Sons.

McGILL, P. (1986) 'Sugar Island Children Reap Bitter Harvest of Hunger', *The Observer* (London), 13 July, p. 19.

McLENNAN, M. S. (1969) 'Land and Tenancy in the Central Luzon Plain', *Philippine Studies*, Vol. 17, No. 4, pp. 651–82.

McLENNAN, M. S. (1982) 'Changing Human Ecology on the Central Luzon Plain: Nueva Ecija, 1705–1939', in McCoy and de Jesus, eds., pp. 57–90.

MEARS, L. A., AGABIN, M. H., ANDEN, T. L. and MARQUEZ, R. C. (1974) *Rice Economy of the Philippines*. Quezon City: University of the Philippines Press.

MELLOR, J. W. (1986) 'Agriculture on the Road to Industrialization', in J. P. Lewis and V. Kallab, eds., *Development Strategies Reconsidered*, New Brunswick, N. J.: Transactions Books for the Overseas Development Council.

MELLOR, J. W. (1987) 'Determinants of Rural Poverty: The Dynamics of Production, Technology, and Price', in Mellor and Desai, eds., pp. 21–40.

MELLOR, J. W. and DESAI, G. M., eds., (1987) *Agricultural Change and Rural Poverty: Variations on a Theme by Dharm Narain*. Baltimore: Johns Hopkins University Press.

MILLER, J. (1973) 'Genetic Erosion: Crop Plants Threatened by Government Neglect', *Science*, Vol. 182, pp. 1231–3.

MOFFETT, M. and TRUELL, P. (1988) 'The Man Who Did Mexico's Borrowing Now Works on a Possible Solution. . .' *Wall Street Journal*, 25 January.

MONTES, M. F. (1987) 'Macroeconomic Adjustment in the Philippines, 1983–85', PIDS Working Paper No. 8701, February.

MOORE, B. (1910) 'Forest Problems in the Philippines', *American Forestry*, Vol. 16, February and March, pp.75–81, 149–54.

MORGAN GUARANTY TRUST COMPANY OF NEW YORK (1986) 'LDC Capital Flight', *World Financial Markets*, March, pp. 13–15.

MORRELL, J. (1979) 'Aid to the Philippines: Who Benefits?' *International Policy Report* (Washington, D. C.: Center for International Policy), Vol. 5, No. 2, October.

MOSLEY, P. (1980) 'Aid, Savings and Growth Revisited', *Oxford Bulletin of Economics and Statistics*, Vol. 42, No. 2.

MULTISECTORAL FORUM (1986) 'Position Paper on the Philippine Rice Problem', in *Sowing the Seed: Proceedings of the International Solidarity Conference for the Filipino. Peasantry, October 11–21, 1986*. Manila: Kilusang Magbubukid ng Pilipinas, 1988, pp. 285–96.

MYDANS, S. (1990) 'Recovering Marcos Assets Proves Trying For Aquino', *The New York Times*, 18 November, p. 2E.

MYERS, N. (1988) 'Environmental Degradation and Some Economic Consequences in the Philippines', *Environmental Conservation*, Vol. 15, No. 3,
pp. 205–14.

NASOL, R. L. (1971) 'Demand Analysis for Rice in the Philippines', *Journal
of Agricultural Economics and Development*, Vol. 1, No. 1, pp. 1–13.

NATIONAL ACADEMY OF SCIENCES (1972) *Genetic Vulnerability of
Major Crops*. Report of the Committee on Genetic Vulnerability of Major
Crops, Agricultural Board, Division of Biology and Agriculture, National
Research Council. Washington, D. C.: National Academy of Sciences.

NATIONAL CENSUS AND STATISTICS OFFICE (NCSO) (1985) *1980
Census of Agriculture: National Summary. Volume 1: Final Report*. Manila.

NCSO (1986a) *1985 Foreign Trade Statistics of the Philippines*. Manila.

NCSO (1986b) *1985 Family Income and Expenditures Survey: Volume 1:
National Summary: Final Report*. Manila, December.

NATIONAL ECONOMIC AND DEVELOPMENT AUTHORITY (NEDA)
(1974) *Statistical Yearbook 1974*. Manila.

NEDA (1976) *Statistical Yearbook of the Philippines 1976*. Manila.

NEDA (1986) *1986 Philippine Statistical Yearbook*. Manila.

NEDA (1986b) *Medium-Term Philippine Development Plan, 1987–1992*.
Manila. November.

NEDA, Technical Working Group on Poverty (1988) 'A Monograph for the
Estimation of the 1985 Poverty and Subsistence Thresholds and Incidences'.
Manila, typescript.

NATIONAL STATISTICAL COORDINATION BOARD (NSCB) (1988) *The
Philippine Food Balance Sheet, CY 1973 to CY 1986*. Manila.

NSCB (1989) *1989 Philippine Statistical Yearbook*. Manila.

NATONTON, J. and ABRAHAM, F. B., Jr. (1984) 'Regenerated Forest in
Agusan', in *The Key to Philippine Forest Conservation: The Defense of the
Dipterocarps*. Manila: Columbian Publishing Corp., pp. 100–24.

NAYLOR, R. T. (1987) *Hot Money and the Politics of Debt*. New York: Simon
and Schuster.

NECTOUX, F. and KURODA, Y. (1989) *Timber from the South Seas: An
Analysis of Japan's Tropical Timber Trade and its Environmental Impact*.
Gland, Switzerland: WWF International (World Wide Fund for Nature).

NELSON, G. C. (1988) 'Sugar in the Philippines: Policy Responses to a
Distorted World Market', *Food Policy*, Vol. 13, No. 3, pp. 283–92.

NORTH, D. C. and THOMAS, R. P. (1973) *The Rise of the Western World: A
New Economic History*. Cambridge: Cambridge University Press.

NYBERG, A. J. (1968) 'Growth in the Philippine Coconut Industry,
1901–1966', *Philippine Economic Journal*, Vol. 7, No. 1, pp. 42–52.

O'CONNELL, D. P. (1967) *State Succession in Municipal Law and International Law. Vol. 1: Internal Relations*. Cambridge: Cambridge University
Press.

OFRENEO, R. E. (1985) 'Philippine Industrial Debacle and the Debt Crisis',
Economic and Industrial Democracy, Vol. 6, pp. 161–84.

OFRENEO, R. E. (1980) *Capitalism in Philippine Agriculture*. Quezon City:

Foundation for Nationalist Studies.

OLOFSON, H. (1981) 'Introduction', in H. Olofson, eds., *Adaptive Strategies and Change in Philippine Swidden-based Societies*. Laguna: Forest Research Institute, pp. 1–12.

OOI, J. B. (1987) *Depletion of Forest Resources in the Philippines*. Singapore: Institute of Southeast Asian Studies, ASEAN Economic Research Unit, Field Report Series No. 18.

OPENA, C. L. and PAHM, E. A. (1987) 'Directions of Agrarian Reform in Agribusiness Plantations', University of the Philippines at Los Banos, Institute of Agrarian Studies, Occasional Papers No. 18, April.

ORDEN, M. E. (1987) 'Living Condition, Employment and Income of Landless Households in Favorable and Unfavorable Production Environments', Paper presented at the First Workshop on Differential Impact of Modern Rice Technology on Favorable and Unfavorable Production Environments, International Rice Research Institute, Los Banos, 23–5 March. IRRI Agricultural Economics Department Paper No. 87–15.

ORGANISATION FOR ECONOMIC CO-OPERATION and DEVELOPMENT (OECD) (1985) *Statistics on External Indebtedness: The Debt and Other External Liabilities of Developing, CMEA and Certain Other Countries and Territories at End-December 1983 and End-December 1984*. Paris: OECD.

OECD (1987) *External Debt Statistics: The Debt and Other External Liabilities of Developing, CMEA and Certain Other Countries and Territories at End-December 1985 and End-December 1986*. Paris: OECD.

OECD (1991) *Environmental Indicators: A Preliminary Set*. Paris: OECD.

OSHIMA, H. T. (1983) 'Sources of Philippine Postwar Economic Growth: The Overall Record in Comparative Perspective', *Journal of Philippine Development*, Vol. 10, No. 1, pp. 1–44.

OSHIMA, H. T., DE BORJA, E., and PAZ, W. (1986) 'Rising National Income per Worker and Falling Real Wages in the Philippines in the 1970s', *Philippine Review of Economics and Business*, Vol. 23, Nos. 3 & 4, pp. 151–90.

OTSUKA, K. (1987) 'Technical Change and Land Reform Implementation: A Comparative Analysis of Five Rice-Dependent Villages in the Philippines', Paper presented at the Second Workshop on Differential Impact of Modern Rice Technology on Favorable and Unfavorable Production Environments, International Rice Research Institute, Los Banos, 23–5 March.

OTSUKA, K., CORDOVA, V. G. and DAVID, C. C. (1987) 'Technological Change, Population Growth, and Wage Differential: Favorable and Unfavorable Rice-Growing Villages in the Philippines', Paper presented at the First Workshop on Differential Impact of Modern Rice Technology on Favorable and Unfavorable Production Environments, Thailand and Indonesia, 17–26 November.

OVERHOLT, W. H. (1976) 'Land Reform in the Philippines', *Asian Survey*, Vol. 6, No. 5, pp. 427–51.

OVERHOLT, W. H. (1987) 'Pressures and Policies: Prospects for Cory Aquino's Philippines', in Lande, ed., pp. 89–110.

PAHILANGA-DE LOS REYES, R. and LYNCH, F. (1972) 'Reluctant Rebels: Leasehold Converts in Nueva Ecija', in Lynch, ed., pp. 7–78.

PAIGE, J. M. (1975) *Agrarian Revolution: Social Movements and Export Agriculture in the Underdeveloped World.* New York: Free Press; London: Collier Macmillan.

PANGANIBAN, L. R. (1983) 'Exchange Rate Adjustment: The Philippine Experience', *Central Bank Review*, Vol. 35, No. 9, September, pp. 8–11.

PAPANEK, G. F. (1972) 'The Effect of Aid and Other Resource Transfers on Savings and Growth in Less Developed Countries', *Economic Journal*, Vol. 82, pp. 934–50.

PASTOR, M. (1989) 'Current Account Deficits and Debt Accumulation in Latin America', *Journal of Development Economics*, Vol. 31, No. 1, pp. 77–97.

PASTOR, M. (1990) 'Capital Flight from Latin America', *World Development*, Vol. 18, No. 1, pp. 1–13.

PASZTOR, A. (1987) 'Inquiry Into Payments by Westinghouse to Marcos Aide Expected to be Dropped', *The Wall Street Journal*, 15 December.

PATRICK, H. and MORENO, H. A. (1985) 'Philippine Private Domestic Commercial Banking, 1946–80, in the Light of Japanese Experience', in K. Ohkawa and G. Ranis, eds., *Japan and the Developing Countries.* Oxford: Basil Blackwell, pp. 311–65.

PAYER, C. (1974) *The Debt Trap: The International Monetary Fund and the Third World.* New York: Monthly Review.

PAYER, C. (1985) 'Repudiating the Past', *NACLA Report on the Americas*, Vol. 19, No. 2, pp. 14–24.

PAYER, C. (1991) *Lent and Lost: Foreign Credit and Third World Development.* London: Zed Books.

PAYER, C., ed. (1975) *Commodity Trade of the Third World.* New York: Wiley.

PEAGAM, N. (1984) 'The Spectre that Haunts Marcos', *Euromoney*, April, pp. 46–63.

PEARSE, A. (1980) *Seeds of Plenty, Seeds of Want: Social and Economic Implications of the Green Revolution.* Oxford: Clarendon.

PELZER, K. J. (1945) *Pioneer Settlement in the Asiatic Tropics: Studies in Land Utilization and Agricultural Colonization in Southeastern Asia.* New York: American Geographical Society.

PESARAN, M. H. and PESARAN, B. (1987) *Data-FIT: An Interactive Econometric Software Package.* Oxford: Oxford University Press.

PHILIPPINE COCONUT AUTHORITY (1988) *Coconut Industry Yearbook.* August.

PHILIPPINE-GERMAN FOREST RESOURCES INVENTORY PROJECT (1988) *Natural Forest Resources of the Philippines.* Manila: Department of Environment and Natural Resources, Forest Management Bureau.

PHILIPPINE PEASANT INSTITUTE (1989) 'Unmasking the Rice Cartel', *Farm News and Views*, Vol. 2, No. 4, pp. 2–3.

PICK, F. (1968) *Pick's Currency Yearbook 1968*. New York: Pick Publishing.

PINEDA-OFRENEO, R. (1985) 'The Philippine Sugar Crisis in an International Setting'. Quezon City: University of the Philippines Law Complex, International Studies Institute of the Philippines, Research Report No. 1.

POFFENBERGER, M. (1990) 'The Evolution of Forestry Management Systems in Southeast Asia', in M. Poffenberger, ed., *Keepers of the Forest: Land Management Alternatives in Southeast Asia*, West Hartford: Kumarian Press, pp. 7–26.

POMEROY, W. (1970) *American Neo-Colonialism: Its Emergence in the Philippines and Asia*. New York: International Publishers.

PORTER, G. and GANAPIN, D., Jr. (1988) *Resources, Population, and the Philippines' Future: A Case Study*. Washington: World Resources Institute.

POWER, J. H. (1983) 'Response to Balance of Payments Crises in the 1970's: Korea and the Philippines', Philippine Institute for Development Studies Staff Paper Series No. 83–05.

POWER, J. H. and SICAT, G. P. (1971) *The Philippines: Industrialization and Trade Policies*. London: Oxford University Press, for the Development Centre of the OECD.

POWER, J. H. and TUMANENG, T. D. (1983) 'Comparative Advantage and Government Price Intervention Policies in Forestry', Manila: Philippine Institute for Development Studies Working Paper No. 83–05.

PUTZEL, J. and CUNNINGTON, J. (1989) *Gaining Ground: Agrarian Reform in the Philippines*. London: War on Want.

QUIBRIA, M. and RASHID, S. (1984) 'The Puzzle of Sharecropping: A Survey of Theories', *World Development*, Vol. 12, No. 2, pp. 103–14.

QUISUMBING, M. A. (1987a) 'The Philippine Food and Nutrition Situation: Trends and Policy Issues', in UPLB Agricultural Policy Working Group, *Policy Issues on Nutrition and Welfare*, College, Laguna: UPLB, Center for Policy and Development Studies, pp. 11–51.

QUISUMBING, M. A. (1987b) 'Land Reform for Forest and Upland Areas: Some Suggestions', Los Banos: UPLB, Department of Economics, mimeo, May.

QUISUMBING, M. A. (1991) 'International Transfers in Philippine Rice Villages: Gender Differences in Traditional Inheritance Customs'. New Haven: Yale University, Economic Growth Centre, mimeo, April.

RAFFERTY, K. (1983) 'Thrilla in Manila', *Institutional Investor*, December, pp. 98–104.

RANIS, G. (1984) 'Brief Reflections on the Philippine Economy: Summer, 1984', Prepared statement before the Subcommittee on Asian and International Affairs, Committee on Foreign Affairs, US House of Representatives, September 20.

RANIS, G. (1987) 'Marcos's Economic Legacy: Problems, Policies, and Prospects for President Aquino. and How the United States Can Help', in Lande, ed., pp. 111–21.

RANIS, G. and STEWART, F. (1987) 'Rural Linkages in the Philippines and

Taiwan', in F. Stewart, ed., *Macro-Policies for Appropriate Technology in Developing Countries*. Boulder: Westview, pp. 140–91.

RAVEN, P. H. (1987) *The Global Ecosystem in Crisis*. Chicago: MacArthur Foundation, December.

REID, W. V., BARNES, J. N. and BLACKWELDER, B. (1988) *Bankrolling Successes: A Portfolio of Sustainable Development Projects*. Washington, D. C.: Environmental Policy Institute and National Wildlife Federation.

REINAH, D. (1987) 'Philippine Sugar Industry Market Considerations and United States Policy', in Lande, ed., pp. 141–55.

REISEN, H. and VAN TROTSENBURG, A. (1988) *Developing Country Debt: The Budgetary and Transfer Problem*. Paris: OECD Development Centre.

REMOLONA, E. M. and LAMBERTE, M. B. (1986) 'Financial Reforms and Balance-of Payments Crisis: The Case of the Philippines: 1980–83', *Philippine Review of Economics and Business*, Vol. 23, Nos. 1 & 2, pp. 101–41.

REMOLONA, E. M., MANGAHAS, M. and PANTE, F., Jr. (1985) 'Foreign Debt, Balance of Payments and the Economic Crisis of the Philippines in 1983–84'. Report to the Group of Twenty-Four, UNDP/UNCTAD Project INT/84/021: Studies on International Monetary and Financial Issues for Developing Countries.

REPETTO, R. (1983) 'Overview', in R. Repetto and M. Gillis, eds., *Public Policies and the Misuse of Forest Resources*. Cambridge: Cambridge University Press, pp. 1–41.

REPETTO, R. (1989) 'Nature's Resources as Productive Assets', *Challenge*, Vol. 32, No. 5, pp. 16–20.

REPUBLIC OF THE PHILIPPINES, Ministry of Agrarian Reform (1984) *Working Arrangements and Management Practices in Sugar Lands*. UNDP/FAO 'Expanded Assistance to the Agrarian Reform Program' Study No. 3. Manila, June.

RES, L. (1985) 'Changing Labor Allocation Patterns of Women in Rice Farm Households: a Rainfed Rice Village, Iloilo Province, Philippines', in International Rice Research Institute, *Women in Rice Farming* (Aldershot: Gower Publishing), pp. 91–118.

REVILLA, A. V., Jr. (1984) 'Forest Land Management in the Context of National Land Use', Philippine Institute for Development Studies Working Paper No. 84–02.

REYES, B. Y. and AGABIN, M. H. (1985) 'A History of Credit Programs Supporting Agricultural Mechanization in the Philippines', *Journal of Philippine Development*, Vol. 12, No. 1, pp. 211–25.

REYES, E. A., MILAN, E. and SANCHEZ, M. T. (1988) 'Employment, Productivity and Wages in the Philippine Labor Market: An Analysis of Trends and Policies', Manila: Philippine Institute for Development Studies, mimeo.

REYES, L. B. and REYES-CANTOS, J. (1989) 'PNB and DBP: Business as Usual', *IBON Facts and Figures*, Vol. 12, No. 9, pp. 1–7.

REYES, M. R. (1984) 'Perpetuating the Dipterocarp Forest in Productive

Condition,' in *The Key to Philippine Forest Conservation: Defense of the Dipterocarps*. Manila: Columbian Publishing Corp., pp. 28–60.

REYES, B. Y. and AGABIN, M. H. (1985) 'A History of Credit Programs Supporting Agricultural Mechanization in the Philippines', *Journal of Philippine Development*, Vol. 12, No. 1, pp. 211–25.

RICH, B. (1989) 'Funding Deforestation: Conservation Woes at the World Bank', *The Nation* (New York), 23 January, pp. 73, 88–91.

RIDDELL, R. C. (1987) *Foreign Aid Reconsidered*. Baltimore: Johns Hopkins University Press; London: James Currey.

ROCAMORA, J. and O'CONNOR, D. (1977) 'The US, Land Reform and Rural Development in the Philippines', in W. Bello and S. Rivera, eds., *The Logistics of Repression*. Washington, D. C.: Friends of the Filipino. People, pp. 63–92.

ROLA, A. C. (1988) 'Assessing the Benefits and Risks of Pesticide Use in Philippine Agriculture', Los Banos: UPLB, Center for Policy and Development Studies, Working Paper No. 88–03.

ROMULO, C. P. (1968) 'Strategy for the Conquest of Hunger', in *Strategy for the Conquest of Hunger: Proceedings of a Symposium Convened by The Rockefeller Foundation, April 1 and 2, 1968, at the Rockefeller University.* New York: Rockefeller Foundation, pp. 116–22.

ROOSEVELT, T. (1934) 'Land Problems in Puerto Rico and the Philippine Islands', *Geographical Review*, Vol. 24, pp. 182–204.

ROQUE, C. R. (1987) 'Environmental Futures of the Philippines', in F. S. Jose, ed., *A Filipino. Agenda for the 21st Century.* Manila: Solidaridad, pp. 305–17.

ROSE, B. (1985) *Appendix to the Rice Economy of Asia*. Washington: Resources for the Future in cooperation with the International Rice Research Institute.

ROSENBERG, D. A., ed. (1979) *Marcos and Martial Law in the Philippines*. Ithaca: Cornell University Press.

ROSENBERG, J. G. and ROSENBERG, D. A. (1980) *Landless Peasants and Rural Poverty in Indonesia and the Philippines*. Ithaca, N. Y.: Cornell University, Rural Development Committee, Special Series on Landlessness and Near-Landlessness, No. 3, February.

ROSENGRANT, M. W., GONZALES, L. A., BOUIS, H. E. and SISON, J. F. (1987) 'Price and Investment Policies for Food Crop Sector Growth in the Philippines', Washington, D. C.: International Food Policy Research Institute. Final Report submitted to the Asian Development Bank for the project 'Study of Food Demand/Supply Prospects and Related Strategies for Developing Member Countries of ADB, Phase II'. 20 January.

ROTH, D. (1983) 'Philippine Forests and Forestry, 1565–1920', in R. Tucker and J. F. Richards, eds., *Global Deforestation and the Nineteenth Century World Economy.* Durham, North Carolina: Duke University Press, pp. 30–49.

RUTTAN, V. W. (1969) 'Agricultural Prices and Factor Markets in Southeast Asia', *Economic Development and Cultural Change*, Vol. 17, No. 4,

pp. 501–19.

RUTTAN, V. W. (1977) 'The Green Revolution: Seven Generalizations', *International Development Review*, Vol. 19, No. 4, pp. 16–23.

RUTTAN, V. W. (1978) 'A Postscript on Alternative Paths of Induced Institutional Change', in H. P. Binswanger and V. W. Ruttan, eds., *Induced Innovation: Technology, Institutions, and Development*. Baltimore: Johns Hopkins University Press, pp. 409–13.

RUTTAN, V. W. and BINSWANGER, H. P. (1978) 'Induced Innovation and the Green Revolution', in H. P. Binswanger and V. W. Ruttan, eds., *Induced Innovation: Technology, Institutions, and Development*. Baltimore: Johns Hopkins University Press, pp. 358–408.

RUTTEN, R. (1982) *Women Workers of Hacienda Milagros: Wage Labor and Household Subsistence on a Philippine Sugarcane Plantation*. Amsterdam: University of Amsterdam, Department of South and Southeast Asian Studies, Monograph No. 30.

SABORIO, S. (1990) 'The Costa Rican Debt Accord: Lessons and Implications', Washington, D. C.: Overseas Development Council, mimeo.

SACERDOTI, G. (1982) 'Out of a Cooking-oil Crisis -A Multipurpose Giant', *Far Eastern Economic Review*, 8 January, pp. 44–8.

SACERDOTI, G. and OCAMPO, S. (1982) 'Guthrie and the Angels', *Far Eastern Economic Review*, November 19, pp. 58–62.

SACHS, J. D. (1984) 'Comments' [on Diaz-Alejandro's "Latin American Debt"], *Brookings Papers on Economic Activity* 2:1984, pp. 393–401.

SACHS, J. D. (1988) 'Comprehensive Debt Retirement: The Bolivian Example', *Brookings Papers on Economic Activity* 2:1988, pp. 705–13.

SAITH, A. (1983) 'Development and Distribution: A Critique of the Cross-Country U-Hypothesis', *Journal of Development Economics*, Vol. 13, pp. 367–82.

SANGALANG, J. B. (1987) 'The Coconut Replanting Program', in UPLB Agricultural Policy Working Group, *Policy Issues on the Philippine Rice Economy and Agricultural Trade*. Los Banos: UPLB, Center for Policy and Development Studies, pp. 225–45.

SANTOS, J. (1985) 'Caram Charges Benedicto on Unforwarded Forward Contracts', *Mr. & Ms.* (Manila), 14–20 June, pp. 32–3.

SCANDIZZO, P. L. and DIAKOSAWAS, D. (1987) *Instability in the Terms of Trade of Primary Commodities, 1900–1982*. Rome: FAO Economic and Social Development Paper No. 64.

SCHIRMER, D. B. and SHALOM, S. R., eds., (1987) *The Philippines Reader: A History of Colonialism, Neocolonialism, Dictatorship, and Resistance*. Boston: South End Press.

SCHUL, N. W. (1967) 'A Philippine Sugar Cane Plantation: Land Tenure and Sugar Cane Production', *Economic Geography*, Vol. 43, pp. 157–69.

SCOTT, J. (1976) *The Moral Economy of the Peasant: Rebellion and Subsistence in Southeast Asia*. New Haven: Yale University Press.

SCOTT, M. (1989) 'The Disappearing Forests', *Far Eastern Economic Review*, 12 January, pp. 34–8.

SEN, A. K. (1962) 'An Aspect of Indian Agriculture', *Economic Weekly*, Vol. 14, Nos. 4–6, pp. 243–6.

SEN, A. K. (1975) *Employment, Technology and Development*. Oxford: Oxford University Press.

SEN, A. K. (1981) *Poverty and Famines: An Essay on Entitlement and Deprivation*. Oxford: Clarendon Press.

SEN, A. K. (1984) 'Goods and People', in his *Resources, Values and Development*. Cambridge, Mass.: Harvard University Press, pp. 509–32.

SEN, A. K. (1987) *The Standard of Living*. Cambridge: Cambridge University Press.

SEN, A. K. (1988) 'Sri Lanka's Achievements: How and When', in T. N. Srinivasan and P. K. Bardhan, eds., *Rural Poverty in South Asia*. New York: Columbia University Press, pp. 549–56.

SHAPLEN, R. (1986) 'The Philippines -Part II', *The New Yorker*, September 1.

SHELDRICK, W. F. (1987) *World Nitrogen Survey*. Washington, D. C.: World Bank Technical Paper No. 59.

SIAMWALLA, A. and HAYKIN, S. (1983) 'The World Rice Market: Structure, Conduct, and Performance', Washington: IFPRI Research Report No. 39, June.

SIMON, J. L. (1975) 'The Positive Effect of Population Growth on Agricultural Saving in Irrigation Systems', *Review of Economics and Statistics*, Vol. 57, No. 1, pp. 71–9.

SIY, R. Y., Jr. (1982) *Community Resource Management: Lessons from the Zanjera*. Quezon City: University of the Philippines Press.

SIY, R. Y., Jr. (1988) 'A Tradition of Collective Action: Farmers and Irrigation in the Philippines', in Korten and Siy, eds., pp. 20–30.

SJAASTAD, L. (1984) 'Where the Latin Loans Went', *Fortune*, November 26, pp. 197–202.

SMITH, C. (1986) 'Kickback for Japan: Documents Suggest Marcos was Paid "Commissions"', *Far Eastern Economic Review*, 24 April, pp. 42–3.

SMITH, G. W. and CUDDINGTON, J. T., eds., (1985) *International Debt and the Developing Countries*. Washington, D. C.: The World Bank.

SOBHAN, R. (1983) *Rural Poverty and Agrarian Reform in the Philippines*. Rome: FAO, In-depth Study Series No. 2.

SPRAOS, J. (1980) 'The Statistical Debate on the Net Barter Terms of Trade between Primary Commodities and Manufactures', *Economic Journal*, Vol. 90, pp. 107–28.

STAUFFER, R. B. (1979) 'The Political Economy of Refeudalization', in Rosenberg, ed., pp. 180–219.

STEVE, G. T. and COWITT, P. P. (1976) *Pick's Currency Yearbook 1975–1976*. New York: Pick Publishing.

STREETEN, P. (1987) *What Price Food? Agricultural Price Policies in Developing Countries*. London: Macmillan.

SZANTON, M. C. B. (1972) *A Right to Survive: Subsistence Marketing in a Lowland Philippine Town*. University Park: Pennsylvania State University Press.

TABORA, M. C. D. (1986) 'Overseas Workers: An Important Dollar Earner', *Central Bank Review*, Vol. 38, No. 4, April, pp. 21–5.

TADEM, E. C. (1980) *Mindanao Report: A Preliminary Study on the Economic Origins of Social Unrest*. Davao City: Afrim Resource Center.

TADEM, E. C., REYES, J. and MAGNO, L. S. (1984) *Showcases of Underdevelopment: Fishes, Forests, and Fruits*. Davao City: Alternate Resource Center.

TAKAHASHI, A. (1970) *Land and Peasants in Central Luzon: Socioeconomic Structure of a Philippine Village*. Honolulu: East-West Center Press.

TAKEUCHI, K. (1974) *Tropical Hardwood Trade in the Asia-Pacific Region*. World Bank Staff Occasional Paper No. 17. Baltimore: Johns Hopkins University Press.

TAN, E. A. and HOLAZO, V. (1979) 'Measuring Poverty Incidence in a Segmented Market: The Philippine Case', *Philippine Economic Journal*, Vol. 18, No. 4, pp. 450–90.

TANCO, A., Jr. (1976) 'Food: Directions for the Year 2000', *Philippine Development*, 15 December, pp. 5–6.

TAYLOR, L. (1985) 'The Theory and Practice of Developing Country Debt: An Informal Guide for the Perplexed', *Journal of Development Planning*, No. 16, pp. 195–227.

THOMPSON, E. T. (1941) 'The Climatic Theory of the Plantation', *Agricultural History*, Vol. 15, No. 1, pp. 49–60.

THOMPSON, M. and SLAYTON, G. W. (1985) 'An Essay on Credit Arrangements Between the IMF and the Republic of the Philippines: 1970–1983', *Philippine Review of Economics and Business*, Vol. 22, Nos. 1 & 2, pp. 59–80.

TIDALGO, R. L. (1976) 'Labor Absorption in the Philippines, 1956–73', *Philippine Economic Journal*, Vol. 15, Nos. 1 & 2, pp. 183–237.

TIDALGO, R. L. P. and ESGUERRA, E. F. (1984) *Philippine Employment in the Seventies*. Manila: Philippine Institute for Development Studies.

TIETENBERG, T. (1988) *Environmental and Natural Resource Economics*. 2nd edn., Glenview: Scott, Foresman.

TIGLAO, R. (1981) *Looking into Coconuts: The Philippine Coconut Industry, Export-Oriented Agricultural Growth*. Davao City: Alternate Resource Center.

TIMMER, C. P. (1974) 'A Model of Rice Marketing Margins in Indonesia', *Food Research Institute Studies*, Vol. 13, No. 2, pp. 145–68.

TIMMER, C. P. and FALCON, W. P. (1975) 'The Political Economy of Rice Production and Trade in Asia', in L. G. Reynolds, ed., *Agriculture in Development Theory*. New Haven: Yale University Press, pp. 373–408.

TOLCHIN, M. (1990) 'Rewards of Public Service Are Growing', *The New York Times*, 13 May.

TREADGOLD, M. and HOOLEY, R. W. (1967) 'Decontrol and the Redirection of Income Flows: A Second Look', *Philippine Economic Journal*, Vol. 6, No. 2, pp. 109–28.

TRUELL, P. (1988) 'Bolivia Buys Back Nearly Half of Its Debt to Banks at a Fraction of the Face Value', *Wall Street Journal*, 18 March.

TRUELL, P. (1990) 'Bolivia and Brazil Reach Accord on Plan to Cut $300 Million of Each Other's Debt', *Wall Street Journal*, 11 May.

TRYON, J. L. (1967) 'Internal and External Terms of Trade in Post-War Philippines', *Philippine Economic Journal*, Vol. 6, No. 2, pp. 189–209.

TWAIN, M. (1901) 'To the Person Sitting in Darkness', *North American Review*, No. 531, February, pp. 161–76.

UMEHARA, H. (1974) *A Hacienda Barrio in Central Luzon: Case Study of a Philippine Village*. Tokyo: Institute of Developing Economies.

UMEHARA, H. (1983) 'Green Revolution for Whom? (An Inquiry into its Beneficiaries in a Central Luzon Village, Philippines)', in Ledesma, Makil, and Miralao, eds., pp. 24–40.

UNICEF, Manila (1988) 'Redirecting Adjustment Programmes towards Growth and the Protection of the Poor: The Philippine Case', in G. A. Cornia, R. Jolly, and F. Stewart, eds., *Adjustment with a Human Face, Volume II: Country Case Studies*. Oxford: Clarendon Press, pp. 184–217.

UNITED NATIONS (1988) *World Demographic Estimates and Projections, 1950–2025*. New York: United Nations, Department of International Economic and Social Affairs.

UNITED NATIONS ECONOMIC COMMISSION FOR ASIA AND THE FAR EAST (UNECAFE) (1965) *Economic Survey of Asia and the Far East 1964*. New York: United Nations.

UNITED NATIONS ECONOMIC COMMISSION FOR ASIA AND THE FAR EAST (UNECAFE) (1969) *The Coconut Industry of Asia*. Regional Plan Harmonization and Integration Studies Series No. 1. Bangkok and New York: UNECAFE.

UNITED NATIONS INDUSTRIAL DEVELOPMENT ORGANIZATION (UNIDO) (1983) *Industry in a Changing World*. New York: United Nations.

UNIDO (1985) *Industrial Development Review Series: The Philippines*. Report UNIDO/IS. 527, prepared by the Division for Industrial Studies, Regional and Country Studies Branch, 10 April.

UNITED STATES AGENCY FOR INTERNATIONAL DEVELOPMENT (USAID) (1977) *Philippines: Crop Protection: Proposal and Recommendations For the Review of the Development Loan Committee*. Washington, DC: USAID Project Paper, August.

USAID (1979) *Environmental and Natural Resource Management in Developing Countries: A Report to Congress. Volume I*. Washington, DC: USAID, February.

USAID (1980) *Country Development Strategy Statement, FY 1982: Philippines*. Manila: USAID, January.

USAID (1983) *US Overseas Loans and Grants and Assistance from International Organizations: Obligations and Loan Authorizations, July 1, 1945 -September 30, 1983*. Washington, D. C.: USAID.

USAID (1985) *Country Development Strategy Statement, FY 1986–90:*

USAID/Philippines. Washington, D. C.: USAID, March. [Abridged version: April 1986.]

UNITED STATES CENTRAL INTELLIGENCE AGENCY (1987) *The World Factbook 1987*. Washington, D. C.: Central Intelligence Agency.

UNNEVEHR, L. J. (1983) 'The Effect and Cost of Philippine Government Intervention in Rice Markets', Washington: International Food Policy Research Institute, Rice Policies in Southeast Asia Project, Working Paper No. 9.

UNNEVEHR, L. J. and BALISACAN, A. M. (1983) 'Changing Comparative Advantage in Philippine Rice Production', Manila: Philippine Institute for Development Studies Working Paper No. 83–03.

VALIENTE, A. M., Jr., *et al.* (1979) 'Coconut Socio-Economic and Marketing Study: Southern Mindanao', Manila: Ministry of Agriculture, mimeo.

VIRATA, C. (1984) 'North-South Dialogue' [Interview with Cesar Virata], *Third World Quarterly*, Vol. 6, No. 2, pp. 272–81.

WADE, N. (1974) 'Green Revolution (II): Problems of Adapting a Western Technology', *Science*, Vol. 186, 27 December, pp. 1186–92.

WALLICH, H. C. (1984) 'Capital Movements -The Tail That Wags the Dog', in *The International Monetary System: Forty Years After Bretton Woods*. Boston; Federal Reserve Bank of Boston, Conference Series No. 28, pp. 179–87.

WALTER, I. (1987) 'The Mechanisms of Capital Flight', in Lessard and Williamson, eds., pp. 103–28.

WEINER, B. (1987) 'Advice for Mrs. Aquino: Get Business on the Government's Side', *The New York Times*, 11 January.

WEISSKOPF, T. E. (1972) 'The Impact of Foreign Capital Inflow on Domestic Savings in Underdeveloped Countries', *Journal of International Economics*, Vol. 2, pp. 25–38.

WELLONS, P. A. (1977) *Borrowing by Developing Countries on the Eurocurrency Market*. Paris: OECD Development Centre.

WGBH EDUCATIONAL FOUNDATION (1987) 'In Search of the Marcos Millions', Transcript of *Frontline* No. 511, broadcast by the Public Broadcasting System on May 26. Available from: WGBH Transcripts, 125 Western Avenue, Boston, MA 02134, USA.

WHITELAW, J. (1987) 'Bolivia Crafts Buyback Plan for Bank Debt', *American Banker*, 11 May.

WHITMAN, M. V. N. (1987) 'The Impact of the Debt Problem on International Trade', in R. M. Rodriguez, ed., *The Export-Import Bank at Fifty*. Lexington, Mass.: Lexington Books, pp. 87–96.

WHITMORE, T. C. (1984) *Tropical Rain Forests of the Far East*. Oxford: Clarendon.

WICKHAM, T. H., Barker, R. and Rosengrant, M. V. (1978) 'Complementarities among Irrigation, Fertilizer, and Modern Rice Varieties', in *Economic Consequences of the New Rice Technology*. Los Banos: IRRI, pp. 221–32.

WIDEMAN, B. (1976) 'The Dizzying Pace of Expansion', *Far Eastern Economic Review*, November 26, pp. 54–5.

WITTFOGEL, K. A. (1957) *Oriental Despotism*. New Haven: Yale University Press.

WOLTERS, W. (1984) *Politics, Patronage and Class Conflict in Central Luzon*. Quezon City: New Day Publishers.

WOODRUFF, J. G. (1979) *Coconuts: Production, Processing, Products*. 2nd edn., Westport, Connecticut: AVI Publishing.

WORLD BANK (1962) *Economic Growth in the Philippines: A Preliminary Report Prepared by the Staff of the IBRD*, 4 January. Published as *Appendix II to the State of the Nation Message of President Diosdado Macapagal*, 22 January.

WORLD BANK (1971) *Policies and Operations: The World Bank, IDA and IFC*. Washington, D. C.: World Bank, June.

WORLD BANK (1973) *Current Economic Position and Prospects of the Philippines*. 3 vol. Report No. 78-PH, 20 April.

WORLD BANK (1976) *The Philippines: Priorities and Prospects for Development*. Washington, D. C.: World Bank.

WORLD BANK (1979a) *Philippines: Sector Study: Grain Production Policy Review*. 2 vol. Report No. 2192a-PH, 22 January.

WORLD BANK (1979b) *The Philippines: Domestic and External Resources for Development*. Report No. 2674-PH, 12 November.

WORLD BANK (1979c) *The Philippines: Poverty, Basic Needs, and Employment: An Assessment*. First draft of Report No. 2984-PH; reprinted as *The World Bank Philippine Poverty Report* by Counter-Spy Magazine, Washington, D. C.

WORLD BANK (1980a) *Philippines: Sector Survey: Agricultural Support Services*. Report No. 2177-PH, 23 January.

WORLD BANK (1980b) *Aspects of Poverty in the Philippines: A Review and Assessment*. 2 vol. Report No. 2984-PH, 1 December.

WORLD BANK (1982) *The Philippines: Irrigation Program Review*. Report No. 3545-PH, 15 December.

WORLD BANK (1983) *Philippines: Agricultural Credit Sector Review*. Report No. 4117-PH, 12 May.

WORLD BANK (1984) *The Philippines: A Review of External Debt*. Report No. 4912-PH, 2 November.

WORLD BANK (1985a) *The Philippines: Recent Trends in Poverty, Employment and Wages*. Report No. 5456-PH, 20 June.

WORLD BANK (1985b) *World Debt Tables: External Debt of Developing Countries. 1984–1985 Edition*. Washington: World Bank.

WORLD BANK (1985c) *World Development Report 1985*. New York: Oxford University Press.

WORLD BANK (1985d) *The Philippines Food Processing Sector: Development Potential and Constraints*. Report No. 5503-PH, 11 July.

WORLD BANK (1986a) *The Philippines Sugarlands Diversification Study*. Report No. 6042-PH, 30 May.

WORLD BANK (1986b) *The Philippines: A Framework for Economic Recovery.* 3 volumes. Report No. 6350-PH, 5 November.

WORLD BANK (1987) *World Development Report 1987.* New York: Oxford University Press.

WORLD BANK (1988a) *The Philippines: The Challenge of Poverty.* Report No. 7144-PH, 17 October.

WORLD BANK (1988b) *World Development Report 1988.* New York: Oxford University Press.

WORLD BANK (1989a) *Philippines: Toward Sustaining the Economic Recovery. Country Economic Memorandum.* Report No. 7438-PH, 30 January.

WORLD BANK (1989b) *World Debt Tables: External Debt of Developing Countries, 1988–89 Edition.* Washington, D. C.: World Bank.

WORLD BANK (1989c) *Philippines: Forestry, Fisheries, and Agricultural Resource Management Study.* Report No. 7388-PH, 17 January. [Subsequently published under the title *Philippines: Environment and Natural Resource Management Study.* Washington, D. C.: World Bank.]

WORLD BANK (1990a) *World Debt Tables, 1989–90: External Debt of Developing Countries. Volume 2: Country Tables.* Washington, D. C.: World Bank.

WORLD BANK (1990b) *World Development Report 1990.* New York: Oxford University Press.

WORLD RESOURCES INSTITUTE (1990) *World Resources 1990–91.* New York: Oxford University Press.

WURFEL, D. (1983) 'The Development of Post-War Philippine Land Reform: Political and Sociological Explanations', in Ledesma, Makil and Miralao, eds., pp. 1–14.

YOTOPOULOS, P. A. (1985) 'Middle-Income Classes and Food Crises: The "New" Food-Feed Competition', *Economic Development and Cultural Change*, Vol. 33, No. 3, pp. 463–83.

ZABLAN, F. M. (1961) 'Binga Hydroelectric Project,' *Indian Journal of Power & River Valley Development*, Vol. 11, No. 4, pp. 1–10.

ZEDILLO, E. (1987) 'Mexico', in Lessard and Williamson, eds., pp. 174–85.

Author Index

Subject Index